TRAVELS WITH A
TANGERINE

'With the *Travels* of IB (as he affectionately thinks of him) in hand,
Mackintosh-Smith here follows his predecessor's trail as far as the
Crimea, seeking what remains of the sights Battutah saw, skilfully
evoking those that have vanished, all the while remaining alert to the
deep connections between modern Muslim society and the past.
The result is an immensely engaging book'

Daily Telegraph

'Battutah couldn't enjoy a better champion than Mackintosh-Smith . . .
This is a considerable book, mind-broadening not only in the way that
it revives the history of a remarkable traveller, but also for its representa-
tion of modern Islam as tolerant, hospitable, humorous and cultured'

The Times

'Sometimes, as [Mackintosh-Smith] travels from Cairo to the Crimea,
across deserts, into assassins' strongholds, it seems that Ibn is just a swish
of a robe ahead'

Independent

At the age of twenty-one Tim Mackintosh-Smith headed for the real Arabia. For the past seventeen years, when not travelling, he has lived in the Yemeni capital, San'a – a place which has missed out on many of the more awful aspects of the post-medieval period. His first book, Yemen, won huge critical acclaim and the 1998 Thomas Cook/*Daily Telegraph* Travel Book Award. It has been translated into Dutch, Arabic and Chinese.

Martin Yeoman is a painter, draughtsman, sculptor and etcher whose work can be found in a number of notable British collections.

TRAVELS WITH A TANGERINE

A Journey in the Footnotes of
Ibn Battutah

Tim Mackintosh-Smith

PICADOR

First published 2001 by John Murray (Publishers) Ltd, London

This edition published 2002 by Picador
an imprint of Pan Macmillan Ltd
Pan Macmillan, 20 New Wharf Road, London N1 9RR
Basingstoke and Oxford
Associated companies throughout the world
www.panmacmillan.com

ISBN 0 330 49114 8

A CIP catalogue record for this book is available from
the British Library.

Printed and bound in Great Britain by
Mackays of Chatham plc, Chatham, Kent

'If you are a son of this Maghrib of ours and wish for
success, then head for the land of the east!'

Ibn Jubayr of Valencia (d. 1217), *Travels*

'I have milked the teats of Time, pair after pair,
Wandered the world around,
And rivalled al-Khadir in my circumambulations.'

Abu Dulaf (tenth century), *The Ode of the Banu Sasan*

For
Professor ʿAbdullāh Fāḍil Fāriʿ, of Aden,
and
Professor Alan Jones, of Oxford,
two outstanding teachers

Contents

Prefatory Note

IBN BATTUTAH (hereafter IB) spent half a lifetime on his journeys and travelled some 75,000 miles. I grappled with the logistics of covering his *Travels* in one volume of my own, and lost. This book deals therefore with the first stage of his journey, from Tangier to Constantinople; another one – perhaps other ones – will follow him to further parts. In many places I have shadowed him more or less closely. Elsewhere I have dropped in on him. I have left gaps, and sometimes big ones. I only wish I had the odd thirty years to spare, and IB's enviable knack of extracting large amounts of cash, robes and slaves from compliant rulers.

For reasons of clarity and conciseness, I have made a few alterations to the Hakluyt Society's English translation by Gibb of the *Travels*. Computers tend to treat my Ibn Battutah and Gibb's Ibn Battuta as two distinct persons. They are, of course, identical. The final *h* is a matter of taste, which is not among the criteria of electronic indexing.

Constantino
(Ista

MEDITERRANEA

Tangier
Rabat

MOROCCO

S a h a r a

N
W E
S

| miles |
| 0   300   600   900 |
| 0   600   1200 |
| kms |

TRAVELS with a TANGERINE

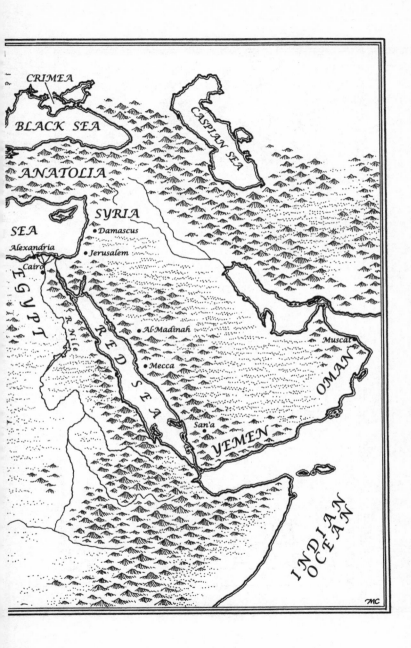

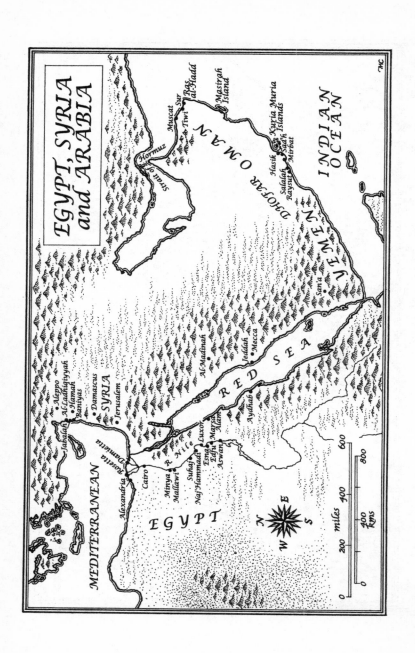

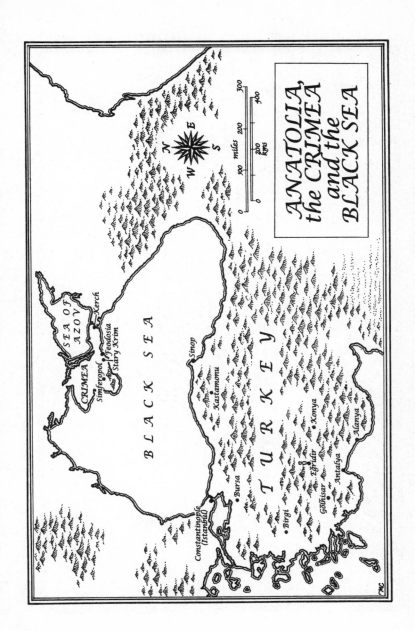

IB was born in Tangier in 1304. His family were of Berber origin but thoroughly Arabized; they belonged to the educated classes and had a tradition of serving as qadis, Islamic judges. Nothing is known of IB's youth, but he probably received the scholastic training usual to his class. At the age of 21 he set out on the Pilgrimage to Mecca. So far so unremarkable; but let us turn to the notice of him from Ibn Hajar's Concealed Pearls, a biographical dictionary of the fourteenth century:

'Ibn al-Khatib says: "Ibn Battutah had a modest share of the sciences. He journeyed to the East in the month of Rajab 725 [1325], travelled through its lands, penetrated into Iraq al-Ajam, then entered India, Sind and China, and returned through Yemen . . . In India, the king appointed him to the office of qadi. He came away later and returned to the Maghrib [the western Islamic world, i.e. north-west Africa and Muslim Spain], where he related his doings and what had befallen him, and what he had learned of the people of different lands. Our shaykh Abu 'l-Barakat Ibn al-Balfiqi told us of many strange things which Ibn Battutah had seen. Among them was that he claimed to have entered Constantinople and to have seen in its church twelve thousand bishops. He subsequently crossed the Strait to the Spanish coast, and visited the Negrolands. Thereafter the ruler of Fez summoned him and commanded him to commit his travels to writing."

'I have seen in the handwriting of Ibn Marzuq the statement . . . that Ibn Battutah lived to the year 770 [1368–9] and died while holding the office of qadi in some town or other. Ibn Marzuq also said: "And I know of no person who has travelled through so many lands as Ibn Battutah did on his travels, and he was withal generous and welldoing." '

Preamble

Lust and Lore

'A book is a visitor whose visits may be rare, or frequent, or so
continual that it haunts you like your shadow and becomes a
part of you.'

al-Jahiz (d. 868–9), *The Book of Animals*

A LETTER HAS just arrived here in San'a from a Russian lady, Nina
Suvorova. She writes on lightly scented paper from the Crimean
port of Feodosia, a place still known to Tatars and to Turks of the
older generation as Keffe. Nina was very pleased, she says, to receive
my letter on the eve of the New Year. 'But there are no more letters
from you. Maybe you went somewhere . . . How is Battutah? I often
recollect your eyes and your expression talking about Battutah, and
how we called you Battutah.'

*

I first met Ibn Battutah – strictly, Nina is incorrect to drop the 'Ibn' –
in San'a, in the Greater Yemen Bookshop, so small that all the
departments are within the diameter of a swung cat. I wasn't looking
for him; it was a chance encounter – better, as the saying goes, than a
thousand appointments.

Not long before, while I was eating a boiled potato from a barrow
on the street outside my house, I felt a tap on my elbow. It was a
neighbour, a man who takes gentle pleasure in publicly eroding my
bookish reputation. 'Where does the word *batatah*, potato, come
from?' he asked. Without waiting for an answer he said, 'Haven't you
heard of IB? Battutah . . . *batatah*,' and disappeared.

It seemed plausible, for about a nanosecond. Then I thought:

surely IB lived in the old, pre-potato world ... didn't he? Of course I
had heard of him. He was the most famous Arab traveller. And that,
I realized, was the extent of my knowledge.

So, while I wasn't looking for him, he was filed under 'Shameful
Gaps in Knowledge' in some dusty lobe of my brain. And there he
was, sitting on a shelf in the Greater Yemen Bookshop and bound in
pillar-box red – or rather his *Tuhfat al-nuzzar fi ghara'ib al-amsar wa
aja'ib al-asfar (The Precious Gift of Lookers into the Marvels of Cities and
Wonders of Travel*; or perhaps, to preserve the original rhymed prose –
an effect called *saj'*, 'the cooing of doves' – *An Armchair Traveller's
Treasure: the Mirabilia of Metropolises and the Wonders of Wandering*;
although maybe, to avoid music-hall levity, the *Travels, tout court*, is
best). I looked at the Contents. There was an introduction, then on
page ten we were off with 'Departure from Tangier'. I turned to the
text: 'My departure from Tangier, my birthplace, took place on
Thursday the second of the month of God, Rajab the Unique, in the
year seven hundred and twenty-five ... ' Chapter and verse: AH 725
was AD 1325, give or take a year – the Middle Ages. Potatoes were still
slumbering in the pre-Columbian sod.

I bought a Yemeni history I had come for; and, as an afterthought,
picked up the *Travels*, not suspecting that I had set the course of my
life into its own middle age.

That afternoon I opened the *Travels* with that slight thrill of anticipation, of a book to be explored greedily, and alone. I turned first
to the section on Yemen, to find out what IB had to say about my
adoptive home, and was soon into his description of lunch with the
Sultan. The doorbell rang. I swore, but pulled the rope that opens the
door down on the street. A minute later Hasan appeared, breathless
from the climb.

Hasan is one of the few people I enjoy being disturbed by. An
afternoon with him will touch on many topics, always interleaved
with jokes, few of them repeatable and fewer translatable. He asked
what I was reading, and I passed him the *Travels*. Arabic is a language
of recitation, and he began reading aloud, as he often does, sometimes
for twenty minutes at a time: ' "*Account of the Sultan of Yemen*. He is
the Sultan al-Mujahid Nur al-Din Ali, son of the Sultan al-Mu'ayyad
Hizabr al-Din Da'ud, son of al-Muzaffar Yusuf ibn Ali ibn Rasul." '

Suddenly, Hasan stopped and looked up. 'That's funny. You know
who Sultan al-Mujahid is, don't you?'

'You've just told me. He was the Sultan of Yemen. IB had lunch with him.'

'No, the point is . . . our family, Bayt al-Shamahi, we're a section of Bayt al-Mujahid. Sultan al-Mujahid is my ancestor. My direct paternal ancestor.'

For a moment, I felt a strange sensation. Perhaps I could call it temporal vertigo: the feeling of looking at a spot in time, far away yet reachable in a single, breathtaking leap. I think Hasan felt it too.

When he left after sunset, he borrowed the book. My glimpse into IB's world had been brief; but it had waited 650 years and could wait a week or two more. As for that temporal glitch, it was something that would return when I came to explore that world on the ground.

*

I have always been conscious of the nearness of time past. It may be the result of coming from an elderly family. My childhood was inhabited by Edwardian aunts who wore their hair in vestigial bobs and said 'orf'. My youngest grandparent, the only one I knew, was born a little before the moving picture. My maternal grandfather dated back to the year in which cricketers were permitted to bowl overarm.

From an early age, I was conscious too of an even more distant past. As a toddler, I would stray on to the founder of Pennsylvania's father, who lay under a slab in front of our pew in church, and try to wake up the fifteenth-century merchant whose effigy slept in a recess in the wall behind. I cannot remember ever being bored. Who could be, in that light-dappled forest of columns? I would sit there and look upwards, and lose myself in its sheer oldness.

Although I didn't know it at the time, our parish church was anything but parochial. In about 1325, the year in which IB set out from his home town of Tangier, a pious inhabitant of my own native city decided to give the church of St Mary Redcliffe a new north porch. The plan of the building, a hexagon, was unusual. The doorway, though, was a fit of eccentricity: cusped and sub-cusped like the mouth of some toothy sea creature, it sprouts a deep undergrowth of foliage from which small figures peep. Pevsner called the structure 'desperately original' and 'curiously tropical', and suggested that it might be 'the first case of *orientalisme* in major Western architecture'. I have shown a photograph of the door to several architectural historians. All but one (she recognized it) have transported it eastwards: prayer niche? some influence from metalwork – Mosul perhaps? Mongol Persia? Islamic India? The porch is truly ectopic, a sort of medieval Brighton Pavilion. But perhaps the outlandishness is not misplaced: the shrine which the porch once contained was a favourite place for travellers to offer prayers, before setting sail a few yards away from the busiest quay in England and, by the grace of God, when they returned. And whatever inspired the design, its date - and that of IB's departure – could hardly be more apt: the first half of the fourteenth century was one of those rare periods when everything was in motion. Writing at the other end of the world in 1350, the Chinese scholar Wang Li said in his *Unicorn Plain Essays*, 'He who travelled 1,000 *li* [about 200 miles], it was as if he had walked across the courtyard; he who travelled 10,000 *li*, as if he had gone to his neighbour's house.' For a few decades – IB's decades – the world seemed to have contracted.

The Crusades were over, the Tatars tamed and Islamized, and the world by and large made not war but love, or at least nuptial alliances. The Mamluk Sultan of Egypt and Syria, whose father and predeces-

sor had begun his career as a Kipchak Turkish slave, was romantically attached to the young Tatar Ilkhan of Iraq and Persia – a descendant of Genghis Khan and thus a cousin of the Yuan Emperor of China – and married to another cousin of the Ilkhan, a daughter of the Khan of the Golden Horde, the latter being married to the Emperor of Byzantium's daughter, one of whose illegitimate stepsisters was Empress of Trebizond and two of whose legitimate stepsisters, the daughters of Anne of Savoy, were married respectively to a Bulgarian prince and a nobleman of Genoa, and whose stepmother was a daughter of Duke Henry the Wonderful of Brunswick.

Marriages were made, and so was money. The east–west road streamed with merchants. Pegolotti, a Florentine merchant banker who compiled a businessman's guide to the east in the 1340s, assured his readers that the road to China could be travelled in perfect safety. Under his checklist of 'Things needful for merchants who desire to make the journey to Cathay', he stressed the importance of a good dragoman, warning that 'you must not try to save money in the matter of dragomen by taking a bad one instead of a good one'. But his chief priority concerned the shibboleth of shaving: 'In the first place, you must let your beard grow long.' (During the Crusades, Franks and Muslims had learned that they had much in common. One point of complete incompatibility, however, was the question of which end of yourself you should shave. 'The Franks shave their beards', wrote one Muslim commentator, 'and only let a nasty, rough stubble grow. One of them was asked about this and said, "Hair is an excrescence. You Muslims remove it from your crotches, so why should we leave it on our faces?" ')

Just as peace made in-laws of far-flung dynasties, so it brought about some exogamous marriages in the world of design and technology. One of these has rarely been matched in fertility. For centuries, Persian potters had been using cobalt to paint underglaze blue decorations. In the early fourteenth century, some bright entrepreneur had the idea of taking it to China. The Chinese potters tried out this 'Muhammadan blue' on their highly prized white porcelain, and in about 1325 started to export the barbarous results back to the Near East. The shapes were based on those of Islamic metalwork, the blue decorations incorporated jolly chinoiseries. Soon, imitations were being made in Persia, then in Egypt and Syria. Later on, the Ottomans took blue-and-white to heart and put tulips on their pots; the seventeenth-century Dutch then fell in love with it, putting windmills and armorials on their pots, and tulips in them. The bastard transfer-printed descendants of blue-and-white still leave Stoke-on-Trent in their willow-patterned millions.

The early decades of the fourteenth century were a period of toings and froings such as had not been seen since ancient times. With the world in such a confusion of currents, it was not so surprising that a piece of exotic jetsam like the porch of my parish church should land up in an English port city.

★

It was into this world that the 21-year-old IB launched himself: 'I braced my resolution to quit all my dear ones, female and male, and forsook my home as birds forsake their nests.' Hasan having returned the *Travels*, I launched myself with him.

It was a world of miracles and mundanities, of sultans, scholars, saints and slave-girls, in which outrageous fortune and dubious dragomen — the sort Pegolotti warned against — steered a course that lurched between luxury and poverty, asceticism and hedonism. IB, I discovered, had a penchant for the picaresque and a storyteller's delight in close shaves, honed along the way by constant recounting in princely courts and caravanserais. He escaped pirates, storms and shipwrecks; he dodged the Black Death, purged himself of a fever with an infusion of tamarinds, survived the near-fatal consequences of undercooked yams and endured diarrhoea caused by a binge on melons; he worked for the Sultan of Delhi — 'of all men the most addicted to the making of gifts and the shedding of blood', who had bumped off his father in a Buster Keaton-style collapsing pavilion operated by elephants — and lived to tell the tale.

Twenty-nine years after he flew the nest, IB returned to Morocco. He had seen a huge swathe of the known world, visiting over forty countries on the modern map and travelling some 75,000 miles by horse, mule, camel, ox-wagon, junk, dhow, raft, and on foot — around three times the distance Marco Polo claimed to have covered. He had got as far north as the Volga and as far south as Tanzania. He had surfed the scholarly internet, meeting fellow Moroccans in China and savants from Samarkand in Granada. His itinerary was as irrational as that of a New Zealand backpacker. At one point, he left Jeddah by sea for India, only to get there via Egypt, Syria, Anatolia, the Crimea, Constantinople, the steppe, Khwarizm, Khurasan, Transoxiana and Afghanistan. Inexplicable spatial blips teleported him across hundreds of miles and then returned him, just as suddenly, to the point where he had left his original road. Along the way, he had been judge, hermit and ambassador, and had plotted a coup in the Maldives. He had earned the title Traveller of Islam, and can justly claim to be the greatest traveller of the pre-mechanical age.

9

Apart from all this, IB was a great travel writer. That irresistible urge to impart information brought on an occasional bout of the Baedekers, if not in IB himself then in his editor. But he was too ill-disciplined, too fond of digression to compile a *reiseführer*. As I read, I realized that he wrote not in guidebook monochrome, but with the colour and detail of a limner. His descriptions are like contemporary manuscript illustrations – crowded, vivid and closely observed, the salient features zoomed into the foreground. Before, I had always looked at IB's age through the inverted telescope of history; now I was viewing with the glass the right way round. Like the temporal vertigo I had felt on discovering the link between my friend Hasan and IB's Yemeni host, it was a dizzying experience.

For several hours a day I read on, carried along by constant changes of scene. I tried to follow IB in the atlas. He evaded me briefly on the Red Sea coast, and more frequently in Anatolia. Further east, he often had me hopelessly lost and hypothesizing wildly: were the dog-faced tribes in Burma or Borneo? did the Amazon-like queen rule in the Philippines or in Japan? My unmitigatedly grotty edition of the *Travels*, devoid of maps and footnotes, was good exercise and had me panting after the author as he disappeared ahead over one horizon after another.

But it was not just the need to know where he'd got to that kept me going. Something else had been happening: the authorial presence, at first wispy and ectoplastic, had filled out. IB was no longer a dead medieval writer. He had become thoroughly, agreeably human. Physically, he remained a blank: he tells us nothing of his appearance except that – like every adult Muslim male of the day save eunuchs and a sect of antinomian depilating Qalandars – he had a beard. But he gradually revealed other bits of himself – a soft heart, a big head, a huge libido. And there was a tender underside to the Great Traveller. He had to leave an audience with the Sultan of Delhi in the Hall of a Thousand Columns because of a boil on the backside; and after one walk, a mostly level eighteen miles, he complained: 'My feet had become so swollen in my shoes that the blood was almost starting under the nails. For six days I was powerless to rise to my feet because of the pains that they had sustained.' The boils and blisters are curiously modern, a well-trodden topos of current travel literature. IB displayed his artlessly. It was because of this endearing tendency to bare himself that, the more I read of him, the closer I got to know him and the more I came to like him. *'C'est quasi le même de converser avec ceux des autres siècles'*, wrote Descartes, *'que de voyager.'* With IB I felt I had done both.

★

In 1348, less than a quarter of a century after that strange porch was added to my parish church in Bristol, a new arrival from the east disembarked at a quay a few yards away. IB, on his way back from China, had already run into this traveller in Damascus and Cairo. Reaching Tangier, he found that the traveller had got there before him and had killed his mother. Scientists call it *Pasteurella pestis*; it also goes by the name of the Black Death.

The golden fourteenth century turned to dust. Europe luxuriated in rampant melancholy and the cult of the body vile. The central Islamic lands fell under a succession of brutish and short regimes. In China, the Ming defeated the Tatar Yuan in 1368. In 1389 the Ottoman Turks, whom IB had seen in Anatolia in the first flush of military success, conquered the Serbs; in the following year they captured the remaining Byzantine possessions in Asia Minor. The century ended with Tamerlane and his neo-Tatars rampaging through the eastern Islamic lands and India. Calamity followed calamity; God seemed to have reverted to his vengeful Hebraic youth, and the world IB had known was never the same again.

And yet that world had survived, in the *Travels*. Like IB himself, it had filled out as I read. Towards the end of the book it had become so visible, so vivid, that I could slip in and out of it – a virtual fourteenth century. And it had become addictive. What would I do when I finished? I could start at the beginning again. But I knew that cerebral travel was not enough: from those very first words – 'My departure from Tangier, my birthplace ... ' my feet had been itching for the physical, visitable past. The more I read of the *Travels*, the stronger became the itch. There was only one way to cure it.

It would be an enormous undertaking. But I felt certain that the remains of IB's world were out there to be tracked down – not just the great buildings of Mamluk Cairo or Palaeologue Constantinople, but also the minor monuments: a scholar's pen box, houses of fishes' bones, half-forgotten graves, buffalo-milk puddings, smells, sounds. And people. (The *Travels* mentions the names of around 1,500 individuals met over thirty-odd years. Ibn Hajar's *Concealed Pearls*, the

Islamic *Who's Who* of the fourteenth century, does only slightly better with 5,400 entries for the entire hundred years. Perhaps there would be other Hasans.) I began to think of my journey as a sort of Proustian, inverse archaeology. Instead of recreating past lives by examining objects and places, I would start with a life – IB's – and go off in search of its memorabilia, fragments of existence withdrawn from time.

I put together a packing list. It included books by IB's contemporaries: the Persian traveller Mustawfi, a recorder of marvels (armless tailors, a milkable turtle, an emetic bridge); the Syrian poet-historian-geographer and warrior-prince Abu 'l-Fida; al-Abdari, the 'Disgusted, Tunbridge Wells' of Moroccan travel; Sir John Mandeville, whose travels (rather more textual than terrestrial) coincided in date with those of IB and who apologized to his readers for failing to describe Paradise; and Friar Jordanus, who made no apology for failing to describe Aran, a part of Azerbaijan. The tenth chapter of his *Mirabilia Descripta* runs in its entirety:

X
HERE FOLLOWETH CONCERNING
THE LAND OF ARAN

Concerning Aran, I say nothing at all, seeing that there is nothing worth noting.

Then there were Friars Symon Semeon, a rather maiden-auntish Irishman, and Giovanni de' Marignolli, who wrote in what one authority calls 'atrocious Latin', and who dropped a diplomatic brick by presenting the Muslim Khan of the Golden Horde with a gift of strong liquor (the Khan probably enjoyed it – according to IB, he was a boozer); the Reverend Ludolph von Suchem, who said that in Cairo 'one can see, above all, elephants and gryphons'; and the somewhat over-hyped Venetian who died a year before IB left home, Marco Polo. I decided as far as possible to forego post-medieval guidebooks, since they tend to omit the most interesting sights such as gryphons.

Later, God willing, I would embark on another journey – to write what traditional Arab authors call a *dhayl*, a 'tail', to IB's *Travels*. According to a seventeenth-century blurb, I could do no more:

All master-works of travel, if you will but look,
Are merely tails that drag at Ibn Battutah's heel.
For he it was who hung the world, that turning wheel
Of diverse parts, upon the axis of a book.

My aim would be the same as his (as expressed by his editor, never a master of the sound-bite) – 'To give entertainment to the mind and delight to the eyes and ears, with a variety of curious particulars by the exposition of which he gives edification and of marvellous things by adverting to which he arouses interest.' IB's European contemporaries called this, more snappily, lust and lore.

Morocco

One End of the World

'Her fingertips, outstretched, sketched a farewell,
Her eyes, downcast, asked when I would return.
And I replied, "What traveller went forth
Who knew the fate God had in store for him?" '

Unattributed, quoted in al-Abshihi (d. 1446), *Al-mustatraf*

IT WAS A truly astonishing revelation. I read it again, this time with
the italics it deserved: according to a short piece on him in the
Royal Air Maroc in-flight magazine, IB had been, 'by turns, an
ambassador in China appointed by the Sultan of India, a judge and *a
Muslim religious official on the Falkland Islands*'.

For a few dizzying moments, thoughts galloped around my head
like Tatar horsemen: IB made it across the Atlantic; he probably did
give his name to potatoes; world history would have to be rewritten;
the reviewer is mad; I am mad.

Fortunately, the magazine was trilingual, and a look at the Arabic
and French versions cleared things up. IB had not dispensed *shari'ah*
on Goose Green. The Falklands were in fact 'Juzur al-Maldif', confirmed by the French 'Iles Maldives'. The Maldives, I realized, must
have rearranged themselves in the translator's mind as the Malvinas.
Geographical howlers have a long and distinguished history, and just
as Shakespeare mentioned the coast of Bohemia, the Baghdad geographer Ibn Hawqal had written of 'the shores of Tibet'. That was a
thousand years ago; but even now, it seemed, in the age of word-
processors and satellite navigation, the Indies could still be misplaced
in the New World. As the plane taxied to the runway, I remembered
spotting in an English digest of the Arabic press an article on the

Chechens – in Arabic 'Shishan' – which the spellcheck-happy translator had entitled 'Muslim Views on the Shoeshine War'.

For a moment I wondered if the pilot might head dyslexically for
Tanjore or Tanjungselor; but, two and a half hours later, he landed us
with perfect orthography at the IB International Airport in Tangier,
in 'A land', the traveller wrote,

> where charms were hung upon me,
> Whose earth my skin first touched.

I had come to Tangier, as I imagined, to visit his tomb and seek his
blessing for my own travels.

My first destination, however, was his hotel – the Hôtel Ibn
Batouta. I wondered, as the *grand taxi* negotiated the steep and
narrow streets above the harbour, what IB would have made of the
address – 8 rue Magellan, off rue Cook. The hotel was terraced into
the hillside and draped with flashing coloured lights; its amenities
included a Pizzeria-Steak House and a Salon de Coiffure. As I signed
the register, I mentioned my quest to the receptionist. 'Ah,' he said,
'you have found IB already!' He pointed to a naïve oil painting above
our heads, which showed a bearded man in a Wordsworthian setting.
Beside the man lay what looked like a school satchel bulging with
scrolls, and in the background a ship lay placidly at anchor.

'Come with me,' the receptionist invited. 'I will show you another
picture of IB.' In the television lounge, he pointed to an old framed
photograph on the wall.

'But it's a photograph,' I said.

'Yes. A very old photograph.'

'And he's smoking a water-pipe.'

'Ah, IB knew that water-pipes are healthier than cigarettes.'

'But tobacco came from America, and photography was only
invented a hundred and fifty years ago.'

'IB', said the receptionist, with unanswerable finality, 'was a very
great traveller.'

I took my room key and went to unpack. I was beginning to
understand why most research on the fourteenth century took place
in the less surprising setting of libraries.

A Syrian contemporary of IB, Abu 'l-Fida, wrote that Tangier was
famous for three things – its grapes, its pears, and the brainlessness of

its inhabitants. At about the same time, another geographical encyclopaedist, a native of the nearby Moroccan town of Sabtah, explained the reason: 'Outside Tangier is a spring called Barqal. Its water is said to cause stupidity. They diagnose their imbeciles by saying, "It's not their fault. They've drunk the water of Barqal."' While in the city, I was careful to mix the tapwater with duty-free scotch, and suffered no ill effects that I am aware of.

Other than these scant comments, my reading had turned up little information on Tangier in the time of IB. The pace of Tangerine events picked up in 1471, a century after IB's death, when the Portuguese captured it; the city later passed through various other European hands, yet managed to retain its Arabness. The Spanish adventurer Domingo Badia y Leblich – a probable Napoleonic spy who travelled and wrote under the name Ali Bey – found early in the nineteenth century that the short passage across the Strait of Gibraltar was like being 'transported to another planet'.

Since then, things have changed. IB would have been hard put to recognize his native city if he had come with me to the boulevard Pasteur that evening, to watch the *paseo*. Among the men, there was not a burnous-wearer in sight; a few even sported shorts. The women were divided into two groups: long coats plus headscarves, and bare arms with skin-tight trousers. From a head-count made over a mint tea at a pavement café, I estimated the groups to be roughly equal in number. IB, I thought, would have regarded the second category with a mixture of pious horror and anthropological fascination. As the call to prayer sounded, distant and weary, I asked myself how one could pray in Calvin Klein; perhaps lycra would help.

I returned to the hotel and climbed the stairs to the Pizzeria-Steak House, wondering if they did a pizza IB: the dough would be made from Luristani acorn flour; Damietta buffalo cheese would take the place of mozzarella; it would be topped by flakes of South Arabian dried shark and coarse-ground Malabar pepper, and presented on a platter of Omani banana leaves. But the chef had not risen to the challenge, and I dined on a discus-solid *quattro stagione* to the beat of Spanish dance music. Completing the Mediterranean scene, couples – the girls were all from the bare-armed group – gazed into each other's eyes and fed each other pizza.

The dance music followed me to bed, in a room beneath the staircase to the restaurant. I lay listening to the pounding bass and the clatter of feet above my head. Other sounds rose from the port below, the strigine hoot of a train and the orotund honk of a ship in harbour. Tangier echoed to the sound of arrival and departure. I fell asleep thinking that the pizza probably tasted better if someone fed it to you.

I was awakened by a brass band blowing *fortissimo* at 4.45 a.m. A very sharp trumpet, a swaggering trombone and a flatulent sousaphone, egged on by a snare drum and a cheering crowd, were blasting away at some comic-opera march. I groaned into the pillow. It was an aural mugging, grievous bodily harmony. But the band moved off, playing as it went, fading into the night; and distance gave the music a strange pathos. I fell asleep again, wondering if I had dreamed it.

In the morning, the receptionist assured me it had not been a dream. 'It was a wedding,' he said. 'They were going to get the bride.'

I went and sat with a coffee and a *pain au chocolat* at the Café de France, one of the best places from which to observe passing Tangerines. There were some oddities. A boy walked past who had a nose like Federigo da Montefeltro's in the famous portrait. A respectably dressed woman in her forties, hurrying to an appointment, suddenly stopped to harangue a tree; then, as suddenly, she looked at her watch, muttered something and was off like the White Rabbit. I suppose I was looking for a reincarnation of the untravelled IB; but if he passed by, he was disguised by the shades and Latinate haircut that seemed *de rigueur* for younger Moroccan men. The girls too, even if they dressed less anatomically than for their evening promenade, looked no different from girls on the other side of the

Mediterranean. Morocco, however, had not been entirely expunged from the place de France, and morning brought out the older generation – a few men in burnouses, and women on their way to market, wearing the red-and-white striped stuff of the Rif and topped by straw hats bearing a heavy crop of pompoms. But in this overwhelmingly European setting they somehow managed to look alien, as Morris men might on Oxford Street. I spotted some other picturesque characters: a stray from Woodstock in a shocking pink T-shirt, beads and a white beard of the sort that only Victorian clergymen and very ancient hippies can grow; and, on the arm of a dapper Moroccan who had clearly once been handsome, a large and elderly Englishman from within whose carapace of summer-weight tweed an Audenesque head moved slowly, periscopically, as if he were a turtle on a constitutional. It seemed that even the recent past, the Tangier of International Zone days, was all but extinct. What chance had I, then, of finding the Tangier of IB? Wherever it was, it was not here on the place de France. I paid for my breakfast and went to look for the tomb.

For many Muslims, tomb visiting is something to be done regularly, like changing the oil in a car: it ensures the smooth running of history. History being people rather than artefacts, IB and other travellers headed for tombs in the places they visited as we might head for art galleries. The deceased, for their part, need human contact as much as the living. A Maghribi traveller who settled in Yemen never ceased to dwell guiltily on his family's tombs lying unvisited back in Morocco, for 'the dead feel pain if separated from their living relatives'; IB's contemporary Ibn Khaldun wrote that the dead have sense perception, and that a dead man 'sees the persons who attend the burial and hears what they say, and he hears the tapping of their shoes when they forsake him'. The idea of burning one's dead is still considered extraordinary. I have not yet admitted to my Muslim friends that I forked my father's ashes into a Lincolnshire flowerbed.

To translate oneself from *ville* to *madinah*, passing through the press of the Grand and Petit Soccos into Tangier proper, is to enter, if not another planet, then at least another continent. The street map I had resembled the biopsy of some many-vesicled organ and was next to useless. Besides, I didn't know precisely where I was going. I headed upwards. Here, the light was different, diffusing off peeling walls of

rose madder and primrose. The smell was different too, and there was
an odour of long habitation, of centuries of simmering *tajines*.

At the top of the climb I reached a gateway. Inside it a dwarf was
sitting on the step of a small shop. I asked him where I was. 'This is
Bab al-Asa, the Gate of the Stick. It's where they used to flog people.
Like this!' he said, springing up and wielding an imaginary birch.
When he had exhausted himself, I explained that I was looking for
the tomb of IB.

'Then you've come to the right place,' said a voice from inside the shop. 'I was IB's *sa'is*.'

His syce? His groom? I looked into the shop and saw a dark-skinned man in a burnous, sitting on a donkey saddle.

'Come in,' said another voice.

I entered the shop, puzzled, and greeted the two men. The owner of the second voice, a lighter-skinned man, explained. 'He means he acted the part of IB's groom in the TV series.' They both laughed. I was given a glass of tea, and the lighter man handed me a business card: 'GROUPE GNAWA EXPRESS TANGER, Abdelmajid Domnati, Maître de Groupe'. The walls of the shop, or rather office, were covered in newspaper clippings, mostly in German; a number showed pictures of my three hosts with other musicians. 'We have many fans in Germany,' Abdelmajid explained. 'They like the spiritual content of our music. The Stonz also were interested in Gnawa music.'

'The who?'

'You know – Brian Jones, Mick Jagger . . . '

'Oh, those Stones.'

'And look at this . . . ' He passed me a CD. Its cover showed a familiar bearded face. 'You see . . . You have found IB! This was sent to us by a German friend, Burchard. He is their *maître de groupe*.' The CD, entitled simply 'Ibn Battouta', was by a German band called Embryo. Frustratingly, the musicians had no CD player. In the space of twenty-four hours I had bumped into IB three times – on the plane, in the hotel, and now on a CD; but he remained inscrutable.

'Come,' said Abdelmajid, as though he had read my thoughts. 'We shall visit the real IB.'

He led me out of the shop, through the Gate of the Stick, and into a perplexing three-dimensional maze of alleyways. We climbed up and down steps and passed through tunnels. Even though Abdelmajid lived in the area, we got lost and ended up against the blank wall of a dead end. Eventually, after asking the way, we turned into a steep and crooked lane – IB Street – and there before us was the tomb chamber, lying in deep shadows cast by tall houses.

'Whoever is responsible for this has little taste,' Abdelmajid said, eyeing some beige and chocolate tiles around the door. He was right: they could have been a remnant from a DIY megastore, and were set in grey cement rendering like the crust on a porridge pan. A boy was summoned to find the guardian. He soon returned with a grave, shaven-headed and grey-bearded man carrying a key. 'Is he a Muslim?' the guardian asked. Abdelmajid said that I was, but without much conviction, and then excused himself. I didn't contradict him.

The interior of the tomb was lined with a dado of blue tiles; above this, the walls were painted pink and decorated with a silver arabesque frieze. Qur'ans rested on shelves, and around the walls hung strings of giant prayer beads. The tomb itself was covered in an embroidered black pall sheathed in transparent plastic, like the upholstery of a brand-new car. I said a brief prayer for the soul of IB, then reclined next to the guardian on a green satin cushion.

We sat in silence, in the presence of the physical IB. I could think of nothing to say, except that I didn't think much of the pink. It wasn't awe, or even anticlimax; it was a kind of extreme neutrality, brought on by everything turning out to be rather as expected. I had experienced the same feeling – or apathy, non-feeling – on first visiting the Pyramids.

A voice broke the silence – my own. 'So this is IB.'

The guardian nodded. 'He was born in this street. And from here he went on pilgrimage to the House of God. Reflect on how far he travelled, on foot and by sea, without cars or aeroplanes.'

I tried, dutifully, to reflect. There was another long silence. Then I remembered a question I had meant to ask. 'Are there any members of the IB family here in Tangier?'

The question immediately sounded silly. It was like asking for the Chaucers in London.

'There are none,' said the guardian.

Wishing that Abdelmajid had not gone, I looked around the chamber for inspiration and noticed a small *mihrab* set into the wall, a niche showing the direction of Mecca. 'Do people pray here?'

'They come to recite the Holy Qur'an, after the dawn prayer.'

This raised my spirits. 'Then I must try to come.'

'It is better for you not to come. There are many drunkards and other wicked people about at that hour.'

Again we sat in silence. I could hear my watch ticking. Then I thanked the guardian, put a donation in the box – 'It is not necessary,' he said – and left with a last look back at the porridge-like walls.

I don't know what I had expected from the tomb. Whatever it was, I had not found it. I suppose I had been hoping for a vibration or two. The tomb's appearance, a combination of municipal washroom and front parlour, had not helped; a poker-work sign ('Dunroamin'?) wouldn't have been out of place. Neither had the poker-faced guardian, whom I could picture ferrying the dead across the Styx. Worse, phrases I had read about the tomb rose up to haunt me – 'authenticity open to question', 'considerable doubt as to the true identity of its occupant', 'possibly some distant relative of the traveller' – phrases which, in my desire to find the real, physical IB, I had conveniently buried.

Who then was the real IB? *The Concealed Pearls*, the Islamic biographical dictionary of the fourteenth century, lists him as Muhammad ibn Abdullah ibn Muhammad ibn Ibrahim ibn Muhammad ibn Ibrahim ibn Yusuf, of the tribe of Lawatah and the city of Tangier, surnamed IB. The Lawatah are descendants of the Lebu, a people mentioned in Pharaonic records – the Libyans of the Greeks – who originated in the region of Cyrenaica. They spread into Egypt early on, and by the ninth century AD had settled in the far south-west of present-day Morocco; there are also said to be Christian Lawatah on Malta. After the coming of Islam the Lawatah, like many of the other tribes collectively known as Berbers, claimed an Arabian origin. There were plenty of stories to back up the idea. One told of a South Arabian ancestor wandering all the way to Libya, a journey of 1,800 miles – a fair distance given that he was looking for some lost camels. Historians from Ibn Khaldun onwards have gleefully trashed such tales; but while their reasoning may be based on sound scholarship, it all seems rather unfair – in the same league as denying Father Christmas. A family like IB's were totally Arabized, and to pick nits about the traveller's Arabness would be like questioning a Cornishman's Englishness because his ancestors were Celts and not Anglo-Saxons. IB himself would have been aghast to be called a Berber, a word which in Arabic as in the European languages has the ring of 'barbarian'.

IB's family name is more of a problem. One theory explains 'Battutah' as a Maghribi diminutive of the Arabic *battah*, 'duck', and a pet version of the girl's name Fatimah. The notion that 'IB' should mean 'Son of the She-Duckling' is charming enough to be plausible. But then so are the various other suggestions that have been put forward: Son of the Father of a Tassel/of an Egg-Shaped Bottle/of a Bad Woman with an Ellipsoidal Body. ('Battut', it should be added, is the Arabic for Donald Duck.)

My uneasy suspicion that I had come all the way to Tangier to visit the tomb not of IB but of some cousin of his many times removed – if its occupant was even that – was partly dispelled by lunch in La Grenouille on the rue Rembrandt. A BBC nature programme on crustaceans, broadcast by a Spanish satellite channel, was showing silently on a television set in the corner. I ate a solitary and excellent meal of snails, sole and *tarte au citron*. Over coffee, I decided to leave Tangier. I needed help, and I had a convoluted introduction to a gentleman in Rabat who might give it.

Later that afternoon I was in the Grand Socco, on my way to thank the kind Abdelmajid, when a man in a grubby white T-shirt sidled up and walked along beside me. 'I saw you at the station,' he said softly, in English.

I had indeed been at the railway station, booking a ticket to Rabat for the following day. I replied in Arabic, 'I'm sorry, I didn't catch what you said.'

'I saw you at the station,' he repeated, in Arabic.

'You are very observant.'

'You did not travel.' He was keeping pace beside me. Neither of us looked at the other.

'What you say is true.'

'You will not travel?'

'God is the most knowing.' I turned to face him. 'I am an amateur of historical geography. Perhaps I might be of service?'

'Thank you,' said the man, reinsinuating himself into the crowd.

I found my way to the Gate of the Stick. The headquarters of the Groupe Gnawa Express were shut, so I continued upwards into the kasbah, the citadel. After several dead ends, I came to a lane which ran parallel to a long, high wall. This was punctuated by a small gateway, like the entrance to a walled garden. I turned into it, and found myself on a cliff overlooking the sea.

The transition from the introverted city to this blustery crag was a complete surprise. For a few moments, I felt dizzied and disorientated, like a sleepwalker who awakens inches from the head of a staircase. I sat on a low parapet perched high above the end of Africa and Islam.

Ludolph von Suchem, IB's German contemporary, wrote that the Strait of Gibraltar was so narrow that 'upon one bank there stands a Christian woman and on the other bank a heathen woman washing their clothes, and wrangling and quarrelling with one another'. I looked in vain for the coast of Europe. (Granted, it was a dim and vaporous day; but Suchem must have been a particularly gullible landlubber, for among the other sailors' yarns he recorded is one about a great fish, 'the Troya marina or sea-swine'. To frighten it away you had to 'stare at it with a bold and terrible countenance'; conversely, you could feed it bread.) Neither could I see, beneath the waves, the remains of a bridge which medieval Arab geographers believed had joined the two continents, and which would be revealed again at the end of time.

Another legend, one which appears in some of the early Qur'anic commentaries, told that this spot had been the point of departure for Moses and al-Khadir. In the Qur'an, al-Khadir – the immortal 'Green Man' – was the Prophet's spiritual guide on an epic quest for the Fountain of Life; he later became a metaphor for far travel and honorary grand master of all Islamic mystical orders. Later, I was to bump into him in Damascus, and by the Black Sea. Now, sitting here on the parapet, I remembered this Islamic Gilgamesh; and thought of that sudden and dreamlike transition through the gate in the high wall, from the intervolved alleyways of the city to this disclosure of the wide sea – where, down in the port, a ship was now calling its passengers, bellowing 'Come! . . . Come!'; and felt that I had stepped into the frontispiece of a book of travels far older than IB.

Even if I ignored the doubts about its authenticity, I could not imagine IB in that tomb, with its pink walls and dismal guardian. But I could picture him up here on this parapet, looking out to sea like a Moorish Boy Raleigh. This was where the vibrations were!

I left the parapet with the sun, and wandered back down through the *madinah*. The cafés on the place de France were full, but I found a table on the boulevard Pasteur and sat down to write up my diary. A few minutes later I became aware of an animated Australian voice at the next table.

' . . . they ain't being themselves. They look like they got special permission to dress like that.' The speaker must have noticed that I'd tapped into her conversation, for she suddenly addressed me. 'Excuse me. Do you speak English?' I nodded. 'It's a bit of a funny question, but . . . what do you think about our clothes?'

My neighbours were two girls of the sun-burnished, tennis-playing sort admired by John Betjeman. One was wearing a long-sleeved shirt and loose trousers, the other a white ankle-length dress and a headscarf.

'She means,' said the other girl, 'do you think we should, well, wrap up a bit more? It's just that we seem to get a lot of ... attention. And look at this lot!' She indicated the daringly clad Moroccan girls on their evening promenade.

'I think you're both most respectably dressed,' I said. 'It's probably just that you're what they call the Other.'

'You *are* a Pom,' said the first girl. 'We thought so. I was just saying – oh, I'm Alison and this is Lucy – that you mustn't get too obsessed about putting on layers and layers, or you end up looking like a bloody snowman.'

'Absolutely,' I said.

'Do you live here?' Lucy asked.

I said I was passing through.

'So are we,' said Alison. 'Like a dose of salts!' They had been in Morocco for about ten days; in that short time they seemed to have covered most of the country. Where did they get the energy? To me, a train ride to Rabat seemed like a major undertaking.

'And we've been on a camel ride in the desert,' added Lucy. I smiled. 'I know, it's a bit of a cliché. But this is our first Arab country. We've already been round Europe – Greece, Italy, France, Spain ... '

I'd always wondered why they did it. 'Why?' I asked.

Alison thought for a moment. 'Oh, you know, there's nothing at home. Just whingeing families. And then you look at the map and you think, "Christ! We're bloody miles from anywhere!" '

'There's so much to see,' said Lucy, 'and so little time to see it in.'

I thought of my own journey that lay ahead – not only the train ride to Rabat, but the further one – and rose and bade them goodnight. A few yards along the boulevard, I turned and waved to them. The café was brightly lit; but, suffused with sun and travel, they seemed brighter. In fact, they positively thermo-luminesced.

★

Like present-day Antipodeans, medieval Maghribis were aware of living a long way from anywhere. IB tells an anecdote to illustrate this:

When I was in Sin Kalan [Canton] I heard that there was a venerable *shaykh* over two hundred years old who neither ate nor drank nor excreted nor had intercourse with women, though his powers were intact, and that he lived in a cave outside the city, giving himself to devotion. I went to the cave and saw him at the entrance. He was thin, very ruddy, showed the traces of his devotional practices, and had no beard. I greeted him; he took my hand, sniffed it, and said to the interpreter: 'This man is from one end of the world and we are from the other.'

The verbal root of 'al-Maghrib', *gharaba*, means both 'to set (sun)' and 'to be remote', and for Near Easterners the Maghrib, the Occident, evoked the distantly exotic in the same way that 'Orient' still does, vestigially, for western Europeans. Persians like the eleventh-century Nasir Khusraw believed that people in al-Andalus, which medieval geographers included in the Maghrib, had eyes like those of cats. Other Persians, among them IB's contemporary Mustawfi, placed in the Maghrib legendary sites like the City of Brass and the City of Women – a sort of Islamic-socialist-feminist commune; the Maghribis set these myths in the East. Even today, a Middle Eastern Arab who regards Cairo as his back yard looks on anywhere to the west of it almost as a world apart. Maghribis are indeed peculiar in subtle ways, using Arabic instead of Indian numerals and retaining in their handwriting fossilized features of Kufic, the script that went out of general use in the Middle East nearly a thousand years ago. Most noticeable of all, they are set apart by their fiendishly incomprehensible spoken dialects. Ali Bey noted that 'when the famous Orientalist *Golius* came into this country [Morocco], he could not understand a word of their Arabic, but was obliged to make use of an interpreter'.

Maghribis, the Antipodeans of Islam, have been both its most adventurous travellers and its greatest travel writers. Such was their output that, even if he never left his study, their educated compatriot could – like Defoe's *Compleat English Gentleman* – make the tour of the world in books. Probably the earliest Maghribi travel writer was Yahya ibn Hakam, who went on two embassies for the Caliph of Cordova, the first in 840 to Constantinople, the second some years later to the King of the Norsemen. On both occasions Yahya, nicknamed 'the Gazelle' on account of his great beauty, serenaded the ruler's wife in troubadour fashion with lyrics of his own composition – a charming form of diplomacy which could well be emulated today to the benefit of international relations. Sadly, the Gazelle's account of his travels is only known from a few fragments.

Another early Andalusian traveller to the fringes of civilization was Abu Hamid, born in Granada towards the end of the eleventh century. He wrote a descriptive geography, liberally truffled with wonders (the rulers of China have miscreants licked to death by a rhinoceros), adventure (the author wrestles with a squid which has tried to steal his knife) and useful tips (sealskin sandals reduce the pain caused by gout). In the middle of the twelfth century, Abu Hamid wandered around the Aral Sea region, travelled up the Volga and spent some years by the Danube, probably in what is now Hungary. In his account of these places and of lands further north he gave an early puff to caviare, 'the finest of all preserved delicacies in the world', and described with an illustration the construction and use of skis. Among the peoples he mentioned are 'red-skinned northerners with blue eyes and flaxen or blond hair, who drink a liquid made from barley; this drink is as sour as vinegar but it agrees with them since, as their diet consists of honey and the flesh of beavers and squirrels, they are hot-tempered', which must be one of the earliest descriptions of the Lager Lout. Abu Hamid's interest in comparative anthropology is shown by a snippet of dialogue between him and the Christian King of Bashghard. The King has heard Abu Hamid encouraging the Muslim royal mercenaries to marry four wives and refrain from wine:

King: This is not logical! Alcohol strengthens the body, and women weaken it. This Islam of yours runs contrary to common sense.

A.H.: But there is a difference between us. You Christians take wine with your food and do not get drunk. But Muslims who drink do so with the express aim of getting inebriated. They lose their minds; they go crazy. On the matter of polygamy, Muslims are naturally hot-blooded, so they enjoy plenty of sex; and you should bear in mind that if you permit them four wives they will father more children, and your army, who are Muslims, will increase.

King: Hmm. Perhaps we should listen to what this *shaykh* says ... In fact, he is most logical!

Abu Hamid and the Gazelle were, however, exceptional in the choice of their destinations. Most Maghribi travellers headed for Arabia, drawn by the irresistible centripetal force of Mecca and al-Madinah. Pilgrimage, a sacred duty for Muslims who are able to undertake the journey, was the primary incentive to travel. The way east led into the heartland of Arab-Islamic culture, and visitors from the end of the world would eagerly set about improving themselves there. Ibn Khaldun, himself a Maghribi, wrote that the East was superior to the West because of 'the additional intelligence that accrues to the soul from the influences of sedentary culture'. For the Maghribis, the whole experience was a sort of Grand Tour: travellers like IB were treading a similar road to the one which eighteenth-century Englishmen, nineteenth-century Americans and the Australasians of today would follow around Europe.

Just as English Grand Tourists dusted off their gerundives and optatives before heading for the Classical world, Maghribi travellers mugged up on their classical Arabic before going east. Few, though, went as far as a scholar of Tangier who boasted, 'I did not enter the East until I had committed to memory 34,000 lines of pre-Islamic poetry.' Later travellers, however, were often disappointed by what they found. Basrah Arabic, like BBC English, was once famous for its perfection but, says IB, 'I was present one day at the Friday service in the Great Mosque of al-Basrah, and when the preacher rose and recited his discourse he committed in it many gross errors of grammar. I was astonished at his conduct and spoke of it to the *qadi* Hujjat al-Din, who said to me "In this town there is not a man left who knows anything of the science of grammar."'

One traveller, al-Abdari, made other people's linguistic short-comings a major theme in the book of his journey to Mecca and back, begun in 1289. A merciless pedant who hailed from the Moroccan town of Hahah, he gloatingly published syntactical blunders together with the names of their perpetrators. When not behaving like a linguistic Red Guard, he still had little to say in favour of anything. He got off to a crabby start – 'In this age of ours, the harvest of virtuous men is blighted' – and thought the Alexandrians 'fetid ... for, as you know, ports are stinking places'. This was only limbering up. The Cairenes provoked al-Abdari into a full-blown rant, purple in face and prose: 'Among them, the generous man is meaner than a firefly, the brave man more timid than a whirring locust, the scholar more ignorant than a moth that flies into a flame, the eminent lowlier than a woodlouse, and the sedate more fickle than a gnat. Their orators stammer like adolescents, their mighty are more abject than beggars ...' and so on, for five pages of elegantly rhymed vitriol. A whole section is devoted to the pernicious Cairene vice — *'We seek refuge with God from such an abasement of morals!'* — of eating in public. Here, and elsewhere, he reminded me of a head-master of mine. And, as is often the case with headmasters, al-Abdari became lovable in the soft focus of memory: his tomb is extant and, like that of the putative IB in Tangier, still venerated.

A far more likeable character, and the author of the most cele-brated book of travel before that of IB, is Ibn Jubayr of Valencia. It was said that the governor of Granada, in a fit of pique, forced him to drink seven cups of wine; the governor later regretted his action, and in expiation gave Ibn Jubayr seven cups filled with gold coins. These funded his pilgrimage to Mecca. He sailed to Alexandria in 1182, travelled up the Nile and crossed the Red Sea to Arabia. Returning two years later through the Levant at the height of Crusader power there, he set sail across the Mediterranean with a group of Christian pilgrims and watched them celebrate a candlelit Hallowe'en at sea. His *Travels* are a priceless record of the interplay between Christendom and Islam; they are also a splendid read. In his descrip-tions of sea travel Ibn Jubayr is an Arabic Conrad. Here he is, becalmed in the eastern Mediterranean:

On Wednesday 23rd a breeze stirred from the east, languid and sickly. At first we hoped that it would grow in strength; but it was no more than a dying sigh. Soon the water was covered by a thin mist, the waves were stilled, and the sea resembled a court-yard paved with glass. Of the four winds not a breath remained. To our eyes the surface of the water seemed like an ingot of silver. And there we lay, bobbing idly, as if lost between two skies.

IB was not unique. He was part of a long tradition of Maghribi travel writers, and it would be a fair guess to suppose that he had read at least Ibn Jubayr before leaving Tangier at the age of 21. If so, I would wager a *dinar* to a *dirham* that one passage, above all, stuck in his mind:

If you are a son of this Maghrib of ours and wish for success, then head for the land of the east! Forsake your homeland in pursuit of knowledge ... The door to the east lies open: O you who strive after learning, enter it with a glad greeting! Seize the chance of freedom from the cares of the world before family and children ensnare you, before the day comes when you gnash your teeth in regret for the time that is gone ...

Ibn Jubayr went on to recommend a sort of medieval Interail, insured by Providence: if you get bored with a place, simply move on, for 'in every village people will shower you with your daily bread'. It is, literally, a philosophy of loafing around. No better copy could have been written to promote the life of the scholar–gipsy.

When the Prophet famously said that Muslims should seek out knowledge even if they have to look for it in China, China still had the metaphorical sense that Timbuktu had for us before the days of the Paris–Dakar Rally. IB, unlike his predecessors, followed the advice to the letter – and having reached the literal China, he then turned around and went to the literal Timbuktu as well. But of this he had no idea as he left Tangier, a not untypical spiritual backpacker.

*

Next morning, I had an early breakfast on the hotel terrace. Overhead, hundreds of swifts screamed and scudded. The girl in charge of the small rooftop kitchen brought my pot of tea, and asked me how long I was staying. 'I'm going when I've finished my breakfast,' I told her.

She glanced around the terrace, then whispered, '*Khudhni ma'ak.* Take me with you.'

I smiled; then realized that she meant it.

*

I was taking a short cut through the cemetery of Rabat, down to the beach, when I was startled by a voice: 'Shall I walk with you, or do you prefer to be alone?' it said, in Arabic. I looked round and saw a tall young man, wearing jeans and an unwashed white shirt.

'Thank you, but on the whole I prefer to be alone.'

'As you wish,' he said, and he branched off on another of the many tracks that doodled between the graves.

I didn't think any more about the meeting; but on the way up from the beach, I bumped into the man again. We greeted each other.

'Like you,' he said, 'I'm a stranger here.'

' "And all strangers are kin to one another",' I quoted.

' "*Wa laysa ghariban man tana'at diyaruhu*

Walakinna man wara 'l-turabu gharibu",' he continued.

It suddenly struck me how improbable the situation was – to be reciting pre-Islamic verse with someone whose name I didn't know, standing on a pavement between a roaring highway and a drainage ditch that, all too evidently, doubled as a public lavatory – and how topical those last two lines were:

> He is not a stranger whose home is far away;
> But he who's laid in earth, he is the stranger.

'How appropriate,' I said. 'We met in a cemetery.' We both laughed.

In a café overlooking the Bou Regreg, the wide river that separates Rabat from its smaller sister of Sala before slipping into the ocean, Khalid told me his story. It was short: he was from Miknas and so far had failed to find work there or anywhere else. 'I'm fed up with the kingdom, the King, the lot. I must go abroad. Ali ibn Abi Talib said, "Abroad, a fortune gives you a home; at home, poverty makes you an alien." '

'But what about poverty abroad? You may not find work.' Or if you do, I thought, what sort of work? Someone I met in Tangier told me that three members of his family were in Italy. They sent home $500 a month and were, he said, 'in things like drug-dealing'. Then there were those reports of violence against Maghribi immigrants in Paris and Marseille, the deportations, the unimaginable shittiness of being an illegal alien.

'It doesn't matter,' Khalid said. 'I prefer *al-taqarfas* abroad to staying here.' He saw me looking puzzled. 'It's a Moroccan word, something like "to fall apart". I don't want a living death at home. Martyrdom on the path of God is far better – I mean, if you go, and fail, you've still succeeded in God's eyes.' I thought of the usual pictures of economic migrants, bedraggled and abject creatures, and compared them with these adamantine martyr's eyes.

We sat and talked about abroad, that mythic place, Lotus Land or Circe's island, until I noticed it was dark. 'I must go,' I said, thinking of my hosts.

'Wait,' said Khalid. He took a piece of paper from his pocket and began writing. An address, I supposed, to be added to the other addresses of people met and conversed with in cafés, in bus stations, on mountainsides. But he wrote: 'In the name of God, the Compassionate, the Merciful ... ' The script was archaic, with sudden swellings and swooping descenders. 'Say: He is God, One, God the Eternal, He has no offspring; neither was He begotten. He has no equal.' The 112th chapter of the Qur'an, a potent amulet. In a world of change, of generation and corruption, it said, there is one constant.

'Take this,' Khalid said. 'It will keep you safe.'

Touched, I thanked him, and put the slip of paper carefully in my pocket. 'You are strange people,' I said, rising to go.

Khalid laughed. '*Inta fi 'l-Maghrib wa la tastaghrib.* You're in the Maghrib: don't consider anything strange.'

In the taxi, Khalid's jingle kept going round in my head. He was right. There was nothing strange or new in wanting to go out of Africa. The motive now was expressed in economic terms, but the language that described it – martyrdom, the path of God – was spiritual. *Ex Africa nunquam aliquid novi.* Perhaps, if I was looking for a reincarnation of the young IB, I had just met him.

The British Ambassador's Residence, at least on the inside, resembled a small English country house, transported to the Bou Regreg and made comfortable by a staff of Edwardian proportions. Its châtelaine, Arlene Fullerton, carried a small remote-control device which I assumed was something to do with security; in fact, it summoned the butler.

William, her husband, was a scholarly Arabist; and with Arab hospitality he had invited me, a passing stranger, to stay. While he dealt with ambassadorial paperwork in his study, I gave Arlene my thumbnail sketch of IB. 'He's a sort of Arabic Marco Polo.' I hated myself whenever I said that. 'But vastly more interesting. And of course he went much further.' I went through IB's destinations, which were also mine. Arlene then began to catalogue her own travels as a diplomatic consort, mostly in the Arab world but with a spell as First Lady of the Falklands. I had noticed the photograph of William, gubernatorially plumed and sword-girt, standing beside the famous London cab. 'Now that's one place IB didn't get to,' she said.

'Oh yes he did,' I retorted. I sensed her asking herself, understandably, if her husband had invited a lunatic to stay, and quickly explained about the Royal Air Maroc in-flight magazine. Arlene, my sanity re-established, seemed relieved.

After dinner, we all retired early. 'We don't often get a night in like this,' William said. 'Where is it tomorrow? Oh yes, Peru.'

Next morning, I rose to find that my hosts had long since left for work. I breakfasted alone and damp, having been chased across the lawn by a sprinkler. At dinner the night before, I had mentioned my conversation with Khalid and his phrase about 'martyrdom on the path of God'. 'Many of the migrants really are martyred,' said William. 'Rafts capsize in the Strait of Gibraltar, people get suffocated stowing away.' Now, opening today's *Libération*, which lay on the breakfast table, I found grim confirmation of his words: five migrants, in this case Tunisians trying to get to Italy, had died of asphyxiation in a cargo hold. The same article also revealed that over the past twenty-eight days alone 2,773 illegal immigrants, nearly all Moroccans and Tunisians, had been caught on and around the tiny Italian islands of Lampedusa and Pantelleria.

It seemed to me that money by itself was not enough to explain this lemming-like exodus. Starvation might force one to gamble with the sea and the Italian coastguard; but these young men, while hard up, were not starving. I wondered if what propelled them was not economics, but genetics. After all they, no less than IB, were heirs to the Arab and Berber pastoralists who had ranged across North Africa. If there is a gene for wanderlust, the Maghribis are sure to have it.

That afternoon I drove to the Villa Baghdad to meet the man who, if anyone, could tell me about the tomb in Tangier. Dr Abdelhadi Tazi, sometime Moroccan Ambassador to Tripoli, Tehran and Baghdad (twice, hence the name of his house), member of the Moroccan Royal Academy and editor of the new Arabic edition of IB's *Travels*, was in his late seventies, but sparkled with energy. I was not surprised when he said he had fourteen children. One of them appeared, a girl of about 12. 'Greet your uncle,' her father told her, and she delicately presented one cheek to be kissed, and then the other. We sat in a room rich with cushions and books, overlooking a lawn on which sprinklers threw out miniature rainbows. Gunpowder tea was brought, and dates in light and melting pastry. 'I have them sent from Baghdad,' he said. 'The dates are from al-Basrah. There are none better!' Basrah dates have been the connoisseur's choice since antiquity; because of sanctions and the Iran-Iraq war, which devastated the Basrah palmeries, they are now a rarity.

'You live in San'a? A most beautiful city! When you return there, *in sha Allah*, you must give my greetings to my brother the Qadi Isma'il al-Akwa', and to his brother the Qadi Muhammad.' He spoke Arabic with panache, savouring selected words as if they were the finest Basrah dates.

He asked me which editions of the *Travels* I had. 'Well, I've got the Hakluyt Society version,' I said.

'Ah, the late Professor Sir Hamilton Gibb. And dear Professor Beckingham. In the study of IB, you Europeans are our masters! I am only ... an *amateur*. And in Arabic?'

'Only the Beirut one done by Dar al-Turath,' I admitted, feeling the reflected lustre of Gibb and Beckingham rapidly fading. 'It isn't much good.'

'Hmm ... These Beirut editions are a grave disservice to the memory of our *shaykh*, IB.'

'I couldn't agree more,' I said.

'Unfortunately, you will not have found a copy of my own edition. His Majesty bought up most of the print run to give away.'

This was bad news. I had already trawled the bookshops of Tangier and Rabat in search of the edition. Now it seemed there was no chance of finding the one thing which, apart from IB's blessing, I had hoped to take away from Morocco. Dr Abdelhadi said he was working on a second edition; but I might have to wait years for it.

For the next couple of hours we talked of nothing but IB. I soon realized that Dr Abdelhadi was no less obsessed with the traveller than I. From time to time, when I came up with some new interpretation or reference, he would utter a little cry, in English, of 'Congratulations!' or 'Bravo!', and jot down a note. On each occasion, my academic ego was given a small lift.

I brought the conversation round to the tomb in Tangier. Dr Abdelhadi smiled. 'That tomb, I fear, is nothing more than a phantasm, a dream! Ibn Marzuq, as you will know, tells us that IB was appointed *qadi* "in some town of al-Maghrib" after his return. Well, Ibn al-Khatib has solved the puzzle of which town: the text of a letter is preserved in the manuscript of his *Nufadat al-jirab* which he addressed to "IB, Qadi of Tamasna". Now, the capital of Tamasna at that time was Anfa, and we may reasonably assume that our *shaykh* is buried there.'

All this was new to me. My pulse quickened at the thought of an expedition to look for the real tomb. But where was Anfa? 'Forgive me, I'm not so well acquainted with Maghribi topography ...'

'Of course. I forget that you are a Mashriqi, an Easterner. A Yemeni! Anfa has disappeared. The Portuguese destroyed it in, I think, 1468.'

'But there must be *some* remains.'

'If there are,' Dr Abdelhadi said, 'they are underneath Casablanca. It was built on the site of Anfa. Remember what Jalal al-Din al-Rumi said:

> When we are dead, seek for our resting place
> Not in the earth, but in the hearts of men.

Later, when I was about to leave, Dr Abdelhadi asked me if I had tried betel. IB devoted an excursus to its botany and its alleged aphrodisiac properties. I said I had chewed it in Aden.

'I too have tried it. IB writes about it as if it were Viagra! Did it ... have any effect on you?'

'I'm not married, or at least only to my books.'

He looked concerned. 'Then, since you are now my friend, I shall give you another wife.' He disappeared briefly, then returned carrying five volumes. 'My edition. The very last copy!'

I left the Villa Baghdad overjoyed and covered in Dr Abdelhadi's kisses.

Back in the Residence I dipped into the edition. The fifth volume, out of which dropped a book-mark from the Dubai Inter-Continental Hotel, was entirely made up of indexes. There was even an Index of Indexes, which contained thirty-four items, including Weapons, Food and Drink, Gems and Jewellery, Scents and Aromatics, and Diseases. (This passion for listing characterized scholarship in the age of IB. The traveller's contemporary al-Nuwayri, for example, compiled a thirty-one-volume encyclopaedia and universal history. It includes over a hundred pages, divided into some ninety sections, on 'What the poets have said about the bodily members'.)

The footnotes were, to say the least, eclectic. They revealed a polymathy worthy of the medieval cosmographers: there were references to Afghan diplomats, to the street map of Moscow, to a paper Dr Abdelhadi presented to the 1981 International Conference on Mineral Water, and to his fifteen-volume *Diplomatic History of Morocco*; there was even a mention of the far-travelled date sweetmeats I had just eaten in the Villa Baghdad and which IB ate in Khwarizm near the Aral Sea; and there were strange juxtapositions – one note mentioned a letter sent to a wife of the Khan of the Golden Horde by Pope Benedict XII, while the next quoted an elegant pornographic verse in allusion to a curious gynaecological feature of this same lady, which IB had described from hearsay. I was going to enjoy the footnotes: like Dr Abdelhadi himself, they sparkled with exclamation marks.

IB's bones, it seemed, lay somewhere under one of the largest cities in Africa; but the following day I went to see the undisputed tomb of someone he had known: Sultan Abu 'l-Hasan of the Marinid dynasty, father of the traveller's patron Sultan Abu Inan. Setting out from the Residence, I followed the walls of Rabat. They had both kept out marauders and greatly simplified life for twentieth-century urban planners, who slapped down a ring road around them. After about a mile, I crossed the road, dodging between the traffic, and made for a small hill also encircled by walls. Inside was the necropolis of Shallah.

The Marinid gateway to the necropolis resembled a giant keyhole. The whole edifice was encrusted with relief carving – spikily exuberant inscriptions and serpentine interweaving strapwork. The corners of the polygonal towers which flanked the gateway were cut away, leaving overhangs that had erupted into stalactites. The towers bore curious, knotty designs which reminded me of the Queen's Award for Industry.

Through the gate, I entered a garden bursting with hibiscus and oleander. Out of the trees poked a Marinid minaret of the usual Maghribi shape, a tall cuboid with a smaller one on top. It was covered with exquisitely carved diapers and surmounted by a large and tousled stork's nest which, while it might have detracted from the silhouette of the building, added greatly in Moroccan eyes to its general mana. (Few stork-revering peoples have gone quite as far as the Maghribis: according to Ali Bey, the endowments of the Fez

lunatic asylum were regularly diverted to pay for the nursing of sick
storks, which were believed to be temporarily transmogrified
humans.)

I wandered along the dusty paths and came to a ruinous but pretty
madrasah, or college of Islamic science. In its courtyard was a pool
lined with turquoise tiles which, when operational, must have presented a Hockneyesque aspect. Outside the ruins were more storks,
nesting on the domed tombs of holy men and in pachydermatous
trees which looked as old as the buildings. The tombs were so generously spattered with stork guano that they seemed to have been
hastily whitewashed. I wondered how so indelicate a creature could
have been invested with such an aura of sanctity. Oblivious of both
their holiness and their personal squalor, the storks clacked away con-
tentedly at each other, sounding like slowed-down football rattles –
hence their Arabic name, *laqlaq*. Where there were no *laqlaqs* there
were egrets, flocks of them, chattering and snickering out of the trees
like guests at a manic drinks party.

The *laqlaqs* of Shallah, however, have to concede in holiness to its
nuns. These live in a gloomy stone-lined pool, attended by an old
lady with a tray of hard-boiled eggs. 'Where are they?' I asked her.

'Wait and look. You'll see them.'

After a few minutes, a mole-like head appeared from beneath the
overhanging side of the pool, followed by a sleek body that glinted
beneath the water. Another one emerged, then a third. These were
the celebrated eels of Shallah. They cruised the pool languidly, then

slid back into their hiding places. There was something sinister and Svengalian about the spectacle.

An obese eel may sound like a paradox, but in proportion to their length of three or four feet these were positively podgy. The old lady explained the reason. 'Women who want babies come here and buy my eggs. They feed them to the eels and, God willing, become pregnant.'

'What about the cats?' About a dozen of them lazed around the pool. 'They look pretty well fed too.'

'The *nuns* get the whites and the cats get the yolks,' she told me.

A young French couple arrived, and asked me if I had seen *les anguilles*. 'You have to give them an egg before they'll come out,' I said, wanting to see the eels in action. The girl bought one from the old lady, who separated the white from the yolk. She motioned to the girl to throw it in.

This time, the eels darted out of their lairs like muscular torpedoes. Watching them voraciously feeding on the fragments of egg, it struck me that while a semiologist would have trouble divining the significance of storks, the link between engorged eels, eggs and pregnancy was obvious to the point of grossness. 'Now, God willing,' I said to the girl, 'you will have a baby.'

'A baby?'

I explained the legend of the Bassin aux Anguilles.

'I don't want a baby!' She glanced at her partner, who was grinning. 'Not yet, anyway ...' The old lady sat beaming with approval, surrounded by her cats.

I had not yet found the tomb of Sultan Abu 'l-Hasan, and asked one of the gardeners for directions. He led me to a ruined chamber open to the sky, and pointed to a slender white marble grave marker. It was the length of a man and the shape of an old-fashioned strawberry cloche. Along its apex ran an inscription. It was as crisp as the day it was cut, and seemed to have been carved not in stone but in some more malleable substance, like icing sugar.

The gardener asked me where I was from. When I told him, he said, 'Then you and the Sultan are in-laws. His wife, Shams al-Duha, was English.'

I was surprised; but the idea was not totally implausible, as Abu 'l-Hasan had close contacts with Christian Europe. His army, with which he brought much of north-west Africa to heel, included a 5,000-strong Iberian Christian contingent. As well as being a successful warrior, Abu 'l-Hasan was a poet. He neatly versified his sultanic manifesto thus:

> I give to God His due both in public and private;
> I defend honour from the defilement of suspicion;
> I am bountiful to such as I choose;
> I smite with my sword the bases of necks.

He would, I felt, have approved of his gravestone, for he was also an accomplished calligrapher who copied and gilded three Qur'ans, one each for the holy cities of Mecca, al-Madinah and Jerusalem.

In 1348, when news of his death in battle near Tunis reached Fez, his son Abu Inan proclaimed himself sultan. Not long after, the dead ruler turned up in Morocco, alive; Abu Inan, deprived of his inheritance by this precocious resurrection (Abu 'l-Hasan had in fact escaped from the battle unnoticed), immediately made war on his father. When IB met the latter, he was back in Tunis and still fighting; but the traveller managed to give him a condensed version of his adventures, in a tower overlooking the field of battle. Abu 'l-Hasan died, this time incontrovertibly, in 1351 and was buried in Marrakesh. The following year, Abu Inan had a belated burst of filial piety and transferred his father's remains to Shallah; IB, at home between trips to Spain and west Africa, took part in the cortège.

The Marinid dynasty to which Abu 'l-Hasan and Abu Inan belonged were known in Europe through Moroccan wool exports – the origin of the name 'merino'. Their fame in the Islamic east resulted from the sensational demise of an earlier sultan: he had dyed his beard and was lying on his back waiting for the henna to take effect when he was stabbed to death by a black eunuch. His successor immediately ordered a pogrom of eunuchs in retaliation for the murder, and to conceal the fact that he had instigated it. Apart from such occasional blips in the succession, the Marinids were exemplary rulers. But a cloud hung over them. Like both preceding dynasties, they were Berbers; unlike them, they developed a complex about their origins – perhaps because they chose for their capital Fez, a hyper-Arab and rather po-faced city founded by a descendant of the Prophet. Eventually, in the manner of many non-Arab rulers before and since, they slammed the door on the skeleton in the cupboard by discovering a definitive pedigree that went back to the Prophet's ancestor, Adnan.

The Marinids further increased their respectability – and simultaneously invested in heavenly futures – by pouring their money into magnificent mosques and *madrasahs*. The finest of these were the ones built by IB's patron Abu Inan, who also founded a Sultanic Academy which included, along with IB on his return, grammarians, rhetoricians, historians, mystics, an archivist and an analyst of dreams. Abu Inan's own scholarly abilities were of a high order, judging by his writings that have survived. A certain massaging of one's literary patron never goes amiss, but IB was not entirely exaggerating when he wrote of him:

> In the disciplines of Qur'anic commentary, Prophetic Tradition, Maliki jurisprudence and Sufi literature, his is the highest attainment; he solves their difficulties with the light of his understanding, and illuminating apothegms are projected from his memory ... I have not seen any of the kings of the world whose concern for religious knowledge attains this degree.

Writing in Rome nearly two centuries later, Leo the African recalled this Marinid cultural apogee – the age of IB and Abu Inan – as a time when the Sultan would give poets laureate not only large sums of cash but also a fine horse, a fine slave-girl and, literally, the shirt off his back. He remembered too standing as a young man at this very spot, by the tomb of Sultan Abu 'l-Hasan, and copying the inscription. I began to do the same but soon gave up, defeated by its self-conscious, almost wilful intricacy. The light was going, and I bade the Sultan farewell.

Nearby, I bumped into a respectable-looking man who asked me for a cigarette. I gave him one; he immediately disembowelled it. I spotted him shortly afterwards, reclining beneath a bush and happily befuddled, surrounded by a cloud of kif and hibiscus and by the clacking of *laqlaqs*.

Altogether, it was a fine spot for a necropolis.

★

Before leaving Rabat I walked across the bridge over the Bou Regreg to Sala. Four centuries ago, in the great days of privateering, the town was home to those premier-league pirates, the Salee Rovers. Today, the place feels as innocuous as Bideford and, despite the short distance over the river from the capital, almost as provincial. I had come to see a building which, however, rivals anything to be found in the Marinid capital Fez.

As with many of the best buildings in Morocco, the *madrasah* founded by Abu 'l-Hasan in 1341 gave little away on the outside. Crossing the threshold into its courtyard was like opening a plain cloth binding to find it contains a pop-up book vividly coloured in greengage-green, sky blue, royal blue, turquoise, ivory and cinnamon. After the initial surprise came another: the inside was too small for the outside. But I realized that, although the courtyard was small, it was made to seem smaller by its decoration. Every single surface was covered either in carving or in polychrome tilework, as if the designer had suffered from acute *horror vacui*. The overall effect was of a very expensive bibelot.

When my eyes had adjusted, I was able to focus on the different areas of pattern. The floor, walls and dwarf peristyle columns were covered with *zillij*, tile mosaic. By turns, I sorted out the various colours; then the individual geometrical elements – stars, triangles and rhomboids; then, as happens with that oversized hound's-tooth check made fashionable by Chanel, my vision began flicking between positive and negative – was that a white star with a small blue one in the middle, or was it a small blue star surrounded by paper-dart shapes? Finally, I gave up looking and saw an ensemble, harmonious as the double helix. The Moroccan national airline chose well when they put *zillij* on their salt packets.

Above the *zillij* was a narrow band of tiles, this time bearing Qur'anic verses. The inscriptions nestled among arabesques like flurries of crisp leaves. Above the tiles, the walls were covered with carved stucco the colour of old bones and bearing more inscriptions, then, higher still, designs made up of swags, lacy bow-ties and sycamore propellers. Finally there was a richly sculpted cornice of dark cedar. It framed the only visible surface which was not in some way adorned: the sky.

Through an archway at one end of the courtyard was a small prayer-hall. Here the lower part of the walls was left plain, so as not to distract the worshippers' attention. At the opposite end of the courtyard I spotted a marble tablet. It was inscribed with a verse: 'Rejoice,' it said,

> for within this splendid building,
> In this extraordinary interior,
> You are in select company.

Looking about me, I agreed that the *madrasah* had good reason to be proud of itself.

The guardian took me up a staircase to the first floor and showed me the students' rooms, now empty. They were as plain as monks' cells. 'When the Sultan built this college,' he said, 'he was following the verse in the Holy Qur'an which tells us that knowledge is the true sultan.' Above, there was another floor of cells. The staircase continued upwards to the roof, where we sat on a parapet overlooking the town. Below us, a group of women walked past. 'Look at them!' exclaimed the guardian in a voice clearly meant to be heard down on the street. 'They go wherever they want. And the men are no better. They sit all day in the cafés, the mosques are empty . . . '

I left him to his reflections and returned to the courtyard, where I sat on the tiled floor with my back against a pillar.

There was something of the quadrangular, self-contemplating air of medieval Oxbridge about the place. But it was Oxbridge hung with brocade, an architecture not of space but of surfaces. The scholars who spent their formative years in such a setting were marked by it for life: the literature of IB's period was as lavishly decorated and inward-looking as its architecture. 'It was an age', a Moroccan historian has written, 'of condensations and exegeses, of condensations of the condensations and exegeses of the exegeses, and of commentaries on all these.' A not uncharacteristic work was an exegesis of the word 'In' in the phrase 'In the name of God'. Not a lot of what was written was new; but a lot was written. The free-thinking Ibn Khaldun disapproved, and wrote a chapter of his *Prolegomena* under the title, 'The great number of scholarly works available is an obstacle on the path to scholarship.' We can only guess what he would have said about our own undammable, computer-generated slurry of words.

Writing in the Marinid period was akin to *zillij*-making. Even the most mundane correspondence put out by the ruler's Department of *Insha* (letterwriting, also style, contrivance and, significantly, construction work) was composed with an obsessive attention to ornament, the prose rhymed and sometimes internally sub-rhymed. Only airmail letters escaped prolixity. Written on lightweight 'bird-paper' and flown by carrier pigeon, they were restricted to what one authority called 'the marrow, the cream of words'.

IB left the Maghrib at the age of 21 and never spent long enough in the literary capitals of the Arab world to develop the required baroqueness of phrase. So, when Abu Inan instructed him to set down his *Travels*, the Sultan brought in the young Andalusian belletrist Ibn Juzayy to empurple the Tangerine's prose. Ibn Juzayy was a literary prestidigitator. Among his achievements was a long ode devoid of the letter *r* (which no doubt became the party piece of labdacism sufferers). For the most part he merely tidied and rearranged IB's original, for much of the *Travels* is written in a plain style, Hemingway to the prevailing Pater. But now and then he pops up in the text like a literary jack-in-the-box: 'Ibn Juzayy says ... '; 'Ibn Juzayy remarks ... '; 'Ibn Juzayy adds: My father (God's mercy on him) used frequently to recite ... ' It is rather endearing, even if today it would be thought ill-mannered.

Ibn Juzayy also added a *dibajah* – literally a length of brocade, literarily an introduction in rhymed prose. Beginning with pious phrases, the passage sets out the idea of the book. It is also a chance to acknowledge its patron. Predictably, it is not a mere 'I should like to thank ... ': Abu Inan's reign 'is conjoined with majesty whose

crown is bound upon the temples of Gemini, and with glory that
sweeps with its skirts the Galaxy of Heaven . . . ' and so on, for several
pages. It is almost impossible to synthesize in translation the original's
rich and sophisticated flavour. A rare English *dibajah* introduces the
great Cambridge orientalist Edward Granville Browne's *A Year
Amongst the Persians*. He recalls 'how in pursuit of knowledge/I had
foregone the calm seclusion of college', before 'from Kirmán and the
confines of Bam/I had returned again to the city on the Cam'.

I sat by my pillar until my backside went numb, unwilling to leave.
The stucco had yellowed, the cedar darkened, and there was a new
nozzle on the little fountain in the centre of the courtyard; otherwise,
what I saw was what I would have seen in IB's time.

Suddenly the reverie was shattered by a gabble of voices as a group
of Spanish tourists entered the courtyard. They thudded across
the *zillij* floor on grape-pressing feet and ran their fingers across the
stucco. A teenaged boy leaned against a pillar with one commando-
soled boot cocked back against the tiles, staring into the sky with
a look of transcendent boredom. I remembered that Andalucia,
al-Andalus, the lost paradise of the Maghrib, gets its name from the
people from whom the Arabs took it: the Vandals. The invasion
lasted no more than five minutes; but the spell of the place was
broken.

I stopped a taxi to take me back to the Residence. 'Avenue Bou
Regreg, please. Just off the *jawlah*, the roundabout.'

'The what?'

I had used a Yemeni word. 'Sorry. I mean the *dawar*.'

'The *what*?'

I searched unsuccessfully for another synonym. 'You know, the
place where the roads meet and the cars go round in a circle.'

'Oh, you mean the *rond-point*.'

'That's it. So what do you call it in Moroccan Arabic?'

The driver looked at me curiously. '*Al-rond-point*.'

*

On the train back to Tangier, I had a longer Franco-Arabic conversation – the French was all hers – with a girl from the south, of
Mauritanian origin. She conformed to no image of Islamic woman-
hood that I had ever encountered: she wore black denim and high
army boots, and she was travelling with a large military-style ruck-

sack which she swung with a grunt on to the luggage rack. Her appearance, and her views – some of which raised eyebrows among our fellow-passengers – had me wondering whether she came from the City of Women, that Amazon-like colony located by eastern geographers in the Maghribi desert.

Everything went well until she asked if I was married. 'Only to my books,' I said, giving my stock answer. She looked sceptical. 'The thing about books', I went on, 'is that they don't answer back, they don't need to be bought clothes. You know what the poet said: "A man's best friend is his library."' The two other men in the compartment grinned; my friend looked hurt. I'd meant it lightheartedly, and now felt a cad.

'*Some* women are not as you imagine,' she said in a low voice.

She left the train at the next station; but before she did so she reached into her pocket and, without comment, handed me a newspaper cutting. It bore a photograph showing her in what appeared to be pyjamas, and the headline: 'Only Woman in Southern Morocco with Karate Black Belt'.

Back in Tangier, the Hôtel Ibn Batouta was full, but the receptionist told me that the place across the road had vacancies. In the lobby of the other hotel I rang a bell and waited, wondering how to take a prominently displayed notice: 'Absolutely No Guests to be Entertained in Bedrooms'. Was it simply a euphemism? Or did it mean that only conversations of a tedious nature were permitted? In a stay of one night, I would probably not be given the chance to find out.

The boy who answered the bell looked like a youthful Boris Karloff. As we climbed the stairs I told him I was writing a book about IB.

'Many famous writers have stayed here,' he said.

'Really? Who?' Remembering the photograph of IB across the road, I half expected them to include Ibn Khaldun and Sir John Mandeville.

'William Burroughs, Allan Ginsberg . . . Jack Kerouac.' He opened a firestation red door to a room that looked as if it might hardly have changed since the days of the Beats. The floor was laid with tiles in pomegranate pink, the heavy, dark oak bedsteads had brown velvet counterpanes, and green gingham covered a rickety table. A bidet squatted behind a curtain that flapped in the breeze from an open window. The room was loomed over by a very large wardrobe, painted glossy black. Surrounded by these potential metamorphs, I wrote up my notes warily. I did not open the wardrobe. It was certainly a setting to inspire, with a little metaphysic and a lot of drugs, *Naked Lunch*. (Further research revealed that the Mouniria was indeed the place where Burroughs, with the aid of his Eukodol-muse, wrote the novel. His room, however, was on the ground floor. Was my upstairs room the one where the Beats gathered to eat magic mushrooms, supplied by the late Dr Timothy Leary?)

Later, as I lay in bed – with half an eye on that wardrobe – I reviewed my brief visit to IB's homeland. In one sense, I had failed signally: I had come to visit his tomb, to ask for his blessing on my journey, and had found it to be a fake - a phantasm, Dr Abdelhadi called it. But on the credit side, I had found IB's spirit very much alive: in Khalid, for instance, the would-be traveller who could quote pre-Islamic poetry; and in Dr Abdelhadi, the far-travelled Maghribi come home to royal patronage. Moreover, IB seemed to have cult status. Apart from the airport, the street and the hotel, one of the ferries to Spain was named after him; there were seminars and conferences on him; there had been a TV series on him, an exhibition of 'portraits', and a Year of IB; they were planning an IB Museum in Tangier, and no doubt, one day, there will be a theme park. Further away, a German group had recorded a CD in his name; a Dutch friend has told me of an IB Scout Troop in Rotterdam; and there is even an Arabic on-line dating agency called 'IB'.

But cults need relics. Although al-Rumi tells us to look for the dead in men's hearts, his own tomb in Konya is one of the most revered and visited in Turkey. I had heard that they even display the great mystic's long-johns. I could only hope that somewhere along my route between here and Constantinople – a route eccentric enough to take in the Kuria Muria Islands in the Arabian Sea – I would find something as tangibly, if not so intimately, connected with IB.

I had a long way to go. A vision came to me, that of the Residence servants in Rabat lined up by the door, waving farewell; it gave way to another – an endless sequence of economical hotels. I slept uneasily, my dreams haunted by the flushing of a nearby lavatory.

As the Tangerine dawn turned to day, I set off for the airport. I was glad not to be following IB overland from Morocco – to cross rural

Algeria in his time was dangerous enough, but today it would have been potentially suicidal. The taxi driver painted a gory picture of events across the border. 'In many ways,' he said, not meaning to be discouraging, 'travel is more difficult now than it was in IB's day.'

As I paid him, he wished me a safe journey; then added, 'You must always remember that IB wanted people to know one another. He was ... ', he thought for a moment, then slipped into Franglais, ' ... *il était un gentleman*. May God go with you.'

He smiled broadly and patted me on the back. And there, I thought, not from a tomb but from the driver of Grand Taxi n° 158, was the blessing I had come for.

IB travelled across North Africa to Egypt. In Alexandria, he had his first inti-mations that he was 'to travel through the earth'. After passing through the Nile Delta he arrived in Cairo, capital of the Mamluks – a military élite of Turkic origin who ruled Egypt and the Levant. From Cairo he followed the Nile into Upper Egypt then crossed the desert to the Red Sea town of Aydhab, intending to sail to Jeddah, the port for Mecca. Political disturbances, however, had halted shipping. IB retraced his route to Cairo.

The Delta

A Dark and Greenish Country

'Real dream vision is an awareness on the part of the rational
soul in its spiritual essence, of glimpses of the forms of events.
While the soul is spiritual, the forms of events have actual
existence in it, as is the case with all spiritual essences. The soul
becomes spiritual through freeing itself from bodily matters and
corporeal perceptions. This happens to the soul in the form of
glimpses through the agency of sleep, whereby it gains the
knowledge of future events that it desires and regains the
perceptions that belong to it. When this process is weak and
indistinct, the soul applies to it allegory and imaginary pictures,
in order to gain the desired knowledge. Such allegory, then,
necessitates interpretation.'

Ibn Khaldun (d. 1406), *The Muqaddimah*, trans. Franz Rosenthal

SIX HUNDRED and seventy-one years, five months and three days
after IB, I walked along Lote-tree Gate Street, by which travellers
from the Maghrib entered Alexandria. 'She is a unique pearl of
glowing opalescence, a secluded maiden arrayed in her bridal adornments, glorious in her surpassing beauty.' IB, or more likely his editor,
was nothing if not flattering. Alexandria was even then of a certain
age. Now she is a very old lady indeed, an empress exiled to a tene-
ment who hardly dares to recall the days when Mark Antony came to
dinner.

Lote-tree Gate Street is a sort of deconstructed Marks and
Spencers, and I had to force my way between shoppers and racks of
nighties (or were they housecoats? Many Egyptians exist in a quoti-
dian sartorial penumbra, in which the division between day and
night attire is blurred and grown men are to be seen in pyjamas at tea-
time). There were tumuli of knickers, and pyramids of bras that,

given a concept, might have passed in Cork Street for feminist sculpture. More pyramids, built of watermelons with the one at the apex cut open, tottered along on horse-drawn carts whose drivers cleared a passage with loud cries. Barrows carried mounds of knobbly guavas and rupturing figs, protected from the flies by smoke from pans of incense. I bought some figs, and as I bit into one I remembered a couplet:

> He said: 'Your lips are split.'
> I said: 'Like only the sweetest of figs . . .'

IB made the long journey from Tangier to Alexandria by land, via Tlemsen and Algiers, Bougie, Constantine and Bône, Tunis and Tripoli, before crossing in the Libyan Desert that invisible line of longitude that divides Maghrib from Mashriq, West from East. In Bougie he caught a fever; by Tunis he had suffered a relapse and arrived at the city tied to his saddle with his turban cloth. Alone, and surrounded by groups of embracing friends, he burst into tears. But he left Tunis as *qadi*, judge, of the pilgrim caravan, and in Tripoli married the daughter of one of its members. In the desert before Egypt, in between avoiding nomadic bandits, he fell out with his father-in-law and divorced the girl. By the time he reached Alexandria, he had remarried.

My own journey into Egypt was less eventful. Mindful of al-Abdari's warning that 'the traveller, from the time he leaves the territory of Morocco until his arrival in Alexandria, never ceases to face death at the hands of malefactors' and of the fact that the difficulties of overlanding through Algeria and Libya were now, if anything, greater, I had flown into Cairo and caught the train. I had missed out the blunt end of a continent. But IB's account of the journey is sparse. The wastes of Barbary were not a place in which to linger.

The other passengers on the Alexandria train were mostly well-to-do families on their way to the seaside. Slowly, we slipped between the grubby suburban fingers of Cairo into the Delta. It was astonishingly green – of a dark, furry greenness shot with irrigation channels that glistened like slug trails – and I could understand the apparent colour blindness that often, in Arabic, confuses green with black. A medieval poet described the landscape we were travelling through as

A meadow of night–dark green like the down on a cheek,
A stream of chisels worked by the north wind's hand.

People still waved at trains. Men in earth-coloured *jallabiyyahs* and carrying mattocks would pause to raise a shovel-sized hand as we went past. Beamy women with trays of washing on their heads strode through the fields along slender paths. At intervals, we passed towns that had erupted into the fields in a rash of scabby cement buildings. Many of the flat roofs had sprouted sugarloaf pigeon towers of mud; the effect was a combination of the Gorbals and Timbuktu. In an utterly horizontal landscape, the tall chimneys of brickworks seemed unduly grand. Their angular inscriptions, picked out in bricks of a contrasting colour, made them into distant cousins of the Timurid tomb-towers of Samarkand.

In the station at Banha, a group of large and very beautiful women sat on the platform like earth mothers. As I looked at them, a small man with a Mr Punch face in a grey safari suit walked up to them and performed an energetic hornpipe. They quivered with laughter. In Damanhur station, the people on the platform had graded themselves according to size and shape, like pebbles on a beach: one bench was for large women, another for slimmer ones, and others were occupied by fat fellahs, thin fellahs and bent old men. Damanhur didn't look to be 'possessed of remarkable attractions', as it was for IB; but few places do from a railway line.

As we approached the coast, the Delta became less bosky. The sky opened out, and increasing humidity gave it a dull pearlescence, like the inside of a mussel shell. A hush of anticipation went around the children. I could remember that feeling, from a long time ago, approaching another sea.

Egypt looks big on the map; but, with nearly all its habitable area lying along the Nile, it is in reality a thin country, thinner than Chile. As if to make up, there are many Egypts, and nowhere more so than in Alexandria. One can read Forster, Cavafy and Durrell on the city, but it is most neatly summarized in the names of its tram-stops: Sidi Bishr, Sporting, Bulkley (officially Isis), Stanley, San Stefanu, Miami, Mustafa Pasha, Glymenopoulos.

I had little idea of what remained of the physical Alexandria IB saw. Of the two structures he described one, the Pharos, was reduced to a magnificent pile of rubble after his visit. The other still stood – the great column raised in honour of Diocletian in AD 300 and known to the Crusaders as Pompey's Pillar. In a city famous for eclecticism since the first Ptolemy set up a committee to design its religion, this at least was a stable point of reference from which to begin some inverse archaeology.

The Pillar stands as it did in the time of IB in a grove of date palms and other trees. Signs said 'To the Pillar' and 'Pillar this way' – well-intentioned but pointless: it was as if someone had put up notice-boards around Trafalgar Square to direct visitors to Nelson's Column. The Pillar rises on a dusty hillock riddled with cisterns, vaults and passages. Reaching the top of this eminence, I came face to face with an exceedingly ugly block of flats. The days were gone when Alexandria's buildings, as IB said, united imposing size with architectural perfection.

It was hot. The noise of Lote-tree Gate Street came on a fitful breeze like the murmur of a distant football crowd. I examined the centuries of graffiti carved into the base of the Pillar, hoping against hope to find 'IB, AH 726'; but the base was of soft stone, now eroded, and all I could make out was 'CICERO' followed by '1822'. I was joined by a group of Indonesian tourists in the charge of a pretty Egyptian guide. She told them that the Pillar was 26.85 metres tall from the bottom of its base to the top of its capital, and that 'it has been attributed since the Crusades' time to Bombay, the well-known Romanian general'. Thus, I suppose, are legends born.

Like many essentially useless objects, the Pillar has generated a number of stories to explain its existence. One account of the time of IB suggests that it was part of the stoa of Aristotle; the same source gives an alternative explanation, that it was one of seven columns brought by the giant proto-Arab tribe of Thamud from near Aswan, each column carried by a Thamudi under his armpit – like the old advert which shows a workman, made superhuman by Guinness Extra Stout, carrying a colossal girder. In the *Travels*, Ibn Juzayy in one of his editorial asides tells another story associated with the Pillar. One of his teachers, 'a much-travelled man', saw a member of the Alexandrian corps of archers sitting on top of it, apparently as some sort of protest. He had made the ascent by shooting a thread attached to a rope over the capital, pulling the rope over and securing it in the ground on the other side, and climbing up it. He then threw the rope off, 'so that people had nothing to guide them to his trick and were astonished by his feat'. Ibn Juzayy does not answer the most interesting question: How did the man get down?

An elegant lady in a small neo-classical building among the palms, who had charge of the Pillar, had not heard of the rope trick. She seemed shocked when I suggested going to the Alexandria Sporting Club to find an archer who could re-enact the stunt. But she did tell me that, in the more recent past, twenty-two people had had a picnic lunch on top of the Pillar.

For the medieval geographers, Alexandria swarmed with legends. One told how, when Alexander was building the city, each day's work would be mysteriously destroyed during the night. A watch was posted, and it was discovered that the culprits were sea monsters. Alexander had a brainwave. He ordered his carpenters to construct a mini-submarine of wood, sealed with tar and provided with glass portholes. Accompanied by the two best court artists, Alexander was lowered into the sea in this contraption, straight into a group of 'satans in human form, with the heads of beasts, carrying hatchets, saws and billhooks'. The artists quickly sketched the monsters and, safely back on land, turned their drawings into statues which they set up along the sea front. When the monsters emerged for their nightly spree of vandalism, they saw their own images, took fright and were never seen again.

Ibn Khaldun, rarely a willing suspender of disbelief, branded the story absurd. 'Were one to go down deep into the water, even in a box, one would have too little air for natural breathing. Because of that, one's spirit would quickly become hot. Such a man would lack the cold air necessary to maintain a well-balanced humour of the lung and the vital spirit. He would perish on the spot.' The force of logic may be on Ibn Khaldun's side; but the submarine story, apart from being entertaining, is a nice allegory for the process by which Hellenic art and science tamed the dark, irrational animal-headed gods of the Pharaohs.

The sea around the site of the Pharos was grey-green and truculent, and I could see how the imagination might people it with monsters. (In fact, a giant statue of Isis Pharia was dredged up at this spot forty years ago.) Here, legends cluster as thickly as the barnacles on the rocks. The historical Pharos was built by Ptolemy II Philadelphos in the early third century BC. One of the classical Wonders of the World, it was 450 feet high and topped by a brazier and a mirror which reflected light far out to sea. Medieval science fiction turned the mirror into a powerful reflecting telescope, through which the departure of ships from any port in the eastern Mediterranean – or, in another version, the world – could be observed. Some accounts add that the mirror was treated with special oils; others converted it into a giant burning-glass which could zap vessels far out at sea. The mirror was smashed by a Byzantine spy; or in the version of Leo the African, who places it on Pompey's Pillar, rendered useless by a Jewish agent who rubbed garlic into it.

More critical writers transmitted such legends with a good basting of scepticism; but the habit of retelling them created a phantom edifice of myth that outlived the physical Pharos. Travellers who saw the building in its senescence felt they had been sold a dud. The pilgrim-guide writer al-Harawi, 150 years before IB, wrote that 'nowadays it is no longer a Wonder of the World – it is no more than a watchtower by the sea'. IB, a congenital optimist, called it 'a square building soaring into the air', but admitted that a whole face of it was ruined. Passing through Alexandria again, twenty-three years later, he found that 'it had fallen into so ruinous a condition that it was impossible to enter it'.

Over a century later, the Mamluk Sultan Qayt Bey built a fine fortress from the remains of the Pharos. It still stands there, out on its tongue of land, riding the waves like a Dreadnought. I was sitting beneath its walls, just above the limpet line, mesmerized by the suck and gloop of the water, when a man with pigmentless hands came and sat beside me. I agreed with him that, praise God, it was a fine spot.

'You are a Muslim?'

I said I wasn't, and he gave me a brief lecture on Heaven and Hell.
'. . . And when your flesh has been consumed by the fire, it is immediately renewed and the process begins again. Don't you want to
escape this punishment?'

I thought for a little. 'I think our Hell is slightly less nasty than
yours.'

He laughed. 'Well, it's your decision.'

It was all very good-natured; we might have been discussing
whether to pass through the red or the green channel in Customs.
The man wished me an enjoyable stay, and went to rejoin his family.

At the tip of the peninsula the sea was angry, thudding against the
rocks and spitting spray. A lone man crouched down by the waterline
collecting limpets, but with one eye on the waves. Whenever a
big one came he scuttled out of its way. Tradition gives the
Mediterranean a malevolent character: it is said that God, after He
had created the seas, asked the Indian Ocean what it would do with
the Faithful who travelled on it. 'I'll carry them on my back,' said the
Ocean. When He asked the same question of the Mediterranean, it
answered, 'I'll drown them!' God blessed the Indian Ocean with
pearls and spices, and cursed the Mediterranean with storms and
Christians.

In his chapter on Alexandria, IB quoted a long prayer, the *Litany of
the Sea*. Reading it at this spot, it seemed to throb and flow with the
rhythm of the waves:

> Subject to us this sea as Thou didst subject the sea unto Moses,
> and as Thou didst subject the fire to Abraham, and as Thou
> didst subject the mountains and the iron to David, and as
> Thou didst subject the wind and the demons and the jinn to
> Solomon. Subject to us every sea that is Thine on earth and in
> heaven, in the world of sense and in the invisible world, the sea
> of this life and the sea of the life to come. Subject to us every-
> thing, O Thou in Whose Hand is the rule over all. *Kaf-Ha-Ya-
> Ayn-Sad* . . .

Fourteen centuries of exegesis have failed to explain those final
letters, and others, which appear in the Qur'an. They are reputed to
be a powerful talisman. Six months later, I was to see them carved on

the stern of a long-beached *sambuq* in a tiny haven, two thousand miles away on the Arabian Sea.

I walked back along the landward side of the peninsula, looking across the bay towards the city. From here it appeared to float like a mirage; through half-closed eyes it might have been the city Alexander built, so dazzlingly white that he had green silk hung around its streets to cut the glare. It is all an illusion, a trick of the light that has taken in generations of visitors. Symon Semeon, in the city a couple of years before IB, wrote that 'Alexandria shines in outward appearance, but in reality its streets are narrow, ugly, tortuous and dark'; al-Abdari thought that 'its form is greater than its substance ... like a beautiful body without a soul'. Few places on earth can have suffered so long and dispiriting an anticlimax.

I walked on, haunted by snatches of the *Litany of the Sea* and 'Eternal Father, Strong to Save'; and ended up feeling maudlin. Chicken livers in Madeira sauce at the Elite Restaurant did nothing to dispel the sensation. Neither did the ambience of the restaurant. The *patronne*, an elderly Greek woman with turkey wattles who wore beads and a striped kaftan, sat with a prematurely grey young man. She smoked and swayed to a tape of sad bouzouki music, counterpointed by the rhythmic clang of a water-seller out on the street. An old Greek couple came in and greeted her. They were dressed as for a wedding; the man carried a white shoulder bag, decorated in the manner of Chanel with large gilt bosses.

I awoke in my hotel room in the twilight, after an overlong siesta crowded by fantastical, chicken-liver inspired dreams. My maudlin state persisted; darkened by the feeling that I wasn't getting anywhere near IB or his Alexandria, it threatened to turn into one of ennui. There was only one antidote: a visit to Lionel.

Lionel was living in graceful retirement in the suburb of Bulkley, named after its tram-stop. The driver of the taxi I hailed to take me to Lionel's explained that Mr Bulkley – he called him 'Bukleh' – was a member of the original Victorian tram company's board of directors, and that the stop was built to serve his villa. Victorian Alexandria now seems hardly less distant than Hellenistic Alexandria, and the road to Bulkley is overlooked by walls of high-rise blocks and clogged with a thrombus of traffic. But it was in the unlikely setting of this traffic jam that I had my first real glimpse into the Alexandria of IB.

The subject of trams led unexpectedly into that of *walis*, 'friends of God' or saints. 'When you British were building the other part of the tramline,' said the driver, 'a strange thing happened. The route you'd chosen was blocked by the tomb of a *wali*, Sidi Abu 'l-Durdar, and you decided to knock it down.'

I protested at the 'you'.

'All right, they decided to knock it down. And, would you believe it, the first workman who raised his pickaxe to strike the tomb found that his arms were paralysed! And the next one, and all of them. So you left the tomb alone. It's like an island between the tramlines. This was a great *karamah* of the saint.'

Talk of saints and *karamahs* – saintly as opposed to prophetic miracles – took me straight into the text of the *Travels*. IB was enthralled by saints, and wherever he found himself he went out of his way to knock on the doors of hermitages, collecting anchorites as avidly as later tourists collected ammonites. It was here in Alexandria that his hagiophilia took off, with a saint called Burhan al-Din the Lame. My research had failed to turn up any references to Burhan al-Din other than IB's, and the driver had not heard of him. I asked him about Yaqut, 'Ruby', another holy man IB had visited in Alexandria.

'Sidi Yaqut? Haven't you seen his new mosque? It's as big as al-Mursi's and right next to it.'

Suddenly, things were dropping into place. IB had called on Yaqut. Al-Mursi – Abu 'l-Abbas of Murcia, in al-Andalus – was Yaqut's teacher; he died before IB's visit, but the Moroccan mentioned his fellow Maghribi in passing.

'By the way,' said the driver as I paid him, 'my name is also al-Mursi.'

'Your family name?' I asked, surprised.

'No, my given name. It's very common here.' Such is the devotion of the Alexandrians to their holy men that generations of sons have been named after a town far away in the south-east of Spain. As I rang the bell to Lionel's flat, I felt I might be getting somewhere.

The flat was half-way up a twelve-storey block. Lionel had filled it with orientalia and made it into a comfortable roost for a migratory, slightly old-fashioned bachelor. We filled in a lacuna of several years since we had last met. 'And now,' Lionel concluded, 'I may be graciously retired. But it's still the same old story: it's not love that makes the world go round. It's *hysteria*.'

'White-hot, incandescent hysteria!' I added, completing Lionel's catchphrase.

I told him about my conversation in the taxi. 'Oh yes, they're *great* ones for saints, the Alexandrians,' he said. 'You'll have to ask my Lord Burleigh about saints. He should be here soon.'

Burleigh, an old Alexandrian friend of Lionel's also known as Muhammad, appeared shortly, resplendent in tweed jacket and yellow silk stock. I asked him about the elusive Burhan al-Din the Lame, but he hadn't heard of him. He did, however, add to the taxi driver's story of Abu 'l-Durdar, the saint of the tramlines. 'They say – and God is the most knowing – that during the Second World War a bomb was heading straight for the tomb when a white cloud appeared and diverted it. A British soldier was standing at the spot and would have been killed. He converted then and there.'

Over supper we talked more about the supernatural. Burleigh told the story of a property developer who had built an office block in the nearby suburb of Rushdi. He made a *nadhr* – a holy pledge usually involving the giving of alms – which he would discharge when the building was finished. 'He forgot about the pledge, or couldn't be bothered with it. And the jinn came and took the place over. No one's ever been able to stay in it. Some policemen once tried spending the night there, for a bet. But they were hurled around – really flying through the air. The building's on the main road and worth a fortune. But it's never been occupied, except by those jinn.'

I tend to be sceptical about scepticism; however, I found it hard to believe that a valuable piece of real estate would be abandoned because of bumps in the night. But as he drove me back to my hotel, Burleigh pointed it out. It stood dark and windowless between brightly lit blocks, like a single rotten tooth. All the openings on the lower floors were walled up. It was a warm evening, but I shivered. A phrase came to mind: *the abomination of desolation.*

Next morning, I set off along the Corniche to call on the two saints mentioned by the taxi driver: Yaqut, whom IB visited, and Yaqut's spiritual master, al-Mursi. Al-Mursi's mosque-tomb was built in the 1940s in the Mamluk-baroque-revival style. It is a tall, creamy, octagonal structure, cathedral-sized and topped by four domes on high drums and by a slender minaret. With its fretted cresting and relief carving, the building looks like a very large ivory reliquary. A relipuary, of course, is precisely what it is. Inside, al-Mursi lies in a tomb covered with a rich pall and surrounded by candles. The enclosure around the tomb is piped with striplights in green, the colour of Islamic sanctity, and by illuminated signs exhorting one to pray; which is what several dozen men and women, the latter decorously separated by a barrier, were doing. A few other men were sitting against columns, reading the Qur'an or dozing, and the place had the rustly, sleep-inducing air of a public library. There was a sort of fervour about the worshippers, but it was laid back. I noticed, framed on a column, a piece of advice given to al-Mursi by his own spiritual master al-Shadhili, author of the *Litany of the Sea*: 'Know God, and be as you like.'

I went and sat with the doorkeeper in the lofty entranceway. It was filled with pigeonholes and resembled an Oxbridge porters' lodge, except that the pigeonholes contained shoes and sandals. The doorkeeper was delighted when I showed him the reference to his saint in IB's *Travels*. Turning the page, he saw the *Litany of the Sea*: 'It is written here', he said, 'that "His disciples still recite it every day." And now, they still do! How old is this book? Six hundred and fifty years! Glory be to God!'

Some other men joined us, and the *Travels* was passed eagerly from hand to hand. 'Look! Here is Sidi Yaqut ... And someone called al-Kindi. No, we don't know him; but listen to what the book says: "He used to wear a turban of extraordinary size. Never either in the eastern or in the western lands have I seen a more voluminous headgear than this."' They all laughed.

'If God wills,' said the doorkeeper, 'you will pray the noon prayer with us.'

I gulped. People were always assuming that I was a Muslim. It was the way I spoke. My Arabic has the rhythms and cadences of the Arabian Peninsula. Besides, I had learned through experience to classicize my speech further: once, offering to carry some bags for the Egyptian wife of a friend, I inadvertently slipped in a Yemeni dialect word and said what sounded to her like, 'Do let me ravish your baskets.' She declined, with a shriek. Now, to the ears of the doorkeeper, my speech – littered with imprecations to prolong my listeners' lives and reward their goodness – was 'Arabic as it was sent down from heaven'. For Arabs one is what one speaks. I could hardly be anything but a Muslim. 'Um,' I said, looking at my watch, 'I must go and visit some more saints first.'

'As you like,' said the doorkeeper. 'Our city is full of *walis*.' He beamed with civic pride. Lionel was right: the Alexandrians were great ones for saints.

I retrieved my shoes from their pigeonhole, took my leave of the doorkeeper and his friends and walked the hundred or so yards to the mosque-tomb of Sidi Yaqut. If anything, it was even bigger than that of his guru, and the juxtaposition smacked of post-mortem rivalry. The building was unfinished, a skeleton of reinforced concrete filled in with red brick. It reminded me of a 'Bako' building set I had played with as a child. Inherited from my pre-Lego elder siblings, it consisted of a base drilled with holes into which you inserted metal rods; between the rods you had to slot grooved bakelite bricks. One of the workmen explained that they were nearly ready to begin sticking on the façades. To see the mosque as yet unclad was faintly shocking, like catching sight of a bishop in Y-fronts.

The workmen pointed out Yaqut's tomb, in a sort of undercroft, then introduced me to Shaykh Hilal, the imam of the new mosque. I explained my reason for coming, and added that I thought IB would have been delighted to see the saint so magnificently remembered.

' "Only he shall inhabit God's places of worship who believes in God and the Last Day, and performs the prayer," ' Shaykh Hilal intoned, quoting from the Qur'an. The word 'inhabit' had a secondary sense of 'build'. 'And it is all being achieved by private subscription, not government funding.'

Standing there on the steps of his unfinished cathedral in immaculate white *jallabiyyah* and graduated aviator shades, Shaykh Hilal looked the part – head of a consortium of spiritual investors. We talked a little more, but I felt that his eyes, just visible through the tinted glass, were looking not at me but into me, probing around for my soul. I saw a question begin to form on his lips and, not wanting to be revealed as an infidel quite so close to where I'd been taken for a believer, I wished the Shaykh success and left.

I had so far found no trace of the Alexandrian holy man who most influenced IB, Burhan al-Din the Lame. Shaykh Hilal had not heard of him; the doorkeeper of al-Mursi's mosque had said, 'Burhan al-Din ... No, I don't know him. But', he added, 'I seem to remember a Maghribi traveller looking for him a couple of years ago.'

That earlier Maghribi, IB, described Burhan al-Din as 'the learned, self-denying, pious and humble imam, one of the greatest of ascetics and a devotee of outstanding personality . . . I spent three days as his guest.' He went on to recall

> *A miracle of his.* One day, when I had entered his room, he said to me: 'I see that you are fond of travelling and wandering from land to land.' 'Yes,' I replied, 'I am fond of it,' although there had not as yet entered my mind any thought of penetrating to such distant lands as India and China. Then he said: 'You must certainly, if God will, visit my [spiritual] brother Farid al-Din in India, and my brother Rukn al-Din Zakariyya in Sind, and my brother Burhan al-Din in China, and when you reach them convey to them a greeting from me.' I was amazed at his prediction, and the idea of going to these countries having been cast into my mind, my wanderings never ceased until I had met these three.

It was frustrating to find out nothing about the man from whom IB learned of his destiny. Later, a trawl through the literary sources proved as fruitless; it did, however, net some other curiosities. I discovered in al-Nabhani's *Compendium of Saintly Miracles* that a supernatural bond existed between the occupants of the two great Alexandrian mosque-tombs. Al-Mursi telepathized the birth of his future disciple Yaqut in distant Ethiopia and, although it was the middle of summer, ordered *asidah* to be cooked in celebration – the equivalent of Christmas pudding in July. Years later, Yaqut, who had been bought as a slave, happened to be with his merchant owner at sea near Alexandria when a storm blew up and threatened to sink the ship. Yaqut's master vowed that if they were saved he would present the slave to al-Mursi. They landed safely, but as Yaqut was found to have scabies, the merchant offered al-Mursi another slave. Al-Mursi refused: 'I don't want this one. I want the slave you pledged to me.' Yaqut eventually became a Muslim St Francis, interceding on behalf of distressed animals and birds. One story tells that a dove rode on his head from Alexandria to Cairo, so that the saint could complain on her behalf to a muezzin who was killing her squabs.

The introduction to al-Nabhani's hagiography lists different types of *karamah*, or saintly miracle. These range from the useful ability to write out texts at great speed, to bodily metamorphosis and the Einsteinian concept of the scrolling up or unscrolling of time and space. Among the stranger miracles are what might be termed tele-phagy – the belly of an absent hungry person is filled simultaneously as the saint eats – and the knack of seeing the names of crimes, including adultery, written in black on the offending member.

Reports of similar miracles are scattered throughout the *Travels*. In IB's time, scholars eagerly discussed and analysed sainthood and mira-cles. Holy men were held to have access to a world of spiritual intel-lection in which all times and places were co-existent – hence their ability to foretell the future, travel with great speed and appear at the same time in different locations. It is the sort of strange hypothetical realm which contemporary physicists explore, more clumsily, with their particle accelerators. In fact, meta- and particle physicists have more in common than one might suppose: both tug, if in slightly different directions, at the knots which hold the cosmos together; both look beyond the immediate world of sense perception into one where cause can only be deduced from effect – a quark is as invisible as an angel; both are confronted by Manichaean polarities – miracles and black magic, cheap energy versus total destruction. For laymen, the theories behind both ways of looking at creation are equally esoteric, and to believe in either of them needs faith.

IB was intrigued by the world beyond the senses and by the holy men who could look into it. In his day there were a lot of them about: al-Nabhani, whose hagiography covers around 1,300 years, lists more saints and miracles for the thirteenth and fourteenth centu-ries than for any other period. Also, a disproportionate number of holy men came from the Maghrib: a contemporary of IB's said that 'saints sprout from its soil like grass'. IB was born not just in a medieval Age of Aquarius, but in its California.

The law of supply and demand applied to sanctity no less than to any other commodity. There were simply too many saints in Morocco and al-Andalus for home consumption, so the region exported them. The greatest holy men of Egypt, like al-Mursi and al-Shadhili, were from the west. In his eastward journey, IB was surfing a wave of sanctity. He himself was often tempted to give up the world; but what he calls his 'importunate self' – his materialist ego – was too strong. He was never more than an enthusiastic amateur of the spirit, a Dr Syntax of mysticism.

Had he joined the mystics, he would have been lost to the world of travel literature, and probably would have gone the way of Herr

Hornemann of Göttingen who, according to Sir Richard Burton, 'set out from Cairo in 1798; became, it is supposed, a Marabut or Santon in Káshná; and disappeared about 1803'. If one didn't disappear, one was liable to be pestered to death – literally, in the case of a holy man of Damawand in Persia who was killed by the inhabitants of the village where he lived, lest he relocate himself and his divine blessings. Even in death one could be horribly molested. The body of a certain Moroccan saint was exhumed and buried so often that he had four tombs in four different villages, each eager for its share of holiness. When the saint's son ordered the graves to be examined, they found his father's corpse in each one.

Walking back along the Corniche, I reflected that the physical Alexandria of today would be all but unrecognizable to IB. But the intangible city – the one built on devotion to saints, holy pledges and belief in miracles – was in remarkably good shape. To travel with IB I would have, in effect, to keep my third eye peeled.

Before I left the country, something happened to me in Upper Egypt, in the desert between the Nile and the Red Sea, which I find hard to explain except in terms of this other, non-physical context. Perhaps it was even a very minor *karamah*.

*

The air from the Rosetta, or Bolbitine, branch of the Nile was fresh, but the teahouse was fuggy with gossip. One of my fellow tea-drinkers leaned towards me and said in a stage whisper, 'You know, Princess Diana was killed by the British intelligence services ... '

'Yes,' another confided, 'and for some time before that she had been wearing a *headscarf!*'

I was in a flippant mood. 'Then I'll let you in on something. Her mother-in-law has been wearing a headscarf for years. She doesn't do it much in public. Mostly when she's out with her horses.'

They smiled. They knew we were playing with symbols, of which the headscarf is a potent one. It can render its wearer a toff or a pleb, a martyr or a traitor (a woman MP in Turkey was recently stripped of her nationality for wearing one in Parliament).

The whole world was buzzing with Diana, but nowhere was as thick with rumours as Dodi's ancestral home. They had settled on Egypt like a plague of locusts, chirping away in cafés and on the pages of the press: Diana was pregnant by Dodi; she was going to marry

Dodi; she had married Dodi; she was thinking of converting to Islam; she had converted to Islam; she had converted after Dodi played her cassettes of al-Sha'rawi, a man regarded by many as a modern *wali*. Columnists compared the affair to that of Antony and Cleopatra, with the Royal Family as the vengeful Octavian; or to the rumoured intention of Richard the Lionheart to marry his sister to Saladin's brother, or to Saladin himself, with the Royal Family as the interfering Pope who stymied the match. An Egyptian was to file a lawsuit against the Queen and Tony Blair: the plaintiff had always cherished the notion that Britain champions democracy and religious freedom, and by plotting against Diana they had caused him psychological damage. The price of this damage, he said, should be $170,000.

I bade the tea-drinkers good-night. I'd had enough of headscarf-and-dagger conspiracies. And I'd had a long day.

IB left Alexandria to visit the greatest living holy man in Egypt, his countryman al-Murshidi, who led 'a life of devotion in retirement from the world, and bestowed gifts from the divine store, for he was indeed one of the greatest saints who enjoy the vision of the unseen'. Al-Murshidi's retirement was, however, metaphorical, for like Diana he suffered from his own celebrity. Despite living in an obscure village thirty miles from Alexandria he 'was sought by the amirs and ministers of state, and parties of men in all ranks of life used to visit him every day'. Many pestered saints take to pillars or other inaccessible spots; but not al-Murshidi. He rose to the occasion, making his hermitage the Garsington Manor of fourteenth-century Egypt. All his visitors were fed: 'Every man of them would express his desire to eat some flesh or fruit or sweetmeat at his cell, and to every one he would bring what he desired, though that was often out of season.' I had left Alexandria on a minibus not knowing if, like Yaqut, al-Murshidi was still revered or whether, like Burhan al-Din the Lame, he had dropped from the hagiography.

One of the largest women I have ever seen hauled herself on to the minibus and sat next to me. She had a child of about four who sat in rather than on her. Whenever he became fretful, she smothered him with her arms and breasts. There are plenty of bulky Egyptians – in Alexandria I noticed a sign saying 'KURHAUS AND OBESITY MANAGEMENT' – but I had never actually come up against one quite so enormous. It struck me that you rarely saw older Egyptians of great size, and I wondered whether a day came when they could no longer fit through the door and had to stay at home, shut away like the Monster of Glamis, getting bigger and bigger. On the cramped minibus seat there was no question of maintaining a demure Islamic distance from female flesh. There was too much of it.

We drove for a while along the busy Cairo motorway, then turned off into an aqueous, nacreous nether land of water and wobbling horizons. In every direction there were dikes and rice fields, some covered in water like sheets of mercury. Animals and birds were everywhere: buffalo, docile as old dogs, following small boys on thin cords; buffalo wallowing in the channels, half submerged like lumpy logs of mahogany; ducks, geese and small boys splashing in the canals. In one village a flock of geese shimmied between the wheels of our bus and those of a lorry, like a drunken *corps de ballet*. Humans seemed to take on the guise of animals. Tall, thin peasants in white *jallabiyyahs* and baseball caps had an avian profile, like the egrets that followed them through the rice fields. A man squatting in a dike glared up at the minibus like an annoyed toad.

My neighbour left the minibus in a village, and I stretched gloriously, released from my soft, damp prison. Soon afterwards we arrived in Fawwah, through which IB passed on his way to al-Murshidi's hermitage. I climbed into a *calèche*, drawn at a lick by a high-stepping roan, and was dropped at the convent of the Khalawati dervishes.

The dervishes are long gone, replaced by the local office of antiquities. The Director was keen to show me the restored portal of the National Fez Factory set up by Muhammad Ali Pasha; the portal was clearly his baby, and he seemed crestfallen when I declined. But he kindly deputed two assistants to take me to al-Murshidi's village. IB's memory or his editor had concertina'd the distance from Fawwah to the village, Munyat Bani Murshid. Rather than being 'separated from it by a canal', it was beyond the town of Mutubis and two more bus rides away.

No one seemed to know what, if anything, remained of al-Murshidi. But Hajj Ali, the elder of my two companions, was a regular of more local tombs, and on the short walk to the bus garage he pointed out several long-dead *walis*. I asked about Abu 'l-Najah, a saint whose tomb in Fawwah IB mentioned. 'Oh, he's just here, behind the Bank of Egypt.'

The tomb-chamber was roofed with a later pot-bellied dome and crowned with a stone turban. It stood on the bank of the Nile; beside it some fishermen were mending their nets. Under the little building flowed a water channel which Hajj Ali said cured all sorts of illness. We looked through a heavy bronze grille and saw a tomb swathed in green, on which a large green turban sat beside an open Qur'an. Hajj Ali told me that the grille had floated to the spot along the river. 'Smell the sweet breeze from the tomb,' he instructed me. 'It comes from the saint, not from any perfumes.' I sniffed, and the air did seem slightly scented – holy air-conditioning, I thought.

In fact, the whole of the western Delta reeked with the odour of sanctity. In Mutubis, between buses, we visited another pot-bellied mausoleum and had tea with the guardian, an ex-policeman who bore a striking resemblance to Ronald Reagan. He proudly showed us the pall he had embroidered for his saint – much as an English parish spinster might display her altar-frontal – and told us that during a drought in 1958 water had suddenly gushed up beside the tomb.

We arrived at Munyat Bani Murshid on a particularly crowded minibus. Hajj Ali and his colleague, another Mursi, were looking dishevelled and sweaty, and I hoped I hadn't brought them on a wild *wali* chase. We stood by a dike, looking lost, until a middle-aged man detached himself from a domino game in a café across the road and offered his assistance. Tentatively, I asked if there were any memories of al-Murshidi, the saint.

'How could we not remember him? All the villages in Egypt were born at the tombs of saints. Our saint is just around the corner.' Then he added, 'Did you know that the traveller IB came to see him in – when was it? – 1326, I think.'

I was astonished. So far in Egypt, IB had hardly been more than a name. Now, in a secluded spot surrounded by rice fields, someone was talking about his visit as if it had happened within living memory. As we walked to the saint's tomb I explained why I had come and the man, who introduced himself as the local schoolmaster, quoted from the *Travels*: ' "Arriving at the cell of this shaykh before the hour of afternoon prayer" – you have come a little later in the day – "I saluted him ... He rose to meet me, embraced me, and calling for food invited me to eat. He was dressed in a black woollen tunic." ' He was word-perfect. As he read, or recited, it seemed that the years which had elapsed since the original visit were insignificant beside the constants of place and memory. I had chanced, I felt, on one of those fragments of existence withdrawn from time.

The mosque-tomb had been added to over the years, and most of it looked recent. The schoolmaster introduced us to the imam, a man in his thirties. Under a red and white turban, he had a bony, chiaroscuro face, the sort IB would have described as 'displaying the marks of his devotions'. We went inside the screen around the saint's tomb and the imam intoned the inscriptions on the tombstone in a deep bass, then the Qur'anic verses on the screen itself: 'The friends of God need have no fear; neither should they sorrow. They are the ones who have believed and been pious, and they shall rejoice in the world below and the world above.' He looked at me, ascetically beautiful as an El Greco saint. 'You are a Muslim?'

'A Masihi.'

There was a pause. Then he smiled. 'Our religion is tolerance. We are not like the bearded ones.'

'In Yemen, where I live,' I said, 'there is a saying: "If whiskers meant anything, tomcats would be pashas." '

The imam grinned and repeated the proverb, chuckling, as he circled the tomb, adjusting its coverings, tucking the saint up.

We went and sat in the vestry, where the imam had a desk with his name engraved on a brass plate. Sport Cola and biscuits were brought. The late summer afternoon was humid with the exhalations from the rice fields. The weather had been the same when IB was here. I opened the *Travels* and read aloud: ' "When I prepared to sleep, he said to me 'Go up to the roof of the cell and sleep there', for this was during the summer heats ... So I ascended to the roof and found there a straw mattress and a leather mat, vessels for ritual ablutions, a jar of water and a drinking-cup, and I lay down to sleep." '

The schoolmaster took over, from memory: ' "That night, as I was sleeping on the roof of the cell, I dreamed that I was on the wing of a huge bird which flew with me in the direction of Mecca, then made towards the Yemen, then eastwards, then went towards the south, and finally made a long flight towards the east, alighted in some dark and greenish country, and left me there." ' It was very quiet in the vestry. You could hear the bubbles bursting in the Sport Cola. He continued: ' "I related my dream to the shaykh and he said: 'You shall make the Pilgrimage to Mecca and visit the tomb of the Prophet at al-Madinah, and you shall travel through the lands of Yemen and Iraq, the lands of the Turks, and the land of India. You will stay there for a long time and you will meet there my brother Dilshad the Indian, who will rescue you from a danger into which you will fall.' " '

And so it came to pass. And then, without warning, something about the setting – I think the late summer heaviness, the pop and biscuits – took me back to a day about twenty-five years earlier when, in my mother's kitchen in Bristol, a Shinto priest had cast my horoscope and spoken about the approximate date of my death. He had hedged his bets: 'Something may change in you, and you will avoid it.' But I was still in the danger period.

I had rarely mentioned the prophecy to anyone, but I told it now. The imam spoke: 'The Prophet – peace be upon him – said: "Astrologers tell lies even when they tell the truth." Knowledge of the future is God's, even if He sometimes permits His prophets and saints to look into it, like Joseph – peace be upon him – with Pharaoh, and like our own saint here with IB. Today there are people who claim to tell the future and to interpret dreams. Most of this comes from the Devil. God knows whether they are impostors. There are also saints, but they keep their identity concealed. Things have changed.'

'And some things have not changed,' said the schoolmaster. 'IB wrote, "He then gave me a travelling-provision of *ku'aykat*, small cakes, and silver coins." We have no silver coins; but do you not think that *ku'aykat* is better Arabic than *baskawit?*' He offered me a biscuit, and we all laughed.

I thanked the imam and the schoolmaster and bade them farewell.

'*Hasalat barakah,*' said the imam, 'you have brought blessings with you.'

'Even if I am not a Muslim?'

'You are a guest. Ours, and the saint's.'

Hajj Ali and al-Mursi left me at the Nile Barrage. I walked across it and stopped in the middle. Upstream, Mutubis was varnished in late-afternoon light like a brand-new Canaletto. The great volume of water flowing beneath me had a plastic, almost fleshly look,

> As if its waves were the wrinkles on a belly,
> And its eddies navels.

I remembered how even the crotchety Symon Semeon, watching the Rosetta Nile, had been entranced by this 'famous and interminable river, navigable from the Mediterranean Sea to Upper India where dwells Prester John'.

I stood there as the sun fell and thought about IB's dream of far travel. For medieval metaphysicians, dreams came not from some spidery Freudian crypt of the psyche but from that bright world of spiritual intellection where events and places are parallel. Ibn Khaldun explained the oneiric mechanism: in sleep, the veil of the senses is lifted and the soul seeks contact with this spiritual world. Detached from the body, it becomes a 'spiritual essence' in which the forms of events past and future have actual existence; but on its return to the body these events appear as allegories, which need interpretation. Ibn Khaldun quoted from an earlier scholar some dream words which, uttered before sleep, prepare the soul for visions: *tamāghis ba'dān yaswādda waghdās nawfanā ghādis.* From the same source, he passed on a recipe for enabling a man to tell the future: put him in a barrel of sesame oil for forty days and feed him on nothing but figs and nuts, 'until his flesh is gone and only the arteries and sutures of the skull remain'; then expose him to the air to dry out. (To me, this seems a long-winded way to achieve the same result as trepanation, which these days can be performed in seconds with an electric drill equipped with a suitable bit and, of course, a steady hand.) The recipe, Ibn Khaldun rightly warns, is 'detestable sorcery'.

Six hundred years on from Ibn Khaldun a Moroccan scholar, in the same fusive tradition that made translations of the Greek work on dreams by Artemidorus popular among medieval Muslim savants, has applied to IB's dream a Jungian-Sufi reading: the great bird is the *simurgh*, for Sufis a symbol of divine revelation; the air it flies in stands for illusion; in the dark and greenish country darkness symbolizes primeval origins, greenness – as in the green palls on saints' tombs – Islamic salvation; the land where IB arrives is 'the real and solid truth'.

I used to dream IB's dream, with certain differences; we probably all have dreamed it. My version came to me recurrently when I was a child: I would fly in a telephone box over nomad encampments set in desert and steppe, and along mountain ranges. I can't remember ever landing, which in Jungian-Sufi terms must condemn me to a life of spiritual dilettantism. Anyone who watched British television on Saturday afternoons in the 1960s and later will immediately put the telephone box down to the influence of *Dr Who*, which came on after the wrestling and the football scores and whose eponym travelled through time and space in a police-box called the Tardis. I am inclined now, perhaps not entirely flippantly, to wonder whether the Tardis and the *simurgh* are in fact one and the same, travelling in the same metaphysical space-time continuum, and whether Dr Who, the Time Lord, is the archetypal Wise Old Man, who like the Qur'anic traveller al-Khadir is immortal and who, in at least one of his incarnations, appears in the patched robe of the Sufi master or of Joseph, the prototypical interpreter of dreams . . .

But I have strayed into the primordial sludge of the collective sub-conscious, Nilotically fertile for poets and madmen, a sprite-haunted quagmire for the rest of us.

★

The following day I left Rosetta, or Rashid, to travel across the hypotenuse of the Delta to Damietta, or Dimyat, where I hoped to find traces of the depilating dervishes known as Qalandars.

Slowly, rice fields gave way to cotton. At a place called Kafr al-Shaykh I got into a minibus and waited for it to fill up. So far the only other passenger, sitting in front of me next to the driver's seat, was certainly no depilating dervish; he was what the imam of al-Murshidi's mosque-tomb would have called a Bearded One. The term 'fundamentalist' is often used by the press, but it is a misnomer: since the principal revelation of Islam came in the text of the Qur'an and Muslims are all by definition fundamentalists, the bearded ones are perhaps better termed puritans. The puritan beard is immediately recognizable: it has a vegetal, weedy quality like the beard of a Roman river god. I was about to make conversation when he looked into the rear-view mirror and began delicately arranging the tendrils of his beard. As I watched him, I thought of the Regency beaux who would spend much of a morning tying their stocks so as to achieve an unstudied appearance. As in this, and in the Japanese art of ikebana, real art lay in concealing art. Other examples of puritan chic include the clipping of the moustache so that it cannot catch and retain parti-cles of food, and the crucial length of the midi-*jallabiyyah* – long enough to cover the unseemly knee, short enough not to be bemerded by the various forms of *najasah*, substances which would nullify the state of ritual purity required for prayer. For puritans of whatever faith, God is in the detail.

I arrived at Damietta in the dark. Crossing the smelly Bucolic, or Phatnitic, branch of the Nile by a narrow road bridge, I was nearly decapitated by a rank of cabrioles, which stuck out of a donkey cart like dancers' legs at the Moulin Rouge. For, as I quickly realized, I was in the home of that type of furniture known as Louis Farouq. An evening stroll around the city was an illustrated history of cabinet-making, taking in the later Louis, Chinese Chippendale, Regency, Empire, Biedermeier and even some Art Deco. Showrooms glittered with gilded *fauteuils*, canapés, commodes, *bonheurs-du-jour*, davenports and whatnots. There were bedsteads that were not just king- but orgy-sized, their headboards designed to incorporate quadrophonic music systems.

The ground floor of the hotel I checked into was occupied by a vast *mubiliyat* showroom that shone with *faux boulle* and ormolu. This

splendour did not, however, extend upstairs. One lavatory was spec-
tacularly blocked; the only other one was working but not inviting.
As with nearly all Egyptian lavatories, the bowl was equipped with a
little pipe – not unlike the mouthpiece of a bassoon – which squirted
water upwards for personal ablutions. The pipe was ringed with a
collar of someone else's turd.

I hesitate to mention the subject, fearing to fall into a national
stereotype of anal fixation and closet copromania; but I suspect that
for more travellers than would admit it, the most poignant memories
of travel originate, as St Augustine said of ourselves, *inter urinam et
faeces*. As a child, my first sight of a squat lavatory in France spoke
more eloquently of foreignness than a different cuisine or language;
later, my Yemeni acculturation was completed when I abandoned
bumf. I cherish many happy memories of defecation in far places –
in a doorless lean-to overlooking the island-studded Sound of Harris,
in the bartizan of a Yemeni castle with the wind rushing up a sheer
cliff face beneath me, lashed by spray in the stern heads of a *sambuq*
off the Kuria Muria Islands, in a wardrobe in an Ottoman mansion in
Safran Bolu (the wardrobe cleverly concealed a miniature bathroom);
and some less happy memories – the time my sweat-lubricated spectacles slid off my nose and into a noisome maw by the Red Sea, and
the horror, the horror of a public crap-house in the outskirts of
Simferopol. I have long thought that what might be termed *la nostal-
gie des chiottes* would be a fertile and only partly frivolous subject of
study; after all Tartaret, a fifteenth-century scholar of the Sorbonne,
is reputed to have written a treatise *De Modo Cacandi*. Later on in my
travels I was delighted to meet a girl in Laodiceia ad Lycum who was
carrying out research on this very topic, with special reference to
Turkey and Eastern Europe. Mhairi, I wish you success with your
scatological monograph.

To be fair to the hotel in Damietta, it wasn't a bad place. But as I
tossed, sweaty and sleepless, at 4.45 a.m. – some of the other guests
were holding an animated conversation on the landing outside, a
constant stream of motorized and horse-drawn traffic rumbled and
clattered by in the street below, a nearby cock crew incessantly the
sinister theme from *The Saint* – I wondered, Why am I doing this?
IB's motive, as revealed by Burhan al-Din the Lame and al-Murshidi,
was compelling: he travelled because he was destined to travel. But
then, would he have pursued his destiny if it hadn't been revealed to

him? My brain, flapping about for sleep like a netted fish for water, imagined a fantastical exchange on a TV travel show:

Interviewer: So, Mr and Mrs Bandersnatch, what made you choose the Algarve? Was it the direct flight? Or the childcare facilities? Or was it all this wonderful, guaranteed sunshine?

Mr B.: Well, we certainly liked the look of the place in the brochure – didn't we, dear – but, to be honest, what really decided us was irresistible, inexorable Fate.

Of course, it's not meant to work like that. Travel these days is one of the ultimate expressions of determinism. People travel because they choose to do so. Or so they are led to believe; for perhaps most of those looking for sun, booze and relaxation are, in a broad sense, fated to end up in the Algarve or certain other places in a closed set of destinations. Free will, as C.S. Lewis said, 'is the *modus operandi* of destiny'. Fate, too, chooses one's fellow hotel guests. I cursed mine inaudibly.

The curse worked, and the pre-dawn debate broke up. Then there was a lull in the street noise; then a horrible gurgle from the cock. Perhaps someone had wrung its neck. Merciful sleep came.

For IB, Damietta was one of the culinary high-points of his travels. He quoted a saying about the city – 'Its wall is a sweetmeat and its dogs sheep' – and noted that flocks of fat sheep and goats wandered freely about its streets. He also mentioned the excellence of its bananas, which Mandeville picturesquely described as 'long apples . . . though ye cut them in never so many gobbets or parts, overthwart or endlongs, evermore ye shall find in the midst the Holy Cross of our Lord Jesu'.

The cultivation of bananas has declined because of cheap imports and, with all the furniture-laden lorries and carts, only the most foolhardy sheep would wander the streets of Damietta today. But the city is still famous for its sweetmeats, and as I walked about its centre the following morning I noticed many shops filled with piles of pastries and other confectionery. IB also praised the quail of Damietta, which he found exceedingly fat, as well as its *buri* or grey mullet and 'various preparations of buffalo milk, which are unequalled for sweetness and delicious taste'. With all this in mind, I decided to spend the day eating.

At the Information Office I enquired about the best place for quail. A tall and skeletal man asked if I had a security permit. 'I don't think he needs one to eat quail,' said one of his colleagues, rolling her eyes. She told me to follow her, and took me out of the building and up a side street to a restaurant called Bazzoom, which depending on the vagaries of Arabic etymology might mean Mighty Biter.

'Quail are off,' said the cook, wiping his hands on a bloody apron. 'You can only get the farmed sort at the moment, and we don't touch them. They're not a patch on the wild ones, and the season for netting doesn't start for another couple of weeks.'

Undeterred, I went to the *suq*. The netting of quail has a long history in the Middle East. The Hebrews of the Exodus, fed up with manna, gorged themselves on quail with disastrous consequences; further south in the Farasan Islands off the Arabian coast the inhabitants were said to have lived from early times almost entirely on the birds. Contemporaries of IB wrote that so many of them flew into Egypt on their migration that the people of the coast near Damietta could net them from their front doors. Now, I was looking for some early birds, and fortune led me to the only ones in the market, a lone brace in a wicker cage. Their owner swore solemnly that they were the netted sort, cut their throats in the direction of Mecca and dropped them into a plastic bag. As I walked back to Bazzoom, they flapped their last.

The cook gave them full marks for freshness. 'They're a bit on the small side, though. But they're the first ones I've seen this year.'

Later, I returned to Bazzoom to find my two little birds roasted with their heads on and stuffed *à la mode de Damiette* with onion, garlic, hazelnuts, sultanas and cumin (there is a similar recipe for chicken, which dates from the time of Saladin); they were served on a mound of rice surrounded by stuffed cabbage leaves, stuffed baby marrows, *tahinah* and pickles. The customers of Bazzoom were serious, elbows-up eaters: a man sitting opposite me was tucking into braised lamb with vegetables and rice garnished with plump kidneys. There were snatches of conversation about commodes and sofas, but the main sound was that of eating. I left the restaurant with a belch, and a blessing for IB. This was inverse archaeology at its most enjoyable.

Now, I thought, for some preparations of buffalo milk, unequalled for sweetness. Nearby I found Taha Taha Fishwar's sweetmeat emporium, where I had a plate of *kanafah*, buffalo cheese buried in layers of sweet vermicelli. Further along the road, at a shop called Futuh, there were great sweating truckles of the cheese, impressed with calligraphic rectangles, and bowls of buffalo-milk rice pudding strewn with sultanas. I ate two of the latter. My payment was waved away with a smile.

A surfeit of puddings can only be cured by a savoury, and there could be few more savoury savouries than *fissikh*. The definitions of the verbal forms in my dictionary give an idea of how the dish is prepared: *fasakh* is 'to be corrupt', *tafassakh* 'to fall off (hair of a corpse)'. *Fissikh* are fish which are left in the sun until they begin to blow up. Next, the gills are stuffed with salt, and after eight days the fish are put in a barrel of brine. Although strictly a departure from my Battutian menu, *fissikh* are a venerable delicacy of the area. The thirteenth-century geographer Yaqut al-Hamawi, writing of the then-famous textiles of Damietta, said that the genuine products always stank of *fissikh* as the Coptic weavers were addicted to it and never washed their hands before working; he added that the cloth was so sought-after that, in the mind's nose of its buyers, it smelt of ambergris. A later writer, however, wrote that for those unused to eating *fissikh*, 'it can cause the accumulation in the body of large quantities of putrid waste matter ... which can generate many fatal diseases'. One account of the defeat of the Crusade of St Louis near Damietta in 1250 attributes it to the Franks' consumption of putrid fish, sold to them by the local inhabitants; this might have been a form of medieval germ warfare, but to me the story has about it more than a whiff of *fissikh*. I had heard, moreover, that each year at the spring festival of Shamm al-Nasim, or 'Sniffing the Breeze', around a dozen people die of *fissikh* poisoning. It was therefore with some trepidation that I approached the shop of Abu Rajab.

Outside the shop was a heron, trussed to a tree stump. At first I thought it was stuffed, but it turned out to be cataleptically alive. I asked Abu Rajab if it was to be eaten, but he said it was 'just for decoration'. Inside, a fat boy guided me around the stinking barrels.

'I want your best quality,' I told him.

'Then try this,' he said, pulling off the lid of a barrel. An almost palpable miasma rose from it; I gagged, and watched as he plunged both hands in up to the elbows and pulled out two fat sprats. He pressed his thumbs into them. The impressions stayed, as they would have done in putty. 'You see, they're the best quality!' He pulled a piece off one of the fish and handed it to me. I shut my eyes and popped it into my mouth.

Like durian, the taste was admittedly better than the smell; it could hardly have been worse. I could feel myself breaking into a cold sweat, and made for the door and fresh air. Perhaps, with the quail, the *kanafah*, the two rice puddings and now this, I had overdone things.

The heron eyed me rheumily. Slowly, my nausea passed, but I still felt as though I'd swallowed a pot of Gentleman's Relish in one go.

'So, did you like my *fissikh*?' Abu Rajab asked. 'It's the best in Egypt!'

I wondered what the worst *fissikh* in Egypt was like. 'Your *fissikh* is ...' – I searched for the right word – '... astonishing. How much do I owe you?'

'It's on me,' said Abu Rajab, beaming.

'May God reward your goodness,' I said.

One more course remained. I had already, in Rosetta, eaten *buri*, the grey mullet admired by IB. It was delicate in flavour, as might be expected of this gentlest of fish which, the poet Oppian said, 'never stains its lips with blood but in holy fashion feeds always on green seaweed or mere mud'. I was now keen to try its roe, considered a great delicacy. Later, I watched the roe being extracted in a village near the coast: a man gently palpitated the bellies of hen *buris* to see if they were pregnant; if they were, he made a neat incision with a small Stanley knife then pulled out the roe in its yellow membrane, reticulated with pink veins. This, he explained, would be salted, pressed, then dried in the sun. Finally it would be dipped in wax. Even in its unprocessed state the roe looked precious; in its final form, as *batarikh* – the French *boutargue*, the Italian, and particularly Sardinian, *bottarga* – it is hugely expensive. The Egyptians say of a successful businessman that *mahfazatuh batrikhat*, 'his wallet has swollen with roe'.

I was forewarned of a high price by the English sign on a shop near Abu Rajab's: SUPER CAVIARE. It was a minimalist shop, containing only a small refrigerator and selling nothing but *batarikh*. The shopkeeper produced a cylinder of paper from the refrigerator and unrolled it to reveal several rosewood-coloured blocks. They resembled mummified human fingers and smelt slightly of football socks. At 260 Egyptian pounds a kilo, *buri* caviare was almost as pricey by Egyptian standards as Beluga in London and I bought the smallest block, a couple of ounces in weight. I told the shopkeeper it was like buying dope. He looked alarmed. 'It's all right, it's perfectly legal.'

After a short siesta to sleep off the excesses of lunch I took my *bat-arikh* to a bar overlooking the river. Alan Davidson, the doyen of ichthyophages, recommends eating it sliced very thin, with a simple dressing of olive oil, lemon juice and pepper. I found pickles and Stella beer a suitable alternative. Like most expensive comestibles it was interesting in texture, and the thin wax casing contained a gooey centre, richly fishy. I nibbled slowly, spinning my two ounces out over several beers, and could not have eaten more.

The coastal region near Damietta, like parts of Essex or Louisiana, is neither entirely of the land nor of the sea. It was long a haunt of hermits and dervishes, the scene of skirmishes and strange goings-on. In Tinnis, a place famous for its textiles, its catamites and for an endemic disease called the Tinnisi Death-rattle, a woman gave birth to a lamb. The town was so often raided by the Crusaders that the whole population was moved to Damietta. Nearer to Damietta itself, where the Bucolic Nile meets the sea, is a place IB calls al-Barzakh, the Isthmus. Here was a 100-cubit chain that blocked the river against the Franks, and some minarets that quivered when touched. It was also a favourite spot for ascetics, and IB spent a night there with them, 'in prayers, recitation of the Qur'an, and liturgical exercises'.

Damietta originally stood across the mouth of the river from al-Barzakh. Like Tinnis, the city was continually raided throughout its Islamic history, by Byzantines, Sicilians and finally Crusaders; the chain deterred the Franks for a while, but in 1219 they arrived in a force of Gulf War proportions, which Egyptian sources say included a 750-foot iron-clad destroyer. The Franks cut the chain and occupied Old Damietta for two years. The Jimmy Carter of the day was St Francis of Assisi, who seems to have held peace talks with the Sultan. A less pacific saint, the French King Louis, led a later crusade in 1249 which once more captured Old Damietta. It ended a year later – possibly, as mentioned above, because of mass *fissikh*-poisoning – with the Franks routed and Louis in fetters, guarded by a eunuch gaoler. A popular song of the time, in the manner of 'Boney Was a Warrior', warned al-Fransis, *le françois*, that if he came back Sabih the Eunuch would be happy to entertain him again. All the same, the Sultan removed temptation by destroying Old Damietta and relocating its population to the present site a few miles upstream.

Old Damietta between the two Frankish occupations was home to the leader of one of the stranger movements in Islamic history. Jamal al-Din of Saveh, in Persia, was an ascetic from his youth, but his good looks caused a woman of Saveh to fall passionately in love with him. As IB tells the story, she enticed Jamal al-Din into her house and pressed him to break his vow of chastity. He pretended to agree, but first excused himself to go to the lavatory. He emerged having shaved off his beard, moustache, hair and eyebrows. The seductress, horrified, threw him out.

Jamal al-Din moved to Damascus, then to Damietta, where he lived in the cemetery. His followers, known as the Qalandars, imitated his shaving habits and shocked a society in which beards were the rule. In the manner of the Cynics, they also gave up other social norms, 'abandoning polite intercourse', a contemporary account says, 'and attaching no importance to their appearance or to what was thought of them'. Some of them even gave up praying. This was asceticism taken to the limit, mortification not of the flesh but, as Albert Hourani put it, of self-esteem. The august *Encyclopaedia of Islam* compares the Qalandars to hippies; but perhaps their philosophy was closer to a sort of pantheistic punkism – the Persian *kalandar*, the probable origin of the name, means 'an ugly or ungainly man', which is not far from the original definition of 'punk'. (Their spiritual cousins the Haydaris, another group of Persian origin, were even more punkish, practising body-piercing and in extreme cases wearing rings in their penises.) The Qalandars, predictably, got a bad name, and were accused of being dope-heads and lechers. Sa'di, the great Persian poet, said that there were two sorts of people who will always feel remorse: the merchant whose vessel has been wrecked, and the heir who has become the associate of Qalandars. Substitute for Qalandars punks/hippies/New-Age travellers, and the late twentieth-century bourgeois fear of the antinomian has been, in substance, the same.

After my Qalandar-like day – Sa'di also said that 'they stuff till they have no room in their stomachs to breathe' – I decided to spend the following morning looking for traces of Jamal al-Din of Saveh. I first headed for the Isthmus, with high hopes of finding a saint or two. But as I approached the sea my hopes fell: the road was lined with hotels and hoardings; there was an International Circus and a Damiettex Cinema. The architecture was bewilderingly eclectic – here a Chinese roof, there a lotus colonnade in reinforced concrete – and the whole place had the jerry-built look of somewhere that has started off temporary and become all too rapidly permanent. The bus driver took it as a compliment when I compared it to Las Vegas.

He dropped me off at the end of his route, and I walked towards the Isthmus past a string of deserted fast-food joints and the Hanging Garden Pool Room and Amusement Park. Empty hamburger boxes skittered past in the breeze. The Isthmus itself was a long, narrow promontory sheathed in concrete. At the end of it was a stubby light-house; opposite, on the other side of the river mouth, was another of the same design. The anti-Frank chain was, of course, gone; so were the quivering minarets, the pious brethren and their hermitages. The Isthmus, it seemed, would have gone too were it not for the great piles of caltrop-like blocks of cement designed to break the force of the waves. A man fishing with rod and line told me that there had been an old mosque here – conceivably the place in which IB stayed – but that the sea had washed it away. The blessed land of Egypt and the cursed Mediterranean used to maintain a sort of equi-librium, as the silt that came down the Nile in its annual flood made up for what the sea took. Now, since the building of the High Dam at Aswan, there had been no flood, no silt, and the sea was winning.

The only other passenger in the ferry across the river to Old Damietta, now called al-Azbah, was a pretty girl dressed and coiffed like a starlet of half a century ago. We shared a taxi, a pea-green Dodge of 1951, which went with her appearance. Most of the vehi-cles were of a similar age, except for the flocks of motor-scooters, which the taxi driver called *batt*, ducks.

We dropped the starlet off and chugged slowly around, asking in cafés if anyone had heard of Jamal al-Din and the Qalandars. The men we spoke to had a slight swagger about them, an air of ex-cons on the Costa. Abduh, the driver, told me that most of the men of the place had been in the Greek merchant navy; he himself had worked for Onassis. Their faces were quite unlike those of the lumpen fella-hin of the inland Delta: they had the large eyes and fine features of Roman mummy portraits.

There were reminders of the Hellenistic and, in the Dodges, Plymouths and Chryslers, of 1950s America; but none of Jamal al-Din. No one had heard of him. What seemed to be the oldest mosque was 400 years too late. The old cemetery, perhaps the one haunted by the Qalandar leader, had been turned into a market.

I collared the local preacher but he only knew of another Jamal al-Din, buried in present-day Damietta. He was pessimistic about my search: 'Damietta is not a learned place. The people here are too interested in making money.'

Something told me he was right, that Damietta, a city of swollen wallets, with its good food, its gilded *fauteuils*, its snappy haircuts, seaside leisure facilities and international maritime connections, would have forgotten Jamal al-Din and the Qalandars long ago. They were exotic migrants, too exotic for even the dervish-loving Egyptians: in 1360 the Sultan caught sight of the then leader of the Qalandars and was so horrified by his hairlessness and his 'heretical, frightful Persian attire' that he ordered any Qalandar who did not grow a beard and dress properly to be flogged and expelled.

That evening I consoled myself for not finding the Qalandars with another session of beer and *batarikh*. The only other customer in the bar by the river was a woman in a wedding dress. She was sitting alone, arrayed like IB's Alexandria in her bridal adornments. I imagined her as the Miss Havisham of Damietta and, heady with Stella, considered offering her a nibble of my *batarikh*; but prudence prevailed, and greed.

Cairo

The Palace on Crimson Street

> 'They came to a spacious, well-appointed and splendid hall . . .
> In the middle stood a large pool full of water, with a fountain in
> the centre, and at the far end stood a couch of black juniper
> wood, set with gems and pearls.'
>
> *The Arabian Nights*, trans. Husain Haddawy

FEW VISITORS HAVE liked Cairo on first sight. '*Uff!*' exclaimed an eighth-century caliph, 'She is the mother of stenches!' Later, a geographer wondered why anyone should have wanted to build a city 'between a putrid and mephitic river, the corrupt effluvia of which cause disease and rot food, and a dry and barren mountain range devoid of greenery'. The ground teemed with rats, scorpions, fleas and bugs, the air with miasmas. In Cairo Symon Semeon buried his companion Brother Hugo, who had succumbed to an attack of dysentery and fever 'caused by a north wind'. My guidebook, compiled a century after IB's visit, was disturbingly frank about the dangers of living in a polluted high-rise city where light and air rarely penetrated the dark alleyways. Its author, al-Maqrizi, warned that 'the traveller approaching Cairo sees before him a depressing black wall beneath a dust-laden sky, from which sight his soul shrinks and flees away'.

I too approached Cairo with a sinking heart. My last daylight view of it had been from a friend's flat on the Muqattam Hills: the city lay below, gasping under an incubus of fumes; in the distance the Pyramids were hazily visible, as if seen by a *pointilliste* with failing eyesight. But now, as the taxi passed the Eastern Cemetery, a perfectly timed sunburst spread thick, buttery light over the Mamluk tombs and turned them into towering versions of Mrs Beeton's centrepiece puddings. My heart began to rise.

Just as there are many Egypts, there are many Cairos. IB realized that the city was a multiple oxymoron: 'Therein is what you will of learned and simple, grave and gay, prudent and foolish, base and noble, of high estate and low estate, unknown and famous; she surges as the waves of the sea with her throngs of folk, and can scarce contain them.' All visitors have agreed with the last point. Friar Symon complained that it was 'so thronged with barbarous and common people that it is only with the greatest difficulty that one succeeds in getting from one end of the town to the other'. Al-Abdari related an accident which befell his mule in a Cairo traffic jam: a friend had borrowed it, and while he was riding along the main street 'the crowds pressing about him caused him to be knocked from his saddle. The mule was swept away in the throng of people, and my friend was unable to catch up with it. He could only look on helplessly while the animal receded into the distance. And that was the end of my mule.'

Today, the worst of the jams have moved west to Tahrir (Liberation) Square. But there are three days in the year when the old centre of Cairo reverts to its former self with a vengeance. Unwittingly, I had arrived at their climax. The square next to the Mosque of al-Husayn surged with slow-moving crowds, as the waves of the sea. The Husayn Hotel, overlooking the square, had one room free.

'You're lucky,' said the receptionist. 'We're fully booked for the Mawlid, but you came at just the right moment.' It seemed that the room had been vacated because of a death; I didn't enquire further.

The Mawlid, or Festival, of al-Husayn commemorates the Prophet's grandson, killed in 681 at Karbala in Iraq. The body of the greatest Islamic martyr stayed where it was; his head, however, worked its way westward, with long stopovers in Damascus and Ascalon, until it arrived in Cairo in 1153. Al-Maqrizi's guidebook tells a story about the high-wattage *barakah*, or divine blessing, which radiates via the relic. When Saladin took over Egypt, reports reached him of a palace servant of the old Fatimid régime who knew where his former masters had hidden a great treasure. The man refused to reveal the cache, and was subjected to a particularly horrible torture: 'Dung beetles were put on his head and bound in place with a crimson cloth. It is said that this is the most unbearable of tortures, since the beetles gradually burrow into the victim's brain.' In this case, although the torture was repeated several times, the beetles died on each occasion and the old retainer was unharmed. When asked what his secret was, he replied, 'When the head of Imam al-Husayn arrived in Cairo, I was one of those who carried it. What secret is more potent than this?'

For centuries, the Mawlid has been a giant beanfeast for the distribution of blessings. Descendants of al-Husayn camp around the magnificent mosque that contains their ancestor's head, accompanied by members of the Sufi orders which they lead. Spectators come from far away, to mill, gawp, drink tea and ingest a little *barakah*. Looking over them from the top floor of the hotel, I guessed there were three or four football crowds'-worth – perhaps 150,000 people. In the surrounding streets there must have been several times more.

Down at ground level I blundered into a slow-motion scuffle taking place around a stall distributing free *mulukhiyyah*, the mucilaginous and delicious dish made from Jew's mallow. Bystanders were helping themselves to water from an enormous green hip-flask, inscribed with Qur'anic verses and strapped to the back of a small and dervish-like man. Someone next to me cut the throat of a sheep. The sheep looked understandably surprised, then its head flopped back with an indignant gurgle. Thick, venous gore spurted over the paving stones. As I was wondering how this would go down in Trafalgar Square, a woman pressed her palm into the blood then stuck her hand down another woman's neck. The butcher strung the sheep up on a lamp-post and peeled away the skin. It came off like a diver's wetsuit.

I drank free Mawlid tea, heavy with cinnamon, with a farmer from south of the Pyramids. He explained that a palm print of sacrificial blood on the spine averts the Evil Eye and cures epilepsy. 'Of course,' he said, taking in the tents and the crowds with a sweep of his arm, 'this isn't Islam. It's pure heresy!' He was grinning, and patently enjoying himself.

The farmer asked if I was a Muslim. I shook my head. 'Did you hear about the American professor who converted? Well, soon afterwards he came to Egypt. And do you know what he said? He said, "Thank God I converted to Islam before I saw the Muslims." You know,' he confided, 'if you became a Muslim you'd be better than us.'

I smiled. I'd come across the same fancy in every Islamic country I'd visited; come across it, or its mirror image, in the *Mirabilia Descripta* of IB's contemporary Friar Jordanus, who believed that oriental converts to Christianity were 'ten times better, and more charitable withal ... than our own folk'. The American (or British, or Russian) professor also popped up regularly from Marrakesh to Muscat. The implication was that by converting one automatically became a sort of spiritual and moral *Übermensch*. It was a daunting prospect for a woolly Anglican, even one who is platonically fond of Islam.

I told the farmer that I envied a certain king of the Caucasus mentioned by the geographer Ibn Rustah. He prayed on Fridays with the Muslims, on Saturdays with the Jews, and on Sundays with the Christians. 'Since each religion claims that it is the only true one and that the others are invalid,' the king explained, 'I have decided to hedge my bets.'

The farmer laughed. 'I suppose it's all right if you're a king and don't have to work. But what about the rest of us? We can't afford to spend half the week praying. And', he added, 'I don't think the *shaykhs* of al-Azhar would think much of it.' I looked across the road to the venerable mosque-university, that bastion of Islamic orthodoxy, and felt inclined to agree. In spiritual, as in physical refreshment, one is expected to show brand loyalty, to drink Coke or Pepsi but not both.

That evening I had supper with some friends who lived in Garden City, Toby Macklin and Rachel Davey. Afterwards, Toby and I returned to the Mawlid. We walked in a stream of people over the flyover, closed to traffic for the festival, that leads to al-Husayn Square. The sound of the Mawlid crowd was an unbroken roar, like breakers in a storm.

We reached the square and were sucked in by the human undertow. It was impossible to stop moving. We caught, just in time, an old man who staggered and nearly fell in front of us. After one complete circuit of the square, we snagged on the tent of the Faydi Shadhili order and stood watching the scene inside. A man was chanting the *dhikr*, verses invoking God's blessing, in a voice amplifed to rock-concert volume. Another accompanied him on a tambourine. Two lines of young men wearing *jallabiyyahs* and facing each other swayed sideways to the beat, moving first the same way, then in opposite directions. In the centre of the line facing us was a tall boy in a pin-striped sky-blue *jallabiyyah* and immaculate white turban. His face was veiled in an unchanging half smile, unearthly but knowing, as if mesmerized by his own suppleness. Toby shouted something in my ear.

'I can't hear a thing,' I bawled back.

'I said, "It's like watching John Travolta." '

John Travolta, though, was too obviously vertebrate; the *dhikr* star in front of us looked to me more like an ecstatic sea-anemone.

The next tent was also occupied by the Faydi Shadhilis. A gaunt and waiterly man in a dark suit beckoned us in, and we took our places in a line of wooden café chairs. Next to us, a berobed gentleman sat receiving hand kisses; most of the other VIPs were in suits and ties and looked like Rotarians. The din was enormous, conversation impossible. We sat for a while sipping hibiscus squash and nodding reverently towards our hosts, then left. During another circumambulation of the square, I was disappointed to find that in the tent of the Rifa'is no one was rolling in fire or biting the heads off live snakes, as IB had seen members of the order doing in southern Iraq; equally, I was mystified by the presence in another tent of a newish Volvo saloon, parked next to the *dhikr* chanter. At around 1.30 a.m. Toby left for Garden City and I for my room in the Husayn Hotel. The crowds and the noise showed no sign of abating, but I surprised myself by falling asleep immediately.

The following morning, except for a few bloodstains that marked the martyrdom of sheep, there was nothing to show that the Mawlid-goers had been there. They had all gone – the chanters, the invertebrate boy, the coloured tents, the Volvo – off to the next festival in the calendar. I thought of my rave-going niece and her sudden disappearances to Nottingham or Hemel Hempstead.

Over breakfast, I reread IB on Cairo. He wrote at length on the Nile, the sweetness of its water and its annual inundation. It was an accurate if workmanlike account. On the Pyramids he was less successful: 'The Pyramids is an edifice of solid hewn stone, of immense height and circular plan, broad at the base and narrow at the top, like the figure of a cone.' To be fair, all medieval writers in Arabic describe the Pyramids as conical – 'pyramidal' was not yet in the dictionary. But to reduce them to a single circular structure suggests that he had no more seen them than had the authors of the European *mappae mundi* who, convinced that they were the granaries of Joseph, drew them as rustic tithe barns. What mattered in Cairo, and formed the bulk of IB's chapter, was its illustrious Muslims – those who lay in the city's vast cemeteries and, especially, the living scholars, judges and Mamluk grandees who ran the greatest city in the Islamic world. Like IB, I turned a blind eye to the pharaonic and started, instead, at the top of the fourteenth-century social pyramid.

I didn't have far to go. Sultan al-Nasir is buried just around the corner from the Husayn Hotel, in a mausoleum on the main street of medieval Cairo. Since being a Mamluk ruler was the political equivalent of leading an infantry charge on the Somme, sensible sultans built their tombs as soon as possible, and always added a *madrasah*, both to the greater glory of God and as a sort of pension plan for the afterlife. Al-Nasir was no exception: he built his college-mausoleum in 1304, at the morbidly early age of 19. Its sombre, almost brutal façade impends over the street like an ironclad in dock, relieved by a Plimsoll line of monumental script and by a gothic doorway pinched from the Crusader church of St George in Acre. The mix of Saracenic and Frankish was a surprise – like my parish church in Bristol, but with the elements reversed. Al-Nasir, in the event, survived another forty years on the throne and, despite having built a perfectly good mausoleum of his own, ended up next door in that of his father Qalawun.

I passed beneath the great barred windows where, in the Mamluk heyday, Qur'an reciters would sit night and day, chanting a requiem for the dead within. Also in attendance were eunuchs, who guarded the sultanic tombs. They were a touchy lot, and al-Maqrizi warns in his guidebook that the eunuchs at the mausoleum of one of al-Nasir's daughters once beat up a Qur'an reader. 'You have dared to come into the presence of our mistress', they shrieked, '*without underpants!*' Al-Maqrizi does not explain how the lapse was discovered.

Unchecked, I entered Qalawun's tomb complex through bronze doors which gave on to a massive slit-trench of a corridor. To the right, another doorway led into the tomb chamber where, suddenly, the dimensions shot upwards and outwards to enclose a soaring octagonal space: high above floated Corinthian capitals, like great gilded Savoy cabbages, and stucco windows set with grass-green and buttercup glass; the walls were encrusted in *pietra dura* and mother-of-pearl in a pattern of hexagons, quincunxes, reflecting Kufic script and

arrow-headed meanders. 'It might have been designed by bees,' said a poet of the newly built mausoleum, 'for in it stone has softened like wax.' Shadows cast by huge knobbled screens of turned wood created a dappled, jewelled chiaroscuro in which Qalawun and al-Nasir shared a diminutive wooden cenotaph, gabled-ended and rather like a Wendy house. Qalawun, born on the steppe in a felt tent and sold as a slave, had ended up in a necropolitan masterpiece.

Across the entrance corridor, the *madrasah* students enjoyed less spacious accommodation. At the time of IB's visit the college was flourishing, with courses in jurisprudence and medicine. A century later, al-Maqrizi wrote that the teaching staff were 'mere boys and unqualified persons – not that anyone listens to them'. On the morning of my visit, the only sign of life in the college was a small cat with foxy ears, patrolling the shadows.

For IB, however, the third part of Qalawun's foundation was the most remarkable. Early in his career Qalawun had been cured of colic in the hospital of Damascus. He was so impressed by the treatment that he vowed to build something bigger and better in Cairo if he became sultan. The result was the *maristan*, the great hospital of which IB wrote, 'no description is adequate to its beauties. It is equipped with innumerable conveniences and medications, and its revenue is reported to be a thousand dinars a day'. The various wards specialized in fevers, dysentery and ophthalmology. Patients enjoyed a Palm Court ambience, with fountains and a resident orchestra. Qalawun took a personal interest in the latest medical technology, and among his prized gadgets was a gold bleeding bowl of Greek manufacture. It incorporated a gauge in the form of a statuette calibrated to ten-drachm intervals, and a fail-safe device: when the amount of blood reached three Damascene ounces, a mechanical voice in the statuette called out in Greek, 'Enough! Enough!'

By the early nineteenth century, the hospital had fallen on hard times. Its inmates, wrote Ali Bey, existed 'in the greatest misery ... while the administrator is clothed in the greatest luxury'. Qalawun and IB, however, would be delighted to know that today, more than seven centuries after its foundation, it is thriving again. Low, temporary-looking buildings have sprung up among the ruins of Qalawun's vaults, a blend of Piranesi and Portakabin.

I called on the director and showed him IB's description of the hospital. He smiled wistfully. 'Today, we are not so well funded. And we're only an eye hospital. But we still deal with about 300 cases a day.'

I said that he must be proud to be part of a 700-year-old tradition.

The director thought for a moment. 'It sometimes makes me think how slowly we've progressed. I mean, we think we know everything now. But the basic technology is the same. Even when your traveller was here, they were performing cataract operations. I always try to remember that verse of the Qur'an: "You have been given but a little knowledge".'

As I left the hospital, I noticed a smudgy mark on one of the old columns: a palm-print, rust-coloured. It was blood, and reasonably fresh. I was surprised; but then, perhaps an eye hospital was the natural habitat for the Evil Eye.

Later, I went back to the tomb chamber with al-Maqrizi and turned to the section on the tomb's joint occupant, Sultan al-Nasir Muhammad ibn Qalawun. The Sultan died, I read, in the Citadel of Cairo in 1341. He was 57 years old and had reigned for forty-three of them, not counting two periods when he was temporarily deposed.

Al-Nasir had been born with his fists clenched. When the midwife prised them open, blood ran from his hands. 'This was taken as an omen, that those hands would shed much blood,' wrote the biographer Ibn Hajar. 'And it was as they predicted.' The three years between the death of Qalawun and the succession of al-Nasir in 1293 were rich in coups, and one of the first acts of the new child-sultan was to execute the murderers of his brother and predecessor – having first had them paraded on camels with their severed hands dangling around their necks. Later, when he had a convicted burglar crucified in drag on Bab Zuwaylah, the southern gate of Cairo, there were murmurings that he had gone too far. 'But', he retorted, 'what else can one do with common people and market types? They only fear a tyrant.' IB was shocked by the severity of al-Nasir's officers in crushing a riot against European merchants in Alexandria: thirty-six of the Muslim ringleaders were sliced down the middle and the halves displayed, Damien Hirst-fashion, on either side of the street. (The public display of anti-western militants is still a feature of Egyptian political life; bisection seems to have been abandoned.)

The Sultan's bloody hands and long reign created unparalleled prosperity. The population of Cairo doubled to half a million – probably ten times that of London – and the city became a full-blown consumer society: the value of left-overs and packaging was said to be a thousand gold dinars a day. Friar Symon thought Egypt in 1323 to be 'the most beautiful, stable and prosperous country in the whole world ... Nobles and peasants ... and foreigners of whatever condition, with no possibility of bribery, are subject to the infliction of the same penalties; and', he continued enthusiastically, 'this especially when it is a case of capital punishment, death being inflicted by crucifixion, decapitation, or cutting in two with a sword.'

The friar was less enthusiastic about Mamluk leisure pursuits. Polo he thought a namby-pamby affair compared with the tournaments of Christian knights, although he conceded its popularity: when the Sultan took part, the spectators raised such a din that 'they seem to hinder the motion of Arcturus, and to crash with the inhabitants of Sodom'. Symon also dismissed the Sultan's attachment to hunting as effeminate. Admittedly, al-Nasir never roughed it. On his hunting expeditions he would take a portable steam-bath, as well as a phalanx of physicians, pharmacists and antimony appliers.

Al-Nasir's greatest passion, however, was building. His palaces, forerunners of contemporary Gulf taste, dripped with gold and lapis lazuli; his mosques – around thirty of them – were panelled with rare marbles. He rebuilt the Citadel mosque entirely, went off the new design, knocked it down and rebuilt it all over again. IB admired the Sufi monastery of Siryaqus, another of the Sultan's foundations and situated in his favourite hunting country. Al-Nasir would drop in on the ascetics after the chase, rather in the manner of the English nobility of the eighteenth century with their resident hermits. (The asceticism was, of course, five-star: the mystics had their own sauna and live-in masseur.)

IB also praised al-Nasir's generosity to the Mecca pilgrims in providing food, water and camel transport for the poor and weak. Few pilgrims, however, travelled in the style of the Sultan's favourite wife. She took a herd of milch cows and a portable kitchen garden, and lunched and dined all the way to Mecca and back on greens and fried cheese, prompting al-Maqrizi to wonder that she did not die of indigestion.

Fried cheese was a regular feature of court life. When the Sultan slept, plates of it were placed nearby, together with bowls of stew, bananas and cream, and glasses of sherbert. The midnight feasts were not for him, but for his bodyguard: he was terrified that they would fall asleep, leaving him exposed to the silent dagger in the night. He knew that the threat came from within, and killed some two hundred of his most senior officers; with the rest he played a furious game of snakes and ladders, promoting and demoting at whim. Only a few fortunate myrmidons escaped these violent swings of fortune, and even with these he could fly into a rage, clobbering them with his boots.

Al-Nasir died, unusually for a Mamluk sultan, of natural causes. His funeral was conducted without pomp. The corpse was placed on a bier borne by two mules and preceded by a single candle. Orders were given for the shops to be closed, and people were prevented from watching the cortège. Here in the tomb chamber waited the director of the hospital, the four grand *qadis* and a few other notables. They washed the body in a fountain outside the mausoleum, wrapped it in a winding-sheet and prayed the prayers for the dead over it. Al-Nasir was then lowered into the grave next to his father. 'Glory be to the One who changes not, nor ceases,' wrote al-Maqrizi. 'This was the greatest ruler in the inhabited world, and he died a stranger.'

It is a nice epitaph. The Mamluks ruled the Arab Islamic heartland for 250 years, and were still a power in Egypt when Napoleon invaded; but they were always strangers – Turkic and Circassian slaves from beyond the far end of the Black Sea, an oligarchy of displaced persons. The Arab establishment never let them forget that they were outsiders. Ibn Hajar wrote at the beginning of his biographical dictionary *The Concealed Pearls*: 'Properly speaking, we should have started with names beginning with a long *a*; but since only Turkic names, like "Āqush", and those of women, like "Āminah", begin thus, I have postponed them so that the names of Islamic scholars may have due precedence.' The Mamluks were not only displaced literally, alphabetically; they were bracketed together with women.

IB lists a few of the Mamluk grandees ('Arghun the Dawadar ... Tushtu, who was known as "Green Chickpeas" ... Bashtak'), but for him their society was impenetrable. For me, too, they were as yet no more than outlandish names carved on splendid tombs.

The following day I set off southwards from the tomb of al-Nasir and Qalawun, along the main street of medieval Cairo. It was here that al-Abdari lost his mule and Ibn Sa'id, another fastidious traveller from the Maghrib, made the mistake of hiring one of the city's 30,000 donkey taxis. 'No sooner was I in the saddle than the beast shot off, raising a cloud of black dust which blinded my eyes and soiled my robes.' Seizing the opportunity of a traffic jam, Ibn Sa'id threw himself off the donkey and did what all Arabs of a literary bent used to do when in a state of extreme emotion: 'I extemporized a verse –

> This city is sheer hell, alas,
> For him that hires a taxi-ass.
> I, driver, on your donkey sit,
> Eyeless in Cairo from the grit,
> While all along the street you tear,
> Tornado-like, behind your fare.
> O driver, show some mercy, please!
> I beg you now, upon my knees,
> Ere in earth's winding-sheet I'm trussed,
> Ashes to ashes, dust to dust.'

I walked, past al-Husayn Square then, dodging the hawkers of scent, through an unfragrant underpass. I paused to eat some *hawawi-shi*, fried mince sandwiches, in a tiny Mamluk-period shop where the walls oozed with generations of cooking oil, then rejoined the ancient street. The crowds were thinner than in IB's time, but the

smells were still the same – incense, smoked fish, crushed coriander, freshly trodden dung, freshly killed meat. The only anachronisms were the post-Columbian odours of tobacco smoke and guava.

'All the *amirs*', wrote IB, 'vie with one another in charitable works and the founding of mosques and religious houses.' The buildings are still there, interposed between the shop fronts and looped about with carving – here an inscription, there an escutcheon bearing some symbol of office. It seemed that every Amir of a Thousand, Keeper of the Pen-box and Lord High Polo Sticks had put up a tomb-mosque.

I passed through Bab Zuwaylah, site of the cross-dressed crucifixion, and entered the Tentmakers' Suq, where they sew appliqué awnings for saints' festivals and have recently diversified into King Tut scatter-cushions. For about a mile, my route was overwhelmingly Mamluk and remarkably free of motor traffic. But after the Saddlers' Suq the timeline began to kink: I crossed a roaring highway, then came to the huge ninth-century mosque of Ibn Tulun with its strange cresting, like stick-men dancing along the parapet, and its helical minaret – a miniature ziggurat, or a giant helter-skelter. I passed under an aqueduct punctured by another highway and, four miles from my starting point, reached the Mosque of Amr.

Founded in 641 by the Muslim conqueror of Egypt and in a state of structural flux ever since, the ancient mosque's only remaining features are its name and its numen. The rebuilds were not a matter of taste, but of necessity. IB noted that the building had become a public highway. Ibn Sa'id, still fulminating from his experience with the donkey taxi, lamented the state of the most venerable Islamic monument in Egypt. People picnicked in it, he grumbled, and threw rubbish in the courtyard; the ceiling was a mass of cobwebs, the walls covered in graffiti. 'And yet', he went on, 'my soul was elated here . . . There was some mysterious sanctity inherent in the mosque. It derived from the Prophet's companions who were present at its building.' Name and numen were, are, in fact, everything.

I passed a bus station, then Babylon, the Roman and Coptic centre of the city. Over the millennia, Cairo has done a triple jump towards the north; my southward route had taken me backwards in time. Now it took me out of the confusing conurbation and into a familiar suburban present, over a metro line, under flyovers, past petrol stations.

IB had left Cairo by the same route, heading for Upper Egypt. In the *Travels* he is uncharacteristically silent about his own experiences in the megapolis of the Islamic world. A disembodied spectator, he tells us nothing about where he slept, what he ate or whom he met. Now tentatively, he walks into the picture again. 'I stayed on the night following my departure at the convent which the Sahib Taj al-Din ibn Hanna built at Dayr al-Tin.' Taj al-Din, who had been Vizier to the young Sultan al-Nasir, placed in the convent some relics of the Prophet: a fragment of a wooden basin, his kohl pencil, an awl which he used for mending his sandals and a Qur'an in the hand of the Prophet's son-in-law, Ali. The Vizier, IB explains, 'endowed the convent with funds to supply food to all comers and goers and to maintain the guardians of these sacred relics'.

For me, a secular relic-hunter, a documented Battutian overnight had irresistible cachet. Even if the convent lay somewhere among the tatty industrial nether regions of the city, I had to find it. I followed the highway towards Helwan, the Dagenham of Cairo. To the west, scabrous skyscrapers overlooked the Nile. Nearer to hand I passed what looked and smelt like a manure recycling plant, then entered a zone of cement factories. Someone directed me through one of these. I scaled the far wall of the yard and found myself, quite unexpectedly, in the country.

'You are a traveller,' said the café owner, waving away payment for my plate of fried aubergines. 'Did you know, Uncle Muhammad, that he's come all the way from Yemen?'

'Yemen . . . ' said Uncle Muhammad. 'I was there in 1964. In the army.' He paused, silently remembering his time in Egypt's Vietnam. 'Do they still chew that drug there – what's it called? – *qat*?' He puffed out his cheek and rolled his eyes.

'They do. In fact, I myself chew it every day,' I said.

He shuddered. 'I seek refuge with God!'

I quickly changed the subject to the Convent of the Relics. Overlooking my admission that I was a crazed dope-head, Uncle Muhammad offered to take me there.

We walked along a dusty road lined with mud-brick cottages, a fragment of rural Egypt marooned among the factories, then turned off into an oasis of palms and other trees. There was a mosque, a fine Ottoman building and at least three centuries too late for IB. Bits of earlier walls stood in the gardens, no doubt the remains of IB's convent. Inside the mosque, Uncle Muhammad showed me the reliquary, a tall thin room lined with blue-and-white tiles. From the ceiling hung a model boat, rather like a Turkish caique and rigged with cobwebs. 'The relics were taken to the Mosque of al-Husayn about a hundred years ago. But', he added, pointing upwards, 'we've still got Noah's Ark.'

We went out into the sunlight and wandered around the garden looking at the remains of the earlier structure. I tried to imagine how it had looked in the 1320s, to rebuild mentally IB's enormous convent, and failed. The relics of his night here were all but gone. Even the Nile, which in his day flowed by the gardens, had receded to the west. Arab poets could conjure up a *genius loci* from the slenderest of materials:

The abandoned dwellings spoke to me, though they were silent:
'Our silence is, in part, a form of speech . . . '

Now, if it was, I couldn't hear it.

On the way back to the café, Uncle Muhammad invited me to stay the night. 'After all,' he said, 'your Battutah stayed here.' I was touched but worn out after my urban hike and looking forward to a solitary evening in the Husayn Hotel. I climbed back over the cement factory wall, returned to the highway and caught the number 201 bus back into town.

★

Travel writing is, after autobiography, the most egocentric form of literature. But in eighteen pages on Cairo, between his arrival there and his night in the convent outside the city, IB himself appears only once. I was beginning to wonder exactly what he had got up to. In late medieval times the possibilities were endless. They included everything from Qur'anic studies through shadow plays and street storytellers to dancing camels and professional farters. Perhaps a well-brought-up provincial Maghribi like IB would have taken one look at Cairo – 'this threshing-floor for the chaff of humanity, this dustbin of the world, this refuge of vice,' his fellow countryman al-Abdari had called it – and fled. He does not record how long he stayed on his first visit; but, passing through again a couple of months later, he says baldly, 'I stayed only one night in Cairo.' I wanted to fill in the gaps, and turned to al-Maqrizi.

Exhortations and Reflections on Settlements and Monuments is a whopper of a book, nearly a thousand dense folio pages. I have called it a guidebook; certainly, a Mamluk donkey driver wanting to mug up on the Knowledge would find it all here: quarters, suburbs, streets, alleys, mosques and tombs. There are fifty pages alone on churches and synagogues. But the topography that al-Maqrizi set out to write, nourished by reading and his own observation, grew into a literary mutant, a panoramic, diachronic combination of Pevsner, Pepys and the *A to Z*.

I began where I had started my walk that morning, outside al-Nasir's tomb. Of all the streets of the city, al-Maqrizi wrote, this was the busiest. It took its name, Between the Two Castles, from a pair of Fatimid palaces which once stood on either side of the road. Formerly, Cairene aristocrats would gather here to read biography, history and poetry, 'and to feast their souls on all manner of goods such as delight the five senses'. By the fourteenth century, however, while it was still by day the grandest shopping street in town, it became at night a haunt of 'unspeakable lewdness and debauchery'. The stream of people was so dense that certain despicable men would 'pleasure themselves against youths and women, to the point of ejaculation', without their victims knowing what was happening.

(According to an English friend who lived in Cairo, at least one descendant of the despicable men is alive and well. He is to be found on rush-hour buses and, judging by her account, is not as discreet as his forebears.) More conventional sex maniacs could nip around the corner into the Candle Market and pick up a tart, immediately identifiable by her red leather trousers.

And all this, I reflected, was going on under the noses of the Qur'an readers, as they chanted their requiems in the window seats of the sultanic mausoleum. The juxtaposition of angelic and priapic, of ejaculations pious and profane in this Mamluk Knightsbridge was, somehow, exquisite. 'Therein is what you will . . . '

I returned the following morning to Between the Two Castles. Its racier inhabitants have moved across the Nile to the Saudi-haunted nightclubs in Pyramids Road and, looking around at the surviving medieval monuments, one might imagine that the Mamluks did a lot of praying, studying and dying, and not much else. One purely secular monument, however, survives: the palace built by Bashtak, one of those outlandish *amirs* whose names IB recorded.

The palace stands on Between the Two Castles, but its entrance is in a sideroad, Darb al-Qirmiz, or Crimson Street (*qirmiz* provides the first five letters of 'crimson'). I passed a guard of tethered geese and entered a courtyard. A massive doorway in a humbug-striped wall of red and white led into an entrance hall, from which rose a staircase.

The first floor was pure theatre. The entire space was filled with a multi-storey atrium with a fountain in the middle and surrounded by columns and *iwans*, vaulted side chambers. Stucco windows high above shone with Bashtak's blazon, a red diamond on a white stripe. Friar Symon had peeped into a similar interior and pronounced it the house of God and the gate of Heaven. Heaven, I thought, must have been freezing in winter. Even now, in September, the place was chilly. I warmed myself in a few blotches of sunlight in a latticed window, and listened to the sounds that rose from the street below – passing feet and hooves, horse bells, hammering, the rasp of files, a ripple of voices, the occasional strongly expressed opinion. Mamluk sounds.

As a living space, the hall must have been desperately uncomfortable. Equipped with a cenotaph instead of a fountain, it would have made a fine tomb chamber. Even the lavatory was sepulchrally proportioned, about eight feet by five, and twenty feet tall. I tested the acoustic with a snatch of 'I Dreamt I Dwelt in Marble Halls'. It was superb. The effect on Mamluk farts must have been megaphonic.

Upstairs, from a screened triforium gallery on the second floor, there was a concubine's-eye view of the hall; more lattices looked down to the street. I found my way on to a terrace and climbed a succession of external staircases. More terraces rose in Babylonian profligacy, clustering around the central atrium. Finally, I was level with the domes of Qalawun's and al-Nasir's mosque-tombs. I caught my breath and looked out.

The street below was a dizzying crevasse. Beyond the domes stood crumbling *iwans* interspersed with later building. From this height, the processes that had shaped the city seemed not architectural, but fungal. Successive structures were parasites on the waste of decayed dynasties, like blewits on a cowpat. Before me was a tell that began with Mamluk masonry, then Ottoman, followed by concrete, then wooden shanties, the whole finished off by an airy *bidonville* of junk – packing cases, rolls of wire, sticks, bicycle frames. It was a living Troy, and all the strata were inhabited simultaneously. I watched the inhabitants of the top layer going about their business, washing, cooking, keeping pigeons and growing things in pots. (Aerial horticulture has a long history in Cairo. An eleventh-century Persian visitor wrote, 'I heard that a certain man made a roof-garden on the seventh floor, and took up a bullock to raise water. He grew oranges, citrons and bananas.')

From the roof of Bashtak's palace a Cairo was revealed which hid itself at street level, a city recycling itself upwards. But Bashtak himself remained buried in the *Travels*, a mere name under *Some of the amirs of Cairo*. It was only when I extended my visit with some textual travel that the bare set of his palace sprang to life. Bashtak's story, I discovered, would have been beyond the most inventive of scriptwriters – unless, that is, they could imagine a scenario in which Piers Gaveston joined the cast of *Dynasty*.

From Ibn Hajar's *Concealed Pearls*, I learned that Sultan al-Nasir's crush on the young Mongol Ilkhan of Iraq and Persia – 'the most beautiful of God's creatures', as IB later described him – was so unbearable that he instructed his slave-buyers to find him a *mamluk* who resembled him. They came up with Bashtak, 'a graceful, lightly bearded youth' from the steppe. Al-Nasir was immediately besotted. He showered Bashtak with fiefs, *de luxe* slave girls, and a fresh wardrobe every day – everything, Ibn Hajar says, from brocade cloaks lined with squirrel fur down to gaiters.

Not surprisingly, Bashtak turned into a dandy. Mamluk fashion-victims would analyse and imitate his manner of tying the turban. And, whether despite or because of the supply of concubines, he also turned into a monstrous lecher who even seduced, it was whispered, peasant women and fishwives. As al-Maqrizi put it, 'he was quite incontinent with respect to vaginas'.

A few years after IB's visit to Cairo, Qawsun - another star of the Mamluk brat-pack – bought and refurbished a particularly fine palace on Between the Two Castles. Bashtak was beside himself with jeal-ousy. He immediately bought a mansion directly opposite Qawsun's, wheedled the Sultan into giving him a large piece of land adjoining it and built the palace which I had visited – demolishing, in the process, ten small mosques. 'And thus', says al-Maqrizi, 'did the street once more live up to its name of "Between the Two Castles".' Perhaps as a final nose-thumb at his rival, Bashtak, the quintessential spoilt horror, turned the ground floor of his mansion into a sweet-shop.

Sultan al-Nasir's Cairo was the nearest the fourteenth century got to Hollywood. Most of the *mamluks* from the steppe ended up as menials and extras; but those with looks and luck like Bashtak, and the others who elbowed, backstabbed and flirted their way to the top, found themselves in a world of fabulous wealth. Qawsun married the Sultan's daughter and pursued gold and rare gemstones as hungrily as Bashtak chased women. When another palace of Qawsun's was plun-dered during a temporary fall from grace, so much gold flooded the Cairo bullion market that the price dropped by nearly half. Bashtak, after his death, was found to have amassed 1.7 million dinars in cash alone – about seventy million dollars' worth at today's prices. Those who didn't get their hands on gold, jewels and the Sultan's daughter could always spend a vicarious evening in Between the Two Castles, listening to the latest episode of *The Arabian Nights*. And, as in the *Nights* and Hollywood, reversals of fortune could be sudden and catastrophic: Bashtak and Qawsun were both executed after the death of their sugar-daddy, al-Nasir. (Bashtak would have enjoyed his rival's crucifixion: the crowds who turned up to watch it could buy Qawsun-shaped lollipops.)

Even in his lifetime, Bashtak's palace was a white elephant. Reading al-Maqrizi, I recalled my own feelings about that great morgue of a house: 'Whenever he went there, Bashtak's heart would shrivel. His soul knew no joy as long as he stayed in it. In the end, he sold it.'

To wander through the warrens of al-Maqrizi's *Settlements* was as strange and thrilling as exploring the physical palace and city. Bashtak, a name mentioned in passing in the *Travels*, was now made flesh. And when, on several later occasions, I happened to pass the palace, I would look up and imagine him in his window seat, trying to get warm, letching through the lattice.

Now I had set and actors, I spent a morning in the Museum of Islamic Art looking for the props. Dark wood was inlaid with white ivory, brass and copper with silver and gold, and glass enamelled in royal blue and sealing-wax red. The love of colour and geometry reminded me of the Moroccan *madrasah* I had visited; clearly, the same nimble fingers and Euclidean minds had been at work here, too.

The difference lay in the heraldry. Almost every object bore a device: there were lozenges and fesses, fleurs-de-lis and Maltese crosses, chalices and double-headed eagles. The combination of sombre field, rich pattern and blazon was a first cousin of Gothic; such an ensemble seen against the backdrop of Bashtak's great hall would have thrilled Pugin and made Lord Leighton sick with envy.

IB, it seemed, had never penetrated the *grande luxe* world of Mamluk interiors. But when I looked closely, I began to spot points of contact, tangential ones, with his own world, fragments from the *Travels*. There, on a mosque lamp dated 1319, was the blazon of the *amir* Almalik – vert two polo sticks erect addorsed argent. IB had bumped into him at the Delta hermitage where he had his dream of far travel. Among the metalwork I found a brass box inlaid with the arms of Tuquz-damur, one of the *amirs* on IB's Cairo list, whom the traveller later met in Mecca – an eagle displayed in base a chalice. And nearby, on a pierced lantern cover, was a point of contact with my own world – the propeller-like cinquefoil voided of the Rasulid dynasty of Yemen; beside it was the name of Sultan al-Mujahid, IB's host there and the ancestor of my friend Hasan.

The similarity with European heraldry was obvious. The difference was that Mamluk arms were not badges of honour, but of office. Bashtak's diamond represented a *buqjah*, a napkin in which clothes were wrapped; the Beau Brummell of medieval Cairo was Jamdar,

Master of the Robes, in the amirarchy. Later, reading al-Maqrizi on the ranks of the Mamluk state, I was reminded of another system. Twenty years earlier I had almost reached its summit: splendid in a tie sprinkled with my own badge of office, a fleur-de-lis (which, in its true heraldic form, is of Mamluk origin), I controlled school lunch queues and cast my vote in the election for captain of cricket. I had been elevated to the vertiginous rank of praepostor.

Dr Arnold and the other fathers of the Victorian public school could well have been students of Mamluk society. For while Sultan al-Nasir went in for a most unheadmasterly form of favouritism when it came to the prettier prefects, the Mamluk system was in general not unlike a drawn-out version of Rugby. Young males – mostly from the Kipchak steppe but also from Anatolia, Armenia, the Caucasus and Cathay – were deprived of their liberty at great expense (five thousand dinars, the price of a first-rate *mamluk*, would at today's bullion rates just about cover ten years of private education; the fees, of course, went to the lucky fathers and slave-dealers). The new boys were regimented into boarding houses. Their main subject of study was Arabic, the Latin of Islam. They played compulsory games of a warlike nature, particularly archery and the use of the lance. A matronly presence was there in the shape of eunuchs, who supervised the boys' domestic lives and looked after their uniforms. Clothing was strictly regulated, although a certain degree of ostentation was permitted to senior *mamluks* – the gold belt was perhaps the equivalent of a waistcoat in Pop. Discipline was fearsome, especially where a suspicion of sex was involved: any boy seen performing the special ablutions required in Islam after sexual activity was submitted to an immediate underpant inspection. If traces of what my dictionary delicately explains as 'seeing evil dreams' were found, all well and good; if not, 'death came to the boy from every quarter'.

(As might be expected, Friar Symon had something to say about Mamluk sexuality. His translator renders it with a blushing ' ... ' The original, however, hardly needs translation: *'Ab Admiraldo [sc. amir] usque ad Soldanum [sc. sultan] inclusive, sunt sodomite pessimi et vilissimi, et eorum multi cum asinis et bestiis operantur iniquitatem.'* The statement is a generalization nearly as gross as the good friar's Latin. But there is a seed of truth in at least the first part: al-Maqrizi noted that in his day homosexuality was becoming so widespread among the better sort of *mamluk* that, in order to attract attention, women had to go *à la garçonne* and wear boys' caps. Elsewhere, he mentioned a mosque founded by a certain Zankadah the Reformed Catamite.)

By the end of the fourteenth century the boarding-house system had collapsed. Delinquent *mamluks* rampaged through the streets of the city, 'more lustful than apes, more thievish than rats and more vicious than wolves'. Al-Maqrizi looked back with a sigh to the time when the playing-fields of Cairo had turned out 'noble administrators of kingdoms, captains steadfast in the path of God, natural rulers who strove to manifest good and to restrain the unjust oppressor'. It might be Sir Henry Newbolt on the muscular gentlemen who ruled Britain's Victorian empire.

Through the texts, I was filling in some of the gaps in IB's strangely impersonal account of Cairo. But there was another book I wanted to get hold of, an earlier guide to the city mentioned by al-Maqrizi and written within a year of IB's visit. Toby, my friend from Garden City, took me to a bookshop where he thought I might find a copy.

The bookseller was sitting outside his premises, a row of lock-up garages. 'By al-Zubayri? I can't say I've come across it,' he said. 'But you could try looking.' We went in.

I laughed. The place was a literary version of Cairo itself, a living tell of books. They were stacked up to the ceiling and had invaded lofts and lean-tos. Even assuming that al-Zubayri's work had survived and been published, and that there was a copy here to be found, finding it would take weeks, perhaps years, of patient excavation. Much of the stock in the lower strata had died off, like coral at the base of a reef. It had become purely structural; any attempt to extract volumes from lower down the piles would have sent the whole edifice crashing to the ground. For anyone with delusions about the immortality of the written word, it was a sobering vision.

A good number of the more accessible books were early twentieth-century works on vampires, ghosts and other aspects of the occult, and on sexology. Even more were concerned with magic and conjuring. I came across *Tricks with Watches*; Toby was tempted by *The Manipulation of Billiard Balls*. From these fragments of dead libraries we constructed a picture of the reading classes of Cairo in the Khedivial twilight – pashas in *tarbush* and waxed moustache, turning pages with moist fingertips, plotting illusions and seductions.

As we left the shop I spotted a row of matching octavos on a table by the door, and felt the slight jolt that comes from seeing the familiar displaced. I checked. It was the same edition as my father's – *Nelson's Encyclopaedia* of 1913 – and had the same slightly animal odour that clings to reference books long thumbed. People had often hinted to my father that it was out of date; I had to point out, when I moved to Yemen, that I was not going to live in a distant *sanjak* of the Ottoman Empire. But he remained loyal to those tatty maroon volumes, his contemporary. I ran my hand along the spines. I too was fond of *Nelson's*, companion of many happy hours on the loo. (How deprived are the squatting nations! Defecation and ingestion of knowledge are such complementary activities.)

As we walked, I enthused to Toby about *Nelson's*. Back at his flat in the mock-Gallic *arrondissement* of Garden City, he announced that I was due for an info-technological update. He opened Stella beers and, on his computer, something called HotBot. 'It's probably the best search engine for your purposes,' he explained.

I said I'd take his word for it. I was happy pottering around the ginnels and culs-de-sac of al-Maqrizi's *Settlements* or *Nelson's*. What

pleasure could there be in whizzing along the flash interstates of the World Wide Web, propelled by a search engine, and one so ludicrously named?

In less than a minute, the Ibns had appeared on the screen – Battutah, Hajar, Jubayr, Khaldun, Sa'id and the rest of them, members of the medieval scholarly internet. I was prepared to forgive HotBot for regarding Ibn Battutah (72 matches) as a different person from Ibn Battuta (205 matches). Toby showed me which buttons to press and went to make supper.

Most of IB's appearances were passing mentions in bibliographies. But there were also some esoterica. IB, I discovered under 'Planetary Nomenclature', had lent his name to a heavenly body. An association of saluki enthusiasts quoted him in their website, and he was cited under Coconuts in 'Johan's Guide to Aphrodisiacs: Fruit and Nuts': 'Among the properties of this nut are that it strengthens the body, fattens quickly, and adds to the redness of the face. As to its aphrodisiac quality, its action in this respect is wonderful.' And there, on the list of an Italian record distributor, was the CD I saw but didn't hear inside the Gate of the Stick in Tangier. A further search led me to a discographic website run by a certain Malcolm. It had an entry on Embryo, the German group who had made the CD: 'They started out as a pretty classic space rock band and then got very jazzy in a fusiony period heavy on vibes, and then Burchard started travelling around the world ... '

I could go on almost indefinitely, I thought, chasing the shadow of IB between cyberspace and al-Maqrizi's *Settlements*. But, like Burchard, I felt it was time to get going.

Upper Egypt

Eastward from Edfu

'I suppose that, wherever one goes, one sees in great measure
what one expects to see.'

Edward Granville Browne, *A Year Amongst the Persians*

'I ARRIVED IN the town of al-Aqsur [Luxor] on the thirteenth day of
the month of Jumada 'l-Ula. It is a fine and large town on the
bank of the Nile, and it contains the tomb of the pious ascetic Abu 'l-
Hajjaj al-Aqsuri. I saw there on the river many boats of enormous
size, like great palaces, with many storeys one above the other. The
markets there are broad and expansive, but many of the goods in
them are tawdry items, inscribed with images in the manner of the
ancients. The people say that these images are a form of writing
devised by Hermes [Trismegistos], who is also called by the name of
Khanukh [Enoch] that is Idris (on him be peace).

'Above the shops where these goods are sold they fix large signs
written in the Afranji [Frankish] script. The reason for this is that
God Almighty in His wisdom has given the inhabitants of al-Aqsur
sustenance from the Afranj, who visit the town in great numbers.
When I was in Alexandria I saw many of these Afranj, merchants
from al-Bunduqiyyah [Venice] and Janawah [Genoa], but never so
many as I saw here. Moreover, the Afranj who visit al-Aqsur are
unparalleled as to ugliness. Most of them are tall and fat, with straw-
coloured hair and white faces tinged with redness. This redness is
increased by the action upon their skin of the sun and, as I was told
by a worthy and pious *shaykh* of the town whose name I have forgotten, because al-Qubt [the Copts] sell them different sorts of
intoxicating drinks. I heard also that some of the Muslims also sell

these drinks, may God Almighty punish them for their wickedness.

'It is an extraordinary thing, but these Afranj do not hide their ugliness. On the contrary, they reveal their members in ways of which I do not wish to speak, men and women alike. Most of them also carry on their backs saddle bags [*khirajah*], both small and large, in the manner of pack-animals. In these they carry their travelling-provisions. It is a most undignified sight.

'Even more extraordinary is the fact that these Afranj, who as is well known are Nasara [Nazarenes, i.e. Christians], also venerate the *berbas* which are the temples of the ancient idolaters. I watched the manner of their veneration. They first present an offering to the gate-keeper who sits at the gate of the *berba*. Next, they circumambulate within the courtyard of the *berba*. Before them walk *mutawwifs* [pilgrim guides, a term usually applied to those at the Ka'bah in Mecca]. These *mutawwifs* are plainly distinguishable by the small pennons which they carry. As they walk, they speak to the visitants, advising and exhorting them in strange tongues. As for the visitants, they reply to these exhortations with a great babble. Also, many of them repeatedly cover their eyes with talismans like small boxes. When I saw this, I was unable to restrain my laughter.

'I heard one of the *mutawwifs* speaking to the gate-keeper in Arabic. He was of the race of the visitants and his speech was barbar-ous and incorrect. I asked him which place he came from in the territory of the Afranj, and he said: I come from Barr Man Jahum. Ibn Juzayy adds: I have read that this place is part of the Island of Anqiltarah [England]. And God is the most knowing.'

(Translator's note: 'Barr Man Jahum' is literally 'the land of him that presented a doleful countenance'. An obscure phrase to say the least, it may be a corruption of 'Birmingham'. This alone would be enough to raise suspicions about the authenticity of the account. Indeed, the whole curious passage, with its glaring anachronisms, is surely an interpolation from the pen of some pseudo-IB ...)

A day in Luxor had got to me. Tourism had made it a pseudo-place, like Eurodisney or Riyadh, to which one could fly direct from Barr Man Jahum. A pseudo-reaction seemed the only one possible.

★

The previous morning, as the train rumbled over the bridge from Cairo to Giza, the Nile had looked particularly mucose. It moved sluggishly, exhaling hanks of mist. I remembered the story of an alchemist who could, it was said, weave tents from its water. The sky-scrapers along the banks were spectral; a two-man scull slid through the vapour. It was going to be another smoggy day. But I was heading south.

A tiny man moved slowly along the train, begging alms in rhyming prose. Hawkers also walked up and down, throwing their goods into our laps. Each specialized in a particular line – news-papers, combs, sticking-plasters or keyrings. If you didn't want to buy, you handed them back when their owners came past again. The only one who seemed to sell anything was an old lady who had diversified: she sold copies of the Qur'anic Chapter of the Merciful, and chewing-gum.

As we left Giza station I thought of the Pyramids and the Sphinx, invisible from the railway line. The thought set off an old ditty, *'The sexual life of the camel is stranger than anyone thinks . . .'* I tried to make mental notes on the landscape, but the rhyme kept intruding, to the rhythm of the train. *'For during the mating season, it tries to bugger the Sphinx . . .'* What was that stuff in the fields like giant rhubarb? *'But the Sphinx's anal orifice is blocked by the sands of the Nile . . .'* I must do something about my abysmal knowledge of botany . . . *'which accounts for the hump on the camel . . .'* Note: palm trees *'. . . and the Sphinx's inscrutable smile.'*

It was no good. I gave up on the landscape and opened the *Travels*.

IB left the Convent of the Relics some time in May 1326, heading for Mecca. He travelled down the Nile, passing through Luxor, then turned east at Edfu. For fifteen days he crossed the desert between the Nile and the Red Sea, calling in on the way at the tomb of al-Shadhili, the greatest of the Maghribi Alexandrian saints and author of the *Litany of the Sea*. And then, at Aydhab, the port for Jeddah, he got stuck. He only had himself to blame. Earlier, in the Nile town of Hu, he had told a local holy man of his pilgrimage plans. 'You will not succeed in going to Mecca on this occasion,' the saint told him bluntly. 'Go back, for you will make your first Pilgrimage by the Syrian Road and no other.' Two months and 1,500 miles after he had left it, IB found himself back in Cairo. He had made the elementary mistake of ignoring that inexorable tour operator, Fate.

Inexorable, inscrutable . . . The Sphinx was threatening a come-back. But a sobering realization laid it to rest: I didn't know quite where I was going. The Nile section of the journey was straightforward; the problems started after Edfu. Humaythira, the remote desert location of al-Shadhili's tomb, was according to IB 'infested with hyenas, and during the night of our stay there we were continually occupied with driving them off'. In the morning, he found that one of the creatures had stolen a skin of dates from his baggage. If the hyenas were not bothersome enough, I had also heard that the tomb might lie in a military zone. The port of Aydhab was more of a problem. I knew where it ought to be – if, that is, anything were left of it – but I didn't know what country it was in. At the bottom right-hand corner of Egypt is a wedge-shaped bit of desert, roughly the shape and size of Sicily, which couldn't decide whether it was Egyptian or Sudanese. Aydhab was in the south-eastern extreme of this disputed territory. Where IB was blasé about destiny, I'd ignored a twentieth-century irritation: borders.

As the train entered Minya, I reflected that at least IB – 'I', the authorial *persona* so elusive in Cairo – was back on form. 'One day I entered the bath-house in this township, and found the men in it wearing no covering. This appeared a shocking thing to me, and I went to the governor and informed him of it.' At IB's instigation, a by-law was immediately drawn up to prevent nude bathing. (An alternative if more impractical method of avoiding being shocked was devised by a later Islamic scholar: you should enter the bath, he said, with two coverings – a waist-cloth and a blindfold. Such precautions were necessary. An early wit, al-Jammaz, described having sex in the bath as one of the three greatest pleasures in life. The other two are 'pissing in a washing bowl, and slapping a bald man on the pate'.) I didn't investigate whether IB's law was still in force; I assume it is, as Minya is now famous for its militant puritans. Toby and Rachel had been there recently and had wandered around the place escorted, they said, by a tank. Younger boys seemed to be exempt from anti-nudity laws. Numbers of them were enjoying an otter-like existence in the canals that criss-crossed the cultivated land; one mooned at the train.

The intense green of crops was broken here and there by a house or hamlet, distempered in a pumpkin yellow that matched the dates ripening in the palmeries. The city of Mallawi, I noted, could not be said today to be 'of pleasant appearance and elegant construction', as IB described it; neither could any of the other riverside towns, which all seemed to hide their charms behind a necrosis of concrete. Suhaj, however, had a few remnants of tropical baroque and was set on a pleasing arc of the Nile. At Naj' Hammadi, 300 miles from Cairo, the train crossed back to the right bank, heading for a line of violet cliffs. As we travelled south the light thickened. An opaque, African dusk was flowing slowly upstream, heading for the Delta. We arrived at Luxor, like Edward Lear,

> when the sun sinks slowly down
> And the great rock walls grow dark and brown,
> Where the purple river rolls fast and dim
> And the ivory Ibis starlike skim ...

Before I did anything else, I wanted to get a travel update on Humaythira and al-Shadhili's tomb. According to IB, the desert road there was 'totally devoid of settlements but' – except for the hyenas – 'perfectly safe for travelling'. Bedouins and dromedaries, he said, were available for hire on the right bank of the Nile opposite Edfu. My notes from Ibn Jubayr confirmed this, and added that passengers rode in sociable two-man camel litters, playing chess or reading. Ibn Jubayr himself finished memorizing the Qur'an as he swayed across the desert to Aydhab. I reckoned that the Luxor office of Thomas Cook would know if one could still visit al-Shadhili in a caravan with a good book, or if – as I suspected – the old road had been taken over by hyenas and soldiers.

They didn't. The apologetic manager could do pharaohs, feluccas and *son et lumière*, but medieval saints were not much in demand. 'I think you'll need a permit,' he added ominously. 'Why don't you ask the Tourist Police?'

The Tourist Police were equally unenlightening. One of them hadn't heard of al-Shadhili; another thought his tomb might be in Aswan. When I told them that it was in the desert east of Edfu, they had a brief conference. 'We think', the senior officer said, 'that it is forbidden for foreigners to go there. Why don't you try al-Mukhabirat al-Askariyyah?'

I thanked them for their advice and left under a cloud. It was compounded of three elements: 'permit', 'forbidden' and 'al-Mukhabirat al-Askariyyah' – Military Intelligence. The idea of going to some Upper Egyptian spook for permission to visit a long-dead saint seemed faintly ridiculous. I decided, for the moment at least, to leave my travel plans in the more reliable hands of Fate.

I wandered around Luxor in a bad mood, responding to the touts' English in my tetchiest Arabic. Karnak and the Avenue of the Sphinxes could go to the jinn. 'Hey, mister,' a boy called out, 'pleased to meet you. My name's Sambo. You want to go on Nile boat trip?'

I glared at him. 'Hear, O . . . *Sambo*, what the poet said:

> Men ask but do not always find,
> Like vessels in a contrary wind.'

Sambo looked puzzled. '*Sprechen sie Deutsch?*'

Word must have got around. No one else tried to sell me a trip while I was in Luxor.

In the Horus Hotel I took refuge on the balcony and anthropologized. The tourists who passed by on the road below fell into two main categories according to trouser length. Among the Shorts two sub-groups were identifiable, the hearty Large Rucksacks and the more earnest-looking Vestigial Rucksacks. The second main category, the Longs, was much smaller. Its members might also be termed Death on the Nilers – several of the women wore chiffon harem pants and little turbans. They were probably staying at the Winter Palace, or wishing they were. I then turned my eye on myself, and saw a misfit in a double-breasted Aquascutum jacket from the Second-hand Suq in San'a.

The tourists had their destinations; I seemed to be busily getting nowhere. Perhaps I should forget about al-Shadhili, hire Sambo's felucca and sail south, down Friar Symon's famous and interminable river to the Land of Prester John.

Then I remembered that at least I had a saint here in Luxor, IB's pious ascetic, Abu 'l-Hajjaj. He had arrived from Mecca in 1193, seeking solitude among the ruins, and remained until he died. In one of those strange architectural marriages the Egyptians go in for, like building mud dovecots on apartment-block roofs, the saint's tomb had been slapped down on the peristyle of Rameses II's temple. It was right in front of me, across the road from the Horus Hotel. The minaret poked up above floodlit columns; over it hung a full moon like a truckle of buffalo cheese.

The following morning, I found the entrance to Abu 'l-Hajjaj's mosque-tomb with the help of a policeman. While it was bang on top of the biggest tourist attraction in Luxor, it seemed in every other respect as far from it as possible. It might have risen out of some distant village, inhabitants and all, flown to Luxor and alighted on the temple roof. Peasants caressed the wooden lattice that surrounded the saint, murmuring prayers. A woman steered her child to the tomb and whispered to him, 'Look! There's Abu 'l-Hajjaj!' The child grinned and waved through the lattice, as though he had spotted a rarely seen uncle. Among the usual holy appurtenances, there was a nice touch – an electric fan, pointing on to the cenotaph as if to cool the saint beneath it.

Abu 'l-Hajjaj's minder sat in a corner reading a Qur'an. It struck me that he might know about the desert route to Humaythira. I waited for him to come to the end of a chapter.

'You want to visit al-Shadhili?' I nodded. 'It's a long way. First,' he said, tracing a map on the carpet with his finger, 'you take the road from Edfu towards the coast. Then you turn right at Sidi Salim – he's another saint – and go south for about 120 kilometres. It's asphalted all the way. You wouldn't believe the crowds that go there! Al-Shadhili's in the middle of nowhere, but he gets as many visitors as our Abu 'l-Hajjaj.'

Encouraged, I thanked the guardian.

'Come and tell us if you get there,' he said.

Outside the tomb I met the policeman who had given me directions. 'Did you pray?' he asked.

'Well . . . I'm not a Muslim.'

He thought for a moment. 'That's not a problem. Saints are common property.' Then he patted me on the back.

Having paid my respects to Abu 'l-Hajjaj, I walked around the perimeter of the giant temple enclosure to visit his rather grander undercroft. IB had omitted to notice it; but he was not entirely blind to pharaonic monuments. Down the Nile at Akhmim he had described briefly the carvings on the ancient temple. 'People tell a number of fanciful stories on the subject of these images', he concluded, 'over which it is not necessary to linger.' Other travellers and geographers were not above recounting yarns about buried gold, booby-trapped vaults and curses on mummies; they knew their box-office value. A few took a more scientific interest in the pharaonic past. The physician and historian Abdullatif al-Baghdadi, for example, went into raptures over the ancient Egyptians' knowledge of anatomy displayed in their sculpture, and branded vandals and tomb-robbers 'ignorant idiots'. More often, visitors saw the monuments not in terms of aesthetics, but of morals. The guidebook writer al-Harawi, contemplating one of the colossi at Luxor, came up with an Ozymandian verse –

> Where are the giants and emperors of old?
> They and their treasure-houses none could save.
> The void itself was straitened with their hosts,
> As they lie straitened now within the grave.

– then went one better than Shelley, by inscribing it on the statue's chest. Beneath the lines he added a colophon: 'May God have mercy on him that pondered, and drew a moral.' There could be few more elegant graffiti.

I paid the entrance fee and entered the pylon of the temple between seated colossi. There was a board showing a plan of the site: I noticed that while the other features were labelled simply, 'Pylon', 'Peristyle Court' and so on, the mosque had an adjective: 'Imposing Mosque of Abu 'l-Hajjaj'. It seemed strange: the mosque was relatively speaking a loft extension, dwarfed by the structure on which it perched. To call it 'imposing' one would have to suffer from the sort of spatial delusion that plagues estate agents. And yet, as I explored the temple, something happened to my own sense of space. The temple managed somehow to be both vast and claustrophobic. Down among the forests of papyrus columns I felt like a mouse trapped in the works of an organ. Nearly every wall was covered with inscriptions and gods, a fearfully complex and crowded pantheon. The mosque was dedicated not just to a single deity, but to the Empedoclean god whose centre is everywhere and whose circumference is nowhere. It was, in theological terms, immeasurably imposing.

I was beginning to understand how IB had not seen the temple, at least in his memory's eye, and how conversely the tourists of today could give Abu 'l-Hajjaj's tomb little more than a passing glance. It was partly fashion: in the West, eighty years after Howard Carter, Tutmania is still in; Islam is more out than at any period since the Crusades. More important, the whole idea of travel has changed.

In IB's time, the Islamic Age of Aquarius, *siyahah* – now simply 'tourism' – had the specific sense of mystical, transcendental travel. Would-be mystics had to keep on the move, not only to visit holy men but also to avoid spiritual stagnation. In the Maghrib, that land of itchy feet, *siyahah* was part of the higher education curriculum: promising students were taught chronology and astronomy so that they could calculate the time and direction of prayer, then packed off to the desert to wander around, eat lizards and browse through the infinite library of the Cosmos. Some authorities believed that the shortest period of spiritual outward-bound for a dedicated mystic should be twenty-four years.

Travel was seen as a sort of incubation. As well as providing encounters with Sufi gurus along the way, constant nomadism enabled the embryonic mystic to hatch out into a higher state of consciousness. Through travel, wrote the great dervish-master al-Rumi, a certain holy man had reached the state where he could 'see in a drop of water an ocean, a sun enfolded within a mote'. Few had the stamina for this sort of travel; those who did often attracted derision. People looked at al-Rumi's Blakeian mystic and muttered, 'The brain of this poor wretch through long melancholy and austerity has turned rotten, like an onion.' But, rather like the pioneering hippy-trailers seven centuries later, the few genuine spiritual hard-nuts were followed by more earthbound overlanders, part-time mystics like IB.

Later, transcendental tourism got a bad name. Al-Maqrizi wrote of mystic travellers in the early fifteenth century:

> From Sufis in this age and day a mere six vows are due:
> To swank and sing, to dance and booze, to eat hash-cakes,
> and screw.

Or, as a later poet put it, sex and drugs and rock 'n' roll.

Lurking among the columns of Luxor Temple and observing contemporary *siyahah*, I recalled a piece of advice given to the Persian scholar Edward Browne by a Persian gentleman: 'Do not, like the majority of Firangis, occupy yourself with nothing but dumb stones, vessels of brass, tiles and fabrics; contemplate the world of ideas rather than the world of form, and seek for Truth rather than for curiosities.' But perhaps tourists too, from time to time, when their gnostic faculties are sharpened by Stella beer and Nile sunsets, have Ozymandian intimations or see the world in a grain of sand. I certainly couldn't pass judgement: my search for IB made me, more than any tourist, a seeker after the material.

That evening, near the hotel, I noticed a sign: 'DANTE BAZAAR JEWELLERY – We Write Your Name in Hieroglyphic'. My defences were momentarily down – I'd had a couple of Stellas – and I allowed myself to answer a siren call from within. At least, I thought, I could investigate whether any of the medieval Arab beliefs about hieroglyphics had survived.

The conversation, however, took a different turn. The owner admired the ring I was wearing, a large agate with white spots, and I explained that it had been examined on a sort of mineralogical ouija board in the Great Mosque library in San'a. Following various incantations, it had apparently slid by itself into a section of the board marked 'To Cure Styes, by the Will of God'. Since I had started wearing it I had never suffered from a single stye. 'Not', I added, 'that I ever did before.'

The goldsmith frowned. 'Of course, all this is nonsense. And it's forbidden, particularly for us Christians.' He drew back his sleeve to show me a small blue cross tattooed on his forearm.

I felt that I should defend the occultists of Yemen, and related several strange phenomena that I had witnessed there or heard about.

The Copt remained unimpressed. 'And', I went on, 'there are people who can see thieves and stolen goods in bowls of water — as if they're watching a security video.'

Suddenly, the goldsmith lit up. Recently, he explained, there had been a theft from his shop. 'Three gold chains, worth $1,000 each. I went around all the Muslim seers in Luxor — of course, there aren't any Christian ones — and they all said, *independently* mind you, that the thief was young, and not a customer!'

It was hardly a dramatic revelation. Now, if they had said unanimously that the thief was an albino with a venerean strabismus . . .

'But the priest got to hear about what I was doing and put a stop to it.' He leaned forward and went on in a low voice, 'Can I ask you a favour? I've heard that the Arabians are the best seers in the world. Now, if you could ask them for me . . .'

I smiled. 'It's a long way from Luxor to Yemen. They'd need a satellite link.'

'Someone in Cairo identified a thief in Luxor, and that's a long way.'

I said I'd try. 'But I'm not promising anything. And wouldn't you have to be there too?'

The goldsmith thought for a moment. 'I'll give you something from the shop . . . What about a business card?'

'That', I said 'will do nicely.'

★

MI6, the KGB and Egyptian Military Intelligence, during a brief period of détente unrecorded in the annals of espionage, once got together for manoeuvres in the Eastern Desert. The mission: to stalk and capture a gazelle in the fastest time possible. The MI6 men were back with their quarry within three hours; the Russians, experienced in tracking escaped dissidents across the Siberian tundra, were slightly quicker. But the sun set, the morrow dawned, and the Egyptians didn't return. Anxious for their fellow agents' safety, the foreigners formed a search party. After a morning spent combing the desert, they finally spotted them. The search party approached, but the Egyptians were oblivious. They were totally absorbed in what they were doing, which was alternately bawling at, then flogging, a prostrate donkey. The donkey appeared to be dead.

'What are they saying?' the Russian spymaster asked M, a noted orientalist.

'What d'you expect, old boy? "Confess to being a gazelle!"'

I remembered the story as I approached the gates of Military Intelligence (Aswan Sector), and wondered what lay inside.

The day had got off to an inauspicious start when I was ejected from a Luxor-Edfu minibus. 'You must go with your *fawj*,' the driver told me.

I replied that I was a *fawj* – a group, or herd – of one.

'Sorry,' said the driver, 'but it's government orders. No tourists to travel by minibus.'

I prickled. 'I'm not a tourist, I'm a ... '

'It's for your safety.'

'Go on the ordinary bus,' whispered one of the passengers. 'It's cheaper.'

My face was saved; but something was going on, and it was annoying not to know what it was.

Two hours later, the ordinary bus driver took my fare without hesitation. I wasn't sorry to leave Luxor. IB's 'pretty little place' had disappeared beneath hotels and papyrus showrooms. An enormous XVIII Dynasty temple had appeared. Even the Nile, pre-Socratically, was not the same river IB had seen. Only Abu 'l-Hajjaj's tomb remained as a fragment withdrawn from the traveller's time.

I soon forgot the incident of the minibus and was back in the *Travels*. Esna was a town of wide streets with busy markets and fine orchards, just as IB had described it. South of Esna, the bus followed the divide between cultivation and desert, a precise pinstripe of road between a thick band of green and an endless block of tawny yellow. It was a minimal, almost abstract landscape, like an enlarged Rothko.

At Edfu, I walked over the bridge to the right bank of the Nile. There were no bedouins or dromedaries; neither was there any other form of transport. The only activity was the slow ingestion of tea and *shishah* smoke in a roadside café. There, after some discussion, it was agreed that I had missed the only eastbound bus of the day.

Looking back, I know what I should have done: ordered a tea and a *shishah* and gone into suspended animation. Instead, something – a desire for movement, an ancestral respect for the constabulary, or perhaps some masochistic streak – took me to the police station to ask if I needed a permit to visit al-Shadhili. It was like walking into an undergraduate philosophy seminar and saying, 'Discuss: "Is this a question?"'

And so – a debate, a wait, a bus-ride and a long walk later –
I found myself in the waiting-room at Military Intelligence, Aswan.
IB hadn't been to Aswan; and he had never, not in twenty-nine years
on the road, asked if he needed a travel permit. I thought of him, and
of those intrepid travel writers of today who slip nonchalantly, visa-
less, from Afghanistan into China, and cursed myself.

The room resembled the lobby of a very seedy hotel. There was a
large and battered reception desk; the walls were stencilled in bilious
colours with a repeating spermatozoic pattern and lined with collapsing horsehair sofas. A dishevelled underling appeared. He
cracked his knuckles and straightened his hair. I explained why I had
come.

'This is a matter for the Colonel,' said the underling. 'I'm afraid
he's busy at the moment.'

An image flashed across my mind – the Colonel, sleeves rolled up,
bearing down on a small and cowering donkey.

'Are you an orientalist?' asked the underling.

I winced inwardly. It was a word with undertones, dark ones: an
orientalist went round in native dress, carried a pocket theodolite and
worked for the ultimate and total dominance of the West. 'I just have
a general interest in *walis*.'

'Then', he said, brightening, 'you must certainly visit al-Shadhili.
You know that in the desert he often met up with al-Khadir?'

I was more than slightly surprised – not that the saint should have
encountered al-Khadir, the Green Man, the immortal prototype of
travelling mystics; but that I was hearing about it in Military
Intelligence, Aswan.

The man introduced himself as Nashwat. For the next hour we
talked of nothing but saints – al-Shadhili, al-Mursi and Yaqut of
Alexandria, Abu 'l-Hajjaj of Luxor. When he mentioned
Abdulrahim al-Qinawi, I pulled out the *Travels* and showed him IB's
reference to 'the pious sharif . . . author of many marvellous proofs of
sanctity and celebrated miracles'.

'Sidi Abdulrahim is still performing miracles,' Nashwat told me.
'Not long ago, he got a friend of mine off military service. He prayed
at the tomb and asked the saint to intercede, and when he came up
before the selection board, they said, "We've changed our minds. We
don't want you."'

Suddenly, Nashwat glanced at his watch. '*Ya Salam!* I didn't know it was that time. You must excuse me. Come back later – perhaps the Colonel will be free.'

I left Military Intelligence thinking that, of all the people I might have expected to encounter there, the last would be an amateur hagiographer.

That evening, I returned to find Nashwat behind the reception desk and apologetic. 'The Colonel's gone,' he said. Perhaps, I thought, nobody speaks to the Colonel. 'But don't worry. I'll try the Major.' Five minutes later he was back. His expression wasn't promising. 'The Major says you need to go to Cairo and get a *tasdiq*, a letter of approval.'

I rolled my eyes. The round-trip to Cairo was a thousand miles.

Nashwat leaned across the desk and patted my shoulder. 'Just go,' he whispered. 'If al-Shadhili wants you to visit him, you'll visit him.'

Next morning, I caught the 6.30 bus from Aswan. Its dogleg route took it north towards Edfu then east, past a checkpoint and on to the desert road, and finally down the coast to the point where the disputed territory began. (I hadn't broached the subject of Aydhab, IB's Red Sea port, with Military Intelligence; I had already stirred up a can of worms and didn't want to graduate to a nest of vipers.) The problem was the checkpoint. Nothing worse was going to happen there, I glibly assumed, than an ignominious ejection from the bus and a long wait for transport back. All the same, apprehensions began to wriggle in my stomach as the bus turned east.

As we left the cultivated strip, I noticed a large roadside hoarding for al-Ahliyyah Insurance. Presumably the idea was that nervous motorists would do a U-turn, race back into Edfu and insure themselves before crossing the desert. But two things intrigued me about the sign: the firm's slogan, 'In the care of God' – which begged the question of why insurance was necessary – and its logo, a pharaonic deity. The message seemed to be that a consortium of al-Ahliyyah, Allah and Anubis would cover all eventualities.

My musings came to an abrupt end. The bus was slowing down. I could see the checkpoint approaching. I silently, syncretically asked for al-Shadhili's intercession.

A man in plain clothes boarded and asked everyone to get their papers ready. With a sinking heart, I pulled out my passport. For someone expecting a nice fresh firman from Military Intelligence, it would be singularly off-putting: stained and dog-eared, it gave off an indefinable, spicy smell compounded of tropical sweat and a brief but total immersion in a stagnant *wadi*; the photograph it bore was of a person who had long since ceased to be me. The official moved slowly up the aisle, checking documentation, and went past me without a glance. He was saving the foreigner, the anomaly, until last. I heard him coming back and prepared myself for the gentle hand on the shoulder, the apologetic eviction. He walked past me again, and left the bus. The driver restarted the engine and pulled away.

The passengers, who had hardly spoken until now, began chatting. My neighbour across the aisle introduced himself as Ali Id – Ali Festival. He was dark-skinned and, like most of the other all-male passengers, wore the fine linen turban of Upper Egypt and Sudan; he also carried a sort of swagger-stick. There was an appealing reticence in his speech and gestures, and I was pleased when he said that he too was heading for Humaythira. When I told him my name he repeated it softly, several times, as if trying to solve a conundrum.

I too was pondering a mystery: how I had got through the checkpoint unchecked. Had I been rendered temporarily invisible? I thought of asking Ali Id; but the question, on so short an acquaintance, would have been alarming. Whatever the explanation, I was glad I'd put my faith in the saint and not in the unseen Major.

The landscape we were passing through was also all but invisible: the driver's mate had drawn the curtains of the bus and slotted a cassette into the on-board video player. As the titles came up, Ali Id clapped his hands: 'Fifi Abdou! You'll like this film.' I was sceptical; but the film, an Egyptian kung fu-belly dancing-vengeance-comedy-fantasy, was enthralling. What it lacked in plot it made up for in sheer bizarrerie, as the acrobatic heroine humiliated villain after villain. As the film approached its climax, the driver's mate paused Miss Abdou in mid-kick and announced our arrival at Sidi Salim, the turn-off for Humaythira. Cheated of the denouement, Ali Id and I left the bus and watched it drive off.

We were on a gravel plain scattered with low, desiccated hills like gnawed bones. It was midday. The sun bore down like a jackhammer. No other passengers had got off.

The saint, Sidi Salim, lay behind a high wall inside a cube that turned into an octagon then a dome. Around the tomb huddled a few shacks, an unfinished first-aid post and a café that doubled as a small shop. Across the road there was a mosque of recent date; next to it a broad cement staircase rose to a grandiose block of latrines. We went over to the café, a roof on free-standing pillars, installed ourselves on a bench and ordered *shishahs*. All the necessities of desert life were here – shade, tobacco and cool water stored in sweating earthenware jars – and I felt suddenly and utterly contented.

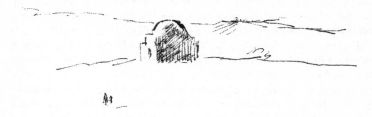

The other occupants of the café were also on their way to Humaythira. One of them was a young teacher, the other four old men, the oldest one in a turban so ancient that it might have been put together from recycled mummy wrappings. Soon after our arrival the café keeper, who doubled as muezzin, called the noon prayer in a fine unamplified voice. Everyone went to pray except Ali Id and me.

In addition to the café keeper, Sidi Salim had one other permanent resident. Prayers were still going on in the mosque when a bulky figure emerged from the tomb compound. Ali Id nudged me. 'That's Hajjah Layla,' he whispered. 'She lives in the tomb.' The woman waddled towards an oil-drum of water, glaring at us as she went past. She seemed to share a couturier with the oldest old man, and was cloaked in what looked like an exhumed shroud, secured above her head by three large knots. Considering her place of residence, it was appropriate. Beneath the shroud she wore a pair of pantaloons so generously cut that the crotch dragged along the ground behind her. Her feet were bound in rags, and finished off with a pair of antique carpet slippers. But even more extraordinary than her wardrobe was the little retinue that followed her. It consisted of three black sheep: a) a portly old ram, b) a medium-sized ewe and c) a silky, pubescent ram. Every few steps, c) tried unsuccessfully to mount b), while a) threw disdainful glances over his shoulder. On each of Hajjah Layla's subsequent appearances, I noticed that the order and activities of the little procession never changed. The whole strange tableau was a ghoulish, grown-up version of 'Mary Had a Little Lamb'.

Hajjah Layla watered her sheep in a trough by the oil-drum, then turned to lead them back. She glared again, and addressed us in a gruff voice: 'Why aren't you two praying like the others?' Then, at Sidi Salim's gate, she stopped and wheeled around with surprising agility. 'You're nothing but a couple of *kafirs*,' she screeched. 'We don't want your sort here!' Oblivious of the attempted coitus at her feet, she fixed us for a full minute with a terrible, gorgon gaze, then disappeared into the tomb.

I heard a splutter beside me. It was Ali Id, choking on his *shishah* smoke. 'They say . . . that in her time . . . 'Ali told me between splutters '. . . she was a great beauty.'

The mosque-goers returned, and we all shared a lunch of buffalo-cheese balls and pancake bread. Hajjah Layla and her sheep made another appearance. The sun began to slide slowly down the sky. We measured out the unspooling day on *shishah* refills. A pick-up turned on to the Humaythira road, but the cab was full and the back contained two camels, roped in a sitting position so that only their heads were visible. It was followed later by a convoy of minibuses but they too were packed, taking families to visit al-Shadhili. Then, at sunset, an empty pick-up came. Ali Id and the teacher negotiated with the driver but came back shaking their heads. 'We offered £E35, but he wouldn't budge from £E50,' Ali said as the pick-up set off to Humaythira, empty. He didn't seem at all bothered. I thought of running after it and paying the difference; but I was enjoying the inactivity of the café. We would visit al-Shadhili in his own good time. Besides, it would be discourteous to abandon his fellow-saint, Sidi Salim. (Not that anyone approached the tomb: it would have meant running the gauntlet of Hajjah Layla.)

As darkness fell, I brought up the subject of the checkpoint. To have passed through it unchecked seemed surprising, if not miraculous. Ali Id smiled arcanely but offered no opinion. The teacher spoke: 'There could of course be some rational explanation. But why shouldn't a *karamah* operate by rational means? After all, miracles aren't the same as magic.'

I asked if he thought al-Shadhili would perform a *karamah* for a non-Muslim.

'If your intention in visiting him is good, why not?' said the teacher. '*Karamahs* certainly take place *through* non-Muslims. I heard a story that happened recently in Cairo.' The café keeper brought a lamp and placed it on a table beside us. 'You know the Mosque of al-Husayn? Well, a poor man was sleeping there when a thief came and stole his money – fifteen pounds. When the man found out, he didn't know what to do, so he stayed where he was. In the night, he saw Sayyidna al-Husayn in a dream. Al-Husayn said to him: "Catch the number 52 bus to the Quarter of Such-and-Such, and you will meet a priest who will help you." In the morning, the man did as he was told – he still had a couple of coins in his pocket for the bus – and found the priest in his church. The priest said to him, "*Salli ala 'l-nabi*. Pray for blessings on the Prophet." So the man said, "May God give the Prophet blessings and peace." Then the priest said the same thing again: "*Salli ala 'l-nabi*," and the man responded again. This went on and on. The man didn't know what was happening, so he said, "How many times am I meant to pray for blessings on the Prophet?" The priest said, "Well, you've done it fifteen times." Then he took some money out of his robe and gave it to the man. It was fifteen pounds.'

Ali Id's eyes were large in the lamplight; the old men muttered approvingly in the shadows. As they sucked smoke and reflected on the story, I got the *Travels* out of my bag and turned to the account of al-Shadhili's death. IB had heard it in Alexandria from Yaqut, who had been told it by his master, al-Shadhili's disciple al-Mursi. I read aloud. Every year, IB wrote, al-Shadhili went on pilgrimage to Mecca via Upper Egypt and the desert. 'One year . . . he said to his attendant, "Take with you a pickaxe, a basket, aromatics for embalming, and all that is necessary for burying the dead." The servant said to him, "Why so, O my master?" and he replied "In Humaythira you shall see."' When they reached Humaythira, IB went on, the saint prayed and then dropped dead on the spot. His servant buried him where he fell.

As soon as I finished reading, the old man in the mummy-linen turban spoke: 'Who wrote this book of yours? He missed the most important part!'

We all looked at him.

'It was al-Mursi who was with al-Shadhili when he died. While he was digging the grave, a man turned up and gave him a hand. Al-Mursi didn't know who this stranger was, because his face was veiled. In fact, it was the Prophet himself, may God give him blessings and peace! Al-Mursi kept thinking, "Who is this man? Who *is* this man?"'

In the end, he couldn't stop himself and ... ' the old man swept his hand in front of his face ' ... he pulled the veil away.'

The old man paused to get his breath back. No one spoke.

'Now, it is forbidden to see the face of the Prophet. So who did al-Mursi see? What do you think he saw?'

Everyone looked at me. I looked at the old man.

'He saw al-Shadhili's face,' his voice was cracking, '*al-Shadhili burying himself!*'

In the long silence that followed, I imagined the raw drama of the telling processed into a footnote ('Among the popular accretions to the account of al-Shadhili's death ... '). It would be a folkloric curiosity, a datum, transfixed on paper like a moth on a pin. While they went and prayed, I took out my notebook and began the slow business of transfixion.

The café keeper cooked a supper of beans. After we had eaten, he turned on his radio. The news was grim. Earlier in the day, nine German tourists and their driver had been burned to death in a coach outside the Egyptian Museum in Cairo. According to the report, an escaped lunatic and his brother had petrol-bombed them. I made a bed on a cement bench that ran along the wall of Sidi Salim's tomb. Ali Id spread a mat on the ground beside me. 'I shall guard you,' he said.

Soon after I had turned in, I heard a distant howl, then an answering bleat from one of Hajjah Layla's sheep. My mind went straight to IB's night at Humaythira − 'infested with hyenas ... continually occupied with driving them off ... ' Ali was still awake, investigating sleeping positions on the hard ground. '*Ya Ali,*' I whispered.

'What?'

'That bit I read out about IB and the hyenas ... What was that noise?'

'What noise? Anyway, there aren't any hyenas now.'

I lay on my back, between the saint and Ali Id, looking up at the Milky Way. It looked solid, like a stroke of whitewash. I had never seen it so bright.

Something woke me. I froze: I could hear a frenzied lapping nearby. Then heavy panting, and the footfalls of a prowling beast. Ali had said there weren't any hyenas; he had also said there weren't any mosquitoes, and there was one whining right by my ear. Slowly, I turned my head. The moon was up, the desert electroplated with light. An animal was padding away from Hajjah Layla's trough. Even without my glasses I could see that it was, incontrovertibly, a dog.

In the small hours I was awoken again, by growling monsters. Sidi Salim had turned into a truckstop, and the café keeper was serving the drivers beans and tea. When they had eaten, they climbed into their cabs and the lorries set off for the sea, snorting and farting. I was beginning to doubt Ali Id's abilities as a bodyguard; despite the din, he hadn't stirred.

It was in the morning that he proved himself. I got out of my sheet sleeping-bag and was about to put my left foot on the ground when Ali, who was already up and drinking tea, shot across the café forecourt and whacked the gravel with his stick, inches from my bare toes. I put on my glasses, and saw a small and very squashed scorpion.

Beyond the periphery of the café, the surface of the desert seemed to have come alive. The movement came from large numbers of partridge, busy in the early sunlight. Before long, Hajjah Layla emerged from the tomb with her ovine cortège. Then, at about eight, a minibus arrived from the Humaythira road. The passengers, mostly women and children, stood giggling and chatting by the roadside while the driver went to the shop. One of the children spotted me, scuttled across the yard with a curious scissor gait and shook my hand. He seemed to be suffering from some form of paralysis. Then he turned and fell flat on his face. I picked him up and he hobbled back to the bus, laughing. We waved to each other as the vehicle drove away. 'People are always happy when they visit al-Shadhili,' Ali Id explained.

The day was heating up, and I retreated to the shade of the café. There was no sign of a lift; I began to wonder whether al-Shadhili was having second thoughts about my visit. And then, towards ten, an empty pick-up came. Uncomplaining, we paid £E70 – double our best offer of the day before – and set off. Ali and I had been waiting twenty-two hours, the teacher two days and the old men an unspecified 'very long time'. I watched the domed tomb of Sidi Salim grow smaller over the tail-gate. As saints go, he might lack the charisma of al-Shadhili; but when he had guests, he held on to them jealously.

Before us, the plain was narrowing and the rocky hills closing in and growing into mountains. Here and there amid clumps of thorn bush stood a shelter, somewhere between a shack and a tent, with a camel or two or a few goats foraging beside it. Ali told me that the encampments belonged to the Ababidah tribe, and said they were *a'rab*, 'Arabs', or nomads.

The pick-up entered a series of low passes, a tract of rock nibbled clean by the wind, bleached and ossified by the sun. I tried to picture IB, riding with his *a'rab* through this hyena-haunted waste; and al-Shadhili, seventy years before, travelling with his grave-clothes. For the saint, it was an appropriate landscape in which to die. A hardened transcendental trekker, he once recalled camping in such a spot, surrounded by prowling beasts, as 'the most delightful night of my life'. Clearly, al-Shadhili was made of different stuff from IB and me.

On the route we were following, however, pilgrims like IB and al-Shadhili were the least of the traffic. 'We saw so much pepper going along this road', Ibn Jubayr wrote, 'that we imagined it to be no more valuable than sand.' The pepper and other spices were shipped from the Malabar coast of India, via Aden, to Aydhab; from there they were carried inland, across these passes and through the desert to the Nile, then downriver to Lower Egypt, to the Maghrib, and across the Mediterranean from Alexandria to Venice and the markets of further Europe. The cosmographer al-Qazwini was amazed by the vast extent of trade in his time, the thirteenth century. In an entry on Maghanjah, 'a city in the land of the Franks on a river called "Rayn" ' (probably Mainz), he wrote: 'It is astonishing that, although this place is in the Far West, there are spices there which are to be found only in the Far East – pepper, ginger, cloves, spikenard, costus and galingale, all in enormous quantities.' Looking over the cab of the pick-up, it was hard to believe that through these narrow cols, like sand through the waist of an hourglass, flowed the most valuable trade of the Middle Ages; that this road ensured the success of a *tajine* in Marrakesh or a Rhenish *wurst*.

Humaythira was a surprise: a cluster of government-built houses, a school and some long low buildings which Ali explained were accommodation for al-Shadhili's visitors, all in a depression ringed by low hills of rock. Ali led me past al-Shadhili's tomb chamber, a modern polygonal structure like an oversized seaside kiosk, and into the police post. He introduced me to the commander, Captain Ibrahim, then disappeared. It was the last I saw of him.

The captain noted down my name and nationality, then asked if I would be joining him for Friday prayers. I shook my head. He led me to one of the guest blocks, then excused himself. After the day at Sidi Salim with Ali Id and the other travellers, it seemed abnormal to be alone. The call to prayer sounded. However far I followed IB, there always remained that one last step.

A boy of about ten appeared in the doorway, saw me and ran across the room. He shook my hand vigorously. 'Have you come to visit al-Shadhili?' he asked.

'Of course.'

'Me too. My name's Baha.'

'My name's Tim.'

'*Teem* ... That's the name of a drink. It's a kind of lemonade. Aren't you coming to the mosque? We've got to hurry.'

He was still holding my hand. 'Not today,' I said.

The boy looked puzzled. 'Well, see you later.' He ran off and collided in the doorway with a woman.

'Baha!'

'Sorry, mother.'

The woman smiled at me. 'Was he being a nuisance?'

'Not at all. He's charming ... *ma sha Allah*,' I said, adding the phrase to avert the Evil Eye.

She laughed. 'You can have him if you want!' The Evil Eye was fully averted: what jinn would want Baha when his own mother was prepared to give him away?

Baha's mother was followed by about thirty women, girls and younger children. As they entered, I realized with growing panic that the captain had taken me to the ladies' quarters. By some dreadful accident I had realized the old orientalist dream – penetration of the seraglio – and could see it turning into a nightmare.

The women were advancing. I grinned disarmingly. 'Well, I'd better be on my way ...'

There was an arpeggio of laughter. 'Where are you going?' asked Umm Baha. 'You're our guest.'

She came and squeezed my hand; all the others followed her example. A toddler waved at me and threw a kiss. The greetings over, the women ranged themselves around the hall, untroubled by the stranger in the harem, and nattered polyphonically. They were all pleasingly plump, chocolate-dark and gorgeously wrapped in bright floral prints.

Umm Baha told me that they were from Luxor. 'But we're originally from south of Aswan, from Nubia. Our family had to move
when the High Dam was built. You see, we're all cousins.'

I asked her what had brought them to Humaythira. Again, she
laughed. 'Oh, we just like to come here. In fact, we come whenever
we can afford to. We visit the saint and spend a couple of days here as
his guests – I mean, you can give a donation if you want, but you
don't have to. And', she confided, 'someone else does the cooking.'

I sat listening to the musical Nubian voices. For somewhere that
owed its existence to death, Humaythira seemed remarkably lively. It
was a place of both devotion and recreation – a sort of Islamic
Butlin's. My own reasons for being here were not a matter of discussion; but one of the cousins asked Umm Baha, in a whisper, if I was a
Muslim.

'How should I know?' she said, then turned to me. 'Are you a
Muslim?'

I said I was a Masihi, a follower of the Messiah.

'Oh,' said the cousin, 'one of *iyal ammana*.'

One of our cousins.

The men came back from their prayers and we sat down to a meal
of rice, *mulukhiyyah* and fat mutton. After lunch, they all left for the
long journey back to Luxor. The hall was empty again; but no longer
silent – the Nubian cousins seemed to have set off some harmonic of
the place, and their laughter lingered behind them.

I went to the tomb, and found I was the only visitor. Everyone else
in Humaythira was enjoying a mutton-fed siesta. It was the slack time
for tomb-going. Feeling, for the first time in my sepulchral travels, a
distinct sense of melancholy, I left the saint and went to look for
a ride in the direction of Aydhab.

★

'And what of the third person of your Trinity, the Holy Spirit?' The
shaykh spoke with the precise little twangs and pops peculiar to
speakers of the most elevated Arabic. His pharynx seemed to conceal
a miniature skiffle group.

To many Muslims, the idea of the Trinity smacks of rampant *shirk*,
polytheism. I was hardly the best person to defend it. I could remember my infant self pondering the subject during sermons at Mattins.
God was 3 in 1, like that brand of oil my brothers put on their bikes.

God the Son was easy: He was shown all over the place on His cross and, this being the 1960s, looked like the latest issue of curate. God the Holy Ghost was more difficult, but perhaps to be found in the attic, which was where ghosts lived. The real poser was God the Father. An early burst of logic dismissed the old-gentleman-on-a-cloud version: wouldn't He fall through the cloud? Perhaps God as a whole was very small – the winds and whales of the Benedicite had to magnify Him, which is what my grandmother did to read the newspaper.

To be frank, my understanding of the triune deity had developed little since childhood. Now, I longed to change the subject to something straightforward like the virgin birth, to admit that I had failed Divinity 'O' Level. But the *shaykh* was waiting for an answer. He smiled quizzically from a face as dark as bog-oak that rose out of a horned moon of beard. It was the face of a mage, or a mesmerist. 'Uhm . . . I think that in the gospels Jesus said that another comforter would come after him, and the comforter is the Holy Ghost. Or something like that.'

'This is another case', the *shaykh* said softly, 'of deliberate alteration to the Injil, the Evangel. The original text is in the Holy Qur'an, in which Jesus says,' he touched my hand in emphasis; on one of his fingers glittered a balas ruby the size of a hazelnut, ' "After me there will come a prophet whose name is Ahmad." Ahmad is, as you know, an alternative name for Muhammad. Jesus the son of Mary predicted the coming of our Prophet, may God bless and preserve all three of them. What do you say to that?'

There was no point arguing with the literal word of God, so I said, 'Mmm.'

The other passengers in the pick-up, the *shaykh*'s followers, looked disappointed at my response. They wanted more. From the cab, a *dhikr* cassette broadcast its rhythmic, unitarian mantra: '*La ilaha illa 'llah*, There is no god but God.' I looked out of the whizzing vehicle on to a landscape as blurred and arid as my brain. I could think of nothing except a silly but apposite joke about a Cairene traffic policeman.

The policeman had been posted to the desert, and was desperate to get back to the city. He had to book someone and prove himself, but for months not a vehicle had appeared. Finally, one day, a Christian priest rode up on a motorcycle.

The bike was in perfect condition; the priest was even wearing a crash helmet. The policeman's heart sank. All he could do was issue a mild word of warning: 'Father, don't you know it's dangerous to travel alone in the desert?'

'But I'm not alone,' said the priest. 'I travel with the Father, the Son and the Holy Spirit.'

'Hah! I knew there'd be something,' the policeman exclaimed, pulling out his notebook. 'Four on a motorcycle. You're booked.'

I told the joke. There was the briefest of hiatuses; one of the passengers laughed *sotto voce*. The *shaykh* fingered the knobbly wooden rosary that hung around his neck. 'Perhaps', he said, 'we can say no more about the true nature of God than the statement of His Prophet: "Consider creation, and do not consider the Creator. For minds cannot attain Him, nor sight encompass Him." '

I nodded enthusiastically, and sighed inwardly with relief. My inquisition was over.

Like me, the *shaykh* and his companions had visited al-Shadhili and were now on their way to the coast. As we turned east at Sidi Salim, my thoughts turned to Aydhab. Compared with the more illustrious pepper ports – Mangalore on the Malabar coast, Aden, Alexandria, Venice – Aydhab was the poor relation. Gibb's footnote in the *Travels* sounded bad enough: 'Its ruins have been identified by G.W. Murray, *Geogr. J.*, LXVIII (1926), 235–40, "on a flat and waterless mound" on the Red Sea coast, 12 miles north of Halaib, at 22°20′ N., 36°29′32″ E.' But the note concealed the true awfulness of Aydhab in its heyday. Ibn Jubayr wrote that pilgrims were forced to pay outrageously high taxes. For those who refused, the port authorities 'devised various inhuman tortures such as suspension by the testicles'. Only one letter, he noted, separates 'Aydhab' from *adhab*, 'punishment'. Things improved when Saladin abolished uncanonical dues; but travellers still had to contend with Aydhab's fake holy men, randy landladies and, most notoriously, rapacious skippers. Their vessels leaked through their coir stitchings and stank of shark oil and bilge gas. Into these, Ibn Jubayr says, the pilgrims were packed one on top of another 'like chickens in a cage'. If anyone complained, the response was, 'You look after your soul, and I'll look after my hull.' The sea was dreadful, a warren of reefs with names like 'the Shoal of the Devil's Mother' and home to ravening sharks. The Persian traveller Nasir

Khusraw, stuck in Aydhab for three months, heard of a camel which died at sea and was flung overboard. A shark swallowed it whole, all but a leg which remained sticking out of its jaws. Then came an even more monstrous fish that swallowed his smaller cousin *farci de chameau*.

Ibn Jubayr made it across the Red Sea, but only just. On several occasions he heard the heart-stopping crunch of hull striking coral – 'We died and were resurrected many times,' he recalled. Disembarking queasily at Jeddah, he resolved to return overland via the Levant: Crusaders were a minor worry compared with the skippers of Aydhab, 'a place which, if at all possible, it were best never to set eyes on'.

One hundred and fifty years later, IB didn't even make it aboard. As today, there was a dispute about who actually owned the port. A third of it belonged to Sultan al-Nasir and the rest to the Bejas, a local and only partly Islamized tribe, 'black-skinned people, who wrap themselves in yellow blankets'. Arriving at Aydhab just as the joint rulers had fallen out, IB discovered that the Beja chief had sunk all the ships in harbour. As the holy man of Hu had predicted, he turned his back on the sea and retraced his steps to Cairo. Continuing territorial squabbles put traders off the port, and within a few decades of IB's visit commerce there had all but fizzled out. Since then, Aydhab has been forgotten – and perhaps deservedly – by all but a few scholars of medieval geography.

The pick-up began to descend a long, narrow valley. I noticed a hint of salt in the air, and peered over the cab roof into the buffeting wind. In the distance, just visible between mustard-coloured rocks, was a dab of royal blue – the Red Sea. I asked the *shaykh* if he had heard of a place called Aydhab.

He looked surprised. 'Aydhab is in our territory. It belonged to our ancestors . . . '

'So you're Bejas!' Fragments of reading on these strange people rushed into my mind: camels trained to sniff out prey like gun-dogs, ritual excision of the right testicle, a female subsection of the tribe who lived as Amazons. European writers identified the Bejas with the Blemmyes, that freakish race whose faces were on their chests. I scrutinized the *shaykh* more closely: admittedly, his face was in the customary position; but he did have a rather short neck. He also looked taken aback.

'The Bejas', he said testily, 'are a people who wear *sticks* in their hair. We are Bishariyyah. Our ancestor was that great warrior and scholar, the Prophet's companion al-Zubayr ibn al-Awwam, may God be pleased with him.'

I was disappointed. I thought I'd met a cousin of the Sciapods, Himantopods and Cynocephales of classical geography. But then I remembered a reference to the *shaykh's* tribe. 'I've read', I said gingerly, 'that the Bishariyyah are of mixed descent, Beja and Arab.'

'The Prophet said, "Genealogists are liars." '

'So ... your ancestor was al-Zubayr ibn al-Awwam.'

I was now the inquisitor, waiting for a response.

The *shaykh* smiled beatifically. 'It would be an honour if you came with us as our guest.'

Protocol demanded an oblique refusal. But I was tempted. 'Would I be able to visit Aydhab?'

'Of course. But there is nothing there. Just a few ruins by the sea. *Ka-annaha lam takun.*'

As though it had never been.

I wavered. But another 200 miles to visit a place which it were better never to set eyes on, a place which might never have been? Besides, I had exhausted my knowledge of the Trinity.

In the small seaside settlement of Marsa Alam I thanked the *shaykh* for his offer, and explained that I really ought to go to Syria. He turned south, I north. It was only later that I realized I'd forgotten to ask which country Aydhab was in.

*

Two months later and on the other side of the Red Sea, I was reminded of my night at Sidi Salim by another news item on another radio. There had been a second massacre, this time at Luxor. Militants had killed sixty foreign tourists and eight Egyptians.

The promiscuous babble of trippers and touts ended in bullets, then sirens, then silence. Luxor went into shock. No Stellas were drunk in the Horus Hotel; the dollars dried up in the Dante Bazaar; Sambo's boat dropped its sails; there was no *son et lumière* after the sound and fury. Luxor, or at least the pseudo-Luxor of the tourists, became a place which might never have been. Unlike Aydhab, it would probably come back to life; but not yet.

The militants had done it, they said, in the name of Islam. I thought of the Egyptians, the Muslims, I had met – Umm Baha and her many cousins, Nashwat of Military Intelligence, the Delta imam with the El Greco face, the farmer at al-Husayn's Mawlid, the possibly Beja *shaykh* – and wondered what they were making of it all.

From Cairo IB crossed the desert to Gaza. He visited Jerusalem and toured the other holy places of Palestine, then visited cities and castles in Syria. In the Umayyad Mosque of Damascus he attended classes on hadith, Traditions of the Prophet, *and was given diplomas by some of the leading scholars of the age. On 1 September 1326 he left Damascus for Mecca, travelling in the Syrian pilgrim caravan.*

Damascus

The Shilling in the Armpit

'Obedience spake and said: "I take my seat in Syria"; the Plague
replied: "And I go with you."'

Mustawfi, *Nuzhat al-qulub* (c. 1340)

SOMEWHERE AT THE bottom of a box, I have a photograph taken by
a friend from the battlements of Crac des Chevaliers, looking
down on to the moat. Far below on the greenish surface of the water
floats a tiny creature, pallid and leggy like something nasty found in a
pond. The creature is me, breasting the frogspawn and rusty cans,
drunk on Bekaa Valley wine. As I hadn't kept a diary or taken a
camera, the picture is one of the few pieces of material evidence that
I had been to Syria before.

Now, driving into Damascus under a November sky crazed with
lightning, other recollections flashed across my memory: a line of
towers marching up the Tomb Valley of Palmyra; a plate of pome-
granates in the Aleppo *suq*, bigger than babies' heads; the cry of a
street hawker in the small hours – 'Beerah beerah whisky whisky
beeraaah'. I recalled a fragment of conversation on the aphrodisiac
properties of the pistachio, and a complete dialogue with a bean-
seller on the mountain above Damascus:

'How much is that?'

'Two hundred lira.'

'You're joking.'

'That's my price. A hundred for the beans, a hundred for the rent
of the table.'

'If I'd known I'd have eaten standing up.'

'You're paying for the view.'

'Bugger the view. Would you care to charge for the air too?'

A car with Saudi plates drew up and a man got out. 'Are you a Saudi?' I asked him. The man nodded. 'Then what do you think of two hundred lira for a plate of horrible beans?'

The Saudi looked blank.

'See?' I exclaimed. 'Even the Saudi thinks it's a rip-off.'

I threw a hundred lira on the table and stomped off down the hill, dodging a hail of Damascene damnations.

The bean-seller of Jabal Qasiyun sparked off other discomfiting memories: accusations that I was trying to pass forged hundred-dollar bills; a missed plane and threats of imprisonment because of a minor visa irregularity. (Never, never argue with a colonel in Syrian Immigration – things have changed since the 1876 Baedeker stated that 'the traveller's passport is sometimes asked for, but an ordinary visiting-card will answer the purpose equally well'.)

As I was reminded in Upper Egypt, borders and passports are in general a modern discontent. But there were exceptions. Although Egypt and Greater Syria were both ruled by the Mamluk Sultan, IB had to show a piece of paper at the frontier. He noted that the sand was smoothed around the border crossing so that any illegal trespasser could be tracked down. 'And', he added, 'they never fail to catch him.' The danger, the traveller explained, was subversion by Mongol agents. In the recent past, it had been a very real threat: the Mongol Ilkhans wrote regularly, if in vain, to the monarchs of Christendom, inviting them to attack the Mamluks in tandem. The present Suez Canal zone was the trap through which an invasion from the east would have to pass. For Mamluk Tatarophobes, this was their Iron Curtain.

In the text of the *Travels*, IB continued from the border to Jerusalem, then made an extravagant northward loop through Syria before reaching Damascus. Since he also says that he took only three weeks to get from Cairo to the Syrian capital, there is little doubt that he cobbled together more than one visit – something travel writers do with few qualms. I, too, cheated in a small way, and stepped out of an aeroplane where IB's literary trip ended.

'What the poets have said in description of the beauties of Damascus', wrote Ibn Juzayy in one of his asides to the *Travels*, 'is beyond all computation.' The next three pages are an anthology climaxing in a gushing eulogy –

This dwelling-place of joys, where doves attune their song
                                        to dancing bough,
And flowers that galliardwise strut through her meads, a gay
                                        and scented band.

– followed by an editorial ahem: 'So let us return to the narrative ...'

IB reached Damascus in August, as the fruit was ripening. I arrived when the year had turned the corner into winter. Instead of fruit, there was a vigorous crop of very large presidential portraits captioned, 'Welcome to al-Asad's Syria'. For a man so often photographed, Hafiz al-Asad was strikingly unphotogenic. Pictures of his neighbour, Saddam, bespeak a certain brigandish braggadocio; al-Asad, however he was portrayed – uplit, downlit, backlit, in bas-relief, in the round, in mosaic, in multiple like Warhol's Marilyn – always managed to look like a grocer.

Images of al-Asad's son Basil also proliferated along the airport road. They showed him in a neatly clipped beard and aviator shades, and sometimes on a rearing charger, the pose borrowed from the famous David of Napoleon. Basil was dashing; but he was dead, smashed to bits in a Mercedes on this very road. This qualified him to be, according to the captions, 'A Symbol for Coming Generations'. Basil's brother Bashar, the new heir apparent, was less in evidence and at least in looks took after his father.

I told the taxi driver the name of the hotel I'd been recommended. 'You don't want to stay there,' he said. 'I'll take you somewhere much better.'

'Oh yes?'

'A flat. Your own flat, with a minibar. And there are people to ... look after you. Girls I mean.'

'Thank you, but historical geography's more my thing.'

We drove on in silence. Fat gobbets of rain began to explode on the windscreen.

'Your Princess Diana ... Was she a good woman?'

'She had a big heart,' I said.

'She was an adulteress. She tricked her husband. Women should be honourable.' He dilated on the theme for a while, then ran out of inspiration and switched on a cassette. It was a mosque sermon.

I could hardly believe the swiftness of the transition from whore-mongering to homily, from minibar to minbar. But after the initial surprise, I began to wonder if the driver was not so much a hypocrite as a sort of moral cubist, taking a biangular look at human nature. Perhaps it was a Damascene trait. 'Man is prostrate with the fishes and serpents,' wrote a cosmographer of the city at the time of IB's visit, 'but his mind is like the moon and his senses the planets ... ' Suddenly the rain came on with wanton violence. Clouds caved in above us. Static ripped through the sky and made eerie holograms of flyovers and unfinished, exoskeletal skyscrapers. 'The voice of Man is as thunder, his laughter lightning. His flesh is as the earth, his bones mountains.'

We arrived. I shouldered my bag and dived into the rain.

★

In Damascus you can while away a whole day grazing on grilled offal, pastries and crystallized fruit. As Ali Bey wrote, it is 'the best place in the world for animal subsistence'. For my first breakfast there I had a brainburger – a whole lamb's cerebrum poached, peppered and squashed into a bun – and a banana milkshake. The city was sodden and uninviting; but I set off with a full stomach and a light step to visit the Umayyad Mosque, which IB thought 'the greatest mosque on earth in point of magnificence, the most perfect in architecture, and the most exquisite in beauty, grace, and consummate achievement'.

My route took me along a highway and over the Barada, the river of Damascus. Ibn Juzayy, in *Golden Treasury* mode again, said in quotation that

> Her waters glide softly with rippling chains, yet unfettered,
> And healthy yet languid the zephyr that plays o'er her leas.

The Barada was a disagreeable khaki colour, and stank. But then, poets are notorious liars – worse even than travel writers. The Persian traveller Mustawfi was unusually frank. Visiting Damascus at about the same time as IB, he admitted that 'its waters are choked with mud, its air bestinks'. The reason the Barada was polluted, he explained, was that it ran under trees. (The geographer al-Idrisi was probably nearer the mark when he said that the sewers flowed straight into it.)

Damascus has always been an ambivalent place. For the conquering Arabs of the seventh century it was a paradise, a giant oasis of orchards cultivated since the second millennium BC. For others, it was Paradise itself. Mandeville, writing on 'the Kingdome of Surry', noted that 'in that place was Adam made as some men saye, for men called sometime that place the felde of Damasse'. But fecundity and fetidness go together. The Arabic name for the Damascus oasis, al-Ghutah, is cognate with the words for dungheap and defecation. Here, hardy Arabians died in urban epidemics and were unmanned by Romano-Persian over-indulgence. Damascus was a paradise sitting in a cloaca.

That morning, the city bestank too with diesel fumes and dank clothes. The voices of sock- and cigarette-sellers rang plangently above the din of the traffic. I turned into the Hamidiyyah, the long covered market that leads into the heart of the old city. Here there was a sudden confusion of colour, of brides' dresses, napery, drapery, tinsel and tat, displayed in a gigantic cross between the Burlington Arcade and Woolworths. There seemed to be few imported goods – Damascus has always been a place where things are produced (damask cloth, damask roses, damascened steel, damsons). I ran into a low-flying flock of falcons, stuffed ones proffered by importunate hawkers, and escaped into an ice-cream parlour.

At first glance, it looked like a gymnasium. A line of sweating men were wielding heavy clubs, grunting rhythmically as they pounded vats of a white, glutinous substance. This was no ordinary ice-cream, but *kaymak*, made with the powdered twin tubers of an allegedly aphrodisiac orchid known to the ancient Greeks as *satyrium* and to Arab pharmacologists as 'fox testicles'. Despite the early hour and the potentially arousing combination, I ate a bowlful studded with crushed pistachios. The ice-cream had the consistency of melted mozzarella and a pleasantly feral aftertaste.

When I re-emerged from the gaudy tunnel of the Hamidiyyah, nearly half a mile long, the day seemed drab and underexposed. Facing me was a barrack-like wall built of large stone blocks that were patched and pockmarked. This first glimpse of the most exquisite mosque on earth is an anticlimax.

And then I looked through the door, and remembered those near-death tales, the Garden glimpsed through a gate. All the light in Damascus seemed to be gathered here, bouncing off the white marble paving of the courtyard and rippling along slender arcades. The interior was light in both senses, luminous and buoyant. It was everything the exterior was not, like an angel in a shabby old mac.

I went in. There was only one other person in the courtyard, a monkish figure in a hooded black gown inscribed on the back with a word in Arabic script. I wondered if the person was an adherent of some obscure dervish order, and strained my eyes until I could read the inscription: *mutawassit,* 'medium'. The figure turned. She was European and the gown, I realized, not a mystic vestment but a cover for unsuitably clad medium-sized Nazarene females.

IB devoted ten pages to the Umayyad Mosque, more than to any other building he saw except for the two sanctuaries of Mecca and al-Madinah. Never a reinventor of the wheel, he based much of the account on that of Ibn Jubayr. The earlier traveller's description needed little updating; even today the mosque looks substantially the same as it did when it was finished in 715, despite six earthquakes and seven major fires. IB noted that the Umayyad Mosque had been a church. (He might have added that before that it was the temple of Damascene Jupiter, and, earlier still, of his Aramean counterpart Hadad.) Supposedly it lies half way between Mecca and Constantinople, so it was fitting that for a time the Muslim conquerors shared the huge temenos with their Christian subjects. The Umayyad Caliph al-Walid appropriated the church in 708; but even this was not the end of the Christian presence for, IB says, 'al-Walid applied to the King of the Greeks at Constantinople, bidding him send craftsmen to him, and he sent him twelve thousand of them'.

Within the mould of the old temple walls the Byzantine artisans, together with others from Persia, India and the Maghrib according to earlier accounts, cooked up a perfect architectural soufflé, solid yet weightless, delicious in its combination of flavours. Nowhere is the fusion more successful than in the mosaics that surround the courtyard, 'cut stones of gold,' IB wrote, 'intermingled with various colours of extraordinary beauty'. Because of Islamic strictures against depicting animate creatures, the mosaics are empty of men and beasts. Instead, they show gardens filled with buildings and streams. Trees grow up the spandrels of the arcades, thick and juicy as asparagus, done in intense pistachio- and spinach-greens and outlined in squid-ink purple. They are not so much stylized as super-real, hypertrophied like Jack's beanstalk. As in the fairy-tale or archetypal dream-scene, little buildings are lost in the woods – pavilions, follies, proto-Palladian boathouses. Some are fantasies of the order of Petra or Portmeirion; others resemble the gabled and colonnaded

Byzantine villas that still survive in parts of northern Syria. It is a real world, but one processed by the dreaming mind. With no perspective, there are sudden confusions of scale – is that a very small palace or a very grand kennel? – and with no visible people, there is something minutely disturbing about the whole scene: *Et in Arcadia Nemo*.

On certain holy nights, twelve thousand lamps were lit around the courtyard; incense drifted from two gilded openwork spheres, standing on columns and looking like ormolu orreries. The sight was said to be one of the wonders of the world. I looked up at the mosaics and imagined their tesserae, those millions of shimmering pixels, flickering in the lamplight, all but animate.

Since it cost seven years' taxes for the whole of Syria, the mosque must be among the most expensive buildings ever constructed. Al-Walid is said to have burned the eighteen camel-loads of account books, saying, 'We have done this for God, and need no accounting!' The sheer prodigality of the building shocked the next caliph but one, the saintly Umar ibn Abdulaziz; he planned to remove the gold from the mosaics and put it to a more altruistic use. In the nick of time, a Byzantine delegation arrived and was shown into the mosque. 'Their leader looked about', the geographer Yaqut recorded, 'and turned pale. "We Byzantines imagined", he said, "that you Arabs would not endure long. Now I have seen otherwise." ' Umar changed his mind about the gold.

The Umayyad dynasty lasted a bare three decades after the death of Caliph Umar in 720. But the Arabs have endured, and so has the Umayyad vision of paradise – an earthly if not a heavenly one – on the walls of their mosque. Arriving in Damascus, I had felt cheated by the poets and their brooks, leas and glades; here, at any rate, they survived in perpetual springtime.

The medium-sized woman had left the courtyard. The only other visitors were pigeons, scores of them, pecking up seed from the paving. Then a crocodile of schoolchildren came in chattering excitedly, and the pigeons took off with a great downdraft of wings and an aviary whiff. They wheeled overhead, a flock of flying circumflexes. The children were followed by a party of Iranian pilgrims, mostly women in black but with a few men in old dark suits, led by a pair of turbaned and bearded clerics. Some of the women scattered seed for the pigeons; one came over to me and gave me a date, ready stoned.

I followed the Iranians into the Shrine of al-Husayn, a large room at the eastern end of the courtyard. Here, in a recess behind a be-ribboned silver grille, the martyr's head had touched base on its journey to Cairo. No connection with al-Husayn and his descendants is too tenuous for the Iranians who, one by one, kissed the recess passionately. When I told the guardian of the shrine that I had recently been to the Mawlid of al-Husayn in Cairo, he smiled. 'That's just a legend. The Cairo head isn't Sayyidna al-Husayn's. It belonged to his grandson, Zayd. The real head went back to Karbala in Iraq.'

'And God is the most knowing,' I said.

If shrine publicists ever had a catchphrase it must have been, 'If you want to get ahead, get a head'. The main prayer hall of the mosque has one as well, that of St John the Baptist. (Or, the Christians say, St John Damascene; or, IB thought, of the Baptist's father, Zechariah. Since I later visited Zechariah's head in Aleppo, there seems to be some confusion.) The Ottomans honoured it with a fine marble reliquary in the style of Leeds Town Hall. Among the clutter inside, I noticed on a table by the cenotaph a pair of Victorian decanters.

In addition to the resident head and the visiting head, the mosque also used to have one of the earliest copies of the Qur'an, a bit of the stone from which the springs sprang when Moses struck it, and some pillars from the Queen of Sheba's throne. For good measure, Jesus will land on the south-eastern minaret on Doomsday. There seemed to be something for everyone.

The Iranians were enjoying themselves gravely. Some of the ladies had their photograph taken next to the pulpit, and then one of the clerics began delivering a homily interspersed by beautiful tenor Qur'anic recitation. I heard a hushed chattering behind me. It was another pilgrim party. They were Indian Isma'ilis, the women in floral print dresses and matching capes that looked as if they had been run up from valances and pelmets, the men in white trousers and tunics of a stuff so sheer that a good Damascus downpour would have rendered them transparent. They hardly looked to be the spiritual descendants of the Assassins.

In IB's time, the prayer hall was home to circles of instruction in which professors, both male and female, would teach the orthodox Sunni sciences. 'It contains also', he wrote, 'a number of teachers of the Book of God, each of whom leans his back upon one of the pillars of the mosque.' As I was about to leave, I noticed the scene he had described, a group of men gathered around a column at the far west end of the hall. They chanted in unison, frowning with concentration, their master stopping them every two or three words to correct minutiae of intonation and elision. The rigidly orthodox IB would have been relieved to see that, despite the preponderance of Indian and Iranian Shi'ites, someone was keeping the Sunni side up.

The Qur'an class was taking its time, in contrast to IB who, in this same prayer hall, attended a sort of Islamic crammer. The course involved listening to a reading and exposition of the entire corpus of the Prophet's sayings in fourteen sittings. IB listed more than a dozen scholars with whom he rubbed shoulders here in the Umayyad Mosque, and who gave him *ijazahs*, or diplomas. These were the heavyweight traditionists of their day: a contemporary reader would have heard the solid clunk of dropping names. They included Ibn al-Shihnah, a centenarian yet, according to a contemporary, 'sound of knee ... He took a daily cold bath and still enjoyed conjugal relations'; al-Birzali of Seville, who had studied under two thousand masters and had diplomas from a thousand of them; A'ishah bint Muhammad, also a professional seamstress; and the doughty spinster Zaynab, who had travelled much in the East and spent her daylight hours transmitting traditions. By listing these scholars who had converged on Damascus from across the Muslim world, IB was showing that he had plugged himself, in a somewhat wobbly fashion, into the medieval Islamic internet.

I left the mosque by the west door to inspect a nearby fountain mentioned by IB. It is now a chic meeting-place, with a gallery and a café frequented by young people in existentialist black. There were many polo-necks, floppy hairdos, and floppy hands draped over chair-backs to reveal wrist-watches. The café is post-Battutian but still old: two hundred years ago Ali Bey described it as 'crowded with the idlers of the city' and − like me − was mildly shocked to see Damascene ladies smoking water-pipes. The reek of *longueurs*, languor and carefully cultivated ennui mingled with the tobacco smoke.

'This place', said the man on the next table in English, 'is full of ... how do you say? ... *mutathaqqifin.*'

I had already met him as he was guiding tourists around the Umayyad Mosque. 'Well, *muthaqqafin* are "cultivated people", so *mutathaqqifin* ought to be "would-be cultivated people".'

'I love the way you can play around with Arabic,' said my neighbour's companion. He spoke with a hint of the English Midlands, and turned out to be a Kashmiri from Nottingham. Just before, I had heard him talking to the guide in a low and portentous voice about 'that certain subject'. Now, the ice broken, he let me into his secret. 'My family are always on at me to get married. To be honest, I'm more interested in studying Arabic. So I thought I'd come here, find a wife, and kill two birds with one stone. Ahmad's helping me. But the trouble is, I've only got a fortnight.' He sighed.

I explained why I was in Damascus. 'If it's any consolation,' I said,

'IB was here only a few days longer than you, and he managed to get married *and* study the entire *Sahih* of al-Bukhari.'

The Kashmiri looked glum.

I left them to their marital machinations and headed back to the hotel. It was a fine Ottoman building in the Saruja Quarter, with a black-and-white marble fountain in the courtyard. My room gave on to a rickety balcony above a pergola'd street; a large coop on the roof opposite contained several perky hens. On the landing outside the room there was a shell-shaped porphyry washbasin, which it seemed a sacrilege to use, like brushing your teeth in a font.

Most of the other guests were New Zealand backpackers. Like the girls I had met in Tangier, they suffered from a national claustrophobia and treated it with large doses of travelling. 'I'm just moseying around,' one of the travellers told me. 'I've done thirty-three countries so far ... Think I can make it sixty.' Most of the talk, however, was on the shifts and wrinkles of travel – jabs, visas, how to make a few dollars by smuggling cigarettes into Jordan.

The theme continued in a series of notebooks kept at the reception desk. They formed a fascinating codex of information. There were pages of Swedish in a looping, girlish hand, beautiful hand-drawn maps minutely annotated in Japanese, scrawls by Rob from Wellington. If *Lonely Planet* is the pilgrim guide of our times, then notebooks like these are an ever-expanding, polyglot apparatus criticus. Some of what I could read was in the 'regional characteristics' genre beloved of medieval geographers: Iranians are extremely hospitable, Cairene shopkeepers dodgy, certain men in Istanbul slimy. There were several references to 'gropers': 'Attention Girls: if you've got a nice round bum and 36DD tits, keep out of the Aleppo souk – it's full of septic tossers and you'll get shababbed out of your mind!' (*Shabab* is Arabic for 'young men'.) A marginal note to this entry read: 'If you fancy yourself that much, stay at home with a mirror.' A marginal note to the marginal note said: 'Chauvinist toss-pot.'

The Sudanese receptionist heard me chuckling. 'These notebooks', he said, 'are full of *aja'ib*.' He couldn't have chosen a better word: *aja'ib*, the wonders of wandering, the mirabilia of metropolises.

None of this helped me to find the one place in Damascus that I particularly wanted to visit. The Sharabishiyyah Madrasah, the college in which IB lodged, was in his time a recent foundation by a wealthy merchant named al-Sharabishi, the Hatter. (*Sharbush*, plural *sharabish*, is a variant of *tarbush* and the ancestor of the fez.) A rapid tour of other Damascus *madrasahs* that afternoon had given me no leads. The guardian of the tomb of Saladin, all that is left of the Aziziyyah Madrasah, hadn't heard of the Hatter's College and was more interested in improving his English. We acted out a dialogue from a textbook, in which a couple called Pedro and Lucille discussed Dickens, Thackeray, Byron and Oscar Wilde; in the background God's warrior slumbered in his tomb beneath a lewd chandelier that precisely resembled a bunch of prodigious, pendent condoms.

The condoms seemed to be standard issue. In the Adiliyyah, head-quarters of the Arab Academy, they depended again above Saladin's brother al-Adil. Also in the tomb-chamber was a bust of the great one-eyed poet al-Ma'arri. He was a surprising character to find in a college of religious science. Verse of his such as

> There are two types of people:
> Those with brains and no religion,
> And those with religion and no brains

earned him the nickname of 'the Heretic'. The poet seemed to have some awful skin problem – the bronze leaf was peeling off him to reveal white plaster beneath.

No one was in evidence to ask about the Hatter's College, so I tried the Zahiriyyah across the road. It was similarly deserted. The tomb-chamber, despite its fine mosaics and marble dado, reeked of neglect. Mouldering empty vitrines occupied niches around the walls. It was a sad end for al-Zahir Baybars, the early Mamluk Sultan and hammer of the Crusaders – but perhaps no more bathetic than the circumstances of his death, brought about by a dreadful mix-up involving a lunar eclipse and a goblet of poisoned koumiss.

Only one *madrasah* showed signs of life, the Qur'an College founded by Tankiz, Sultan al-Nasir's vice-regent in Syria. IB described him as 'a governor of the good and upright kind'; his many public works included the removal of the city's frogs, to the croaking of which he had a particular aversion. But poor Tankiz fell victim to cold-war paranoia: al-Nasir got it into his head that he was a Mongol mole and sent Bashtak, builder of the palace on Crimson Street in Cairo, to arrest him. Tankiz died soon after, in gaol in Alexandria.

I knocked on the college gate, set in a fine portal inscribed with the date AH 727, the year after IB's visit. There was an answering echo within, followed by footsteps. A pretty teenaged girl opened the door and led me in. Inside there were display cases containing novelty rubbers and other juvenile stationery; murals of cartoon schoolkids covered the walls and even the mihrab, or prayer-niche, in which an angelic cousin of Dennis the Menace sat reading the Book of God. Mamluk purists would stretch their eyes, but at least Tankiz's Qur'an College was still exactly what it was founded to be. 'And', the director told me, 'it will remain so for ever, *in sha Allah*, as long as people do not abandon Islam.' I left having drawn another blank on the Hatter's College, but thinking that the good and upright Tankiz would be delighted, once he had got over the shock of seeing his school Disneyfied.

★

That evening, after another cerebro-burger and a pink grapefruit juice, I explored the newer parts of central Damascus. There was a chill in the air, and the doleful descant of sock-sellers. I was drawn by a neon sign saying VICES CENTER; a closer inspection, however, revealed that the first part of the sign had not lit up – COMMUNI-CATION SER. Next door to this disappointment was the Hejaz Railway Station, the northern terminus of the line that Lawrence and his Bedouin blew up in Arabia. A German locomotive dated 1908 was parked outside on the station approach; on top of it was a sign in the shape of a smaller steam engine, advertising a restaurant in unseemly pink neon. Then, in a sidestreet by the station, I spotted something that more than made up for the absence of vices: a row of bookshops.

The first specialized in science textbooks. 'If it's history and geography you're after,' said the owner, 'then go to Hikmat Hilal. He's two doors away.'

One should try – indeed, one is encouraged by a tradition of the Prophet – to refrain from thinking about the meanings of Arabic personal names. There are too many men called Jamil, 'Beautiful', who are not; Saddam ought to be 'one who crashes frequently', and is the usual word for the bumper of a car; Khadijah, a common girl's name, is cognate with the word for an abortive she-camel. But Hikmat Hilal – Wisdom of a Crescent Moon, or Philosophy of a Parenthesis – had the right ring for a bookseller. To me the name suggested a stooped, ascetic figure in reading glasses.

Mr Hikmat did wear glasses but looked prosperous rather than ascetic. He sat, suavely suited, beneath a framed calligraphic panel in superb gilded script. It was a familiar fragment of verse: 'A man's best friend is his library.' Near it hung another calligraphic panel, the Qur'anic Chapter of Daybreak:

Say: I seek refuge in the Lord of Daybreak from the mischief of His creation; from the mischief of the night when she spreads her darkness; from the mischief of the witches who blow upon knots; from the mischief of the envier, when he envies.

Mr Hikmat saw me looking at the text. 'There is great beauty and great terror in those few words, is there not?'

'I think it's one of the finest pieces of Arabic prose in existence.'

'You are a Muslim?' he asked, tentatively.

'No. A Masihi.'

'So am I. A Roman Catholic.' I glanced again at the prominently displayed Qur'anic text. 'You think I am a little ... syncretic? Well, in the Qur'an itself God says: "We have revealed the Qur'an in the Arabic tongue." *I* am an Arab, of the tribe of Tayy.'

I decided immediately that I liked Mr Hikmat.

A quick look around the shelves revealed that most of the stock was on the Islamic sciences of Tradition studies, jurisprudence and Qur'anic interpretation. I asked if there was anything on the history of *madrasahs* in Damascus.

'But of course. Al-Nu'aymi's *Al-daris fi tarikh al-madaris.* Absolutely indispensable. Let me see ... ' He flicked through a ledger. 'Ah, as I thought. It's in the flat. As it happens, I was about to shut up and go there. Why don't you come? There may be one or two other things of interest to you.'

As we drove into the suburbs, Hikmat explained that in addition to the shop and his own library at home, he had a flat to house most of his stock on history and geography. Eventually we arrived at a nondescript block. Other than a small table, a few chairs and a television – left on and blaring adverts – the flat contained nothing but books. They lined the walls in ceiling-height shelves and covered much of the floor in neat stacks. Hikmat began to look for *Al-daris* but was quickly sidetracked.

'Look, here's al-Ramhurmuzi's *Wonders of India*. A fascinating work, but of course rather too early for IB ... The *Travels* of Rabbi Benjamin of Tudela, the Arabic translation. That's a little closer to your period. Ah, here we are ... Abu 'l-Fida's geographical encyclopaedia, contemporary with IB. So sad they never met!'

I went off on my own trip, and rapidly became intoxicated. Hikmat had moved to another room, but I could still hear his running commentary: 'poetry on the Mongol invasions ... a history of the Assassins ... an original Leiden imprint – *very* rare and expensive ... '

The doorbell rang rudely. Hikmat emerged from the other room with a pile of books, put them on the table and opened the door. Two women came in, whom Hikmat introduced as his wife and sister-in-law. There was a prolonged kerfuffle about some article of feminine clothing. 'How should I know where it is?' Hikmat exclaimed petulantly. He strutted about, waving his hands and mumbling. Finally, the article – an elaborate frock – was found behind a pile of books, together with a bottle of Red Label. Mrs Hikmat poured generous slugs and we sat around the table. The ladies questioned me about my background.

'And precisely how long have you been in Yemen?' asked the sister-in-law. She had a curious, unstable half-smile like a Siamese about to pounce.

'About fifteen years.'

'Just as I thought. It's a girl, isn't it? You've fallen in love, haven't you? But don't take that step! Don't convert! Promise me you'll never do it. Who is more important – that girl or Jesus?'

Hikmat was looking at the ceiling. He spoke gently. 'I think you have nothing to fear. Tim is a ... an orientalist.'

She seemed to relax a little, but kept eyeing me warily.

Soon afterwards, the ladies left and we continued our tour of the bookshelves. Much later, I glanced at my watch and noticed that it was eleven o'clock. I suggested to Hikmat that he might want to go home.

'I was waiting for you to say that you'd had enough,' he replied. 'Oh! And what about Abu 'l-Fida's *Short History of Mankind*, with the continuation by Ibn al-Wardi? Very important ... *Completely* indispensable.'

Hikmat found me a taxi and I returned to the hotel with a pile of

books. Up in my room I turned straight to the chapter in the *madrasah* history on the Sharabishiyyah, the Hatter's College. 'It is in the
Street of the Sha"arin' – the Hair-Sellers? – 'adjoining the Bath of
Salih, north of the Bird Market, inside the Gate of the Water-trough.'
I could hardly have asked for a more precise address, and was so
delighted that I almost overlooked a footnote: 'It has completely disappeared. Not a trace of it remains.'

Undeterred, I set out the following morning with the address on a
scrap of paper. The diligent inverse archaeologist should, after all,
adopt a diachronic perspective; doubtless, my expedition would generate a laconic footnote – 'The site of the Sharabishiyyah is now
occupied by a motorcycle repair shop', or some such.

The easy bit was Bab al-Jabiyah, the Gate of the Water-trough.
Inside, I entered an endless walk-in wardrobe called Suq al-
Qumaylah, the Market of the Little Louse, and selected an elderly
clothes merchant. He pondered over the address. 'The only thing
that means anything to me is al-Sha"arin,' he said at length. 'They
were the people who sold the goat-hair cloth that the *badw* use for
their tents. There's still one of them left.' He summoned a boy to lead
me to the sole remaining goat-hair tent-fabric merchant. I felt a
growing excitement.

The goat-hair merchant was mystified by the address but passed
me on to an uncle, another elderly man. He read the address over
several times. 'There were plenty of *sha"arin* around here when I was
young. But I've never come across the Bath of Salih, or the Bird
Market, and my family's had this shop for five generations. You could
try Hajj Yusuf.'

Another boy led me to Hajj Yusuf, a very old man who was sitting
outside a shop on the Street Called Straight. I perched beside him on
a low stool. He was a bit deaf, so I explained my quest very slowly
and loudly. A small audience gathered.

'Who? Baddudah? Can't say I know the fellow.'

'He was here a long time ago. Nearly seven hundred years.'

'I know I'm a *shaybah*, a greybeard, but I'm not that old.'

The audience laughed.

'What about the Bath of Salih?' I shouted. 'And the Bird Market?'

Hajj Yusuf was silent for a long time. He seemed to have gone into
a trance. Then his face began to twitch. A dreadful thought crossed
my mind: he's having a stroke. 'Really, don't worry if . . . '

'That's it! Elizabeth will know!'

The name rang a bell ... perhaps someone at the Institut Français. 'Who's Elizabeth?'

'Elizabeth the Second, Queen of Great Britain. Who else?' He grinned, grabbed me by the beard and gave me a smacking, slobbery kiss on the cheek.

The audience laughed; and after the initial surprise I, the fall-guy, joined in. As I watched Hajj Yusuf shaking and wheezing, a vision came to me: of an earnest Syrian walking into a shop in the City of London in the late 1990s and asking for directions to something that sounded suspiciously like the Wild Goose Market, at the Sign of Ye Olde Cock and Bull.

I gave up on the Hatter and his college and went to console myself in the Bath of Sultan Nur al-Din. IB said of its builder, Saladin's predecessor, that he was 'a man of saintly life of whom it is told that he used to weave mats and live on the proceeds of their sale'. Since the bath was flourishing at the time of IB's visit, it is more than likely that the traveller was a customer there. The bathkeeper locked my valuables away, and I removed my clothes in a carpeted enclosure beneath a substantial dome – it was more like a basilica than a changing-room – then donned a waist wrapper and a pair of the platform clogs known as *qibqab*. (In 1263 this delightful onomatopoeia, something like 'clip-clops', featured in the execution of an Ayyubid prince. He had unwisely raped the wife of Sultan Baybars, subsequent victim of the poisoned koumiss. Captured afterwards by the Sultan, he was handed over to the dishonoured Sultana who had her slave-girls bludgeon him to death, slowly, with their bathtime footwear.)

I qibqabbed through the innards of the bath-house and found the hot room, where my spectacles steamed up and I blundered into a group of fleshy and amused Kuwaitis. Later, pink and clean, I cooled off for a while in the tepid room, into which the management had introduced an otiose and barbarian addition – a sauna.

As I was about to re-enter the changing area, a hand went for the towel around my waist. 'Thank you,' I said firmly to its unseen owner, 'I'm sure I can manage on my own.' The hand came back. I thought of going for my *qibqabs*; but, in a flash, the towel was off and, simultaneously, replaced with a fresh one. The operation was so deft that even IB, that crusader against bath-house nudity, wouldn't have complained. The attendant wrapped more towels around my shoulders and head, and I returned to the domed hall, where I chatted with the Kuwaitis over camomile tea. Speakers in the vault relayed the Tritsch-Tratsch Polka. It went rather well with all the clipclopping.

While he would have drawn the line at Johann Strauss the Younger, Sultan Nur al-Din might not have disapproved in principle of music in his bath. When he founded his hospital, he appointed as its first medical director one Abu 'l-Majd ibn Abu 'l-Hakam who, as well as being the foremost physician in Damascus and an accomplished astronomer, was also a talented lutenist, hautboyist and amateur organ-builder. His musical abilities perhaps came in useful in the new post, since music was held to be 'efficacious in expanding the chest and revitalizing the spirit, thus strengthening the heartbeat and ensuring the proper function of the organs'. The hospital – inspiration for the great *maristan* that I had visited in Cairo – still stands, not far from the bath.

According to IB, the funding for the infirmary came from the sale of some copper kitchenware that a saintly alchemist had turned into gold. The gatekeeper dismissed the story with a laugh. 'What really happened', he said, 'was that Nur al-Din captured a Frankish prince and was going to put him to death. But the prince offered a ransom, and gave the Sultan five castles and half a million dinars. Not that it did the Frank any good. He died on his way home.'

Inside, the hospital was laid out like a *madrasah*, with a central court and surrounding *iwans*. In the main *iwan*, the director would sit between ward rounds and lecture. Treatment continued here until the nineteenth century. Today, the building is a museum of science and medicine.

Some of the exhibits were intriguing. There was an anaesthetic gag, which the label said would be soaked in a concoction of hashish, opium and belladonna; a pair of Ottoman prepuce snippers; and a birthing-chair from the same period – it had tall balusters attached to the armrests, to be gripped for extra purchase, and a cut-out in the seat that made it resemble a regal thunderbox. My favourite item, however, was an ancient and etiolated *suqunqur*, a type of skink, salted and displayed in a glass jar. According to the label, this nasty-looking creature was for centuries the sovereign aphrodisiac of the Islamic world – more potent even than Aleppan pistachios or the fox-testicle orchid.

Curious to learn more about the *suqunqur*, I later turned to the thirteenth-century pharmacopoeia compiled by al-Muzaffar, another ancestor of my Yemeni friend Hasan. Only male skinks are used, al-Muzaffar explained. The best time to hunt them is in the spring, when they rut. They are disembowelled, stuffed with salt and suspended upside down in the shade – like game, they improve with age. Thereafter they are best preserved in a wicker basket. As well as the skink's flesh, its fat and kidneys may also be administered with honey, rocket seeds or, where permissible, vintage wine possessing a fine bouquet. (The physician and Egyptologist al-Baghdadi also suggests the addition of powdered cocks' testicles.)

IB mentions several aphrodisiacs in the *Travels*. None was more effective than the pills which a certain yogi made for the Sultan of Madurai in southern India. 'Among their ingredients were iron filings, and the Sultan was so pleased with their effect that he took an overdose and died. The Sultan was succeeded by his nephew, who', he adds drily, 'showed high consideration for that yogi and raised him in dignity.'

My research threw up a number of aphrodisiacs which had eluded IB: a fish with a face like an owl's and a crest like a cock's, the effect of which al-Idrisi says is the same as that of the skink, found in a certain reservoir in Xinjiang; a preparation, noted by al-Mas'udi, obtained from the sebaceous excretions of Indian elephants; a root found in the Atlas Mountains and so powerful, Leo the African wrote, that a man accidentally urinating on it will ejaculate immediately, while the hymen of a virgin girl doing so will be ruptured; and an aquatic version of the *suqunqur* mentioned by the geographer al-Zuhri, found in the Caspian, which if kept in the mouth enables a man to have sexual intercourse a hundred times in succession, 'or indeed until he drops dead or spits it out'. Compared with this last statement, claims made for the *suqunqur* proper are modest. Al-Zuhri's Caspian variety, I suspect, is more closely related to the Sudanese Blister Beetle discovered by Roald Dahl's fictional Uncle Oswald.

One of the most fertile sources of recherché *materia medica* is al-Qazwini's twelfth-century cosmography, *The Wonders of Creation*. Some of the remedies sound enjoyable (chewing frankincense prevents amnesia); some less so (to cure an itching anus, insert a few cloves of garlic); some are alarming (to calm an epileptic fit, place a live electric catfish on your head); others nauseating (hepatitis is alleviated by drinking a pint of urine from a pre-pubescent boy, boiled with honey in a copper vessel); one sounds positively kinky (nursing mothers can improve lactation by massaging their breasts with the sweat of wrestlers). Perhaps I have chosen a flippant selection; but then, the medieval Iraqi practice of using mould from water jars as a salve sounds silly – until we recall penicillin.

That evening, the hotel receptionist was in no need of aphrodisiacs; but he did need a translator. He was in love with a French girl, and wanted to send her a *billet doux*. I grimaced, remembering the last such thing I had translated – on papyrus, for a Copt in Luxor. It is hard to put your heart into a love letter when you are *per pro*.

The receptionist handed me a folded page. It was a verse by the contemporary Syrian poet Nizar al-Qabbani. I read it through, then began to write:

Love for you has taught me to try the medicine of apothecaries,
To knock on the doors of fortune-tellers,
To leave home and comb the pavements,
To hunt for your face in the rain and in the headlights of cars . . .
Love for you has taken me into cities of sadness
Which I have never entered before.

As a love letter written in Damascus, in November, it could hardly have been bettered. I went to bed and lay there, listening to the distant swish of cars and the rain dripping through the pergola.

The rain persisted over the next few days, as I visited some of the sites in and around Damascus that IB had described. There were plenty of them, and it was hard to know where to begin. In the end, I began at the beginning.

'When night drew its shadow over him,' the Qur'an says of Abraham, 'he saw a star. "That", he said, "is surely my God." But when it faded in the morning light, he said: "I will not worship gods that fade." When he beheld the rising moon, he said: "That must be my God." But when it set, he said: "If Allah does not guide me, I shall surely go astray." Then, when he beheld the sun shining, he said: "That must be my God: it is larger than the other two." But when it set, he said to his people: "I am done with your idols." '

The cave where, according to Damascene legend, Abraham was born and later hit on the idea of monotheism lies at the northern end of Jabal Qasiyun, the slab of mountain overlooking the city. The mountain, IB says, 'is the place of ascent of the Prophets (on them be peace)' – and, I would add, of the sellers of overpriced beans (on them be a plague). The traveller explained that up the spiritual elevator of Qasiyun went Adam, Moses, Jesus, Job, Lot and a job-lot of seventy anonymous prophets – these days downgraded to forty martyrs – who starved to death in the Cave of Hunger. 'They had with them only one loaf, and it continued to circulate amongst them, as each preferred to give it to his neighbour, until they all died together.' IB does not explain why they played pass-the-parcel instead of nipping down to the nearest grocer's.

To visit Abraham's alleged birthplace, I hired a taxi belonging to a small and neat retired army officer called Abu Ala, who wore a tweed suit and striped tie. With us came his son-in-law-to-be, Munir, who described himself as 'a topography graduate'. We drove through the drizzle along a highway lined with gaunt tower-blocks then, where the road began to rise, turned off into the ex-village of Barzah, a higgledy-piggledy suburb strewn across the hillside. There, despite the presence of Munir the topographer, we got lost.

We chose a house and tapped on the gate. A man in late middle age opened it, and we asked if he knew the Cave of Abraham.

'This is it,' said the man.

He led us into a yard. Before us rose a small cliff, topped by a few cement-block houses; tucked away under the cliff was a door. Through this was a roomy mosque. Inside, we climbed a stone staircase up to a gallery, rather like an organ loft, where a large ginger tom was dozing at the entrance to a tunnel. The sequence of transitions was unexpected, and intensely dreamlike.

We squeezed into the tunnel, which was whitewashed and barely big enough for the four of us. It ended in a pit, a deep hollow in pink rock polished by many hands. The pit glistened in the feeble lamplight, like some bodily cavity seen through an endoscope.

'This', said our guide, 'is where the Prophet Abraham, peace be upon him, was born.' He quoted the Qur'anic story of the prophet, then added that the act of praying four times in the tunnel, which points directly to Mecca, returns the worshipper to a sinless state, 'as if he had emerged from his mother's womb. And God is the most knowing.'

As the little lecture was going on, I remembered a remark of IB's:

'I have also seen in the land of Iraq a village in which Abraham (on him be peace) is said to have been born.' Al-Harawi's pilgrim guide, the authority on such matters, plumped categorically for Iraq. Abu Ala voiced my thoughts. 'What about the tradition that Abraham was born near Babylon?'

The guardian gave Abu Ala a sharp look, then climbed down into the cavity. 'Look! Here are the marks of his mother's feet, where she squatted to give birth.' He squatted. 'And here are the marks of her fingers where she grasped the rock.' He grasped the rock. 'How can you disbelieve?' He stared at each of us in turn, challenging us to argue. None of us spoke. As we left the tunnel, the ginger cat shifted and grinned in his sleep.

★

The next day, I followed IB to the tomb of 'the pious devotee Rislan, known as the Grey Falcon'. Rislan, IB says, was a disciple of the famous twelfth-century Sufi *shaykh*, al-Rifa'i. One year, at Mecca, the two of them bumped into an old friend; al-Rifa'i remembered that he had left a cluster of dates unharvested on one of his palms near the Iraqi town of Wasit, intending to give it to this friend. Undeterred by the thought of a 1,600-mile round-trip, 'Rislan said to him, "By thy command, O my master, I shall fetch it." The *shaykh* gave him permission, and he departed at once, came back with the cluster and laid it in front of him. Al-Rifa'i's followers at Wasit later related that on the evening of that day they saw a grey falcon which swooped down upon the palm tree, nipped off the date cluster and bore it away into the air.'

According to the hagiographer al-Nabhani, Rislan was also in the habit of flying through the air in human form, sitting cross-legged. A visit to the saint's tomb, he noted, improved one's prospects for the afterlife: 'Shaykh Rislan used to say, "Any flesh which has entered my sanctuary will not be consumed by the Fire." A certain man went to pray there. With him he had some meat from the butcher; when he got home and cooked it, it remained raw.'

The tomb didn't look a restful spot. It was situated on a traffic island, and its nearest neighbour was a funfair. Inside the gate, however, the sounds of traffic and jollity were muted. A large man was standing by one of the windows of the tomb-chamber and reciting the Fatihah, the opening chapter of the Qur'an. When he finished, he turned and saw me. For a few moments, we stared at each other. I had never seen anything like him: he had the physique of a wrestler and wore a voluminous black cloak and a red headcloth secured with a double rope of camel hair, and he carried a silver-knobbed malacca cane. His enormous beard was of a luxuriance and blackness seen only on pantomime pirates. Strangest of all were two thick, glossy dreadlocks, tucked behind his ears. This apparition strode over to me, majestic and fiery-eyed like a figure from an Assyrian frieze, and offered me a Marlboro.

He smiled broadly when I greeted him in Arabic, and gripped my arm. 'Did you know that Khalid ibn al-Walid pitched his tent just over there?' he asked, pointing to a spot not far from the tomb. 'He was the bravest of our commanders!' He went off into a long and vivid reminiscence about the seventh-century Muslim conqueror of Syria. I wondered if I was listening to a ghost ... But a ghost who smoked Marlboros?

Eventually, I extracted myself from his grip and showed him IB's account of Shaykh Rislan. 'Ah, the Grey Falcon,' he said. 'I know the story.' He kissed the pages and shut the book reverently. 'Can you not see the light of faith emanating from the tomb of Shaykh Rislan?' he asked, turning to give the tomb a smart military salute. 'You know, about twenty years ago they were going to knock this place down and turn it into a pleasure garden. A *pleasure garden!* Can you believe it? They brought a *bulduzir* ... '

'And', I interrupted, 'the machine broke down.'

'You know the story!'

'I've heard it before,' I said, remembering the saint of the tramlines in Alexandria. 'Or a similar one, about another *wali*. I visit a lot of *walis*.'

'Then you are a Muslim, as I thought.'

'Well, actually, I'm not.'

He looked concerned, held his palms skywards and recited the Fatihah – this time not for the soul of a dead saint, but for that of a live infidel. 'May God guide you to the true path of Islam', he concluded, 'and save you from the everlasting Fire.' He struck another Assyrian attitude, saluted and strode away.

Over at the tomb-chamber I peered through a grille decorated with ribbons and branches of greenery. All I could make out in the gloom inside was a few words of an inscription – 'Rislan, he who knew God . . . ' I thought of the story of the steak rendered miraculously rare. Presumably, a visit to Shaykh Rislan's tomb only fireproofed *halal* meat; it wouldn't safeguard Christian flesh.

I walked back along the Street Called Straight, entering it through the Roman Gate of the Sun. The pagan structure supports a minaret finished off with a short sharp spire – an alternative Messianic landing site on the Last Day. To my right was the Christian Quarter, on my left the Jewish Quarter and, ahead, the Muslim Quarter. All three faiths were convinced that if you didn't convert, you would end up as a kebab on the Everlasting Barbecue; or in the vegetarian Hell of more recent Christianity, that you would be excluded from God's presence for ever and ever, or condemned to a sort of theological nuclear winter, or at the very least end up somewhere that wasn't as nice as it might have been. Looking up at Jabal Qasiyun, I reflected that things had been a lot easier in Abraham's day, when you could get away with being a plain old monotheist.

On my next expedition, again with Abu Ala and Munir the topographer, I became an involuntary and very temporary convert. We were driving southwards on another drizzly morning, on our way to another venerated site, the Mosque of the Footprint. Munir was telling me that the dreadlocked, Marlboro-smoking Assyrian was a devotee of Shaykh Rislan. 'They say that Rislan had the same *kawafir*,' he explained. I was savouring the incongruity of the French loan-word – *coiffure* – when, suddenly, Abu Ala slowed down.

'Since you're into tombs,' he said, 'we must take you to visit Sayyidah Zaynab.'

I was reluctant. IB gave Zaynab only a passing mention, lifted from Ibn Jubayr's *Travels*; but Abu Ala assured me that I would be impressed. He turned off the highway into a suburb distinguished by, if anything, its utter lack of distinction. A few minutes later, he pointed ahead. Two minarets covered in dark blue, turquoise and gilded tiles rose above the grey buildings. We parked the car and entered a courtyard of white marble, in the middle of which was a large, square mosque-tomb, also encrusted with tiles and crowned by a golden dome.

I admitted that I was, now, impressed. 'And I suppose that's real gold leaf.'

Abu Ala smiled. 'No. Real gold *bricks*. You know what the Iranians are like about anyone related to the Prophet ... Well, Sayyidah Zaynab was his granddaughter, and when the Shah was overthrown Khomeini put a lot of the royal wealth into reconstructing this place.'

The building was certainly of an opulence seldom seen since the days of Shah Abbas. Most of the visitors were also Iranian. They moved around in awed groups led by subfusc mullahs. As we followed one of the parties into the tomb, I heard the shoe-monitor say to Abu Ala, 'The foreigner isn't allowed in.'

'He's a Muslim,' Abu Ala replied, giving me an almost imperceptible wink.

We made our way around two men who were fervently kissing the threshold. 'That's a bit over the top,' Munir whispered audibly in their direction.

'We all find our own paths to God,' I hissed back, trying to sound conciliatory. But the threshold kissers were evidently too engrossed to have heard.

It was prayer time, and we found ourselves almost treading on worshippers in mid-prostration. Above us, the vaulted space shone with chandeliers and mirror mosaics in a glitter of crystal, glass and silver – Coleridge's sunny dome with caves of ice reinterpreted by Barbara Cartland. The tomb itself was surrounded by a cage of solid silver, no dainty feminine affair but an industrial-grade structure strong enough to contain an angry rhino. Beside the cage was a sort of large letter-box. I saw a lady in a chador drop a gold bangle into the slot.

As we retrieved our shoes, I noticed that I was panting. My breath, quite literally, had been taken away – by the excitement of being an interloper, by the hyperdecoratedness of the place, but above all by the sheer fervour that permeated it, like a nerve gas. It hardly mattered that the centre of attention – Sayyidah Zaynab, al-Sitt, the Lady – was, in the opinion of the highest medieval authorities, a case of mistaken identity.

We returned to the highway and resumed our journey south. In July 1348, while he was on his way home from the Far East, IB watched a procession taking place along this road. I had been reading about the background to it the night before in one of my purchases from Hikmat, the two-volume *Short History of Mankind*. This work came to an abrupt end in the same year, 1348 – a year in which the history of mankind itself seemed to be ending.

In its final few pages the Syrian historian Ibn al-Wardi, who had taken over the writing of the annals after the death of the original author seventeen years earlier, quoted at length from a treatise of his entitled *Al-naba an al-waba*, *The Pest Investigated*. Despite the subject, it is written in jaunty rhyming prose, full of jingles and wordplays. The Black Death, he wrote, emerged fifteen years before from the Land of Darkness: 'Ah, woe to him on whom it calls! It found the chinks in China's walls – they had no chance against its advance. It sashayed into Cathay, made hay in Hind and sundered souls in Sind. It put the Golden Horde to the sword, transfixed Transoxiana and pierced Persia. Crimea cringed and crumpled . . . ' I apologize to Ibn al-Wardi for the levity of the translation: he was not exactly trying to be funny. Then again, perhaps there is a *touch* of humour, of the deepest black, the literary equivalent of the grinning, cavorting cadavers of Holbein's *Dance of Death* – as if the author were releasing a nervous titter in the face of the approaching horror.

All too soon the pestilence was close enough for him to report on its symptoms: 'He who spat blood found, within two or three nights, a lodging in the ground, while those around him knew their own days would be few.' The obituaries began: 'News reached us of the death of Qadi Zayn al-Din in Safad, of Shaykh Nasir al-Din in

Tripoli, of our friend Shaykh Abdulrahman in Aleppo, of my brother
Yusuf ...' There was a report of lights seen flitting around the tombs
in the town of Manbij; then of the death in Damascus of the scholar
al-Umari, 'Who once sent me some verses in his own hand:

> In the town of al-Ma'arrah live a family of scholars –
> The Wardis, authors of every glorious work ... '

Ibn al-Wardi had copied out his own epitaph. The book ends two
lines later.

When I showed the passage to my Yemeni friend Hasan, a medical
man like his pharmacologist ancestor, he pointed out that the symptoms noted by Ibn al-Wardi – spitting blood, death within two or
three days – are those of pneumonic plague. Alongside this came the
bubonic form heralded by the swellings known variously to Arab
commentators as almonds, cucumbers or *kabab*, meatballs. Michael
Dols, in his essential work *The Black Death in the Middle East*, cites the
third term as the origin of a Cairene curse, still current – 'A meatball
upon you!' to which the reply is, 'And two meatballs on *you!*'

Time, and science, have taken the terror out of buboes; it is now
almost impossible to comprehend the fear they excited. Few descrip-
tions, however, could be as elegantly, surreally nasty as that of the
Welsh poet Ieuan Gethin, writing less than a year after Ibn al-Wardi:
'Woe is me of the shilling in the armpit; it is seething, terrible, wherever it may come, a head that gives pain and causes a loud cry, a
burden under the arms, a painful angry knob, a white lump. It is of
the form of an apple, like the head of an onion ... a grievous thing
of an ashy colour ... '

Arab physicians recommended a range of prophylactic measures.
Among those mentioned by Dols are eating pickled onions before
breakfast, drinking syrup of basil or a suspension of Armenian bole,
avoiding cabbage, garlic and aubergines, carrying pomanders, sleeping in a room open to the north wind, keeping jolly company – as
Boccaccio's characters did in the *Decameron* – and wearing talismans,
certain ringstones and clothing in particular colours. It was also held
to be beneficial to read books, particularly the Qur'an, histories and
humorous works – although presumably not *The Pest Investigated*.

When all else failed, as it did, one could always pray. Someone saw
the Prophet in a dream and passed on his prescription to the

Damascenes: the Qur'anic Chapter of Noah to be recited in the city's mosques 3,363 times. (The Black Death brought on a fashion for precise figures: the Pope was informed after the epidemic that the global death-toll was 42,836,486.) The recitation must have had little effect; six weeks later, IB watched a last-ditch attempt:

> At the time of the Great Plague at Damascus [on 24 July 1348, according to a contemporary historian], the viceroy ordered a crier to proclaim that the people should fast for three days. At the end of this period all conditions of men assembled in the Umayyad Mosque, until it overflowed with them. They spent the night there in prayers, liturgies and supplications. After the dawn prayer, they all went out together, barefoot, carrying Qur'ans. The entire population joined in the exodus, male and female, small and large; the Jews went out with their book of the Law and the Christians with their Gospel, their women and children with them, all in tears and humble supplications, imploring the favour of God through His Books and His Prophets. They made their way to the Mosque of the Footprints and remained there in supplication until near midday.

In Christendom, the calamity of the Black Death provoked religious persecution: the Jews were widely believed to be spreading the pestilence in a well-poisoning campaign abetted by the Moors of al-Andalus. They paid the price in pogroms. In Damascus, however, the three Religions of the Book got together. It was appropriate for the place that claimed to be the origin of monotheism.

To a certain extent, it worked: 'God lightened their affliction; the number of deaths in a single day reached a maximum of two thousand, while in Cairo it rose to twenty-four thousand.'

'Glory to God!' exclaimed the guardian of the Mosque of the Footprint (now singular), as he handed me back the *Travels*. 'This story reminds me of years ago, when I was a boy, and there was a great drought. We all went to the Shrine of Moses, not far from here, and prayed for rain. Then we slept among the graves. I couldn't get to sleep, and I saw the figure of a man in a white robe walking along the wall of the shrine. I called out to the others, but the figure vanished. And then the rain started falling. You see, prayers are answered in this place.'

I hadn't expected this postscript to IB, but it tied in with the traveller's tentative ascription of the footprints, 'which are said to be those of Moses'. The guardian, however, disagreed. 'Your writer's information was wrong. They were made by the Prophet Muhammad. When he was 12 years old he came to Damascus from Mecca in a caravan of merchants. But he didn't want to go into the city. You see, it was the earthly paradise, and he thought it would distract him from the heavenly one.'

I remembered Mandeville – 'and in that place was Adam made as some men saye'.

'So', the guardian continued, 'he couched his camel here and alighted. This was the nearest he got to Damascus.'

Al-Harawi's guidebook was noncommittal: 'It is said that they are the footprints of prophets.' On the next page, however, he claimed to have tracked down a footprint of Muhammad in one of the city's *madrasahs*. (He was something of a connoisseur of the subject: later, he bought his very own footprint of the Prophet in Abbadan for the bargain price of twenty-four dinars.) As a footnote to the confusion, an English visitor in 1601 saw Muhammad's print, 'a great hudge foote of stone', on Jabal Qasiyun.

Like the pavement outside the Chinese Theatre in Los Angeles the Islamic world is littered with celebrity footprints. They come in all sizes. The rule of thumb is, apparently, the earlier the celebrity the bigger the foot. Old Testament means outsize: I have inspected a footprint of Job in the Qara Mountains of Dhofar which was at least a size seventeen. And the law works exponentially – IB judged Adam's footprint on his eponymous Peak in Serendip to be eleven spans, or over seven feet long. (Since the matching print was said to be on the seabed, twenty-four sailing hours away, our common ancestor must have been of extraordinarily Mannerist proportions.) Celebrated animals, like the Prophet Salih's she-camel, have also left their marks.

Questions of faith apart, not many of these marks are especially footlike. A few, though, are too good to be true: in Anatolia, I was told the story of a Turkish princess who threw herself from the roof of a mosque to avoid being raped by Christian soldiers. 'She landed on her feet,' my informant explained, 'and so hard that she made these marks here.' He pointed to a pair of dainty size threes impressed in a slab of marble. I was surprised to see that the princess had been wearing stiletto heels; a closer scrutiny, however, revealed that the marks were those of bolt holes. The slab was the empty podium of a classical statue.

The Damascus footprint was let into a marble window sill, and was reasonably convincing. It looked about the right size for a 12-year-old boy, and had the splayed, spatulate toes of a desert traveller. Beside it was a jug of water. 'I wash it every day,' the guardian explained.

One question had been bothering me. 'I thought that Ibn Jubayr counted nine footprints. Where are the others?'

The guardian looked ruffled. 'They are . . . I hate to say . . . covered by buildings and asphalt.'

I was shocked. This was no way to treat relics.

'But', the guardian added hastily, 'we do have the historian Ibn Asakir. He's buried out there.' He pointed through the window to a jungly patch behind the mosque. There was no indication of a grave. 'I know the spot exactly,' the guardian explained, 'because one day I was doing some gardening and I, er, dug him up. But I put him back.'

That evening over tea in the bookshop, Hikmat chuckled when I told him about the accidental exhumation of Ibn Asakir. Soon, we were joined by a small gentleman with a library complexion, and a glamorous woman in leggings, one of those Levantine ladies with Steinway legs and intimidating hair. Talk turned to pre-Islamic poetry. A worried-looking man came in and inquired, in undertones, whether there was anything on *shari'ah* ordinances regarding conjugal relations and the menstrual cycle; he departed with a thick volume and a look of relief. Then a youngish couple turned up and picked Hikmat's brains on editions of the *Sahih* of al-Bukhari, the corpus of tradition studied by IB in the Umayyad Mosque. Hikmat discoursed knowledgeably.

'If I may ask,' the woman said to Hikmat, 'to which *madhhab* do you yourself belong?'

Hikmat beamed, archly. 'The Roman Catholic one.'

There was a tiny pause, and an exchange of glances from the corners of eyes.

'A chasuble', said Hikmat, 'doesn't make a priest, nor an *aba* an *alim*.' He poured another round of tea.

I left them in the middle of a good-natured argument on whether, historically, Christians or Muslims have been hungrier for power.

'Remember what the Christians said in Spain: "Never have we seen a more gentle conqueror than the Muslims."'

'The whole history of imperialism has been . . .'

'Just look at the state of Yugoslavia. Now, if . . .'

' . . . the Islamic conquests . . .'

Hikmat's voice followed me out on to the street. 'Please! With respect, the *Arab* conquests. I am an Arab, of the tribe of Tayy!'

Northern Syria

Old Men of the Mountains

'Above Jebilee, there dwell a people, called by the Turks, *Neceres*,
of a very strange and singular character ... being such Proteus's
in religion, that no body was ever able to discover what shape or
standard their consciences are really of.'

Henry Maundrell, *A Journey from Aleppo to Jerusalem
at Easter AD 1697*

IBN BATTUTAH MET a great many people during his travels. But, as
Hikmat had said to me in his book-flat, it was a pity that he never
met Abu 'l-Fida. The Syrian nobleman was one of those rare person-
alities who, in retrospect, seem to have embodied the spirit of an age.
Born in 1273 into a branch of Saladin's family which had until
recently ruled the town of Hamah, he was introduced to a further
world by his tutor Ibn Wasil. This aged scholar had spent some
months in southern Italy in the intellectual *Schatzkammer* of the
Emperor Manfred, whom he later held up as a mirror for the young
prince. 'He used to tell me', Abu 'l-Fida recalled, 'that Manfred
knew ten theorems of Euclid by heart.'

Abu 'l-Fida's upbringing was martial as well as academic. Aged 12,
he witnessed the expulsion of 'al-Ustibar', the Hospitallers, from
their great fortress of al-Marqab; four years later at Tripoli he gagged
at the stench of rotting Crusaders; not long after, he was in charge of
dragging a giant mangonel through the snow from Crac des
Chevaliers to the siege of Acre. Later, he skirmished with the
Mongols and took part in the ever-popular sport of Armenian-
raiding. Then, as peace descended on the fourteenth century, he
turned from swordplay to wordplay, composing verses whose nearest
literary equivalent in English is the *Spectator* crossword.

He was a close friend of Sultan al-Nasir, who regularly had him brought to Cairo by the *barid*, the Mamluk Federal Express, to hunt near the Pyramids with panthers and gyrfalcons. Al-Nasir invested Abu 'l-Fida with robes of ermine and cloth-of-gold, and eventually with the title of Sultan of Hamah which his ancestors had borne. The occasion was celebrated with a magnificent procession in Between the Two Castles.

Abu 'l-Fida, warrior, hunter, poet and sultan, was also an accomplished astronomer and botanist; the chief physician in Cairo deferred to him on medical matters; he wrote that useful *Short History of Mankind*, continued by Ibn al-Wardi and finished off by the Black Death; his volume of geographical tables was the most up-to-date thing of its kind, and became a major source for European mapmakers from the Renaissance on. Under this remarkable man, Hamah became an Islamic Parnassus.

At the time of IB's first Syrian trip, Abu 'l-Fida was writing hard, continuing his history and revising his geography. He was working under pressure of time, and he knew it. 'I do not believe', he would say to his courtiers, 'that I shall outlive my sixtieth year, for no member of the Ayyubid house of Hamah has done so.' At the beginning of that year he composed a verse in the Andalusian manner and in sentiment somewhere between Horace and Piaf:

> I do not rant at Time or blame him,
> For with diversions have I tamed him.
> I've lived a blessed life, full of delights
> That please the senses – sounds, and tastes, and sights –
> With pure cups carousing, in paradise browsing.

True to the family curse, Abu 'l-Fida died in 1331 aged 59 years and 8 months by the Islamic calendar. He was buried in a mosque-tomb complex he had built in the outskirts of Hamah, set in a garden by the River Orontes and, in his own words, 'one of the most delectable of spots'.

The Islamic Museum in Cairo owns a personal relic of Abu 'l-Fida – a brass pen-box inlaid in gold, silver and copper with a dense herbarium of arabesques in which lurk the Sultan's blazon. I had looked for but failed to find this apotheosis of the pencil-case. Now I left

Damascus, in search of Battutiana and to visit the delectable tomb of the polymath prince of Hamah.

★

Hamah, set on the banks of a river and the verge of genteel ennui, a city of teashops, public parks and fizzing weirs, of fine old buildings restored with a bridgework of new ashlar, has something of the feel of Bath. In an age when most cities have spilt out of their ancient settings it is still relatively compact, almost hidden in the Orontes valley, recognizably IB's comely town 'surrounded by orchards and gardens, supplied by water-wheels like revolving spheres'.

Dusk was falling when I arrived. I walked down to the river, drawn by the sound of the water-wheels, or norias. They were as tall as three-storey houses yet twirled as easily as spinning-wheels, powered by the slick black belt of the Orontes. The noise was deafening. ('Noria' comes via al-Andalus from the Arabic *na'urah*, itself connected with a root signifying the gushing of liquids and the roaring of beasts.) A man was watching one of the wheels. Suddenly he turned and spoke to me. 'The poets have written much on the subject of norias.' It sounded more like Ibn Juzayy than a conversational opener. 'To what would you liken the sound of this one?'

Perhaps he himself was a poet who had run out of similes. I said the first thing that came into my head: 'A woman giving birth?'

He looked closely at me. 'How did you know? My wife's in hospital. She's just had a baby. A boy. I must go.'

'Congratulations ... ' I called to him, as he slipped away into the dark. I stood there, listening to the music of the wooden spheres at heavy-metal volume and thinking about the strangeness of the encounter.

The following morning, I went to look for Abu 'l-Fida's tomb. I crossed to the right bank of the Orontes, where there was a garden with giant plastic toadstools and, nearby, the carbuncular Cham Palace Hotel (the French-style transliteration was a wise choice – 'Sham Palace' would have been accurate in more senses than one). On the opposite bank was an orchard, dense, tangly and hiding houses and domes. My path gave out and I recrossed the river by an old bridge and followed a lane where guinea fowl pecked in the dust. Another old bridge took me back to the right bank and Abu 'l-Fida's mosque – Masjid al-Hayaya, the Mosque of the Serpents.

I spotted them immediately. In the centre of a double arched window overlooking the river was a column in the form of intertwining 'snakes', so deeply cut that it seemed plaited, not carved. The door was locked, but two bearded carpenters from a nearby workshop found the key. Together we visited Abu 'l-Fida's tomb, in a chamber beneath a small lemon-squeezer dome. It was plain but elegant; so too was the prayer hall of the mosque, a white space relieved only by a dado of rare marbles and a gilded inscription band. Clearly, the Sultan was a builder of taste. But the best part of the building was the view through the snake window.

One of the carpenters pointed out the sights of Hamah – the bridges, the citadel hill, the giant Muhammadiyyah noria. As he spoke he fondled the snakes, already burnished by generations of caresses. 'That garden', he said, indicating a jungly orchard that disappeared around a bend in the river, 'is called Tin al-Dahshah.' The Figs of Amazement. Abu 'l-Fida was right: it was a delectable spot.

I thanked the carpenters and continued downstream towards the Figs of Amazement. There, I found myself in a scene described by Ibn Jubayr in sensuous rhyming prose, 'a place of secret, hidden beauty. Wander, penetrate the shade, for there are gardens whose boughs overhang the banks like soft, dark hair, while the river winds through its lair among the shadows.' Fig trees intertwined with pomegranate and apricot. A little noria turned arthritically, irrigating the gardens. Frogs rasped in the water-channels. A tortoiseshell cat eyed me from the undergrowth. A dog barked, sending a flock of white doves flickering out of the branches.

I followed a lane that twisted through the orchards between mud walls, then crossed the river by an ancient bridge of many arches. Here there was a confusion of weirs, some to work mid-stream mills, others norias. The biggest wheel of them all was the giant I had seen through the snake window. Once every revolution it came to a stop. Then it seemed to psych itself up; it would shudder, gasp, emit a few loud reports, and spasm into action again.

I sat by the wheel, opened the *Travels* and turned to an appropriate verse:

> Many a noria, compassioning my sin,
> As from afar she saw my fell intent,
> Tenderly wept and voiced her grief – enough
> That even the timber weeps 'the Impenitent'!

The Impenitent is al-Asi, 'the Rebel' – the Arabic name for the Orontes. 'It is said to have been called by this name because it seems to one who looks at it as though its flow were from down to up,' said IB obscurely. An early theory claimed that the river was contrary because it dared to flow from Islamic Syria into Christian Asia Minor. But the usual explanation is that, unlike other Syrian rivers, the Orontes flows from south to north.

I began trying to memorize the verse, thinking that it might come in useful if I bumped into any more riverbank poets.

'*Allah!*' said a voice, right in my ear.

I jumped.

'Sorry. I didn't mean to startle you.' I turned and saw a young man. He had been reading the verse over my shoulder. 'I just liked the poem. I've got another one like it,' he said. He frowned, then recited,

> The Rebel, in contrition, bared his breast,
> Grief-stricken like the elegists of ancient years;
> Heart pounding like a noria in his chest,
> He shed upon the stones his penitent tears.

'*Allah!*' I exclaimed. The young man recited several more noria verses. I realized I could never compete with the poetical Hamawis.

Ahmad was in his last year at school. His father owned a fig orchard beneath the noria. 'They're the best figs in Hamah,' he told me. 'Better than the Figs of Amazement.'

'I can see why,' I said, as I watched a cow tethered beneath a tree release a sputtering stream of premium organic fertilizer into the mud.

Ahmad showed me an inscription on the aqueduct that led away from the noria. We made out 'for the Great Mosque ... in the year ...' The date was illegible, but there was a very fourteenth-century-looking Mamluk blazon. I wondered if the Muhammadiyyah was one of the norias IB had seen, revolving like spheres. Materially, of course, the wheel wasn't the same. Its timbers had been renewed over the years, piecemeal, as they rotted. But perhaps its peculiar timbre, and that complex rhythm of creaks and sighs, had endured – like a piece of inherited poetry.

We walked to the Great Mosque. Ahmad told me it had been a pagan temple, then a church. 'Like the Umayyad Mosque in

Damascus,' he added, with unconcealed Hamawi pride. Much of the building, however, seemed newly built. We went through a door – an aluminium one that said 'Push' on the handle – into the tomb-chamber of one of Abu 'l-Fida's ancestors. The interior, too, looked recent; the cenotaph was a makeshift thing like a packing case.

The ancient Great Mosque of Hamah, I realized, was one of the victims of 1982. In that year, the city was taken over by militant orthodox Muslims opposed to the ruling junta's even more militant autocracy. President al-Asad responded to the rebellion in the Syrian Bath, Abu 'l-Fida's Islamic Parnassus, by bombing much of it to bits. At least eight thousand Hamawis were killed, and possibly three times as many.

In the prayer hall, Ahmad pointed to a tablet set in the wall. I was surprised to see that it was inscribed in Greek. 'Can you read it?' he asked. 'No one here knows what it says.'

I said I'd try. I squinted, and read: ΑΝΔΡΑΜΟΙΕΝΝΕΠΕ . . .

I stopped. Here on a stone which, unlike most of the building, had survived the bombing, were the opening words of the *Odyssey*.

Ahmad looked at me. 'So what is it?'

'It's a poem,' I said. 'A very old one.'

Later, I had lunch in the shop of a butcher called Abu Husam (the Father, by coincidence, of a Sharp Blade). He showed me his newly hatched canary chicks while my kidneys sang and hissed on a spit. Abu Husam's boy served them, sprinkled with cumin, at a table between hanging split carcasses. And as I ate I puzzled over the verse from the mosque, which I had transcribed. Beyond those first words it was not the *Odyssey*; that was as much as I could tell. I mourned the death of my Greek.

★

The following morning, Abu Firas the taxi driver and I breakfasted from the boot of his 1963 Mercedes on mountain figs and crystallized pumpkin. The Orontes plain lay below; directly above was a castle, raggedly outlined against a very blue sky.

Masyaf is one of a chain of fortresses which, IB wrote, 'belong to a sect called the Isma'ilis. None may visit them save the members of their sect. They are the arrows of Sultan al-Nasir, by means of whom he strikes down those of his enemies who have taken refuge from him . . .

They have poisoned knives, with which they strike the victim of their mission.' Masyaf was the mother of these castles and headquarters of the Nizari Isma'ilis, popularly called Assassins. Their mountain territory was a semi-fictional world where the medieval imagination ran wild. Picture a plot by Frederick Forsyth, enacted by members of the Branch Davidians on drugs, then translated into troubadour Provençal, and you will have a fair idea of how the Middle Ages viewed the Assassins and their leader, the Old Man of the Mountains.

I left Abu Firas and went to explore the castle. Masyaf was a mazy, introverted pile thrown together like a stork's nest. At the top of it all was a polygonal turret chamber with thick walls and arrow slits. Despite the Bishop of Acre's description of the Old Man's hideouts as *locis secretis et delectabilibus*, Masyaf was hardly secret – it could be seen from miles away – and it would have needed a hefty interior-design budget to make it delectable.

A miniature from the fifteenth-century *Livre des merveilles* shows the fantasy version of Masyaf, a turreted enclosure set among tusk-shaped mountains. Outside, human-headed deer prance or flop on the grass and a simpering harpy flaps through the air. Within the walls gormless-looking youths and damsels dance before an elderly king. The king has just raised his finger to point at the nearest youth; the dancers stare at him, frozen in mid-movement.

The picture, one of the most vivid images of the Orient in the post-crusading mind, illustrated a pervasive legend: the Old Man lured innocent youths, doped them out of their minds on hashish (hence *hashshashin* and 'Assassins'), and gave them a taste of paradise with the girls in his secret garden. Every so often he would pick one or more of the young men to go into the outside world and assassinate an enemy. The killers couldn't lose: if they got away, they would be readmitted to the garden; if they were killed they would take the short cut to heaven. Within the Old Man's perverted *hortus conclusus* are all the elements of the stereotypical cult – a megalomaniac leader, seduction and brainwashing of the young, membership of the elect, paradise guaranteed. As with a Hollywood script, successive writers gave a tweak to the more filmic features or, if they didn't exist, made them up. The biggest name in the credits is that of Marco Polo.

The reality, like the beige walls of Masyaf, was less highly coloured. Drugs and orgies were probably no more a feature of Nizari life than were–deer and harpies. Admittedly, the Nizaris were a missionary organization, with various stages of initiation into esoteric knowledge and with total obedience to their leader. They occupied mountain fastnesses which, if not paradises, were well provisioned – in the other main Nizari region south of the Caspian, one of their castles survived a Mongol siege for fourteen years. And, being a temporal as well as a spiritual power, they naturally disposed of opponents. Like the umbrella-wielding Bulgarian secret service in the 1970s, they just did it more neatly and publicly than anyone else.

The assassinations were not always successful. One of the more celebrated failures was the attempt on the future King Edward I of England, at Acre in 1272. With him was his favourite writer of romances, Rustichello of Pisa – who, as fate had it, landed up a quarter of a century later in a Genoese gaol with Marco Polo. It would be a fair guess to assume that Rustichello's memories of Acre, mixed with Polo's garbled second-hand knowledge of other north Persian sects who undoubtedly did use hashish, produced the farrago of the full-blown Assassin legend. The story assured the two Italians of a goggling readership.

At the time IB was travelling, the Nizaris had long ceased to be a political power. Sultan al-Nasir, however, used them occasionally as contract killers; one of his targets was Qarasunqur, a Mamluk cold-war defector to the Mongols. 'Al-Nasir sent suicide killers against him time after time,' IB wrote. 'Some of them gained entrance to his house, but were killed before reaching him; others hurled themselves at him as he was riding, and were struck down by him.' One contemporary account says that eighty Assassins lost their lives; another doubles the figure. Had the fabled jackals become a bunch of bungling pink panthers? Probably, to some extent; but the sensible Qarasunqur 'used never to leave off his coat of mail, and never slept except in a room built of wood and iron'. Then, in 1328, the Mongols and the Mamluks agreed to a mutual extradition of defectors, or at least of their severed heads. Before he could be arrested Qarasunqur, in the best tradition of the spy story, 'took a ring of his, which was hollowed out and contained a deadly poison, wrenched off its stone, swallowed the poison and died on the spot'. A less melodramatic historian than IB says that Qarasunqur died of diarrhoea.

It took me some time to find my way out of the castle. Abu Firas was sitting on the bonnet of his car, looking out over the plain. We were joined by an old lady, who wore a corsage of wild flowers and nattered at us. When she had gone, Abu Firas said, 'They're a funny lot, you know, these Isma'ilis. When a man leaves his house to go to work, he first kisses his wife's, um ... her you-know-what, and he says "Out of you I came, and into you I shall return." '

I could see the old lady picking flowers as she walked down the path from the castle. She looked, I thought, a bit like Miss Elsie, my piano teacher – and about as likely as Miss Elsie to submit to having her you-know-what ritually osculated.

We left Masyaf and drove higher into the mountains, following minor and diminishing roads in what we hoped was the direction of al-Ullayqah, 'the Bramble'. The castle had eluded medieval geographers – even Abu 'l-Fida, who lived twenty miles away and determined the co-ordinates of towns in China, hadn't mentioned it. At every junction, Abu Firas would stop, mutter '*Bismillah*', then make a divinely inspired guess. We saw no other vehicles and only a few sparse, crofter-like villages. People were windblown and ruddy and stared at the car; there were girls with freckles and men with Hitler moustaches. We asked for directions perhaps a dozen times, but the responses were always halting and equivocal. 'You see,' said Abu Firas, 'they are afraid.'

'Afraid of what?'

'Of everything.'

We passed into a region of chalk-white limestone, then into one of cracked and patinated karst dotted with wind-gnawed boulders. In the bigger cracks huddled tiny terraces of red earth, separated by white walls and planted with tobacco. There were occasional patches of myrtle and oak scrub, dwarfed by the huge effort of growing.

We came on al-Ullayqah unexpectedly. It sat on a little pap of rock surrounded by bare and silvery walnut trees, like a wen in an old man's beard. I left Abu Firas and climbed up tobacco terraces that had invaded the outer walls, then through the main rampart via a breach defended by a thorn bush. I emerged bleeding but victorious. On the summit, all the flat spaces were cultivated. A hole in a field led into an underground cistern, and other shafts disappeared into mattamores and oubliettes. A few arches still stood, but most of the masonry had collapsed, prised apart by the roots of sumac and terebinth. The fortress was slowly reverting to its landscape, crumbling like a sand-castle in an incoming tide of vegetation.

The Bramble was certainly a secret place. But on the far side of the summit there was a surprise: I had climbed up a pimple and now found it to be a crag beetling over a deep and shaggy valley. In the extreme distance I could see a town with puffing factory chimneys and, beyond it, the sea – which, by some trick of perspective, seemed to go uphill.

Abu Firas joined me, unscathed, having found the easy way up. 'That's Baniyas,' he said, pointing to the town. 'And that wadi down below us is called Jahannam.'

Gehenna. It seemed apt that one of the Old Man's paradises should overlook a valley called Hell.

We drove down towards Baniyas, passing signs advertising holy men's shrines, little cubes topped by ping-pong-ball domes and set among stands of holm oak. Abu Firas explained that they belonged to the Alawis. I was hoping to find out something about this secretive sect, to which President al-Asad and the ruling junta belonged, in the coastal town of Jabalah. For the moment, however, we were on a different diversion.

During his excursion along the coast IB passed by another castle, al-Marqab, 'a mighty fortress on a lofty mountain, which was captured from the hands of the Christians by Sultan Qalawun; his son al-Nasir was born close by'. Qalawun, wrote a contemporary Egyptian historian, mustered the latest ordnance from his *makhazin* and *dar al-sina'ah* (the two terms have given us 'magazine' and 'arsenal'); it included

Frank- and Devil-class mangonels, iron projectiles and flame-throwers. Surrounded by this high-tech weaponry, with sappers gnawing at the foundations like rats in the wainscot, the Christians – Abu 'l-Fida's 'Ustibar', the Knights Hospitaller – sensibly sued for peace. From IB's viewpoint, these events had happened only a generation before; but, like the Cuban Missile Crisis from ours, they belonged to a closed chapter of history.

We dropped down to the coastal plain and drove south. Soon, Abu Firas pointed upwards to al-Marqab. I could see where the name came from – a *marqab* is a look-out post. Turning off the coast road, we wound up to the castle and passed beneath its fat black rump. The view from the top was stupendous: there was Baniyas in a wide arc of bay with a bleary Mediterranean behind and, to the south, mile after mile of plain on which polythene greenhouses glistened against the dark green of olives.

The Hospitallers' basalt command-centre seemed unreasonably massive and fascistical. Compared with the Old Man's untidy mop of a castle at Masyaf, and the creeping alopecia at al-Ullayqah, this was a piece of sheer skinhead effrontery. Alone, I explored the interior, beating paths through acres of scrub and brambles, then feeling my way into vaults so dark that only the echo of my footsteps gave any impression of size. In the inner court there was a hole with a can on a rope next to it. I let the can fall, watched the rope uncoil, then heard a slap and a long, ringing reverberation. I hauled the can up and drank, then let it drop again and timed the echo: a full fifteen seconds. I was standing on a cathedral of water. A doorway off the court led into the Hospitallers' chapel. Inside, an endless column of wind poured through the window of the apse and left by the west door, setting off a faint aeolian plainchant. It was a coldly beautiful interior, perfect for soldier-ascetics.

By now it was mid-afternoon, and we still had to find al-Kahf, 'the Cavern', the most secluded of the Assassin castles. But on my way out of al-Marqab the gatekeeper asked if I'd seen the paintings. I was surprised: decorations in this temple to militarism? 'They're in a small room off the chapel,' he explained. 'We only discovered them this year. They'd been whitewashed over.'

I returned to the chapel, and in a small sacristy to the north of the apse found a fresco. Part of it had flaked away, but it clearly showed the twelve apostles in various stages of youth and age, beardedness and baldness. They looked down from the low vaulted ceiling; I felt that I was the one under scrutiny. Then I noticed that the saints were blind: their eyes had been carefully removed – according to an old belief, the powdered pigment cured ophthalmia. I imagined Qalawun's forces entering the deserted chapel, surprised by this sudden burst of faces; and, perhaps, by their ordinariness. It was only a fancy, but I wondered if these fragile images might be portraits. The Hospitallers began to seem more human.

As we drove back into the interior of the mountains, we passed a sign to a village called al-Khanziriyyah, 'Piggy'. Abu Firas's gruff explanation was that there were 'some funny places around here'. A little further on he pointed out the Bramble, up on its perch above the Valley of Hell. 'And look down there. We could have taken that road through the valley. It would have cut out miles. They didn't tell us about it because they were afraid.' I rather fancied a trip to Hell in a yellow Mercedes; but the shadows were lengthening and it was no time for Dantesque frivolities.

Rashid al-Din Sinan, the most celebrated leader of the Syrian Nizaris, died in 1192. His successor was keen to show outsiders that, like the old Old Man, he was a disciplinarian. According to Crusader historians, the opportunity arose a couple of years later when he was entertaining Henry of Champagne at the Cavern. In the midst of the diplomatic niceties, the Old Man ordered two of his warriors to leap from the battlements. And leap they did – ending up, as one romance put it, *'mors et fenis/ Sur les roches agues desrompis corps et pis'*.

It is one of those elastic stories that get stretched to different times and places. Sometimes the witness is not Henry (who died soon afterwards, parodically, in an accidental defenestration at Acre) but Frederick II von Hohenstaufen; sometimes it takes place in northern Persia; Alexander the Great, in the medieval legends, ordered a death leap; Peter the Great is said to have commanded a Cossack to jump from a tower in Copenhagen, to impress the King of Denmark. In the case of the Nizaris it seems to be more than a myth, for the sober and veracious Ibn Jubayr wrote about their leap of faith well before it entered European literature.

Something inspired us to offer a lift to an off-duty soldier who, it turned out, was going in the direction of al-Kahf. He seemed reluctant to accept, and as we drove off he began frantically clicking his prayer beads. Abu Firas smiled at me, his diagnosis of endemic phobia confirmed. But the soldier gradually calmed down and even pointed out a couple of landmarks, the shrines of Adam's son Seth and of the Prophet Salih. The light faded, the road deteriorated and the scene became increasingly druidical. Finally, on an eminence above a densely tree'd valley, the soldier told Abu Firas to stop. 'That's al-Kahf,' he said, pointing to a line of cliff, tousled with vegetation, at a spot where the valley split.

I looked at my watch, then at the castle, and reckoned I could just make it back to the car before total darkness descended. 'Right. If you could wait, Abu Firas, I'll be back as soon as possible.'

Abu Firas didn't look happy. The soldier clicked his prayer beads in alarm. 'Don't go,' he said. 'The forest is full of boars, huge ones. They can cut you in two with their tusks!' He made a horrible diagonal slicing movement across his chest.

Two things came to mind: al-Khanziriyyah, 'Piggy'; and a passage I had recently come across in the memoirs of a boar-hunting man, the local twelfth-century nobleman Usamah ibn Munqidh – 'I remember seeing a boarlet, about the size of a kitten, attack the hoof of my page's horse. The page drew an arrow from his quiver, speared the animal and held it up in the air. I was astonished that so tiny a creature could be so ferocious.'

I asked the soldier how big the boars got. He stretched his arms out to their full extent. 'And more. Maybe two metres.'

'I'm not going,' I said.

We stood for a while, looking up the valley. I pictured its Gadarene

inhabitants . . . a crazy dash through Rackhamesque thickets. The sun was setting, turning the clouds pink. They seemed more solid than mere vapour, to have a sponginess about them, like freshly excised lungs.

Back in Hamah I dined once more at the butcher's, and ordered the only thing possible after a day of Assassin castles: hearts *en brochette*.

★

The mountains of Syria seem to breed fictions and heterodoxies. As well as the Nizaris there was a sect who, IB wrote, 'hate the Ten [Companions of the Prophet] and – an extraordinary thing – never mention the word "ten". When their brokers are selling goods at auction in the bazaars and come to ten, they say "nine-and-one". One day an [orthodox] Turk happened to be there, and hearing a broker cry "nine-and-one", he laid his club about the man's head saying, "Say ten!"; whereupon the broker cried "Ten! . . . for the sake of the club."'

IB was equally intrigued by the Nusayris, now usually known as Alawis because of their devotion to the Prophet's son-in-law, Ali. Although they were nominally Muslims, the Mamluk authorities had to force them to build mosques; but, IB wrote, the house of God was often used 'as a refuge for their cattle and their asses. Frequently too a stranger on coming to a village of theirs will stop at the mosque and recite the call to prayer, and then they call out to him, "Stop braying! Your fodder is coming to you." ' An orthodox Syrian contemporary of IB was equally scathing, and described the Alawis variously as infidels, hypocrites, ignoramuses, pantheists, trinitarians, metempsychosists, Manichaeans and pseudo-Sabians. 'In short, their only invariable doctrine is to ensure plentiful supplies of food, drink and sex.'

The Alawis have generally had a hard time from the orthodox majority, and on one memorable occasion were raided by a force sent by the Pasha of Acre and commanded by Lady Hester Stanhope. The greatest catastrophe to befall them, however, took place seven years before IB's visit. In the traveller's version of events, a charismatic leader claiming to be the Awaited Mahdi persuaded the Alawis to arm themselves with myrtle branches. 'They made a surprise attack on the town of Jabalah while the [male] inhabitants were engaged in Friday prayers, and entered the houses and dishonoured the women.' In the backlash, IB says, about twenty thousand Alawis were killed. The only reason they were not completely wiped out was that 'they were the labourers of the Muslims in the tillage of the soil'. The labourers had their revenge on the forces of orthodoxy 663 years later, in Hamah, armed with more than myrtle branches.

Although the Alawis have now run Syria for the past thirty years, their beliefs are still little understood. Most of my scant information came from orthodox medieval sources written in indelible vitriol. But I had also read in more recent and impartial accounts that, true to IB's comment, they had begun to build mosques voluntarily only in the 1970s; that, like the Nizari Isma'ilis, they had degrees of esoteric initiation; and that their knowledge had been transmitted down the generations through a succession of illuminati called Babs, 'Doors'. Perhaps, I reasoned, a visit to the shrine of the eighth-century Ibrahim ibn Ad'ham, an orthodox Sufi saint also regarded by the Alawis as a Door, would provide a glimpse into the obscure corridor of their beliefs.

Ibrahim ibn Ad'ham is a complex figure, at times mysterious, orphic, asleep in a garden as a viper fans him with a bunch of narcissi; at others touchingly human, an ascetic haunted even in his dreams by the tempting smell of *sakbaj*, a sort of oriental *boeuf bourguignon*. He is also a well-travelled saint. Born into one of the ruling families of

Transoxiana, he underwent a Buddha-like conversion to the holy life then made his way to Syria. Late medieval accounts claim that he lived for a time in a hermitage near Fez, and at the same period stories about him travelled east to India and Indonesia. He even popped up recently in Somerset, while I was having tea with an aunt. We were talking about memory. 'How strange it is', said Aunt Madge, 'that I can still remember poems I learned when I was a girl! There's that one about Abou Ben Adhem. I can see myself now, standing there and reciting it . . .

> Abou Ben Adhem (may his tribe increase!)
> Awoke one night from a deep dream of peace,
> And saw, within the moonlight in his room,
> Making it rich, and like a lily in bloom,
> An angel writing in a book of gold . . . '

She recited, or incanted, in a voice so light that eighty years seemed to slip away from her.

I drove to visit the tomb in Jabalah in a Mercedes even older than that of Abu Firas. As we passed a particularly large portrait of Basil, the driver mentioned that the President's late son was buried nearby. 'In Qirdahah. That's where they come from. You ought to see the tomb – it's like a very big villa. They've put up a five-star hotel. Oh, and there's an international airport.'

I assumed he was having me on about the airport; perhaps even daringly poking fun at the ruling family. Then I saw something that made me literally rub my eyes: a large sign to the 'Martyr Basil International Airport'. It was an accolade normally reserved for superpower presidents and *rinasciamento* painters. If the Alawis honoured Basil thus, I must be in for a sepulchral treat in Jabalah.

Ibrahim ibn Ad'ham's tomb was in a mosque next to the bus station. It was empty except for a thin sleeping man and a fat comatose one. Paint was flaking like dandruff off the ceiling and piers of the prayer hall. In the tomb-chamber a mass-produced rug hung on the wall, showing the Atatürk Bridge in Istanbul. Ibrahim's cenotaph, a giant bedlike structure with football-sized knobs, lay beneath a very dusty chandelier. Where was the parcel gilt, the smoking thurible charged with eaglewood? Where the riddling gnostic *shaykhs* looking beyond the door into infinity?

The fat man had followed me in and was hovering behind the tomb. I asked him if he could tell me any stories about the saint; in response he pointed to a brief framed biography, which told me nothing I didn't already know. He then shadowed me heavily out of the mosque. As I was leaving the main entrance, an old man zipped through it on a red scooter. The doors of Alawi perception remained firmly shut.

I had meant to ask about Ibrahim al-Jumahi, the 'notable devotee' who ran the saint's guest-house in IB's day; and about the annual visitation described by the traveller, when devotees and dervishes came from across Syria bearing candles, and a great fair was held on the outskirts of the town. But something told me that the carnival was long over.

Disappointed by medieval Jabalah, I snubbed it and made for the Roman theatre. In an office in the vaulted entrance I found a genial man who introduced himself as Abdullah Zakariyya. He chatted learnedly on the theatre, which he was restoring, and on the town's later history. When I steered him on to Ibrahim ibn Ad'ham, he confirmed my expectations about the great annual visitation of the saint's tomb. 'You have to remember that you're talking about a long time ago,' he said.

I admitted that I often forgot; then, forgetting again, asked if the name Ibrahim al-Jumahi meant anything to him.

'It's al-Jumahi with a short *a*,' Abdullah replied, correcting my pronunciation. 'Ibrahim al-Jumahi was the intendant of the saint's hospice in the fourteenth century. The traveller IB called him "a notable devotee".'

I was impressed.

'And', he went on, looking pleased with himself, 'I am his descendant.'

★

Perhaps it was the after-effects of temporal vertigo, or perhaps it was the graffito I spotted near my hotel – *b'ahibbak b'ahibbak w'allah b'ahibbak!* ('I love you I love you, *God* I love you!'), followed by a large $; whatever, I couldn't take al-Ladhiqiyyah seriously.

When IB visited the port city, it was famous for a hospitable monastery where Muslim visitors were given ploughman's lunches. Today, the entertainment is more sophisticated: in the hotel lobby, a

185

Beirut satellite channel was previewing the annual Miss Lebanon contest, '120 lovely girls, next Thursday, 8 p.m. GMT, 11 Saudi time'. I escaped to my room and the autobiography of Usamah ibn Munqidh, who had written on the ferocity of boarlets. The memoirs of a nonagenarian written eight hundred years ago were the perfect antidote to dollar signs and dolly birds. I opened the book and read my way out of al-Ladhiqiyyah.

Usamah was fascinated by being so old:

> I wonder that my hand, too weak to hold a pen,
> Speared lions long ago, in its young day;
> That when I walk with stick in hand the ground,
> Though solid, clings beneath my feet like clay.

He also wrote of the effect of time on his memory. 'One for whom the passage of years has been long may be excused a certain forgetfulness – which, after all, is the inheritance of Adam's sons.' But like his coeval, my Somerset aunt, Usamah could recall fragments from the past with remarkable clarity: Lu'lu'ah for instance, nanny to three generations of the Munqidh family, trying to do her washing with a piece of cheese; al-Yahshur, a pampered hawk that slept on a fur-lined bed; and his father's favourite Zaghari bitch – 'At night the pages would play chess by the light of a lamp which they placed on her head. She would sit there, without moving, until her eyelids drooped. My father, God bless his soul, would scold the pages and say, "You've blinded my hound!" But they never took any notice.'

I fell asleep imagining that last tableau, a game of chess far away on a tiny continent of light.

★

'Al-Sarmini, Purveyors of Soap' was almost the first thing I saw inside the Aleppo *suq*, and it had Battutian resonances. IB wrote that Sarmin 'is a pretty town with a great quantity of orchards, their principal tree being the olive. Brick soap is manufactured there and exported to Cairo and Damascus.' I had failed to find the place on the map; but here in Aleppo was a Sarmini still in the ancestral business. Mr Sarmini took a brick of olive-oil soap and broke it open. The inside was veined with green from the juice of laurel leaves. (I sympathized with Usamah's nanny – in poor light, the soap would have been indistinguishable from a lump of Sage Derby.) 'As recommended by Avicenna', Mr Sarmini said, 'for the treatment of dandruff, lice, impetigo and *quba*.' I bought a year's supply. Whatever the last complaint was, it had an unpleasant ring to it.

Mr Sarmini directed me to the Great Mosque, a building admired by IB. 'In the court there is a pool of water surrounded by a pavement of vast extent; the pulpit is of exquisite workmanship, inlaid with ivory and ebony.' As in Damascus, the mosque is a surprise, a sudden open space set in the circuit-board complexity of the surrounding markets. IB's vast pavement is laid out in bordered rectangles, imitating the carpeted interior of a prayer hall; it was dotted with elderly Aleppans who dozed in chairs or read. The prayer hall itself has two notable features. The first is a large brass grille protecting the burial place of Zechariah's head. According to the *Short History of Mankind*, the relic was discovered a few years after IB's visit. Rumours had been circulating about a sealed room. Against all advice, one of the mosque officials located the chamber and opened it up. Inside was a marble ossuary. 'He removed the lid and found a portion of a skull. At the sight of it those present fled in awe.' The official resealed the chamber; 'but thereafter he was smitten with the falling-sickness. In the final attack he bit his tongue clean off, and died soon afterwards.' It was a warning to the curious.

The other notable feature was the minbar, the pulpit of exquisite workmanship IB had mentioned. It was new when the traveller saw it, a gift from Sultan al-Nasir. I was delighted to see it in place and not removed to a museum; then, as I approached the door that closed off the staircase, appalled. Some unspeakable person had covered it with a thick coat of varnish. The colour and finish reminded me of an old tuck-shop favourite called Caramac.

And then something else caught my eye – the dark gleam of polished ebony – and I realized with renewed delight that the sides of the pulpit were in their original, uncaramelized state. 'The leading Greek geometricians', wrote Ibn Khaldun, 'were all master carpenters. Euclid, the author of the *Book of Principles*, was a carpenter and known as such. The same was the case with Apollonius, the author of the book on *Conic Sections*, and Menelaus and others.' Similarly, the carpenter who made this pulpit must have been a master geometrician: its surface was an interlocking mass of marquetry polygons in fruitwoods, set off by deep-cut ivory trefoils and miniature screen-work of crisscrossing ebony balusters with tiny ivory knobs at the nodes. A few bits of inlay had gone missing; otherwise, it was as crisp and fresh as when IB had seen it. The workmanship was indeed exquisite. With its interplay of polychromatic parts, it was a Bach fugue for the eyes.

Next to the pulpit a man was lining himself up to pray. 'Look!' I said to him, making him flinch. 'Isn't it beautiful!' He studied me for a few seconds and seemed to decide that, if I was a nutcase, I was a harmless one. I left him contemplating the minbar, distracted from his devotions.

At the Baron Hotel, nothing had changed since my last stay: the same dark-panelled dining-room and BOAC calendars, the same books and little marquetry thrones in the reading-room. I even had the same bedroom with its Turkey carpets, big chintz curtains, solid furniture and chocolate-tiled bathroom. It was rather like staying with an Aunt. There have been murmurings about the Baron's standards of hygiene; but if it was good enough for – as one is informed by a leaflet – the kings of Iraq and Sweden, Kemal Atatürk, Lawrence of Arabia, Princes Bibesco and Cantacuzino, Mr and Mrs Theodore Roosevelt, Dame Freya Stark, Yuri Gagarin, Valentina Tereshkova, Sir Hugh Knatchbull-Hugessen and Mrs Doris Duke (who may have got on to the list because of her noble-sounding surname), it was good enough for me. I had a beer in the bar and exchanged nods and semi-smiles with an English-looking man of my own age, similarly jacketed, who looked suspiciously like a travel writer.

Lunch at the Shabab Restaurant across the road knocked inverse archaeology squarely on the head, at least for the rest of the day. I chose an item on the menu described simply as 'Birds'. At a table opposite me sat a fat red-faced man in a check jacket. He was completely bald, bearded, and had a hole in the centre of his forehead, perhaps the result of a hasty frontal lobotomy. The face was strangely familiar.

The Birds arrived spit-roast, heads, beaks and all, half a dozen of them, each about an inch and a quarter long. They were crunchy and sharp-tasting – the waiter explained that they were migrants from Russia that fed exclusively on figs and mulberries. To go with them I ordered a half-bottle of 'Duck' brand arak, the label confusingly decorated with a swan. Even more confusingly, *battah*, the Arabic for 'duck', appeared on the cap as *bat'hah* – which might have been a variant of the word for 'swamp' or 'depression' but should, strictly, have meant 'a throwing upon the ground'. If a warning was implied, I didn't heed it. Towards the end of the bottle the bald man's jacket began scintillating, as checks do on a TV screen. Then, as he got up to leave, I realized in a flash of arak inspiration where I'd seen him before: in a picture-book by Rex Whistler that showed faces which could be viewed either way up.

I had only one road to cross to get to my bed at the Baron.

Next morning on my way to the Citadel, I stopped at a juice bar. A plump lady with shopping bags beamed at me. 'You speak Arabic.'

'*Al-hamdu li 'llah*,' I said.

'And you're a Muslim!'

'No, a Masihi.'

She looked concerned. 'Of course, the main thing that separates us is that Trinity of yours.'

I remembered Upper Egypt and my theological wrigglings with the mage-like *shaykh*, and replied with an 'Mm'.

'You can't have three people running the same firm, you know. It just wouldn't work.'

On al-Shahba, the Citadel of Aleppo, Ibn Juzayy quoted a verse by a certain al-Khalidi – or in fact two al-Khalidis, a pair of brothers whose joint productions made them the Gilbert and George of tenth-century Arabic poetry:

> Lo! on her grim and massy rock
> That holds to scorn the foeman's shock
> With lofty tower and perilous steep
> Majestic stands Aleppo's keep.

For once the description is not over the top. IB wrote, awestruck, of al-Shahba, 'the Iron-Grey' – of its walls and deep moat, its marvellous belvederes, and of the prodigious fact that it had withstood a siege by the Mongols.

I climbed up a steep stone viaduct, over the moat and into a gatehouse. The incline continued up to a second gatehouse, a massive, intimidating barbican put up, the inscription read, by the thirteenth-century Ayyubid al-Zahir Ghazi, the Just, the Great Sultan, the Victorious, the Prince of This and That . . . the inscription went on and on. So did the gatehouse, within which there were three separate portals, each furnished with iron doors like the bulkheads of a battleship and guarded by fearsome stone animals. The first portal was topped by dragons with foxy heads, writhing around and nipping each other. Next came the Gate of the Two Lions, not the slim-line heraldic sort but a pair of sparring bruisers. I dog-legged upwards past a cenotaph draped in green, a shrine to al-Khadir, that energetic, mystical traveller who like IB and me had begun his journey in Tangier. Still higher, I reached the third and last portal, the Gate of the Laughing and Crying Lions. They were deployed in bouncer formation on either side of the doorway looking outwards, pudding-faced like Hogarth pussy cats. (The difference in their expressions has generated much empty speculation. To me the reason was obvious: the happy lion has four claws on each paw, the unhappy one only three.)

After all the twists and turns and talismanic guardians, I expected to emerge into nothing less than the City of Brass. But the buildings on top were an anticlimax, the view depressing. A cement suburbia stretched to the horizon, covering the vineyards and orchards which IB had seen. That epithet of the Citadel, the Iron-Grey, had slid down and clothed all Aleppo.

Late that afternoon I bumped into al-Khadir once more. Again, it happened in a gateway – Bab al-Nasr, the Gate of Victory, the northern entrance to the old city of Aleppo. (The patron saint of travel had a habit of popping up in transitional places – entrances and exits, mountains by the sea, tracks across the desert. He was for ever coming or going, arriving or disembarking.) Part of the structure had been turned into a stationer's; al-Khadir's cenotaph was in the other part, covered by the usual green pall and identified by a plaque. It stood in a padlocked enclosure, surrounded by lighted incense-sticks.

Opposite was another enclosure. This one was empty, but I noticed a smooth block of stone with deep holes in it, let into the rougher masonry of the gate. The stone was covered in oily smears and seemed to be inscribed, but in the failing light and the gloom of the gateway I could make nothing of it.

IB hadn't mentioned the site, but back in the Baron I turned up a reference to the stone in the pilgrim guide of al-Harawi, a native of Aleppo: 'Set into the Gate of the Jews, also called the Gate of Victory, is a stone to which pledges are made. People annoint it with rose water and scented unguents. The Muslims, Christians and Jews have diverse beliefs about it, and it is said that beneath it is the tomb of one of the prophets or saints.' I decided to go back. Whatever those diverse beliefs were, it seemed they were still current.

I returned the next morning and found the man with the key to the shrine, who kept a smaller stationer's opposite the gate. He was a stately, elderly gentleman with a smooth round face and an expression of deep melancholy that reminded me of the sad lion of the Citadel. I asked him why there were two shrines to al-Khadir in Aleppo, and he told me that the saint had passed through a tunnel that joined the Citadel with the Gate of Victory, to rally the Muslims when they besieged the city in the first century of Islam.

'And what about the stone with the holes in it?'

He hesitated. 'Some people believe that if you have arthritis and put your finger in one of the holes, you will be cured. But health comes only from God. He cures whom He wishes.'

I asked about the inscription. The old stationer told me it was *mismari*, 'nail-writing' or cuneiform. 'And they say that two people from the cuneiform age are buried beneath the stone.'

'Could I have the key? I'd like to have a closer look.'

'You ... you should go to the Directorate of Antiquities.' I was going to press further, but he continued with sudden passion. 'Al-Khadir is still alive. And Elijah. And Jesus. They are the three who do not die! And Jesus will come on the Last Day and then he himself will die. And Elijah and al-Khadir. And ... ' I looked into the smooth face and saw tears in his eyes, ' ... and that will be the end of this world.' His voice had tailed off to a whisper.

The call to prayer sounded and he appeared to recover. He put on a turban of yellow brocade wound around a crimson *tarbush*. 'You will pray with us?'

I told him that I was a Masihi. He said nothing, but took my hand for a while, then released it. He locked up the shop and left.

I went back inside the gateway and squinted through the bars at the stone. The inscription was not in cuneiform but Greek. As to what it said – whether it was Homer or a Byzantine no parking sign – I couldn't tell. It was just too far away, too obscure. I contemplated going to the Directorate of Antiquities; then decided to leave it as a mystery. Besides, an old man talking about death by the empty tomb of a traveller had reminded me, as if I needed a reminder, that I had to get going.

★

Back in Damascus I picked up several more absolutely indispensable volumes from Hikmat. Like Dr Abdelhadi of Rabat, IB's exclamatory editor, he gave me his *salams* to pass on to various scholars in Yemen and, for myself, a farewell kiss.

I then went on a final expedition with Abu Ala and Munir the topographer. We drove to al-Kiswah, a village south of Damascus where IB joined the Mecca pilgrim caravan (not uncharacteristically leaving behind an impregnated wife). The village sat on a rise facing the desert. There was not a lot to it – a few houses, a ruined Mamluk caravanserai containing anatomized lorries and pools of oil, and the ghosts of many departures.

I couldn't follow IB to Mecca. Even Abu Ala, who had got me into the tomb of the Lady Zaynab, admitted defeat on that one. 'Unless, that is, you converted.' He gave me a sly wink.

'I couldn't convert just to do research! It would be . . . '

'No, I mean *really* convert.' Now he was looking at me unblinking. 'We could do the Pilgrimage together in my taxi. At my expense.'

'And I could come too,' said Munir the topographer.

An image came to mind: of Abu Ala at the wheel of his Damascus taxi, driving out of the iron-grey north into Arabia, southward into the sun, wearing his striped tie and tweed suit.

He was still looking at me. 'But then,' he continued, starting the car, 'guidance comes from God.'

I was of course heading south to catch up with IB. The other side of Mecca we would shake off our literary travelling companions, Ibns Juzayy and Jubayr, and their constant if well-turned interruptions. We would leave the Mamluk heartland and travel centrifugally – to

Oman and the Coast of the Fish-eaters, to Turkoman Anatolia and
the Crimea of the Golden Horde, and to Constantinople, where the
long sunset had begun in a blaze of Palaeologue mosaic.

IB travelled from al-Kiswah; I from Damascus Airport which,
perhaps in the apotropaic tradition of the Aleppo Citadel and the
temples of the Hittites, you enter past a large stone sphinx with an
Assyrian-looking gentleman on top of it. (Could he, I wondered, be
the real reason behind the sphinx's inscrutable smile?)

I checked in, then found the bar. Behind it, bottles of Black Label
were spotlit in little alcoves, relics in a shrine of booze. Opposite,
several dozen Iranian women in black chadors squatted on the floor,
glowing quietly with the reflected sanctity of the Lady Zaynab and
al-Husayn's head. I sat in the middle, the only customer, and drank
beer. It was a curious juxtaposition of elements, and over it all
watched the grocerly, ubiquitous face of Hafiz al-Asad. Looking up
at him, I couldn't decide what he was: Big Brother; a new Alawi Old
Man of the Mountains; or a genius at synthesis.

IB left Mecca with the Iraqi pilgrim caravan, and made a tour of Iraq and southern Persia. He then returned to Mecca and stayed for nearly three years as a 'sojourner', a long-term pilgrim and student. In 1330 he sailed from Jeddah to Yemen, visited the Yemeni sultan, al-Mujahid, then crossed from Aden to Somalia. After a brief hop down the port cities of East Africa he crossed the ocean to the Arabian enclave of Dhofar, then under Yemeni rule. From here he coasted to Oman.

Oman

The Coast of the Fish-eaters

'A man that spurs his mount through empty tracts wrests
wonders from the hands of Time.'

Ahmad ibn Muhammad al-Haymi (d. 1737), *Itr nasim al-siba*

I WAS THE one who was meant to be following him. But for a
moment I was sure of it: he was following me. I stopped and
turned. There was nothing there – a track across a gravel plain
between the mountains and the sea, but no shades.

More to the point at high noon on the Gulf of Oman, there was
almost no shade; just a few crew-cut trees quivering in the heat haze.
I turned off the track, made for one of them and lunched on Bombay
mix in a meagre fretwork of shadow. Then I opened the *Travels*: 'I
turned off the road', wrote IB of this same track, 'and made for a tree
of *umm ghaylan*.'

If anything was haunting me, it was the text. I couldn't recall what
an *umm ghaylan* was, but it sounded close enough to 'mother of
ghouls' for discomfort. And weren't ghouls that species of jinn that
haunt graveyards and mislead travellers in lonely spots? Whatever,
beggars couldn't be ... 'Aeeugh!' I exclaimed. A horrible sound. A
dry, horrible clattering thing. A death-rattle ... *Right here in the tree.*
I slowly turned my head, and found myself eyeball to compound
eyeball with a large grasshopper.

I was testing a theory: that, at this particular point in his journey,
the Prince of Travellers was a wimp. In 1329 he arrived by sea at Sur,
the most easterly town in the Arab world. 'From there,' he wrote, 'we
saw the city of Qalhat on the slope of a hill, and seeming to be close
by.' After a six hundred-mile voyage along the southern coast of

Arabia, he was missing civilization. Qalhat, a sort of medieval Dubai, shimmered seductively. IB was told that the walk would take a couple of hours. He set out with a fellow passenger from the boat, Khadir the Indian, and a crew member as guide and porter.

The walk was a disaster. IB soon became convinced that the guide wanted to steal his luggage. By chance, the traveller happened to have a spear with him and every so often, he says, 'I brandished it so the guide went in awe of me.' After a detour around a tidal creek, they entered the plain, 'a waterless desert, where we suffered from thirst and were in a desperate plight'. Khadir the Indian fell ill. They struggled through gullies and rocks by the shore, and six hours later flopped down for the night beneath their tree – presumably an ancestor of mine. IB didn't sleep: 'I stayed on watch, and every time the guide moved I spoke to him and showed him that I was awake.' Next morning they finally arrived at Qalhat, 'in a state of great exhaustion. My feet had become so swollen in my shoes that the blood was almost starting under the nails ... For six days I was powerless to rise.' It all sounded a bit melodramatic for a walk of eighteen miles.

To be fair on IB, my reconstruction of his walk was not entirely authentic, for I had some advantages over him: I had set out at first light, he at midday; it was now February, while IB had been here in 'the season of heat'; and I had a pair of stout walking shoes of a type not available in the fourteenth century. I thought of giving myself a handicap and bringing my bag with its heavy travelling library, then decided that the age difference – I was ten years older than IB – was also a consideration.

The topography of IB's route was, not surprisingly, unchanged;

but its human geography had altered. Sur had grown, Qalhat –
Marco Polo's Calatu, 'a noble city ... frequented by numerous ships
with goods from India' – had all but disappeared. And there was a
new toponym, al-Anji. I heard the name in Sur while asking a tug-
master for directions, and rifled my memory for a mention of the
place. It certainly wasn't in the *Travels*, and it seemed to have eluded
Ibn al-Mujawir, whose thirteenth-century anecdotal geography is
the best guide to the bottom half of Arabia. 'You know,' the tug-
master said. 'The end of the pipeline.' It clicked: al-Anji was 'LNG' –
the Liquified Natural Gas terminal. And there it was, visible from
beneath my *umm ghaylan*, a couple of giant gasometers and a lot of
oversized Meccano strewn across the plain.

When I had asked how long the walk to Qalhat would take, there
was something hauntingly familiar about the tug-master's response:
'Oh, not more than a couple of hours.' Unless I ran all the way, it
seemed wildly optimistic. All the same, I had set off at a lick along the
beach, escorted by a dawn patrol of dragonflies. An occasional heron –
which the Arabs call 'the sad bird' – contemplated the shallows. On
my left was a strong smell of frankincense from the matutinal fumiga-
tions of Suri houses and, on my right, of tideline iodine. Suburban
Sur ended in a line of large villas. One had pharaonic columns
coloured like Edinburgh rock, another Blenheim-style iron gates, a
cornflower-blue dome and no fewer than three satellite dishes.

The first humans I saw were some boys, fishing with a line. As I
passed, they caught something, dropped it and scurried up the beach.
Then they edged back, chucking rocks. I went to investigate and
found a small drab moray eel, writhing and snapping its last. The
boys called it a *hawin*. 'It bites really hard,' they told me, 'specially
when it sees something red.' I looked at its nutcracker jaws and made
a mental note never to swim in Omani waters wearing red bathing
trunks.

Half an hour further along the beach I came across Rashid and
Hamad, who were doing things to a boat. They invited me to their
village, across the plain at the foot of the hills. In the interests of my
reconstruction, I declined; then changed my mind at the mention of
coffee – breakfast had been a joyless pre-dawn omelette and luke-
warm Nescafé. They promised to return me to this exact spot, and
we drove across the plain in an old pick-up.

In an airy seaward room they brought not only coffee but also

dates, apples, oranges and a Suri sweetmeat – a crunchy jelly that
tasted of cardamom, ginger and Barmouth biscuits. Such Omani
invitations are unrivalled in delicacy, the fruit so precisely cut, the
dates in dainty containers on doilies, the coffee – in tiny cups a
quarter full – to be drunk reasonably quickly and with appreciative
but not over-audible slurps. Rashid instructed me in coffee protocol.
'Only the women fill the cup. You're slurping too loudly. No, never
put the cup on the floor! And you wiggle it like this, from the
bottom, after the third cup.'

They drove me back to the shore and I resumed my journey,
restored. Eventually the track entered the sprawling gas terminal of
al-Anji. Behind high fences sat rows of air-conditioned Portakabins,
humming, inhabited refrigerators. Off-duty Indians stared at me
through the wire mesh; buses filled with more Indians passed by, each
time with a simultaneous turn of heads. A couple of brand-new
Landcruisers also went past, driven by Westerners. They were the
ones who stared hardest. Perhaps I had inadvertently wet myself,
or grown a horn. Everything, though, seemed in order. The only
possible explanation for the stares was that I was walking.

Beyond al-Anji the hills met the sea, and the track rose. Up ahead
was a cuboid building, the first sign of Qalhat. After a mile or so I
passed through the city wall and entered a vast area of scrub and ruins –
more walls, vaulted cisterns and tombs with collapsed domes like
breakfast eggshells. The whole place trembled minutely: Qalhat was
covered with locusts. My solitary grasshopper must have got left
behind. It was an apocalyptic scene – this noble city in ruins, infested
by millions of rustling, nibbling insects – and I recalled a story I had
heard in Sur. The last ruler of Qalhat was having an affair with his
daughter. His advisers dropped hints, but he shrugged them off.
'Why', he asked, 'should I give to others the ripest fruit of my own
garden?' So the city was destroyed, Sodom-style, in a fit of divine
wrath. (The agent of ruin is variously said to have been an earthquake, a tidal wave, or the Portuguese.)

I wandered about the site, treading at almost every step on shards
of jade-coloured celadon ware. When IB was here Qalhat's citizens
were 'traders who live on what comes to them from the sea'; the
smashed luxury porcelain underfoot, imported five thousand miles
across the Indian Ocean, was the fruit of their commerce. IB also
noted Persian tiles covering a mosque built by Bibi Maryam, a saintly

lady who ruled the city until a few years before his visit. The mosque has disappeared, but Bibi Maryam's tomb-chamber still stands, the cuboid building I had seen from the road. As recently as the 1830s, Lieutenant Wellsted of the Bombay Marine reported that the mausoleum was also covered with tiles 'on which are inscribed, *in rilievo*, sentences from the Koran'. Now the tiles are gone, the dome has caved in and plaster is falling off the coral stone walls.

The tomb, however, seemed to be a locust-free zone, and I lay down in the shade of the wall. I was weary from the walk, although hardly in need of six days' bed-rest. IB clearly was a wimp. But then, I thought as I dozed off, I bet he wasn't frightened of grasshoppers.

Still half asleep, I became conscious of a whirring sound. It was closing in. A headline flashed across my mind – 'Killer Locusts: Writer Nibbled to Death' – and I opened my eyes apprehensively. Bibi Maryam and I were surrounded by a dozen foreigners taking photographs. I escaped into the tomb and darted lizard-like glances at the tourists – Germans – from behind the door jamb. Their Italian *gruppenführerin* joined me.

'I hope you've told them about IB,' I whispered to her.

'Er ... Please remind me of him.' I gave her the *Travels* in a nutshell, which she then passed on in German. One of the tourists, I was pleased to see, took notes on the *grosser mittelalterlicher Weltenbummler*.

I felt I had done well by IB; perhaps even made up for poking fun at his blisters.

I cadged a lift from the Germans – who might themselves have been termed gross middle-aged worldbummers – to IB's next destination, the village of Tiwi ten miles up the coast. My own feet were in fair shape, but the time for heroics was over.

IB described Tiwi as 'one of the loveliest of villages and most striking in beauty, with flowing streams and verdant trees and abundant plantations ... They grow the banana called *marwari*, which in Persian means "pearly".' It was still an accurate description of the wadi behind the village. With its pea-green pools, tumbling streams and terraces of bananas and dates, the scene was a total contrast to the waterless waste between Sur and Qalhat.

Under an old gnarled tamarind I questioned some old gnarled men about the *marwari* banana; they didn't know it, but made up by listing the other types that they grew – *billi*, *faridi*, *abu baraghim*, *ahmar* and *aghbari*. Then one of them thrust a bunch of whitish stems in my face. I sniffed them. 'Er, lovely,' I said, not knowing what reaction was expected.

The man laughed. 'They're palm penises. We climb up the trees and stick them in the female parts. You see, the Prophet said, "Be generous to your paternal aunts, the palms." He used this term to describe them because, it is said, the palm was created from left-over clay when God had made Adam.'

I later came across the same tradition in al-Qazwini's *Wonders of Creation*, together with the following useful tip:

> If a palm fails to bear fruit, you should take an axe and approach it, saying aloud to another person, 'I want to cut down this tree because it doesn't bear fruit.' Your companion should reply, 'Don't do that. It will bear fruit this year.' Then you must say, 'No it won't. It's good for nothing,' and give it a couple of light blows with the axe. Your companion must then seize your hand and say, 'Leave it alone. It's a good tree. Give it one more chance. If it doesn't bear fruit this year, then do what you like with it.' If you follow this procedure, the palm will produce an excellent crop.

The technique, surely the ultimate in talking to plants, is said to work equally well with other fruit trees.

The afternoon was getting on but I had no difficulty hitching back to Sur, thanks to a Pathan scrap merchant, a group of Keralan caterers and, finally, a PR man from al-Anji. Adil, a native of Sur, offered a solution to a small geographical query. At the beginning of the walk to Qalhat, IB's way had been blocked by a tidal creek. He saw some men swimming across it, and the guide indicated that they should do the same. But he and Khadir the Indian smelt a rat – 'we were convinced that he meant to drown us and make away with our garments' – and insisted on walking inland to look for a ford. The Omani historian al-Salimi identified the creek as Khawr Rasagh, an inlet not far from the north end of suburban Sur. This, however, was such an insignificant channel that I had almost missed it on my walk that morning. 'I suppose the configuration of the shore could have changed,' I suggested.

'It's possible,' said Adil. 'But I think IB was talking about Khawr Sur, the Sur Creek itself. I reckon he didn't land at Sur proper, but at al-Ayjah on the other side of the *khawr*. People used to swim across if the ferry wasn't working, with their clothes on their heads. If IB had walked up to the ford he would have added quite a bit to his journey.' The blisters were beginning to make more sense. I felt increasingly guilty about scoffing at IB.

We reached the outskirts of Sur in the furry light of late afternoon, and to the unexpected thwack of cricket balls. It was the start of the weekend, and Indian matches were taking place on wickets of dust. Adil dropped me off at Khawr Sur by the *Fat'h al-Khayr*, a fine *ghanjah* – a large sailing ship – dating back to the 1950s and now preserved on dry land. I looked up at the prow, carved with an elegant kiss-curl, and wished that such vessels were still sailing. Still, a humble diesel-engined *sambuq* would do to take me to Dhofar, down what the first-century *Periplus* called the Coast of the Fish-eaters. I would be reversing the direction of IB's voyage; but bureaucracy had insisted I begin my visit to Oman in Muscat, and the word there was that Sur, not Dhofar, was the place for boats.

A moment of elementary reasoning would have revealed that if any coasting vessels actually did sail from Sur to Dhofar they would be obliged, barring shipwreck or global circumnavigation, to return by the same route. Somehow the syllogism escaped me.

★

Bureaucracy has its advantages. The Omani Ministry of Information put me up at the Muscat Gulf Hotel and Resort, a place designed for a thoroughly different class of traveller from me. Over the next few days, big silent American cars took me on a round of official visits.

Muscat has changed since IB passed through. Then, it was a fairly insignificant fishing port. Little was different even as late as the 1960s. Now, under the 'Renaissance' presided over by Sultan Qabus, Muscat has become not so much a city as a consuburbation linked by gleaming freeways, where the residential areas are traffic-calmed into a state of permanent weekend hush. The Omani capital was once notoriously filthy; today you can be fined for driving a dirty car.

A process of architectural homogenization is going on. Villas sprout vestigial crenellations, machicolated air-conditioner surrounds and castellated plastic water tanks. Bus shelters and telephone kiosks are also designed in the Omani-baronial taste. At the same time, old Omani forts have been restored so thoroughly that they resemble the villas. It is all rather like making sandcastles with those cheat buckets that mould a perfect one every time. And the deception goes further. I met a man in Fez who had worked as a fort restorer in Oman. 'We workers were all Moroccans,' he said. 'But if any journalists showed up, they hid us away and brought out Omanis, who pretended to work for the cameras.'

When it comes to road beautification, however, the designers' imagination breaks free. Vast incense-burners jostle for attention on roundabouts with outsize coffee pots and rosewater-sprinklers; fibreglass oryxes, Bambis and merry-go-round horses prance over verges; pirate chests brim with hoards of fake treasure, and giant oysters gape, disclosing nonsuch plastic pearls. I recently noticed a review of a book called *The Artificial Kingdom: A Treasury of the Kitsch Experience*. The title took me straight back to Muscat.

Some highway art, however, transcends the kitsch. In the north of Oman, I saw a roundabout near Suhar with an apparently simple decorative concept – a circle of concrete palm trees. What made it remarkable was the context: all around were acres and acres of real palms. I could only assume that the concrete palms, like Meret Oppenheim's furry teacup, were making some metaphysical statement about form and matter.

The theme park theme overspills the Capital Area. The city's surroundings, described by an early traveller as 'vast and horrid mountains', are an ideal setting for leisure pursuits like rock-climbing, and wadi-bashing – which one does in a plush jeep, very carefully, so as not to jolt the ice-box unduly. One can even go on a guided tour to Umm al-Samim, Thesiger's dreaded quicksands.

To stock up for a wadi-bash, a single visit to the supermarket is sufficient. Here, the only indication that you are in Far Arabia is the separate Pork Room. Living in porkless Yemen, the first time I saw one I found the display of naked flesh and huge mottled salamis as shocking, as fascinating as a sex-shop. I ogled; IB would have fainted on the spot.

My official visits over, I got in touch with a friend of a friend, a man of *shaykh*ly lineage. He suggested meeting that evening at the Ghala Wentworth Golf Club. Although it was my first experience of a golf club, I imagined the ambience of the place – the honours boards and trophies, the personal tankards above the bar, the bon-homie – to be pure Surrey. The members, however, were more exotic. Portly scions of the ruling houses of Muscat and Zanzibar held court and stood rounds; a heroically pissed Irishman was, he said, 'keeping an eye on things for, hic, shecurity reasons'.

Here in the Royal and Ancient – or rather Sultanic and Modern – of Muscat, we dined splendidly on mussels, beefsteaks and cherry pie. The claret was, according to one member of our party, an experienced courtier in a navy and cream co-respondent *dishdashah*, most acceptable. 'You see,' he said, swirling and sniffing a sample from yet another bottle, 'I am what is called *un bon viveur* – or does one say *vivant*?' The question provoked heated discussion. Then, as the bottles emptied, we began swapping poetry and jokes. The only one that has survived the night's oblivion concerned a certain Gulf ruler. During a television interview, he was asked what his favourite leisure activity was. 'Fucking,' he replied. 'Cut! Cut!' cried the Minister of Information, one of the ruler's sons. 'Father, this is a family show. Can't you say something *nice*? Reading, for instance.' Take two: 'And what is Your Highness's favourite leisure activity?' 'Reading ... ' the *shaykh* said, 'about fucking.'

Some time after midnight, my companion and I followed the courtier back to his house. Gilded gates glided open automatically, and we parked inside next to a Bentley. We entered a gorgeous salon, all marble and glass, hung with nineteenth-century orientalist oils and echoing with Sinatra. A silent Indian cupbearer kept us supplied with burgundy. Thereafter I remember only fragments: a line of empty bottles; peeing wildly at a lavatory decorated with tiny hand-painted roses; the courtier's voice saying, 'Aaah! Savour those plums . . . '

I awoke late next morning fully clothed, down to my walking shoes, back in the house of the British friend who was putting me up. Beside me was the evidence, the Cinderella's slipper that proved the night had not been a fantasy – a large box of Romeo y Julieta Churchills. My head was remarkably clear, and occupied with a single, nagging thought: not much inverse archaeology is getting done.

Not much could be, here in Oman proper. After his disastrous walk from Sur to Qalhat, IB had made only a brief excursion into the interior before crossing the Strait of Hormuz to Persia. The bulk of what he wrote on what is now the Sultanate of Oman concerns its southern province, Dhofar, and the adjacent coasts and islands. My Battutian checklist for the region was varied: it included betel, frankincense and dried sardines, houses made of fishes' bones and, a very long shot, a saint's cell in the Kuria Muria Islands – one of the most out-of-the-way spots in the history of eremism.

★

Sur, then, was the place for boats. The morning after my hike to Qalhat, I walked down to the creek. Clearly the place to start was over in the skippers' suburb of al-Ayjah, which I now believed to be IB's landing place.

'Yesterday,' the ferryman told me, 'Khalfan's *sambuq* left for Salalah.'

This was promising news. I was quite happy to wait for the next one.

'It's a pity you missed it. The last time anyone did the trip was, oh, years ago.'

This was appalling news. I dismissed it at once.

Al-Ayjah was a salty old place. Rocky outcrops rang with the blows of shipwrights' hammers. Down on the shore the swelling bellies of *sambuqs* grew plank by plank from *munaybari*, Malabar teak. Old sailors sat in doorways carved in the manner of Calicut and Zanzibar, wearing *dishdashahs* with embroidered yokes – the Omani equivalent of the Aran sweater; like Superman they wore their underwear, a checked waistcloth, on the outside, to protect the skirt of the robe from fishy stains. Everyone confirmed that Khalfan had sailed for Salalah the day before; no one held out any hope of another Dhofar-bound boat. My plans drifted steadily up the creek.

'The trouble is', said the ferryman on the way back, 'no one does the long distances any more. They just put out at night to fish and come back in the morning.' I stared, disconsolate, into the reflective waters of the creek, thinking of the days when Sayyid Sa'id had ruled a seaborne empire of cloves and slaves; when, between them, the Omanis and the British had controlled the western Indian Ocean. 'You could try the new harbour,' the ferryman suggested, sensing my despair.

The new harbour was still being built. In the works office I called on the Project Manager, a bearded Keralan in his fifties. He gave me his card: MR K. JOHNSON ITTY IPE. (I never discovered whether the last two elements were part of his name, or his professional qualifications.) On the wall of the office hung charts detailing shapes and sizes of accropodes – which sounded like some species of Gulf crustacean, but are in fact large T-ended concrete lumps used for building moles – and a quotation from the Letter to the Hebrews, 'Follow peace with all men'. Mr Johnson implemented the advice with a stream of workers, cantering nimbly between Malayalam, English and Hindi. When the stream slackened we went to the harbour.

The mole was growing slowly, like an immense three-dimensional jigsaw puzzle. 'It's my fifth,' Mr Johnson said as we walked along it. We talked of IB's visit to Kerala – Mr Johnson remembered studying the account from the *Travels* at school, in Malayalam – of God and His role in Mr Johnson's escape from al-Khafji when the Iraqis invaded, and of his career. 'I wanted to be a film director,' he told me, 'but my father made me study engineering.'

I looked at the harbour, at the huge and expensive equipment, the disciplined workforce. 'Don't you think directing a harbour is rather like directing a film?'

Mr Johnson's eyes shone. I couldn't imagine him as a Bollywood type. He seemed more of an individualist, a Werner Herzog, perhaps, of the mole-building business.

We hailed a man on a tug and asked where it was going. 'To al-Anji,' the man called back. Further off lay another vessel, a fine

wooden *bum*. I looked at it across the bright water, shielding my eyes
from the sun, and saw a gleaming brass-sheathed prow and brass portholes. Again, illogically, my hopes rose: if any vessel were going to
Dhofar, this had to be it. Mr Johnson summoned a Maldivian
boatman, and we puttered over the water to the *bum*. It was about to
sail: for Dubai, on the return leg of a businessmen's outing. My hopes
sank like a heaved lead.

On the way back into town, I reflected that while the old patterns
of travel seemed to have disappeared, some things hadn't changed. A
Maldivian boatman, an engineer from the coconut coast of India,
teak from Malabar – the network of Indian Ocean ramifications IB
had known was still in place. Here in Sur, Gujarat was closer than
Salalah, and not only in terms of cartographic distance. Knots of
Indian subcontinentals loitered in the late-afternoon sun; others
crowded into moneychangers' shops, busily remitting their earnings
home. In the fourteenth century, Arabs like IB had headed for the
Sultanate of Delhi, drawn by its immense wealth. In the twentieth,
however, the demographic tide turned: the Gulf is now as much
Indian as Arab.

A by-product of this vast movement of labour has been the appearance of a new language, Indo-Arabic. Vocabulary is slimmed down to
an anorexic minimum, and the vigorous branches of the Arabic verb
pruned to a binary *fi* ('in' = 'there is') / *ma fi* ('not in' = 'there is not')
+ infinitive. (A neat example is that of an Indian Muslim who passed
a graveyard. His version of the traditional *memento mori* – 'You [the
dead] are those that precede; we are those that follow' – came out as,
'You there is go; I there is come.') Omanis seem to be bilingual;
I never quite got the hang of it.

That evening, my plans in tatters, I could face neither my diary nor
any of the books I had brought. The only other reading matter in the
hotel room was the telephone directory. It began with the Green
Pages, which list members of the Sultan's family and other dignita-
ries. I considered brightening the evening up by paging a princess, or
even ringing the Sultan himself. Then a thought struck me: I had
heard that Qabus employed a court organist, whom he summoned
from time to time in the small hours to play a chorale prelude from
Bach's *Orgelbüchlein*. I was still on the right side of that career
Rubicon, forty, and it wasn't too late for a change ... I had been an
Oxford organ scholar (admittedly not at one of the more musically

famous colleges) and, briefly, organist of a Levantine cathedral; perhaps I could insinuate myself into what sounded like a pleasant sinecure. The Sultan would surely thrill to my organ arrangement of Mozart's 'Adagio and Rondo for Glass Harmonica'. And who knew where it might lead? In the 1920s Bertram Thomas, another amateur musician and Arabian traveller from Bristol, had virtually run Oman as vizier to Qabus's grandfather. The Sultan's personal number, however, was listed neither in the Green Pages nor under his portrait at the beginning of the directory.

I studied the face in the portrait – the copper skin, white beard and black eyebrows beneath a magenta, purple and orange turban. The image, so formal in pose yet so surprisingly coloured, might have been taken from a Mamluk miniature; indeed, I thought, it may be that in his magnificence, his capriciousness, in the absoluteness of his rule and his manner of achieving it (like IB's two great patrons, the sultans of Delhi and of the Maghrib, Sultan Qabus overthrew his father) he is, of all contemporary monarchs, the one most like those of the *Travels*. That organist's job needn't be a career change: it could be a chance to do some really profound inverse archaeology. Or could have been, had not the winged chariots of mortality been bearing down on me.

Having exhausted the possibilities of the telephone directory, I turned to my map. If I couldn't sail down the Coast of the Fish-eaters, I would have to motor down it. This, of course, was assuming that I could find transport. Most of the coast road was classed as 'Graded'; however, where the Wahibah Sands – a dune desert the size of Wales – meet the Indian Ocean, it became an 'Other Track'. More worryingly, there was a short but significant-looking gap in this Other Track. Then, five hundred miles from Sur, on the shore of Kuria Muria Bay, the road reached a place called Qanawt, and ran out. In the middle of the fifty-mile lacuna before it picked up again, and marooned like an onshore island at the base of the 6,000-foot Jabal Samhan, lay the small settlement of Hasik, visited by IB. From here onwards stretched misty, thuriferous Dhofar, along the coast to Salalah, then to Raysut, Rakhyut, Khirfut, Dalkut and the modern border with Yemen, beyond which the toponymic monorhyme continued.

Strangely, despite the gaps in the route and the uncertainties of hitching along six hundred miles (not counting the kinks) of some

of the most thinly populated coastline in the world, my spirits had
risen. Robert Burton was right: maps are a certain cure for melancholy. Even the small print at the bottom of this one – 'The depiction
of a road or track does not imply a satisfactory motorable surface.
The general public should not attempt to travel along routes not
served by maintained roads.' – did not diminish my new feelings of, if
not exactly optimism, then at least agreeable fatalistic acceptance. I
almost allowed myself to wonder if I might catch up with Khalfan's
sambuq.

★

Next morning I crossed the creek to al-Ayjah and walked a mile or so
to the *bikab* (pick-up) stop for Ras al-Hadd, the Arabian Land's End
where the Gulf of Oman becomes the Indian Ocean. I'd been
waiting only a short time when a boy came up. 'Are you the one
who's looking for a boat?' he asked. I nodded. 'Well, there's a *sambuq*
in the creek leaving for al-Khuwaymah.'

The Evil Eye, according to some Arabs, has a partner called the
Eye of Joy. Its speciality is disappointment. Count chickens before
they hatch, and the Eye of Joy will addle the eggs. 'You're having me
on,' I replied, hoping the Eye of Joy had ears to hear.

'No, it's true,' he insisted.

As a further placatory gesture to the Eye, I left my bag with an
Indian shopkeeper by the *bikab* stop. 'I there is come, same-same bag
half hour *in sha Allah*,' I ventured. 'There is known?'

'Okey-doke,' said the shopkeeper, wobbling his head.

I walked back to the creek slowly, conscious that the Eye was
peeled for any overt signs of optimism.

The *sambuq* was indeed going to al-Khuwaymah, a small place at
the end of the graded road and a whole fifth of the way to Dhofar!
I returned briskly to the shop, picked up my bag and trotted back
down to the creek. I hoped the short voyage would take as long as
possible: my diary badly needed writing up; and there would be
turtles to watch, and dolphins.

The skipper was profuse in his apologies. There was something
very wrong with the engine; the *sambuq* was not going to al-
Khuwaymah, or anywhere else. The Eye of Joy winked lubriciously.

I trudged back to the *bikab* stop, cursing the Eye, my heavy bag and
my walking shoes which, out of sheer spite, had given me a Battutian

blister. In consolation, a *bikab* arrived immediately. It dropped me twenty miles on at an *istirahah*, a 'rest room' – euphemism for a busless bus shelter – outside the village of Ras al-Hadd. There were boats everywhere, miniature *hawri*s, *bum*s and *sambuq*s on columns and triumphal gateways, mocking my travel plans as the sea had mocked the Ancient Mariner's thirst.

The outskirts of Ras al-Hadd were deserted. Knowing now that to travel hopelessly was the only way to arrive, I made myself at home in the shelter and contemplated the long wait ahead. As a result, a series of lifts – Keralan, Goan, Pakistani and Omani – took me down the coast with wondrous rapidity. Every so often we passed a little pavilion on the shore, in the middle of nowhere. Except that nowhere was completely nowhere: at regular intervals there were wooden shops, 'Food Stuff Sale and Luxuries', run by Indians. I wondered if they were victims of some dreadful inundation in Malabar, swept out to sea by the monsoon and washed up here, goods and all.

By mid-afternoon I was in al-Khuwaymah. It was the end of the road and felt like it. With its single street of Indian-run shops, it might have stood in for Tombstone, Arizona, if Bollywood ever made a chapatti Western. There was, it seemed, no hope of transport on the Other Track that headed south between the Wahibah Sands and the ocean and which, by all accounts, was 'very bad'. I remembered the enigmatic gap on the map.

Down on the beach I expressed my feelings towards al-Khuwaymah by chucking a pebble at a stupid, kitschy model boat on a pedestal. Another column supported a crudely painted terrestrial globe on which Africa, Arabia and Asia were separated by blue sea. Another ritual lapidation; then violence gave way to the morbids. I felt islanded, like those drifting continents.

Two Pakistani brothers, motor mechanics, took pity on me and fed me *roti* and *dhal* in their workshop. My depression lifted slightly as we discussed the recent débâcle of the bumpy test pitch in Jamaica (the brothers were from Sialkot, the cricket bat capital of the world), the political début of Imran Khan (which they found amusing), and Qur'anic and Biblical accounts of the Ascension (tricky in a mix of Indo-Arabic and English). Afterwards I bedded down outside the workshop, to be woken twice in the night – by a shower of rain, and by a rat scuttling over my head.

Breakfast was *roti* and *dhal*. The brothers started working on an outboard motor, while I went and sat by the road under a matt sky. As the morning wore on, the sky took on a slight polish. I looked at my watch. The morning hadn't worn on at all: I had been sitting there for five minutes. Time is never so elastic as when one travels. It is motion measured; when motion stops, so does time.

At ten o'clock I made the decision to turn back; then realized that in practice it was meaningless for there was no transport either way. The Pakistanis, however, seemed keen for me to stay. They were shocked at the idea of payment, but at least I could give them English lessons and novelty value. I resigned myself to *roti* and *dhal*, to measuring out the days, perhaps the weeks, *lento*, in lentils.

Then, towards noon, came the sound of approaching cars. My hopes rocketed; then fell like a spent stick – it was an army patrol. They skidded to a halt, three jeeps bulging with jerrycans and bristling with guns and aerials. The soldiers leapt off, raffish in desert camouflage, headscarves and goggles. 'So you didn't find your boat,' one of them said.

I recognized him as a taxi driver who had given me a ride in Sur. 'No. And now I'm stuck here.'

The soldier spoke privately to the lieutenant, who then turned to me. 'We'll give you a lift.'

I almost kissed him.

Two minutes later we were whizzing along the beach – the Other Track – under a now mercurial sky between two oceans, of sand and of water. We chased flocks of gulls, sending them shrieking and glittering into the air. It was as good as sailing. I thumbed my nose at the Eye of Joy.

The duties of the Sultan's Armed Forces Shore Security Patrol were not onerous. We stopped to buy a small shark from some fishermen, then to examine what looked from a distance like a piece of modernist civic sculpture. It was a long-dead beached whale. 'It is full of worms,' said the lieutenant, as it quivered under our exploratory proddings like a great grey blancmange. I tried to imagine this inert, axungious blob alive, flexing and somersaulting through the deep ocean between Hasik and the Kuria Murias. The thought reminded me of IB's houses made of fishes' bones.

Some forty miles from al-Khuwaymah we reached the gap in the map: a series of tremendous dunes like beached white whales. This last convulsion of the Wahibah Sands was banked up against rocks

that fell straight into the sea, forming a barrier that looked insur-
mountable. The other two jeeps attempted the easiest dune, charging
its flank then, before reaching the crest, sliding back down sideways.

It was our turn. 'Hang on with all your strength,' the lieutenant
shouted. I grasped the machine-gun mounting. 'And don't hold us
responsible', he yelled as the sky raced towards us, 'for any . . . ' We
took off. My stomach hit my tonsils.

We landed, and glissaded elegantly down the far side of the dune.

As if shamed into action, the other two jeeps leapt the crest immediately. While we were exchanging congratulations, I noticed a
wetness about my trousers. I looked down and saw a red stain on the
right leg: I must have bashed my shin as we took off. The soldiers
bandaged it up deftly while the lieutenant looked on, concerned.
'Don't worry,' I said, as the pain came on. 'It'll be a fine souvenir of
our trip together.' I still have the scar.

They dropped me off at a place called al-Shannah, a café and a
quay on the margin of a mirage-haunted salt-flat. Again, the main-
spring of time wound down.

At first I was the only customer. But over the long course of the
afternoon the population of the café grew as other passengers arrived –
by the sensible, inland route – for the ferry to Masirah Island. One of
them thought I was a Moroccan. 'I just wondered,' he said. 'You look
like one. And not long ago a Maghribi traveller came through here.
He said he'd visited thirty countries.' A sensation passed through me
as it had on the track to Qalhat – that faint, follicular thrill that comes
when you realize you may not be alone.

The ferry came after sunset, and I boarded with the other passengers. A visit to the island would be something of a departure from IB.
'We came next to the Island of Masirah,' he wrote, 'to which the
master of the ship that we were sailing on belonged. It is a large
island, whose inhabitants have nothing to eat but fish. We did not
land on it, because of the distance of the anchorage from the shore;
besides, I had taken a dislike to these people.' IB had been put off the
Masiris by their violation of an important dietary rule of Islam: earlier
in the voyage, they had stopped at an uninhabited island and stocked
up on edible seabirds. They killed the birds, however, not by slitting
their throats but by wringing their necks, a shocking thing for a pious
Muslim like IB.

In contrast to IB, I had rather taken to the only Masiri I had met (many years before, at a performance of Humperdinck's *Hansel und Gretel*). Now, curiosity was leading me to the island, but also a thread of hope. I was reasonably confident that Khalfan's *sambuq* would visit Masirah on its way down the coast; even if I had missed it, there might be other possibilities. After all, the very best ancient and medieval authorities wrote of Masirah's importance as a shipping centre – the first-century *Periplus*, for instance, spoke of a constant trade with the Yemeni frankincense port of Qana. 'Yonder looms the island,' I hummed as the ferry waddled across the straits, 'yonder lie the ships . . . '

The harbour, of course, was empty. I found my way to the island's only hotel. It was locked and unlit, but a scrap of paper on the door said 'Welcome. Hotel Open'. I knocked, then called into the darkness. Eventually, a sleepy Indian appeared from the shadows. He unlocked the door, found the register and motioned that I should sign myself in.

On the Indian's part, the transaction took place in silence. All my efforts at conversation were met with mute smiles. Finally I tried the most basic approach possible: 'I,' I said, pointing at myself, 'Tim. There is name, you?' I pointed at him.

'Abu Kalam,' he said, grinning. The Father of Speech.

Abu Kalam showed me to a large room that had that newly unwrapped smell of wood-glue and fresh polythene. I had the feeling I might be the first tourist on Masirah.

In the morning I could see why. Masirah was not exactly the Ibiza of the Arabian Sea. You could eat fish, as in the days of the *Periplus*. You could watch planes taking off from the airforce base. You could use your Visa card in the Oman International Bank, and call direct to the Windward Islands from the public phone box. You could buy a packet of Frosties in the Food Stuff and Luxuries, or a 'tummy trimmer' – I listened in admiration as a lady in a wet-look mask discussed its benefits with the shopkeeper in fluent Indo-Arabic. What you could not do was find a boat to Dhofar.

Down at the quay I learned from some fishermen that I had indeed missed Khalfan's *sambuq* again. They seemed to regard coasting to Salalah as a quaint and slightly foolhardy form of travel. 'Our fathers' generation', one of them told me, 'used to sail to al-Mukalla, Bombay, everywhere. Now the Sultan's built roads and airports, and we just go out fishing around the island.' The words of Abdullah al-

Jumahi of Jabalah came back to me, not for the first time: 'You have to remember you're talking about a long time ago.' It didn't matter whether the time difference was a generation, six hundred years or – in the case of the *Periplus* – two thousand. In Oman, everything pre-Qabus was a long time ago.

'Of course, you might be able to get a lift in the *sikayfan*,' suggested another fisherman. I looked blank. 'From the airbase,' he explained. The exotic-sounding word, I realized, must represent something like 'Skyvan'. It sounded most undignified.

'If you want to be IB,' the first fisherman said, 'then you'll have to buy your own boat.'

On the character of the Masiris both IB and the *Periplus*, which called them 'a villainous lot', are gravely mistaken. Hamud, an employee of the bank, invited me to lunch at the house of his wife's family. It was a series of rooms set around an airy courtyard, entered via a little gothic doorway. We ate a mound of rice and mutton – the meat slaughtered, I have no doubts, according to the strictest Islamic principles.

After lunch Hamud's young brothers-in-law showed me their school history textbook. It contained a chapter on 'IB in Oman' followed by comprehension questions and an essay title – 'Compare and contrast today's Oman with that described by IB, with special reference to the civilizational progress which the Sultanate has witnessed.' It was, I told the boys, rather what I was trying to do. (I didn't add that, being a fourteenth-century fogey, I wasn't making the assumption implicit in the second phrase.) As we read through the text together, I realized that something was wrong: it had been *censored*. The grumbles about un*halal* seabirds and the guide from Sur to Qalhat had evaporated off the page; suggestions elsewhere that the Omanis enjoyed eating donkeys, and that 'their womenfolk are much given to debauchery', had also been excised. It was a travesty of the *Travels*.

I recalled a bowdlerized Egyptian edition I had come across, published in 1939 for the use of students. 'We cannot conceal from the reader', the introduction said, 'the fact that IB's pen, in unguarded moments, recorded words and expressions from which pudency should avert its gaze. We have therefore diligently sought out and erased such passages, in order zealously to preserve the modesty of students whose eyes might otherwise have fallen upon, or whose ears overheard, that which they would consider shocking.' Sales of the unexpurgated edition must have soared.

After lunch, Hamud presented me with an Oman International Bank diary drenched in scent. He then sprayed me and the tassel of his *dishdashah*, which the Omanis use as a sort of pomander, with what seemed to be a good half-bottle of *eau-de-toilette*. Reeking like a pair of courtesans, we set off in his Landcruiser for a tour of the island. As I had already suspected, IB hadn't missed much. Masirah seemed to be composed of expanses of khaki gravel, set at slightly different inclinations and dotted with occasional shack-like settlements. 'Mainlanders always think we're a bit of a backwater,' said Hamud. I nodded sympathetically. 'But we have a saying: "Masirah's not short. Masirah is the neck of Oman." ' He wasn't entirely sure what the saying meant.

That evening I sat in the hotel room and wrote up my diary. Outside, the wind sighed along the shore. I got to the end of the day's entry, then had a thought: why not carry on writing? Mandeville had made up large parts of his *Travels* and so, according to recent scholarship, had Marco Polo. The hotel was cheap by Omani standards, and I certainly wasn't going to be disturbed by the Father of Speech. On second thoughts, I realized that you couldn't get away with it these days. The time was long past when travellers, according to the old proverb, might lie by authority.

I looked at the map and saw that I was only a third of the way from Sur to Salalah. There was absolutely no doubt in my mind that IB, in my position, would have gone to the airbase and wheedled a lift in the *sikayfan*. Perhaps that was the answer. I would decide tomorrow.

The following morning I sat in a café eating fried eggs and delaying the decision. In the event, it was made for me. I had been complaining to the only other customer about the lack of boats, when he told me he was about to leave for a village on the mainland to pick up some fish. 'It's a couple of hundred miles nearer Salalah. Why don't you come along?'

I studied him for a moment. With his insouciantly tied headscarf, thick beard, gold teeth and nascent paunch, he had the look of a podgy pirate. He also looked highly amused by the mere idea of the trip. 'Why not?' I said.

He regarded me quizzically; then, as if he had just got a punchline, burst out laughing.

On the way to the quay, Khamis explained that he had a boat at the distant village, together with half a dozen fishermen and a pick-up with a giant ice-box on the back. When the ice-box was full, he would drive across the desert and sell the catch in the Emirates. For the moment, we would be hitching.

To cross to the mainland we boarded a launch which they called a *stimah*, pronounced 'steamer'. Seconds after it had got going, Khamis began waving his arms and shouting, in English, 'My snake! My snake!' We returned to the quay. Khamis had forgotten his camel-stick. After the false start, we flew across the waves. The twenty-mile crossing, an hour and a half in the ferry, took twenty minutes. I now understood why I had seen launches with names like *MIG Fighter*.

Our first lift dropped us at a small settlement where Khamis had relations by marriage. We went to their compound and found a group of solemnly beautiful men sitting around a mat. Greetings were *badw*-style, a long fluid concatenation of prayers and inquiries after health, punctuated by a delicate meeting of the tips of noses – the southern Arabian kiss – and ending in, 'Is there news?' 'No news.'

'Is there information?' 'No information.', after which the news and information, such as they were, were exchanged. We took our seats around the mat and a boy poured coffee. Then a masked lady arrived and extended her hand to each of us. The hand was covered in the gauziest of veils. I grasped and shook it; then noticed that the others were merely brushing the tips of her fingers. With shocking clarity, a comment of Bertram Thomas's came to me: 'For a man to squeeze a girl's hand, or clasp it as in a European handshake, is to make an improper overture, for which the girl's relations may take blood.'

Later, waiting by the side of the road, I asked Khamis about the blunder. '*You shook it?*' he exclaimed, horrified. He made a sickening throat-slitting gesture, then collapsed in laughter.

A short way into our next lift, in a lorry driven by a Goan, Khamis asked if I wanted a drink. I said I wasn't thirsty, but he reached into his bag and pulled out something which confirmed, in his case at least, IB's thoughts about the impious Masiris: a bottle of 'Major Gunn's' Scotch whisky. The bottle was followed by a flat object of curious shape, like a symmetrical ink-blot. It was a small shark, split, boned and dried. We bounced along, swigging scotch and eating shark, Khamis tearing at it with his gleaming pirate's teeth. The Goan turned down the offer of a drink; he kept glancing at us and drove as fast as possible, as if wanting to be rid of these obviously dangerous passengers.

I asked Khamis about IB's Island of Birds, which lay off the coast somewhere along our route but which was invisible from the road. Khamis agreed with Gibb's suggestion that it was an island called al-Humar. 'It stands straight up in the sea, like a pillar,' he told me, 'and it's covered in birds.' I had found out from an article by Michael Gallagher, the doyen of Arabian ornithologists, that these are Socotra cormorants. Khamis shuddered when I asked if he had tried his ancestral delicacy, and took a hefty slug of Major Gunn's to take away the imagined taste. When I told him that I looked forward to sampling cormorant in the Kuria Murias and, with luck, the masked booby – another island dainty – he looked away and muttered, 'Crazy man'.

Around sunset we had a lift with a large Sikh in the construction business, Mr B.S. Mann. Much of the whisky had been drunk, and I gave in to an inexcusable fit of the giggles.

Khamis elbowed me. 'Crazy man! What are you laughing about?'

I got a grip on myself. 'It's . . . it's the pickwickles.'

'What are "pickwickles"?'

'I don't know. Mr Mann, what are these pickwickles you've been talking about?'

'You are English,' said Mr Mann, surprised, 'and are not knowing pickwickles? They are JCBs, artics, etcetera etcetera.'

' "Big vehicles",' explained Khamis, who was fluent in English, Hindi, Urdu and their various mutations.

It was late when we arrived at the one-roomed blockhouse where Khamis's fishermen lived, and we tiptoed unsteadily across the yard. The door was open. A couple of the men were asleep in the dark corners of the room. In the middle, the others were playing cards by the light of a lamp: they were bare-chested, onyx-eyed, aware of nothing but the game. Khamis was about to speak, but I raised my hand to stop him. I wanted to watch the card-players, far away on their tiny continent of light.

In the morning we launched the boat, four of the fishermen and I, and motored south for an hour or so. We rounded a headland where currents clashed and threw up sharp, short-tempered waves, then anchored in the calm of a wide bay. Talk ceased. The only sounds were the hiss and plop of lines, and of the sea as it nudged the hull, gently but insistently, like a hungry cat rubbing against its owner's legs. The men worked with a rhythmic grace: a flash of hennaed palm, a gleaming parabola across the water, a quick twitch as the fish bit.

We lunched on tinned pineapple and cigars, then the fishing resumed. My diary records the catch:

Sardines, for bait; *shuʿn̄*, which I ate on Masirah (where they call it *ʿayṣab*) with sky-blue squiggles; a big one called *kanāfah*, *subaytī* or *maryūm* (maybe *marjūm* – hard to tell); speckled *naqrūr*; ruddy *ḥamūr*, grouper I think – Jum'ah catches one a yard long that looks surprised as it comes over the edge – big lips, old and grey, something like Kingsley Amis; long silvery *sayf randūh*; black-hatched *bint al-nawkhadhah* (lovely name! ['the captain's daughter']) with orange stripes; *qishbīb*, with gold anodized backs; *takwah*; *ḍāfah*; *afrāh*; also plenty of inedible (they say) *ḥawīn*, those sickly looking moray eels, which they treat with great caution. Marzuq hooks something huge. They don't know what it is until it appears above the waves: a turtle, which they call *missah*. It breaks the line and disappears. Much distress that they haven't been able to pull it in, extract the hook and release it. At one point a large shark's fin circles us.

If we caught a *shīr māhī*, the fish on which IB lived during his voyage through these waters, we caught it under a different name. Now, as I lay between the fishermen, within four parts of silent harmony, four lines so sinuously plied, it hardly seemed to matter. The fourteenth century was far away, and so was the twentieth, as we bobbed in the eternal present on Sawqirah Bay.

★

My sea fever had been cooled by the day's fishing, and I knew I had to get on. Khamis and the fishermen told me that the Kuria Murias were best approached from the Dhofar end, and that the prospects of transport along the coast were slender. The following morning I headed reluctantly inland.

The day began with the greatest imaginable rarity of Arabian travel, an unalloyed *mirabile*, a hen's tooth, a mare's nest: a lift with a woman. She wore a gold mask and treated the straight road and horizontal plain like a downhill slalom. She dropped me somewhere in Jiddat al-Harasis, an East Anglia of gravel where gazelles leap under an immense sky. Another lift, then several hours in a place called al-Aja'iz, the Old Women. On the main Muscat–Salalah road, I was comfortably benighted in the Quitbit Resthouse.

Next morning a lorry of excruciating slowness took me across a minimal, almost a nihilistic landscape – a mere joint between earth and sky, both the colour of plaster. The rare verticals, a milepost or the odd lone bush, assumed enormous significance. At Thumrayt I boarded a minibus.

The change was sudden and disorientating: one minute a Venusian desert, the next, green and rolling moors, cowpats and fat cattle. Then, just as my vision had adjusted, we began to drop down to a shining plain, down to the ocean and Salalah, whose name means the Glittering One.

Dhofar

The Importance of Being Rasulid

' "Are you quite sure you are pure-bred?" '

Bertram Thomas, anthropologizing in *Arabia Felix*

THAT NIGHT, SALALAH glittered. Two society weddings were in full swing, and troupes of plump women and thin girls tottered from one party to the other wearing gilded platform sandals, long-tailed dresses with the trains gathered over one arm, and what looked like the entire stock of the Salalah gold *suq*. The women rattled audibly above the thump of amplified nuptial music; Indian maids shadowed them, like bum-boats in a convoy of treasure galleons. But there was something even more arresting than this mass movement of bullion: the women's faces. Each was thickly plastered in white, the eyes bordered by black lines that swept upwards, geisha-style; three green dots descended the chin, with more green along the jawline; other lines swept back on either side of the nose, which was finished off with large spots of boot-polish black on each nostril lobe. At first sight, it looked as if a game with a make-up box had gone horribly wrong. But seen *en masse*, together with all that gold, the maquillage suggested the splendid as much as the sinister – the Thesmophoriazousae, perhaps, on a shopping spree in Ophir.

I watched the spectacle from a café, wide-eyed. My neighbour, however, was from distant Muscat and was not impressed. 'They are slaves,' he said, looking at the ghostly faces. 'Why can't they resign themselves to their allotted fate of blackness?'

Next morning, Habibah admitted that she often felt a bit under-dressed when out and about in Dhofari society. 'They don't put on all that stuff every day, though,' she explained. 'Only for a ladies' dance called *al-tabl*.' (Joyce Grenfell came to mind:

> So gay the band,
> So giddy the sight,
> Full evening dress is a must,
> But the zest goes out of a beautiful waltz
> When you dance it bust to bust.)

Habibah was the perfect hostess. She was a keen collector of Dhofari lore and gossip, and a talented cook. In Salalah I grew fat on chickens in *mulukhiyyah*, mutton with garlic and okra, and the fish called Sultan Ibrahim, fried and dipped in sesame paste. The *mulukhiyyah* always took me back to Cairo and our first meeting, in the City of the Dead, in a house full of sisters and bewitching smells near the mausoleum of Qayt Bey. Muhammad, a friend originally from Birmingham, had fallen in love with – *inter alia* – Habibah's nose. He took me to plead his case with her father. My speech was finely honed, thickly honeyed; he consented, they married. They worked in Cairo, England and Hungary, and were now living in a villa in the coconutty suburbs of Salalah. From here, Muhammad inspected schools while Habibah explored areas of local culture which few outsiders have penetrated. Who else could have told me that Dhofari men like hair on a woman's legs?

'Don't expect us to drink your bathwater,' she had warned me when I arrived.

'I'm sorry?'

She picked up a book – a Lebanese edition of the *Travels* – and opened it at a marked page: ' "When we washed our hands after the meal," ' she read, ' "one of the sons of Shaykh Abu Bakr took the water in which we had washed, drank some of it, and sent the servant with the rest of it to his wives and children, and they too drank it. This is what they do with all visitors to them in whom they perceive indications of goodness." ' She shut the book. 'You see, I've been doing my homework.'

I was impressed. Habibah went on: 'The tomb and hospice of Shaykh Abu Bakr, where they entertained IB, are a bit of a problem. They're somewhere inside the Ribat Palace complex, so they may be difficult to get to. The same goes for the tombs of the Rasulid sultans.

But you'll be pleased to know that we're almost next door to al-Balid.'

Again, she had thrown me: *al-balid* means 'the silly man'. 'Who's he?'

Habibah gave me a hermetic look, suggestive of ancient wisdom. 'Al-Balid is a local pronunciation of al-Balad, "Town". In other words IB's City of Zafar, where he stayed with the preacher Isa ibn Ali. I think', she said, smiling, 'I have passed the test to be your research assistant.'

My list of Battutiana for Zafar, or Dhofar, was long, and I could do with help in tracking them down. The list was also varied. Fourteenth-century Dhofar was a cosmopolitan place which belonged not so much to the Arabian Peninsula as to the monsoon. Now far from the familiar central Islamic lands, IB was confronted by the new and the strange: coconuts, dried sardines as animal fodder, slave women running the *suq*, and elephantiasis and scrotal hernias 'from which God preserve us!' All of these I intended to investigate, together with various sites mentioned by IB. It was unfortunate that the hospice and tomb of IB's holy host were out of bounds inside the Sultan's palace; but, as it happened, I had already found the saint's tomb, or part of it, without even trying.

In England several months before, I had happened to ring up an old friend, an historian of Islamic art. We chatted about my travel plans. 'I suppose you'll go looking for that Dhofari holy man IB mentioned,' Venetia said.

'I didn't know you were a fan of IB.'

'Oh, I dip into him now and again. And I co-authored an article on his *shaykh*'s tombstone. It's in London. In the V&A.'

And so, by a fluke, was I, ringing from a public phone in the basement.

The tombstone is covered in dense and accomplished script and decorated with deeply carved mosque lamps. As Venetia points out in her article, it is Gujarati work, probably from Cambay. Also in the Victoria and Albert Museum are two similar stones from the tomb of al-Wathiq, the Rasulid governor of Dhofar and a very great-uncle of my Yemeni friend Hasan. All these monuments had been seen by IB, who noted that the tombs were places of refuge for criminals and discontented soldiers. He would of course have been utterly appalled by their removal – and no less amazed that

they should have ended up in a wonder-house in the distant, barbaric island of Anqiltarah.

The arrival of IB's ship at the city of Dhofar took place in state:

> The sultan's slaves come out to meet ships in a *sambuq*, carrying
> with them a complete set of robes for the owner of the vessel or
> his agent, and also for the captain and the *kirani* [Anglo-Indian
> 'cranny'], who is the ship's clerk. Three horses are brought for
> them, on which they mount and proceed with drums and trum-
> pets playing before them from the seashore to the sultan's
> residence, where they make their salutations to the vizier and
> the *amir jandar* [the commander of the army]. For three nights,
> hospitality is supplied to all who are in the vessel. These people
> do this in order to gain the goodwill of the ship owners, and
> they are men of humility, good dispositions, virtue, and affection
> for strangers.

The sultan of the time, al-Mughith, was a grandson of al-Wathiq
of the V&A tombstone. IB was staying next to the palace but did not
meet him personally. Al-Mughith, he says, was only seen at Friday
prayers; when he emerged from the palace at other times, he always
travelled in a camel litter 'covered with a white curtain embroidered
in gold; the sultan and his familiar ride in it in such a way as not to be
seen' – the medieval equivalent of a limousine with tinted windows.
Moreover, anyone caught gawping was severely beaten:
'Consequently the inhabitants, when they hear that the sultan is at
large, run away from his route.'

Dhofar had been incorporated into the Rasulid state of Yemen by
al-Muzaffar, the great-grandfather of IB's reclusive sultan. I have
quoted this energetic sovereign on the aphrodisiac properties of the
skink; he was also a prolific author on other subjects as diverse as
Islamic jurisprudence and the science of stain removal. Despite his
busy writing schedule, he still found time to conquer Mecca and
extend his rule in other directions. When, in 1278, the Hadrami ruler
of Dhofar impounded a ship from Aden, al-Muzaffar had a perfect
pretext for an expedition. The Rasulid force took so long on the road
that al-Muzaffar grew thin from worry and the rings dropped off his
fingers; but in the event Dhofar fell after a brief resistance. 'Our

troops', he said, 'took five months to reach their goal, and five days to take it.'

The city prospered under the Rasulids, and IB saw it at the height of its wealth. The dynasty, however, fizzled out early in the fifteenth century. As Muhammad and I left the villa to explore the medieval town, I wondered what had happened to the descendants of al-Muzaffar, al-Wathiq and al-Mughith. Judging by my experiences so far, I half expected to bump into a late-twentieth-century Rasulid; then reminded myself that it was all a long time ago.

We came to a break in the coconut groves and a large fenced-off area. Inside was a high mound, the site of the palace which IB called 'the Castle' and an earlier traveller, Ibn al-Mujawir, 'al-Qahirah' – Cairo, the Victorious. We climbed the tell, passing incongruously new-looking walls, and stood in the breeze on the summit. Before us lay a tufty ruin-field that ran down to the shore and the creek, now silted up, where IB had arrived from Africa. Behind, beyond a shining empty interspace lapped by coconut palms, rose the Qara Mountains. This inland vista resembled some imagined geography – the great Gromboolian plain, perhaps, and the Hills of the Chankly Bore.

Towards the shore we found the remains of the dog-legged Sea Gate through which the ships' masters and merchants, crannies, supercargoes and IB had come to Cairo-on-Sea, brought by the monsoon, greeted by fanfares and splendid in robes; now it is lost in a waste of tussocks, smashed bottles, rotting limestone and windblown sand. The mosque, however, presented a different picture: much of the masonry of its walls had been plundered, but the interior had sprouted a small forest of brand-new polygonal columns. Here we were joined by a European archaeologist, who enthused about the process of consolidation which was, he said, only just beginning. He had a gleam in his eye, and clearly belonged to the Knossos school of archaeology.

'I thought archaeologists were meant to dig down, not build up,' said Muhammad after the man had gone.

I had my suspicions about the columns, the new masonry on the palace mound, the cement-block paths which were being laid across the site, and the designer lamp standards which wouldn't have looked out of place by the pool of the Holiday Inn along the road. The site, it seemed, was being turned into a tourist attraction, like the homogenized sandcastle forts of the north. I pictured a visitors' centre where they would display excerpts from IB – minus, of course, nasty smells, messy betel and scrotal hernias. The city of Dhofar had been systematically robbed of its stone by old Sultan Sa'id; now, under his son, the little that remained was being systematically tarted up. 'Places,' quoted al-Maqrizi,

> when you reflect on them, resemble men:
> Some are inclined to happiness, others to grief.

At present, the *genius loci* of the city of Dhofar was not a happy one.

Back home, Qahtan came to tea. He had driven the minibus on the last leg of my journey to Salalah, refused my fare and given me a tour of the city. My first encounter with a Dhofari on home ground confirmed IB's views about their virtue and affection for strangers. Now, Qahtan agreed that the medieval site had an unhappy atmosphere, but put it down to earlier events. 'Al-Balid', he said, 'was destroyed by God. Some people say its inhabitants were wasteful, that they wore fine silks once and then threw them away. Others say that the king was, well,' he looked at the carpet, ' ... going with his daughter, or even that it was the City of Sodom.' These destruction stories were like locusts, swarming, landing in one spot, then passing on elsewhere.

A couple of miles to the west of the medieval city of Dhofar is an area called al-Haffah. Habibah had identified it as IB's commercial suburb, 'al-Harja ... one of the dirtiest, most stinking and fly-ridden of bazaars, because of the quantity of fruit and fish sold in it'. It is still the main shopping centre; but in the Qabusian age the smells have been banished. One aspect of IB's description, however, had not changed.

IB noticed that 'most of the sellers in the bazaar are female slaves, who are dressed in black'. I was delighted to find that, at least in the scent bazaar, nearly all the shop signs bore women's names. Several were staffed by Indians; but in the others the proprietresses themselves were in charge, matrons whose prerogative seemed to be to sit on the pavement. While none was dressed in black, several wore brown, which happened to be that year's black. My eye, however, was caught by a bulky African-looking lady swathed in jazzy prints.

She wore a small gold rosette in one nostril, and a huge coral-studded ring hung, bull-fashion, from the cartilage of her nose, giving her a fearsome aspect. She sat amid her stock, which overspilled the shop on to the pavement – hundreds of bottles and flasks, ranks of incense-burners, and jar upon jar of ingredients to be pounded, compounded and combusted by the ladies of Salalah. She looked like a high priest-ess of olfactory obeah. Her name, according to the board above the shop, was Radiyyah bint al-Da'n Ashur.

I squatted before her like a supplicant at Delphi, and asked about her best grade of frankincense. 'I only stock *najdi*, from the uplands,' she said testily. 'Most of the other stuff's rubbish. But if you were here in the autumn I could give you *hawjiri*.'

'Where's that from?'

'Jabal Samhan – the mountains behind Hasik.'

Hasik! The settlement of fish-bone houses where IB had observed the export of frankincense. I explained what had brought me to Dhofar, and added that women – diplomatically, I omitted the mention of slaves – had run the retail trade in IB's time.

'Did you hear that?' she called to her neighbour. 'He says we women were running the *suq* . . . when? . . . 670 years ago!' Radiyyah beamed. Her slight initial severity had melted away. I took the oppor-tunity of asking her about the unusual make-up worn by wedding guests.

She laughed, a deep contralto. 'Oh, we put that on because we're *khuddam*, slaves.' I flinched at the word IB had used; political correct-ness had clearly not reached Dhofar. 'With these white faces you can't tell the difference between us and the Arab women . . . Anyway, that's the idea. And the other reason is that when there's a wedding on, men think a lot about sex. If their wives are made up like this, the husbands won't look at other women. Their own wives look like brides.'

'But surely it makes the problem worse: *all* the women look like brides.'

'Ah,' she said, 'you are a clever man. Perhaps our men are stupid, no?'

I noticed the 'no', and realized that Radiyyah's speech was littered with these little rising interrogatives. IB too had heard them: 'Every sentence they speak they follow up with "no?" So for example they say "You eat, no? You walk, no? You do so-and-so, no?" ' He located the phenomenon in Qalhat. In both Sur and Tiwi I had kept my ears

open for it. Now I realized that either the dialectic quirk – the equivalent of the 'innit' of Estuarine English – had migrated, or IB had
misplaced it by several hundred miles.

Not a great squatter, I found my legs had seized up. Radiyyah,
however, seemed firmly rooted to the pavement. I noticed a padded
stool inside the shop and asked her why she didn't sit in comfort.
'Oh, I'm much too old to be getting in and out of *chairs*.' She made
them sound like instruments of torture.

I couldn't guess her age. Radiyyah might have been forty, or sixty.
She was no coquette, but she had a twinkle in her eye as she opened a
little phial of scent and dabbed it on my wrist. I noticed the label,
Asmah Li – 'Permit Me ... ' – and suggested that it was a good name
for dropping hints.

She laughed. Then she looked at me with her initial sternness.
'You're married, no?' I shook my head. 'You must marry now,' she
said gravely. 'We never know the hour of our death. Do it before it's
too late.'

'I think it's probably too late already in my case. Unless you've got
something', I said, glancing at her stock, 'to make me young again.'

'Hah! You're still a boy. Anyway, scents can't make you young.
They can only bring back memories of youth.'

She had put her finger on it: of all organs, the nose is the most
nostalgic.

'Then,' I said, looking at this philosopher of smells, 'what about
something to enchant a beloved?'

She thought for a moment. 'No. Only the heart can enchant a
beloved.'

Not much happens in Salalah by day, other than activities connected with personal grooming and adornment. I had a haircut, then
went to get a ring adjusted. In the silversmith's I met a grey-bearded
gentleman who was supervising the repoussé encrustation of his
camel-stick. We compared rings, introduced ourselves and were
delighted to discover that Shaykh Hasan bin Ghafaylah had once
been the guard of a very distant kinsman of mine in Hadramawt. He
also belonged to the Bayt Imani, the clan of Wilfred Thesiger's desert
travelling companions. I asked after his famous cousins Bin Kabina
and Bin Ghabaisha, whom I had met in 1990.

'They've gone,' said Shaykh Hasan. 'And most of the Bayt Imani.
There are hardly any of us left now. The others all moved.'

I remembered the Bayt Imani tribesmen asking my advice. 'We're in a quandary,' they said. 'We live in the borderlands between three countries, Oman, Yemen and Saudi Arabia. What nationality should we be?'

'Yemeni,' I had replied immediately, loyal to my adopted country. 'Failing that Omani. Never, never Saudi.'

Now, fearing the worst, I asked what had become of them.

'They went to Abu Dhabi. Shaykh Zayid gave them money and villas.'

I breathed a sigh of relief.

At night, a thick tropical lethargy descends on Salalah, and even less happens in what Bertram Thomas called 'the land of sloth'. The evening after my conversation with Radiyyah, I went for a slow spin with three men in a Landcruiser. The exhausting business of going to the café to gossip has been superseded by the *jisiyam*, the 'GSM' mobile telephone, and my three companions spent most of the time chatting, simultaneously, in Swahili and two dialects of Arabic.

Feeling left out, I excused myself on the corniche and walked slowly back towards Muhammad and Habibah's villa. The seaward pavement was dotted with sandals, laid out neatly like choreography symbols. Down on the sand groups of men sat around glowing water-pipes, for at night the beach turns into a great open-air smoking-room. One group had a pair of cockatoos. The male, they explained, lived in al-Haffah, the female in the further suburb of Awqad; they brought them together here every evening. The birds were obviously much in love.

I walked on, in soulful mood, then turned inland through the coconutteries. Above, fronds rustled in the light sea-breeze. The grove was dark and arras-like. I remembered IB's legend about the genesis of the coconut palm. Like the date, it has a human origin: a certain Indian philosopher, the traveller wrote, took the severed head of a vizier, 'planted a date-stone in his brain, and tended it until it grew into a tree and produced this nut. The story', he admits, 'is a fiction, but we have related it because of its wide circulation.'

The wind picked up, and there was a heavy thud nearby. I wondered about the probability of being brained by a falling coconut. The thought reminded me of the conversation in the Scent Suq, and Radiyyah's Horatian advice on marriage. Another thud: perhaps it was already too late . . .

> La vie est brève
> Un peu d'espoir
> Un peu de rêve
> Et puis – Bonsoir.

I made it back to the villa, however, and recounted the events of the day to Muhammad and Habibah. It was good to have people, and not just a diary, to share discoveries with – particularly one as important as Radiyyah and her fellow shopkeepers. Later, as I lay in bed, I recalled a similar sense of excitement from long ago. As a child, I had been briefly addicted to *I-Spy* books. Someone who styled himself 'Big Chief I-Spy' had designed the series to instil a laudable sense of empiricism in the young. The little volumes covered subjects such as trees, nationalities and motor cars; when you spotted one of the items listed – a hornbeam, for example, or a Belgian – you put a tick against it and earned points according to its rarity. I never sent a completed book to Big Chief I-Spy, but I could still remember his address: 'The Wigwam', Bouverie Street, London EC4. Perhaps inverse archaeology was a sophisticated version of I-Spy, in which a female shopkeeper was the equivalent of, say, an Aston Martin and worth at least seven points. Coconuts would be on a par with Ford Populars, a paltry one point. A scrotal hernia, however, or a Rasulid, would - like the virtually unattainable Studebaker Golden Hawk – score a whopping ten.

Habibah, too, had had an eventful day. Her Yemeni carnelian ring had caused a fit of hysteria at a ladies' party in Taqah. 'The women were convinced that the stone was possessed by a jinni,' she explained. The supernatural was a special interest of Habibah's and she collected spells involving blood and armpit hair. For her Dhofar was fertile ground: as long ago as the thirteenth century, Ibn al-Mujawir had noted that 'Dhofari women are sorceresses on account of their proximity to the Island of Suqutra. They go from Dhofar to Java in a single night.' Even in recent years, the witches of Dhofar apparently held knees-ups by the lagoon at Khawr Ruri, arriving on hyenas.

We sat and talked of magic, then decided it would be prudent to light some of Radiyyah's frankincense. Habibah took a *fass*, a 'gem-stone' of it, and placed it on glowing charcoal. It bubbled like toasting cheese, then the fumes rose, spooling slowly upwards in a thick cob-webby skein. The jinn smelt it, and fled.

The days, and weeks, unwound. My watch, which usually gains, ran slow. Nadia, Muhammad and Habibah's 6-year-old daughter, trilingual in Arabic, English and Hungarian, discovered a way of controlling me that was more potent than any Dhofari sorcery. The direct method – '*Please* don't start another conversation about *history*' – failed; so she took to kidnapping my diary, to me more precious than all the gold of al-Haffah. '*I've* got your book of secrets . . . ' she would say. And I would only get my secrets back when I had watched *Aladdin* with her.

We went on trips. Mughsayl, towards the Yemeni border, reminded me of the Dorset coastline from Charmouth to Golden Cap, but with camels on the beach. Further west, at Rakhyut, we snorkelled with sardines, and watched an osprey fishing and a ray gliding through the water, maroon with white spots like a Jermyn Street handkerchief. Behind the village we picked up a yokel in a wooded coomb. 'We got loads of cows in these parts, no?' he told us. 'Some people's got herds of six hundred, no? All local cows, mind. Them foreign cows can't live here, no?'

The man was speaking Arabic, but it was not his first language. Dhofar and the neighbouring regions are part of the Arabian Celtic fringe and home to a number of pre-Arabic tongues. At least one, Bat'hari, seems recently to have gone the way of Manx. Jibbali is alive and well, but with the increasing Omanization of Dhofari life its future looks bleak.

Jibbali is more correctly called Shahri, after the Shahrah people who are the oldest inhabitants of the area. Incomers, the Qara, subjugated them and propagated a 'black legend', which claims that the Shahrah are the Qur'anic people all but wiped out by God because they slaughtered the Prophet Salih's she-camel. The story is illustrated, strip-cartoon fashion, on a rock in downtown Salalah. Impressed in limestone are the camel's footprints, the marks of Salih's walking-stick, and a notch where the camelocides sharpened their knives. Finally come some black smears, said to be the beast's blood.

The Qara conquerors lorded it over the Shahrah and married their women, thus ensuring the survival of Shahri as the mother tongue of succeeding generations. It is a lisping, liquid language rich in poetry and metaphor. Miranda Morris, an authority on Modern South Arabian languages, has translated a verse about a beautiful woman:

> Shaikha is the cargo-ship of the Sultan,
> Already far from New York.
> Her cargo has been unloaded in a secret place ...

Among men, Shaikha is 'adored as are milch camels'; other women, however, envy her down to her toes, which, 'dyed with henna / ... were a source of pain to the co-wife'.

It seems at first strange that IB the nascent ethnologist failed to mention the indigenous languages of the region; but he clearly went no distance inland from the Arabophone city of Dhofar. Later visitors reacted variously to the Dhofaris of the hinterland. In the 1830s Captain Haines thought their figures 'would have delighted the eye of Canova' and added that 'they were frequent lookers on at my crew when playing cricket' (O for the Dhofari view of the game!). Sixty years later, Theodore and Mabel Bent were less impressed by the Qara: 'We never had to deal with wilder men in our lives ... They got hold of our Christian names, and were for ever using them, to our great annoyance.' Bertram Thomas, however, visiting in the 1920s, was fascinated by Qara life and keenly recorded practices such as the stimulation of lactation in cows by twat-blowing.

Qara and Shahrah life are now changing fast. Miranda Morris writes that the Shahri word *ezirit*, 'a track that is temporarily in heavy use; especially to water and to settlements where beautiful women are to be found', is now also used for motor roads. And Muhammad told me that one day in Salalah he saw a mountain man in full traditional dress – an indigo loincloth, dagger and .303 rifle – pull a plastic card from behind his dagger sheath and take money out of a cashpoint machine.

It was bad enough to be tainted with the blood of Salih's she-camel; but the Shahrah have also been identified as a remnant of Ad, the people whom the Qur'an says were destroyed by a hurricane for opposing the Prophet Hud. The association may explain why there is a tomb of Hud in Dhofar – even though there is a perfectly good one in Hadramawt, famous since at least the beginning of Islam. IB visited the Dhofari tomb, 'half a day's journey from the city, on the sea-coast'. Late one afternoon, Qahtan took me in his minibus to the mausoleum seen by IB, a short drive east of Salalah and in sight of the sea. As with most Dhofari monuments which have not been rebuilt in the international Islamic taste, the little four-domed building had been enthusiastically restored. I went in but Qahtan, whose innate reticence seemed to extend to the dead, lingered at the door. 'Aren't you going to greet Hud?' I called. He entered, mumbled a quick Fatihah with downcast eyes, and was out of the door.

The sun set. Qahtan did his ablutions from a well, then chanted the *adhan*, the call to prayer, in a high quavering voice. Unless it was an invitation to me, there was no one else around to join him. I sat inside the darkening tomb while he prayed outside on his Michelin Man windscreen shade.

As we drove back towards Salalah Qahtan said, 'I felt a great fear around that tomb.'

I smiled. 'So it was the jinn you were calling to prayer.'

There was no reply. I was beginning to regret the flippant comment when Qahtan spoke again. 'There was once a Mahri girl who disappeared. You see, she had married a jinni. One day, years later, a man who knew the jinn turned up and offered to get her back. He said, "I'll lead one of you down to her. To save her, this man must take hold of her arm. She will change into a wolf, a rat, a snake and other beasts, but he must not let go of her. And he must neither look at her nor mention the name of God." But no one was brave enough to go.'

I thought of Eurydice, and of all the tales that must have wandered around the world before cultural boundaries began to harden. 'I bet there are lots of old stories like that,' I said, hoping to hear more.

Qahtan took his eyes off the road for a moment and looked at me. 'It's not an old story. I was one of the ones who was asked to get the girl.'

Later, we drove out of Salalah and on to the *jurbayb*, the plain between the ocean and the Qara Mountains. At night it became a vast drive-in salon, dotted with cars and groups of men who reclined on cushions, drinking coffee and eating dates. 'We Arabs', said Qahtan as we left the road, 'have three concerns: *al-bawsh wa 'l-hawsh wa 'l-qahwah fi 'l-hawsh* – camels, flocks and coffee in the yard.' But this was no ordinary yard: paved with platinum, vaulted with sapphire, lit by a topaz moon – no sultan, no Solomon had conceived such mystical architecture.

We joined a group around Qahtan's chief, Shaykh Musallam of the Qazzoz subsection of the al–Bahr section of the Khawar sept of Bayt Kathir. At first we talked about jinn; then the *shaykh* steered the conversation on to Mubarak bin London, the traveller Wilfred Thesiger. In *Arabian Sands*, Thesiger grumbled at the Khawar for banning him from their territory in the late 1940s. Recently, the book had been translated into Arabic. 'He called us avaricious,' Shaykh Musallam said. 'Nothing but praise for our neighbours; but we Khawar are avaricious!'

It was around midnight when Qahtan drove me home. On the way I reflected that, just occasionally, a character in a travel book could turn critic. It was a sobering thought.

The following day I turned to another item on my Battutian checklist, *tambul*. In his description of Dhofar, IB included a page-long ethnobotanical excursus on *Piper betel*. 'The specific property of its leaves', he wrote, 'is that they sweeten the breath, remove foul odours of the mouth, aid digestion of food, and stop the injurious effect of drinking water on an empty stomach; the eating of them gives a sense of exhilaration and promotes cohabitation ... I have been told, indeed, that the slave-girls of the sultan and of the amirs in India eat nothing else.'

I had originally assumed that the plant was brought to Dhofar by the Rasulids, who were responsible for introducing so many Indian species to Arabia. In fact it had arrived long before, as I discovered in the *Plains of Gold* of the tenth-century geographer and historian al-Mas'udi: 'In our time,' he said, 'betel has overtaken all other breath-fresheners and is quite the fashion among the people of Mecca, the Hijaz and Yemen.' (The information was an aside in a passage on Indian self-immolation. On his way to the pyre and bliss in the after-life, al-Mas'udi wrote, the suicide parades through the markets. 'He first has himself scalped, then places live coals, sulphur and juniper resin upon his head. Thus does he walk, the crown of his head smouldering, surrounded by the odours of his roasting brain, chewing betel and areca nut the while.')

Habibah told me at lunch that she had invited a friend over for the evening, an expert on betel. First, though, I wanted to do some field-work. The obvious place to start was in the coconut groves and gardens across the road. There, I followed a track until I came to a little drystone cottage and byre. Outside it squatted a couple of Pakistanis. When I asked if they grew betel they looked surprised, but nodded. One of them led me to a fenced-off plot about thirty feet square. Inside this, palm trunks supported a trellis, thickly covered by shiny, ribbed leaves with sharp points; they would have made an elegant pot plant. IB's description was accurate: 'Trellises of cane are made for it, just as for grape vines, or else the betel is planted close to coconut palms, so that it may climb upon them as the pepper climbs.' The Pakistani plucked some leaves for me, choosing the smaller, yellowish ones. Again, IB was spot-on when he said that the best leaves are yellow.

Back at the cottage I was surprised to see a large American car, and a prosperous-looking Omani sitting on a bed next to the byre. He called me over and explained that he was the owner of the farm. 'In fact, I was born in this very house.' He asked me where I was from. 'Ah, I thought so ... ' he said. Then, to the Pakistanis, 'Be careful.

This is a British spy.' He twirled his camel-stick. 'And where did you learn Arabic?'

'Oxford,' I said.

'Hah! The university of spies!'

'No,' I replied. 'That's Cambridge.'

I had caught him off guard; but he went straight back on to the offensive. 'You British have two vices.'

There was something alarming in his gaze. 'What are they?' I said, swallowing.

'I'm not going to tell you. But I can judge you by your face.' He scrutinized me more closely. 'Hmm. Not bad. Half okay.'

He smiled, and apologized for the ribbing. 'You see,' he explained, 'we are lazy men with nothing to do. I come here every day at four, waste a couple of hours, then go to the mosque.'

'So you're what we would call a gentleman farmer.'

' "Gentleman farmer . . . " I like that.'

My host took me to see the cow in the byre, a miniature Dhofari with a tiny calf. He sniffed. 'Ughh. What an awful smell!' I said I thought it was a perfectly natural smell, but he told the men to light some frankincense. 'It keeps away germs. And *al-shaytan*, Satan.'

He confessed he hadn't the slightest idea about betel. 'What use is it?' he asked. In reply, I read him IB on the properties of the leaf. 'Utter nonsense,' he exclaimed. 'Take my advice and don't touch the stuff. Personally, I keep off all harmful substances. I hardly even drink tea. You do, I suppose. Well, have you ever seen your innards?' I admitted I hadn't. 'Just take a piece of fresh beef and put it in some tea. It does this ... ' he made a horrible, gurning face and blew a raspberry. 'Your guts', he said portentously, 'are like that meat.'

That evening Habibah's friend came to instruct us in *tambul* mysteries. After dismissing her chauffeur she entered the room, removed her veil, and smiled – a meteor-burst of flashes passing over a round, dark moon of a face. At first, Thumna was self-deprecating. 'It's my aunts who are the real authorities on *tambul*. One of them chews it as soon as she gets up in the morning.' But, encouraged by Habibah, she produced a little bag of ingredients – she called it her *mudayghah*, her 'little masticatory' – and began work: two leaves one on top of the other, glossy sides down, a few chips of *kusayr* (areca nut), a scraping of *kat* (catechu – an astringent extract of acacia), a few dabs of *nurah* (paste of caustic lime), all folded into a neat green package. She worked with dexterity and a touch of drama, like a barman mixing a Singapore Sling.

Thumna took the first wad and popped it into her mouth. She had used the leaves collected on my afternoon expedition, and she pronounced them to be of excellent quality. As she chewed she looked saucily from one of us to the other, as if caught at a midnight feast. I heard the crunch of areca nut. The next wad she gave to me. The leaf was spicy, as one might expect from a member of the pepper family. Almost immediately I felt a slight contraction of the oesophagus; this was followed by a liquefaction in the mouth and a visit to the lavatory to spit out a quantity of tomato-red saliva. Soon, all four of us were chewing. Thumna was celebrant of the *tambul* eucharist, Habibah, who brought a smoking incense-burner, thurifer; Muhammad, master of the music, obeyed a subliminal urge to pun and put on 'Sergeant Pepper'. By the third wad I, the bemused neophyte, began to feel faintly trippy; but perhaps it was the Beatles rather than the betel.

Talk turned inevitably to the supernatural. I recounted my strange experience on the bus at Edfu, Habibah a stranger one with a statue of Amenhotep III in Luxor. Then Thumna spoke: 'When I was a child,' she said, 'I caught polio and my leg withered up. The British doctors said there was no hope. But the late Queen Mother took me on. She had me locked up in a darkened room and made me eat gazelle meat for forty days. She also sent me poultices for my leg, made from the powdered skins of snakes and chameleons.' She shivered at the memory; I thought of Macbeth's weird sisters, and Ibn al-Mujawir's sorceresses (like them, the Queen Mother was Dhofari). 'I was really scared. But my family would come and whisper to me through the shutters and tell me not to be afraid.' She paused, and smiled distantly. 'And then my leg got better. It ... grew back.'

It was late when Thumna left. Muhammad was already in bed, and Habibah about to join him. As she bid me good-night, I asked her a question that had been on my mind. '*Ya* Habibah ... do you think IB was right about *tambul* promoting, er, cohabitation?'

She gave me her hermetic look. 'I'll tell you in the morning,' she said, and winked.

It was useful to have a research assistant.

★

I found the descendants of the Rasulid sultans of Yemen and Dhofar, as one does, by chance. The sign stopped me in my tracks: 'Al-Ghassani for Domestic Appliances' was as much of a surprise as 'Plantagenet Hardware' would be in England.

The Ghassanids were a noble Arabian tribe who migrated northward from Yemen in the third century AD. They ended up in Syria, where they founded a small but exquisite kingdom with its capital near Damascus. According to themselves and their court historians, the Rasulids were descended from this ancient stock: al-Mujahid, IB's host in Yemen and ancestor of my friend Hasan, billed himself as 'head of the oldest dynasty in the world'. Admittedly their immediate forbear Muhammad ibn Harun Rasul al-Ghassani had more than a touch of the *tarbush*; but they made no secret of their ancestors' marrying into the Turkomans. It was the male line that mattered.

More recent commentators have axed the noble Arabian ancestry and given the dynasty an unadulterated Manjik Turkoman pedigree. If they are right, perhaps the Rasulids were only emulating the fictional Abu Zayd al-Saruji. This lovable wide-boy, the direct ancestor not only of numerous fake counts but also of Tristram Shandy, Baron Munchausen and the Reverend Jimmy Swaggart, 'claimed at times to be a Sassanid, at others a Ghassanid'. As I entered the shop, I reflected that even if I had discovered a dodgy Ghassanid, I might still have turned up a blue-blooded Rasulid.

Ahmad al-Ghassani, the owner of the showroom, confirmed my expectations: he was, it seemed, a descendant of IB's reclusive Sultan al-Mughith. He had a somewhat *badw* look to him; but when he showed me a picture of his cousin, the head of the family Shaykh Abdulqadir al-Ghassani, there was little doubt in my mind: the elderly gentleman distinctly resembled Hasan's father in distant San'a. The branches of the family had separated seven hundred years ago, and yet those lusty Rasulid genes had conquered time.

Ahmad and a cousin, unable to show me their dead sultanic forbears in the Ribat Palace grounds, led me to a nearer graveyard and a more recent ancestor. It was Shaykh Abdulqadir's father, 'the Pious and Erudite Shaykh, Salim ibn Ahmad ibn Muhammad al-Sayl al-Ghassani'.

'Why "al-Sayl"?' I asked, reading the tombstone. It was an unusual name: the Flash-flood.

'It's the flood at Marib mentioned in the Qur'an,' the cousin elucidated, obscurely. 'The Ghassanis are a very old family.'

Somewhere, a bell was ringing.

It was only later that I realized where I had come across Flash-flood: in Bertram Thomas's *Arabia Felix*. 'Next to me sat old Salim al Sail, another merchant, a God-fearing man and a Solomon among his kind. Human frailty made him claim descent from the noble Bait Ghassan, while all men whispered that he was a foundling child of low Shahari origin that a mountain torrent had swept down in a summer freshet.' There was a further, charming insight into the pious *shaykh*: 'Salim's eyes, as became his eighty years, were growing dim, though were still capable of a twinkle when he begged in secret for an aphrodisiac.'

As I pondered the questions raised by Thomas's revelation I realized that, despite the whispering campaign, logic was on the side of old Flash-flood. A burn in the Qara Mountains sounded only marginally more likely an origin than the left-luggage office at Victoria Station. More important, if the rumours were a fact, why advertise it on your tombstone? It would be like Wilde's Jack having his card engraved 'Mr Ernest Handbag-Worthing'. All the same, I wasn't entirely convinced by the Rasulid pedigree of the Salalah Ghassanis.

God, of course, is the most knowing; for the rest of us, genealogy is more art than science.

Then came another chance encounter of a different sort. Qahtan took me one day into the foothills behind Khawr Ruri, the spooky lagoon where Dhofari witches park their hyenas. Before us lay a most unexpected object – a wall, over a mile long and perhaps five hundred feet high, spanning the gap between two hills. 'That', said Qahtan, 'is the Abyss of Darbat.' As we drew nearer, the feature grew less wall-like and began instead to resemble the business-end of a grubby glacier. We stopped the car and approached on foot through dense scrub. Close up, the true nature of the Abyss became apparent from the little trickles of water that ran down it and continued through the undergrowth. I noticed that the stream-beds were lined with a greyish, calcareous deposit. The Abyss of Darbat was lime-scale on a grand scale.

We returned to the car and drove up a track beside the escarpment. Above it we emerged into a broad flat valley bordered by cave-riddled cliffs; one of the higher caves pierced the rock-face entirely, revealing a patch of sky beyond. The valley floor was covered with close-cropped grass, and dotted with cabin-like dwellings and huge trees. Shepherdesses tended flocks, boys milked camels, cattle mooched and munched, and all this busy hanging garden echoed with bleatings and grumblings. Further along the valley we came to a long meandering lake, not unlike the Serpentine and strewn with heron, coots, moorhens, duck and geese; lakeside trees rustled with doves and egrets. Here the *andante pastorale* of the lower valley gave way to an aleatoric *allegro* – hoots, coos, burbles, chirrups, twitters and clatters of weedy take-offs. Darbat was justly famous for its bird life. (I heard later – from a trustworthy person, as IB would say – that when the Sultan came to visit, art improved on nature: the birds of Darbat had their wings clipped.) Qahtan told me that the place was famous for its profusion of jinn.

While we were strolling along the lake, we came across a bus and a group of about twenty men sitting in a circle, silent and motionless, under a *Ficus vasta*. We greeted them hesitantly; they returned the greeting in unison. Qahtan and I looked at each other, then the men began to announce their names, one by one, as if they were about to take part in some bizarre team game. The last three names and their owners were recognizably non-Omani. 'We are from the Arabic

Department of the Teacher Training College,' one of them explained, 'and we are engaged in an educational expedition.' I looked at him with awe: here was a man who spoke with case-endings.

We joined the circle. I dusted off my inflections and explained what had brought me to Dhofar. One of the foreign-looking men smiled. 'We, that is my two colleagues and I,' he said, 'are from the Maghrib. I, like IB, am a native of Tangier . . . '

I stared at him. In Wadi Darbat, a migrant Tangerine was almost as improbable as a passing penguin.

' . . . and', he continued, 'I am the author of two papers on my illustrious fellow citizen. "The Subjective and the Objective in the *Travels* of IB" explores the continuous narrative interplay between IB's internal reactions to the alien environment, to what one may term the Other – the *aja'ib al-asfar*, the "Wonders of Travel" of his full title – and his reportage of external phenomena – *ghara'ib al-amsar*, the "Marvels of Cities". My second paper focuses on the latter aspect, *c'est à dire l'aspect miraculeux des* Voyages. I am firmly of the opinion that it is a grave mistake to dismiss the miraculous, as some commentators are prone to do; indeed, we must contemplate miracles more closely, for they are an integral part of the *Travels* as a valid historical document.'

I realized that he had paused, and that the circle was looking in my direction. 'Oh, me too,' I said wholeheartedly. For a while I spoke of my own, relatively sublunar approach to IB, of my search for physical and human survivals from his world. Then one of the other professors looked at his watch and whispered something to the Tangerine.

'You must excuse us,' he said. 'We have a very full programme.'

The group rose simultaneously, bade us farewell and bumped off in their bus.

'Well, that was a coincidence, no?' I said to Qahtan.

'One of the wonders of travel,' he replied.

As the afternoon waned, we too left Darbat to its shepherdesses, its birds and its jinn. Qahtan pulled off the track that descended by the Abyss and prayed the sunset prayer on an eminence. I watched a layer of orange light – concentrated orange, tangerine in fact – floating on the humidity of the plain, and thought about the meeting. It was certainly a coincidence; but, like the infrequent transit of planets in different orbits, there was also a fatedness about it.

The light had gone. Qahtan folded his Michelin Man prayer mat, and we set off for Salalah.

That night Qahtan and I joined some of his Khawar kinsmen on the beach. We smoked apple tobacco, and for a time conversation revolved again around Mubarak bin London's attack on the Khawar in *Arabian Sands*. Then, by popular request, Qahtan's nephew began telling a story: 'Uncle Qahtan's family are called Ba'ir.' He tapped my knee. 'You know the meaning of "Ba'ir"? Yes, that's right, a camel. Just checking. They're called this because their immediate ancestor was incredibly strong. He could kill a man just by throwing a sharpened flint at him. Now Sa'id Ba'ir (Uncle Qahtan's father and my maternal grandfather) once found himself in Kuwait and short of money. But he was a clever man. He borrowed some cash from a Palestinian and went to the printer's. He ordered fifteen thousand passports – well, pieces of paper that said: "Government of the Ba'iri State. Temporary Travel Document." Then he sold these, to Indians and so on. He covered his costs, and made quite a bit on top.'

I thoroughly approved of a blow struck against the tyranny of passports; but it all seemed an unlikely tale. Then Qahtan said, 'I once met a Sudanese in Kenya. When he heard my family name was Ba'ir, he said, "You're not by any chance related to Sa'id Ba'ir?" I said, "Yes. He's my father." Then he said, "Well, your father sold me a bit of paper in Kuwait. A Ba'iri State passport." God, I was worried when I heard that. Then he said, "And I travelled all the way to Sudan on it. Nobody ever questioned it." '

Everyone laughed. They must have heard the story many times, but it was one that would never grow stale – like the stories of Abu Zayd al-Saruji, the fake Ghassanid.

The pipe was charged with more apple tobacco. Qahtan's nephew drew on it. The sea sucked at the sand. 'Tell the one about the *bisht*,' they said.

'Ah, the *bisht*.' He tapped my knee. 'You know what a *bisht* is? Yes, that's right – a kind of cloak. Just checking. You see, the *bisht* is important to the story. Well, Grandfather had a particularly fine *bisht*. No one else had one as fine. Anyway, when he was in Kuwait he kept bumping into this Mahri. The Mahri coveted Grandfather's *bisht*. He wanted it more than anything else in the world. On top of this, the Mahris and the Khawar are not the best of friends, and the Mahri kept slagging Grandfather off. One day he said, "You Khawar, you're nothing but slaves." ' He drew on the pipe. 'Now Grandfather was wandering about, feeling really pissed off by all this. Then he spotted this slave, hanging out in the *suq*, a really big black man. Well, to cut a long story short, Grandfather went up to the slave and said, "Come and shag me on the beach." ' I noticed a general turn of heads among the neighbouring groups of beach-bums. ' "Tonight. I'll be sleeping in such-and-such a spot" – he described the place exactly – "and I'll be wearing this *bisht*. You can't mistake it. There's a full moon, and there isn't another *bisht* like it in the whole of Kuwait. Oh, and when you come, don't say anything. Just get on with it as quickly as possible." '

The storyteller paused and peered at his watch. 'Oh dear. It's nearly midnight. Perhaps I ought to break off . . . Or do you want me to carry on?' I nodded vigorously; I knew what Scheherazade's husband must have felt like as dawn approached.

'Okay. Well, Grandfather found the Mahri and said to him, "Look, I know we've had our differences. But I want bygones to be bygones. And as a token of our friendship, please take this *bisht*." The Mahri of course didn't have to be asked twice, and went off wearing the *bisht*. Now, the Mahri always slept in the same spot on the beach. It just happened to be the rendezvous Grandfather had agreed on with the slave. And that night the Mahri had a big surprise.'

'Did the Mahri enjoy it?' I asked when the laughter had died down. It would have been a delicious narrative twist.

'No, he didn't,' said the storyteller. 'He was very angry.'

★

Time rolled on, my watch ran slower, I grew fatter. Habibah's cooking was supplemented by food parcels sent by Thumna – cakes and chickens done in coconut milk. One evening we went to an Olde Worlde Dhofari restaurant to eat *habshah*, a fry-up of tripe and intestines, and a special order: porridge with dried sardines, a thirteenth-century recipe I had come across in Ibn al-Mujawir.

I spent the days gossiping with Habibah, the nights in beach- or plain-salons. Then one morning I came across a poem attributed to the orthodox imam, al-Shafi'i. It was quoted in the introduction to Habibah's edition of the *Travels*, and it shook me out of my pleasant but un-Battutian stasis:

> Travel! Set out and head for pastures new –
> Life tastes the richer when you've road-worn feet.
> No water that stagnates is fit to drink,

For only that which flows is truly sweet.
No lion that spurned the hunt could catch its prey,
No arrow unreleased could earn a score.
A sun that hung immobile in the sky
Would soon become a universal bore.
Sandal's mere firewood in its native grove,
Gold is but dust, unmined within the lode.
Things that are stationary have little worth:
They only gain their value on the road.

Soon afterwards I set out for the Kuria Muria Islands. As I was leaving, Habibah handed me some folded sheets of paper. 'A *hirz*,' she said, 'an amulet – to keep you safe in the boat.'

She had copied al-Shadhili's *Litany of the Sea*, the prayer IB had heard in Alexandria:

... Subject to us every sea that is Thine on earth and in heaven, in the world of sense and in the invisible world, the sea of this life and the sea of the life to come. Subject to us everything, O Thou in Whose Hand is the rule over all. *Kaf-Ha-Ya-Ayn-Sad* ...

Kuria Muria

Minor Monuments

'Men's disagreements stem from names; when they proceed to
the reality, peace ensues.'

Jalal al-Din al-Rumi (d. 1273), *Mathnawi*

KAF-HA-YA-AYN-SAD. There again were those amuletic letters,
this time part of a prayer carved on the stern of a sailing *sambuq*:
'In the Name of God, the Compassionate, the Merciful. I ask for
Your succour, forgiveness and approval, and that You bring us bounty
from whence we know not. Dated 5 Rajab 1371. *Ya-Sin. Kaf-Ha-Ya-
Ayn-Sad. Ha-Mim Ayn-Sin-Qaf.*' Beside this prayer was another one:
'O Protector of souls in hulls, O Saviour of hulls in the fathomless sea,
protect this *sambuq* whose name is *al-Dhib*, O God, O Sustainer, O
God, O Protector.' *Al-Dhib*, the *Wolf*, was less than fifty years old. But
the inscription crossed a sea of centuries – to al-Shadhili's Alexandria,
to Ibn Jubayr's Aydhab with its trembling souls and leaky hulls.

Qahtan and I found the *Wolf* on the beach at Sad'h, a haven
seventy miles east of Salalah at the end of the graded track. A few old
skippers' houses survived from the days when it had been a major
frankincense port; the old mosque, however – 'a simple still space'
with a 'remarkable minaret' – had according to the *Journal of Oman
Studies* been '(demolished 1983, Ed.)'. It was still a pretty place,
although Qahtan shook his head at it. 'I couldn't live here. Ever. Too
shut in.' It was the voice of the claustrophobe from the inland steppe.

We were looking for a boat to take me to the Kuria Murias,
another seventy miles to the north-east. It seemed more than likely
that one of the group of five islands was IB's 'Hill of Lum'an, in the
midst of the sea', where the traveller came across an incomprehensible

and patently very holy hermit. 'Lum'an' is otherwise unknown. But the islands' nomenclature has always been fluid: they were often called after the Bani Ghalfan, the Mahri clan who owned them for much of recorded history; the navigator Ahmad ibn Majid referred to them also as Hayrawan. At any rate, there were no other serious candidates for Lum'an between Dhofar and Sur.

A quick look at the harbour was not promising. Except for the beached *Wolf*, its neighbour the *Tristram* – a tiny blue yacht which clearly hadn't gone anywhere for years – and a few small fishing craft, Sad'h was boatless. As we turned back towards Mirbat, the memory of Khalfan's elusive *sambuq* came back to haunt me.

We drove along the base of Jabal Samhan, a brooding escarpment spotlit by liverish sunbeams. The track passed through a strangely puckered landscape of dry nullahs which Qahtan described as *abasir*. 'It's a Kathiri word,' he explained. To my present frame of mind the word sounded like a mixture of *abis* and *bawasir*, 'frowning' and 'haemorrhoids'. As we approached Mirbat, he added to the general gloom by saying that his father – that man of many wiles, owner of the fateful *bisht* – had been wrecked in a sailing *sambuq* off Mirbat Head. 'He swam ashore', Qahtan said, 'with an old man on his back.'

'Thanks for telling me,' I said, thinking of IB's near miss further along the coast: 'On the Feast of Sacrifice there blew up against us a violent wind after daybreak. It lasted until the sun was up and almost sunk us. A ship belonging to one of the merchants had gone ahead of us, and it sank. Only one man escaped from it – he got out by swimming after suffering severely.'

By the time we reached Mirbat, however, the afternoon had brightened. The water in the harbour was smooth and perfectly transparent; small fish skittered across it like skipping stones. And there, all but motionless, lay two *sambuqs*. Our calls to the first one were answered from the deck by a fat man. 'We're going to Hallaniyah,' he shouted back.

I pretended not to believe it. But the man came ashore and confirmed that he was indeed sailing, on the morrow, God willing, for the only inhabited island of the Kuria Murias. He then added, with a hint of pride, that he had come all the way from Sur.

I held out my hand. 'Captain Khalfan, I presume?'

After his initial surprise, Khalfan seemed delighted at the idea of taking a passenger to the Kuria Murias. He would leave at dawn, and suggested I spend the night on board. I was about to get my bag when a car drew up. 'Oh,' said Khalfan, 'the boss. We ought to check with him first.'

No one who travels can afford to judge people on first appearances. I did; so did the *sambuq*-owner. Our reactions were mutual: he came towards me as a slug might approach a salt–cellar. I hitched up the corners of my mouth into a semblance of a smile, went through the briefest of pleasantries then asked about a return passage to Hallaniyah.

'Two hundred,' said the *sambuq*-owner.

'Baysahs . . . ?' It sounded very reasonable. About £3.

'Two hundred riyals.'

Over £300. 'That's a bit steep,' I said, lamely.

'Okay. One hundred. One way.' He smiled horribly; then turned, oozed back to his car and drove off.

I went and fumed on a bollard, then decided to try the other *sambuq*. The likelihood of both vessels going to the Kuria Murias seemed tiny; but, as I found out from an Indian on board, this one was also heading for Hallaniyah. Gingerly, I asked if I could come along. The Indian's eyes narrowed. 'There is what work? You there is come, there is very problem with government.' He disappeared into the hold.

I found Qahtan and Khalfan discussing my situation. Khalfan handed me a Salalah telephone number. 'Try this,' he said. 'I'm sorry, but it's all I can do.'

As we drove off towards Salalah, Qahtan said softly, 'I think your problem is what we call the Eye of Joy. I saw your face when Khalfan said he was going to the island: you were . . . too happy.'

I nodded silently.

My problem, as I discovered over the next couple of days in Salalah, was not only the Eye. That brief visit to the quay at Mirbat had set off murmurings about shady shark–fin buyers and mystery abalone merchants. There was talk too of fishier business – that I might be engaged in a less innocent version of I-Spy, that I was probably a Yemeni agent bent on taking over the islands (under the old Marxist regime in Aden, they had been a bone of contention with the Omanis). I rather fancied myself in the latter role; however, I established my prosaic *bona fides*. More gratifyingly, I ran into the *sambuq*-owner's son and conveyed various expressions to his father. (The man's name, by the way, is Bin Da'mush; 'Da'mush' may well be a local variant of the classical *du'mus*, an animalcule and, specifically, 'a black water-insect'.)

Having thus vented my spleen – or, as Habibah put it, wiped my liver – I set off again for Mirbat. In my pocket, next to the *Litany of the Sea*, was a receipt from Al-Shahry Trading & Cont. Est. for fifteen riyals, the cost of a passage by *sambuq* to the Kuria Murias.

★

We weighed anchor at 4.30 a.m. I had spent most of the night playing Cluedo out on the plain with a group of Mirbati insomniacs (the men of the town are still, as Captain Haines noted in the 1830s, 'extremely indolent, addicted to smoking, and lolling at their ease'); but I forgot the lack of sleep as we left the harbour, under a full moon and a shoal of drifting clouds.

The Al-Shahry *sambuq* carried a cargo of rice, milk powder, sugar and gas cylinders and had a crew of two: Khalil, the Bangladeshi skipper, who steered with his toes, and a Keralan called Maurice. It was a blessing that the chain of command was so short, for they seemed to have no language in common except for a rudimentary lascar pidgin. The wind rose as we passed Sad'h, and the sun. Dolphins shadowed the *sambuq* as it wriggled and burrowed through the waves. After breakfast – banana sandwiches, 'Les Enfants' cheese triangles and tea with 'Teapot and Swords' brand evaporated milk – I had an exhilarating crap, suspended above the *sambuq*'s wake in a packing case. The head of a large turtle popped up from the water and eyed me with evident disgust. At Ras Nus the cliffs of Jabal Samhan met the water and we struck out for the islands, breasting a big ocean swell. Soon after came the first, hazy glimpse of Hasikiyyah and Sawdah, the two westernmost Kuria Murias.

Poetically if not geographically, the Kuria Murias belong to the same harmonious archipelago as Serendip, the Celebes, Tahiti and Taprobane, Andaman and Nicobar, the Isle of Grain and the Isle of Dogs. I had fallen in love with the name years before, in the atlas. Since then the authorities in Muscat had changed it to the Hallaniyat, after the main island in the group. This further addition to the islands' nomenclature seemed to be based on a misunderstanding – that 'Kuria Muria' was a European invention, connected in some way with the Virgin Mary. It was true that the islands were shown on the fourteenth-century Catalan Map, reduced to two, as 'Dua Maria'.

But they had also appeared well before, and in an eminently respectable Arabic source: in his twelfth-century *Book of Roger*, al-Idrisi called them 'Khurtan and Murtan'. (The *t* is almost certainly a scribal error for *y*; a hundred years later Ibn al-Mujawir gave the more correct form, 'Khuryan and Muryan'.)

According to al-Idrisi, the Kuria Murians were marooned on their islands every winter, 'living in the direst distress and poverty'. At other times, however, they were able to reach the mainland to sell ambergris and turtle shells, which the Yemenis used as bread-baskets and washing-up bowls. There was a postscript, uncharacteristically sensational for al-Idrisi. The Kuria Murians, he says, regularly visit a certain Island of Apes. Here, 'they catch the apes and take them to Yemen, where they are sold for a high price. The people of Yemen, I mean the merchants, keep the apes in their shops as security guards.' (A story told in the tenth century by that great source of sailors' yarns, Captain Buzurg of Ramhurmuz, illustrates the apes' devotion to duty: 'I was told that a man somewhere in Yemen had an ape, and that one day he bought some meat and took it home. He indicated to the ape that it should keep an eye on the meat. But a kite came and snatched the meat. For a time the ape didn't know what to do. Then it had an idea. It climbed to the top of a tree and hung upside-down

with its backside in the air. The kite saw the ape's backside, thought that it was more meat and swooped down on it. At that instant, the ape caught the bird, took it into the house and hid it under a weighted cooking pot. When the man came back, he found that the meat was missing and went to give the ape a hiding. But the ape revealed the kite, and the man understood what had happened. He took the kite, plucked it, and crucified it on the tree.')

From later medieval times onwards, the Kuria Murias got only a few brief mentions in mariners' guides. Then in 1854 Sayyid Sa'id, the ruler of Muscat and Zanzibar, gave the islands to Queen Victoria. The islanders, unaware that they had been subjects of Muscat and were now living on a British possession, were surprised by the arrival of Nazarenes and squads of navvies. This was the age of guano fever, and the Kuria Murias were a rich source – indeed, a not entirely implausible theory suggests that the first element of 'Khuryan Muryan' means 'shitty', from the root *khari*', to defecate. The east-ernmost island of al-Qibli, home to a large colony of masked boobies, was stripped of its valuable crust. Thereafter odd visitors passed by – Colonel Miles noted in 1883 that the houses were roofed with seaweed and shark bones and were 'the height of a walking stick' – but in general the islanders were left to their fishing, the boobies to their slow increment of excrement. At some point the Mahri population left, to be replaced by Shahris. Then in 1959 Sir William Luce, the Governor of Aden, dropped in on this furthest corner of his parish – 'my first and, I sincerely hope, my last visit'. He thought the islanders 'the most malodorous and ill-kempt characters that it has been my misfortune to meet'. Now, as we passed under the lee of Sawdah, the Black Isle, I wondered what time and Sultan Qabus had done to the Kuria Murias.

Hallaniyah was almost unnaturally bright as we approached it, like an image seen in a slide viewer. If this really were IB's Jabal Lum'an, the name was appropriate: *lum'an* should mean something like 'gleaming'. The *sambuq* slid tentatively past underwater rocks and entered the little harbour exactly twelve hours after leaving Mirbat.

Things had changed since the Governor's visit. The crowd on the quay were neatly kitted out in jazzy waistcloths and football shirts. The head islander who received Sir William had worn 'a naval officer's ancient white tunic and very little else'; the present head islander, Deputy Governor Awfit al-Shahri, wore a *dishdashah* of a blue-whiteness rarely seen outside soap powder ads, and a raspberry coulis and mange-tout turban. He drove me in his Landcruiser past the desalination plant, generating station, fish-freezing facility, clinic, school and mosque; then along a street of what he called 'popular housing' – a dozen castellated villas finished off with satellite dishes.

Awfit dropped me at the guest-house. 'I hope you don't mind being a bit cramped,' he said, 'but we've got a team of divers visiting.' I said something about having expected to stay in a hut of fishes' bones and seaweed. The Deputy Governor gave me an unnerving look, and excused himself.

The divers were off diving, but their gear was scattered all about: cylinders, flippers, masks, lumps of coral, turtle skulls and open novels. A sign on the gate said 'Check for Goats under Car before Driving off'. I sat at a table in the yard and tried to fix my position. In one sense I was exactly where I had expected to be: at $17\frac{1}{2}°$ N, $56°$ E, on a lump of granite with a limestone topping, seven miles by four and a half, rising at the north-east to 1,645 feet. In another, I was back in Muscat, or at least in a miniature facsimile of its Omani-baronial suburbs. It was most disorientating.

The divers returned at the end of the afternoon. I had wondered if they would see me as an intruder; but they were immediately welcoming, and introduced me to the arcane world of fins and compressors. Steve Dover, their leader, explained that they were studying coral and other marine life on the wreck of the *City of Winchester*, the first naval casualty of the Great War. 'I've never seen anything like the environment around Hallaniyah,' he said. 'It's pristine. And because we know exactly when the ship went down, it's the perfect place for looking at coral growth.' He invited me to dive with them the following day. 'Awfit's had a go, haven't you, Awfit?' The Deputy Governor, who had just come into the yard, smiled sheepishly. I said I'd think about it; then heard one of the team talking about an under-water encounter that afternoon. 'I turned round', he said, 'and there was this fifteen-foot mako shark staring at me. I don't know who got the bigger shock.' I decided to stick to inverse archaeology.

I read Awfit IB's account of his visit to Jabal Lum'an. ' "Lum'an" ?' he said. 'I've never heard of it.'

'Well, there's nowhere else that would fit, except for one of the Kur . . . the Hallaniyat,' I said. 'I mean, the Hallaniyat do seem to have had several other names. Like the Islands of Bani Ghalfan.'

' "Bani Ghalfan" ? What is this "Bani Ghalfan" ?'

I looked at him in surprise. 'Bani Ghalfan were the Mahri tribe who lived on the islands, probably for centuries.'

'Who told you this? *Who was it?*'

I was taken aback. 'I thought it was common knowledge. Sayyid Sa'id called them the Islands of Bani Ghalfan when he gave them to Queen Victoria,' I said. Awfit grimaced. I had put my foot in it. 'And the name's in Luqman's *History of the Islands of Yemen.*' Squelch went the other foot.

Awfit was looking at me like the aghast chorus in an H.M. Bateman cartoon. I was the Man Who Talked About The Past. '*I* represent the state in the Hallaniyat. All information comes through my office alone. Anyone giving false information will be made to bear the responsibility!' He rose and glided out of the yard. I hadn't realized inverse archaeology could arouse such passion. I sat there, wide-eyed and shaken: Awfit was my equivalent of that fifteen-foot mako.

'Wow!' Steve exclaimed. 'What was all that about?'

'History.'

'He can be a bit sensitive, Awfit, especially about this name business. Evidently there was a Sultanic Decree that made it an imprisonable offence even to say ... ' he lowered his voice ' ... "Kuria Muria". I didn't know about it. We were originally called the Kuria Muria Expedition. I had a load of writing-paper done. Had to bin the lot and start again.'

Awfit was too young to remember much of the pre-Qabusian era, but I had heard that the old head islander was still alive – the one who had worn a navy surplus tunic to receive Sir William Luce. That evening I found him, a handsome man in his eighties, sitting on the gravel in the gateway of one of the villas and wearing a swish *dishdashah.*

Shaykh Sa'id seemed to be expecting me. I had hardly introduced myself when he began a short but vehement speech. 'These are the days of blessing! Before, we had only hovels and caves to live in. Now we have progress! God bless His Majesty the Sultan! If you meet him, give him a kiss from me, from Shaykh Sa'id bin Muhammad!'

I tried to nudge him into the past, but he had nothing more to say. As I rose to leave, his son spoke: 'You must only write good things about us.'

On the way back to the guest-house it crossed my mind that Shaykh Sa'id might have been nobbled by Awfit. Then again, how could I assume that the old man would have wanted to talk about the past? The houses of fishes' bones and seaweed may have represented an unbroken architectural tradition that went back to IB, and presumably long before; but there was no denying that they must have been hovels. I began to understand why the islands had been renamed. To call the Kuria Murias the Hallaniyat was, in effect, to claim that their inhabitants no longer lived in the same old place; that they had moved on, progressed in a more than metaphorical sense. They had been resettled in a new and improved island – one that incidentally occupied the same co-ordinates as their former home. None of this boded well for inverse archaeology.

The Kuria Murias being the Arabian equivalent of Rhum, Eigg and Muck, one might imagine them to be a tranquil spot. Next morning, however, I found myself simultaneously eating breakfast with some of the divers and being videoed by others, interrogated by the Deputy Governor, and videoed and interviewed by a journalist from the Moral Guidance Department of the Omani Ministry of Defence. The power breakfast had also attracted a crowd of about thirty onlookers who murmured a commentary in rapid Shahri.

' "Kuria Muria" is a British invention.'

'Could you pass the jam? No it isn't, it's in al-Idrisi.'

'We're making this short film, and we'd like some impressions of the islands.'

'Twenty-five people have been imprisoned for using the name "Kuria Muria".'

'I'm a bit short on impressions. I only got here yesterday afternoon. I haven't seen anything yet. Look Awfit, "Khuryan and Muryan" is in Ibn al-Mujawir as well.'

'. . . some impressions, please, Mr Makuntush?'

'I said I've only just got here.'

'Ten of them were imprisoned on the island, fifteen on the mainland.'

'. . . impressions?'

'Would "jewels of ever-changing hue set in a placid sea" do you?'

'Have a banana.'

Eventually the film crew went back to the airstrip, the divers went off to dive, and I told Awfit that a rose by any other name would smell as sweet. It lost something in translation, but he seemed to appreciate the sentiment.

I moved the conversation on to the safer subject of birds. Awfit told me that the Hallaniyat were a paradise for ornithologists.

'And not just ornithologists,' I said. 'I've heard that the cormorant, and the eggs of the *dagh*, the booby, are particularly delicious.' Awfit frowned; a ripple of silence passed around the chorus of islanders. 'I mean,' I went on, floundering, 'gulls' eggs are served in some of the best London restaurants, and I wondered . . .'

'I am not aware', said Awfit tartly, 'that any of the present generation has eaten these things. Perhaps the islanders did, long ago.'

Again, the locked door of the past. I approached my major topic with no great hope of success, and read out IB's account of his meeting with the holy man – diplomatically omitting the name 'Lum'an'. There were a few expressions of wonderment. 'Now,' I went on, hesitantly, 'it's just a thought, but I wondered if the hermit might have been buried at the site of his cell.' It was dangerous ground: the past, and faith. 'I don't suppose there are any tombs of holy men on the islands?'

To my amazement, the question released a flood of information. Awfit told me the names of seven holy *sayyids*, six buried on Hallaniyah and one on Sawdah. 'We think they all came from the mainland, some of them a long time ago. And I've got an idea. Your traveller says he didn't understand what the hermit was saying. Perhaps he was speaking in Shahri.' Or, I thought but didn't say, Mahri.

I smiled at Awfit. At last we were getting somewhere.

*

Broadly speaking, the sea was blue. It was also blue-green, green-blue, jade, navy, purple and gold – little worms of colour that wriggled around the slender hull. Sa'd and his brother Ahmad spoke occasionally to point things out: a cave, an osprey, a trickle of water on the cliff face. As we neared Hallaniyah Head the cliffs rose higher, tier upon tier of galleries like a collapsing Colosseum. The sea became more boisterous. Wriggle, kiss and tickle turned to slap then, around the point, to head-butt. The water went blue-black, like a bruise.

IB recalled climbing up to visit his hermit. I had therefore elimi-

nated five of the seven holy tombs, since they were at or near sea-level. This left two, Sayyids Ali Hajj and Sa'id, as candidates for the traveller's holy man. With Awfit's permission, I was going to the far end of the island to visit them.

Island hermits appear from time to time in the records of Islamic mysticism. That prototype traveller and solitary, al-Khadir, would occasionally appear from an island in the Atlantic to guide ships in distress. IB's contemporary Ibn al-Khatib wrote of a Berber holy man who had journeyed 'to one of the islands of the western sea, impelled by divine command to devote himself solely to God'. IB himself came across other island hermits, at the head of the Gulf on Abbadan – at the time an island and a sort of Islamic Athos – and off the coast of India. The only fully authenticated hermit of Hallaniyah was later in date. The man, a retired Iraqi brigadier, was 'living in a stone hut in the village for which he paid rent', the British Consul in Muscat reported in 1954. 'He seems a very simple and harmless type and is perhaps a little mad.'

The Consul would probably have described IB's hermit in similar terms. 'On top of the Hill of Lum'an,' the traveller remembered, twenty-five years after his visit,

is a hermitage built of stone, with a roof of fish bones, and with
a pool of collected rainwater outside it. When we cast anchor
under the hill, we climbed up to this hermitage, and found there
an old man lying asleep. We saluted him, and he woke up and
returned our greeting by signs; then we spoke to him, but he
did not speak to us and kept shaking his head. The ship's
company offered him food, but he refused to accept it. We then
begged of him a prayer on our behalf, and he kept moving his
lips, though we did not know what he was saying. He was
wearing a patched robe and a felt bonnet. The ship's company
declared that they had never before seen him on this hill. We
spent the night on the beach, and prayed the afternoon and
sunset prayers with him. He continued to pray until the hour of
the last night-prayer. He had a beautiful voice in his reciting
of the Qur'an. When he ended the last night-prayer, he signed
to us to withdraw, so, bidding him farewell, we did so, with
astonishment at what we had seen of him. Afterwards, when we
had left, I wished to return to him, but on approaching him I
felt in awe of him; fear got the better of me, and when my companions returned for me, I went off with them.

Awe – the conflict in IB between fascination and fear – had given a
minor encounter on an insignificant island all the remembered intensity of a recurring dream. But while IB recalled the hermit with
filmic clarity, the topographical details are far sparser, edited by time:
the person was, as usual, more important than the place. I had little to
go on, and my idea that the hermit might have been buried at the site
of his cell was no more than wild conjecture. And yet I had to look,
even though I sensed I was looking for something intangible.

Soon after passing Hallaniyah Head we reached a small bay called
Ahawl. The swell was too big to land, so Ahmad dropped the anchor
and Sa'd and I jumped into the water. It came up to our chests. We
waded ashore and climbed up a bluff above a small wadi. Sayyid Ali
Hajj's grave was a boat-shaped pile of stones within a larger oval enclosure. Inside this was what looked like a wooden post-box. Sa'd said it
once contained cups, 'so that visitors could drink coffee'. He also told
me that anyone who removed anything from a *sayyid*'s grave would
be punished. 'Even if you just took a pebble, your boat would be
wrecked.' While he recited the Fatihah, I scanned the surroundings.

Those three clues – the beach, the climb up, the pool – were all I had to follow; the only distinctive one, in a steep island with many sandy bays, was the pool. There was no trace of one.

We swam back to the boat and continued south, Sa'd and I shivering in our sodden clothes. At the bay of Ahalt we were able to beach the *hawri*, and all three of us climbed upwards through rocky gulleys. Sa'd picked up the skeleton of a bird. 'It's a *dagh*,' he said. A booby. 'We sometimes catch them on al-Qibli, then skin them and salt the flesh.'

We climbed on, well out of sight of the beach. My hopes fell. The putative hermitage had to be in sight of the shore: how else would IB have known of its existence? Eventually we reached an eminence of decaying granite. From here the low eastern point of the island was visible, and beyond it al-Qibli, the island of boobies. And directly below us to the south-east lay a shoreline fringed with sand. I felt – was it because I wanted to feel it? – a faint cognitive stirring, like the twitch of the rod in a dowser's hand.

We took off our footwear and approached the grave of Sayyid Sa'id, a low pile of fractured rocks topped by a couple of bleached shells. Slowly, Sa'd and Ahmad walked around it, stroking the stones and kissing their hands. After they had recited the Fatihah, we sat down in silence. Next to us was a shallow depression in the granite where, in time of rain, the water would collect.

'Who was Sayyid Sa'id?' I asked them, breaking the silence.

'God gave us the *sayyids*,' Ahmad said. 'There were many jinn here. The *sayyids* protect us from the jinn and from all evil.'

More silence. Then Sa'd spoke: 'A man from the island was captured by people from the north. They tied his hands and feet and threw him into the sea, off Shinas – that's the small island we could see from Sayyid Ali Hajj's grave. But the man called out, *Ya Sayyid Sa'id!* The next thing he knew, he was sitting here where we're sitting, safe and sound. The pirates' boat was destroyed – bang! like a torpedo hitting it – and they were all drowned. Except for a slave, who swam all the way to Sawqirah. After that everybody knew that if they harmed us, a curse would fall on them.'

'The *sayyids* are very powerful,' Ahmad said. 'You can only visit them if they want you to.'

As we left the grave, I wanted more than at any previous time on my travels to raise the ghost of IB and ask him, *Was this the place?*

Ahmad and Sa'd took me to an old site nearby, called Akhruf. We poked about in the remains of a round structure of big granite pebbles, and found some ancient cane-like netting. 'This is what they used to hold down the seaweed on the roof,' said Ahmad. Sa'd pointed out a flat stone which he said was used for ladies' make-up. It all seemed immensely ancient, like Skara Brae. I said I was impressed by the brothers' knowledge of the past. They smiled, and told me that the house was where their parents had spent the summer months, before Sultan Qabus and popular housing.

We had a snack lunch of *sisan*, dried spinefoot, then a nap in a cave. As I dozed, I was visited by doubts. The scholarly Gibb had been certain that Lum'an was Hallaniyah; but might it be another of the Kuria Murias? Then, could there be some coastal rock elsewhere, too small to appear on the maps? To go into all the possibilities I would need the resources of a major expedition and to be, like the Iraqi brigadier, perhaps a little mad. In short, I would never know if I had found IB's island, let alone his hermit.

I thought back to that depression in the granite, and wished IB had left just a few more clues. Should I return to the grave, and scrabble around for something carbon-datable? But then, I could take nothing away. Except something intangible, insusceptible to calibration and rational investigation: awe.

★

I left Hallaniyah the following morning with Maurice, Khalil, the tentative blessings of Awfit and five tons of fish. Again we passed Sawdah, the Black Island – not so much black as rusty – then the smaller, lower Hasikiyyah. In my imagination, every protruding rock on them became a grave or a ruined hermitage.

The sea simmered with activity. Something slick and black shot out of the water and fell back with a slap. A long slender fin rose above the surface, like Excalibur, then disappeared. All around there were other intriguing surfacings and bubblings in the rich bouilla-baisse of the coastal waters. 'The sea', wrote the traveller Abu Hamid, 'has a greater share of wonders than any other part of creation.' As we reached the mainland at Ras Nus I wrote in my notebook: 'Sea still full of *aja'ib*, even if wonders now = e.g. whale songs.'

Precisely on cue, Khalil nudged me. Only yards away from the *sambuq* a prodigious head was emerging. It lingered, dead still above the water, black, barnacled, beautiful as sea-born Venus. Ponderously, it sank. There was a jet of water. Then a tail appeared – a great glistening V that stood for a moment then slid, slowly, vertically downwards. For all its size, it left hardly a ripple.

Next morning I passed Ras Nus again, in another *sambuq* – the *Sea-Lion* of Captain Rashid of Salalah. The whale was there too, with a friend. They were both whacking the water with their tails. Perhaps my timing was bad, but I told Captain Rashid a story from the *Wonders of India* of Captain Buzurg about a ship in the Red Sea getting rammed by a whale. When it later put into Jeddah, they found the whale's head in the hold, broken off and neatly plugging the hole it had made in the hull. Rashid capped Buzurg's tale with one about a *sambuq* that had entered Dubai, 'not long ago', with a whale impaled on its prow. (I had already heard the story in Muscat, with the whale demoted to a whale-shark. Unlikely though even this sounded, it was told by no less an authority than the Director of the Muscat Natural History Museum.)

The *Sea-Lion* was on its way from Sad'h to Hasik, my final Battutian destination in Oman. Hasik is as much of an island as Hallaniyah for, although on the mainland, it is inaccessible by motor transport and even by radio telephone, marooned under the massif of Jabal Samhan. IB wrote about Hasik's two products, frankincense and sharks, and remembered that like the island hermitage its huts were built with fish bones. By probably no more than delightful coincidence, the root of the name is connected with spiky things – *hasak* is a thistle, a grappling-iron, or a fish bone.

We bounced along, throwing up a fine and drenching spray over the bows. To port, the sea cliffs of Samhan trailed shreds of cloud like the scarves of an exotic dancer. Rashid pointed out a tiny footpath that wiggled along the cliff, used in the monsoon when Hasik was cut off even from the sea. The walk to the roadhead at Hadbin, he said, took seven hours. Just after Ras Nus there was a long bay, a thin line of sand at the base of a towering escarpment; at its far end were a few small buildings. Rashid explained that they housed visitors to the tomb of Bin Hud, invisible in a nook among the rocks. Whoever Bin Hud is – and some think he is the Prophet Salih, son of the Prophet Hud – he has gained a reputation for irritability rather like that of the old Irish saints. Rashid said he was prone to wrecking ships: as if in proof a large cargo vessel lay aground nearby, looking like a bit of jetsam against the backdrop of the escarpment. (I heard later,

however, that since the beginning of Qabus's reign Bin Hud has generally been quite affable.)

Five hours out of Sad'h we reached Hasik, a line of long boxy houses and a stubby minaret. The roads shone with leaping dolphins, and among the five *sambuq*s at anchor there I recognized one: that of Khalfan the Suri.

I now knew that Deputy Governors, like holy men, are not to be trifled with, and approached the chief citizen of Hasik with appropriate awe. Fortuitously, Ali al-Shikayli was a grandson of the owner of the *Wolf*, that old sailing *sambuq* I had seen at Sad'h. When I showed him the transcript of the prayers carved on its stern, he beamed: it was his father, he said, who had done the calligraphy. He spoke nostalgically of the *Wolf*'s voyages, carrying frankincense to Aden, Basrah and India, and *lukham*, dried shark, to East Africa. These were the very products IB had mentioned; but I learned from Ali that in recent years they had declined. Hardly any frankincense was collected these days; and dried shark had been superseded by abalone, that rubbery restorer of the lost youth of Hong Kong businessmen, and by frozen fish. With its new freezing plant Hasik entered the Ice Age, and the trade of centuries, perhaps millennia, disappeared.

Some *lukham* is still produced for home consumption, however, and Ali sent for a piece from an old fisherman. It had the appearance of an old boot sole, and the texture. '*Lukham* needs good strong teeth,' the fisherman told me, 'and a woman afterwards.' As I had neither I gave the object no more than an experimental nibble, and decided that fish-freezing plants were a good idea.

Soon after my arrival Ali was called away from Hasik to a family funeral, and left me the run of the deputy-gubernatorial residence. Indians brought me trays of rice and fish of monstrous size. I wrote up my diary. And I watched satellite TV. A random sampling of Arabsat produced: a debate on medical treatment by Qur'anic recitation (Sudan); a twenty-minute ad for an anti-insomnia pillow (Orbit Shopping); a traffic police docu-soap (Dubai); a discussion on fitted kitchens (Qatar); three old men, drumming and chanting, near to tears (Sudan again); an ad for a tummy-trimmer (Orbit again); a Qur'anic pronunciation class, then Colonel Qaddafi – looking ever more like one of the Rolling Stones, or a mixture of all of them (Libya); and finally the call to prayer, with stills of my home, the old city of San'a (Yemen).

Arabsat was meant to bring it all closer. Instead, it magnified the immense isolation of Hasik. I sympathized with the Dong, far away on his shore, gazing, gazing for evermore.

★

IB got it wrong. 'The frankincense trees', he wrote, 'have thin leaves, and when a leaf is slashed there drips from it a sap like milk, which then turns into a gum.' Shaykh Musallam bin Sa'id al-Naqsh Thaw'ar al-Mahri showed me how it was really done, two hundred feet up the side of Wadi Hadbaram behind Hasik. With both hands, he gripped his chisel-like *manqaf* and with a few downward strokes sliced off a patch of bark to reveal a pistachio-green layer beneath. More strokes left a wound the colour of raw beef. Slowly, beads of white began to appear on the wound, like pus. Musallam called the operation *tawqi'*, a word which can mean 'to gall a camel's back'.

'You mustn't cut to the bone of the tree', he explained, 'or you'll kill it. But you can come back and make more *tawqi's* in the same spot. The more you do it, the more the tree produces. It's like a cow milking better the more calves she has.' The frankincense would take several weeks to seep out, but Musallam had already given me a bag from last year's harvest. This was the *hawjiri* variety praised by Radiyyah in the Salalah scent market, the aristocrat of gum-resins.

Apart from the obvious benefits of smelling nice and driving off demons, frankincense can be used as a tooth-filler, a crack-sealant and a depilatory. According to the Rasulid Sultan al-Muzaffar's book of simples, it heals wounds, staunches blood, clears darkness of vision, burns phlegm, strengthens a queasy stomach, cures diarrhoea and vomiting, expels wind, eases palpitations, protects against the plague and warms a cold liver. Employed as a pessary, it halts vaginal discharge; chewed, it reinforces the teeth and gums, eases speech impediments and combats forgetfulness (of this I took special note, as according to some authorities one of the main causes of amnesia is 'over-attachment to reading the inscriptions on tombstones'). Overdosing, al-Muzaffar warns, can bring on headaches, melancholy, scabies and, in extreme cases, leprosy. I also found in an eighteenth-century Yemeni book on bathing that a mixture of frankincense, olive oil, nigella oil and honey taken in the bath is 'an excellent stimulant of libido in the hundred-plus age-group'.

After the demonstration, Musallam shouldered his hunting rifle and led me down the side of the gorge. Above us on the cliff tops sat a layer of mist, and I remembered the description of the Frankincense Country in the *Periplus* – 'a land mountainous and forbidding, wrapped in thick clouds and fog'. And there was that other, more fanciful mention: that of Herodotus, who thought the frankincense groves were guarded by flying snakes.

Musallam was ready to return to Hasik, but I said I would explore further up the gorge.

'Watch out for leopards,' he warned. 'And snakes.'

I smiled. 'I bet they're flying snakes.'

'Yes. They jump out of the *samur* trees.'

I walked up Wadi Hadbaram into a silence broken only by the rustle of reeds and the beat of pigeons' wings high up on the rock face. I saw some leopard spoor; the *samur* trees I gave the widest possible berth.

★

I wondered if IB had also got it wrong when he wrote about the fish-bone houses of Hasik; perhaps he had been misled by that near homonym, *hasak*. But how could I find out? I had thoroughly explored the village, and found not a vestige of anything pre-Qabus. Al-Habshi, a man who worked in the Deputy Governor's office, explained the reason: Hasik had moved.

Together, we visited the old site of Hasik, a couple of miles to the west. Most of the structures were converted caves in the bank of a dry watercourse, walled in with stone. I had a good poke around but found nothing to indicate a date.

'Let's go to Old Hasik,' al-Habshi said.

'I thought this was it.'

'It is. But there's an older one further west. It's full of remains.'

A short distance along the coast, we came to a large expanse of ruins overlooking an anchorage. Beside the shell of the mosque were some fine inscribed gravestones, which I began to read with growing excitement. None, however, dated to earlier than the eighteenth century. We rooted around the ruins of houses and found shards of Chinese porcelain. Most of them were blue-and-white: post-IB. There was none of the celadon ware in which the site of Qalhat had been so rich; and there were no fish bones. It seemed that Hasik had come up in the world in the centuries following IB's visit, and that all traces of the settlement he saw had been swept away or built over.

We went and sat on the rocks by the sea. I asked al-Habshi if we would find any *sufaylih*, abalone. To lunch al fresco on this most reju-venating of shellfish would, I thought, be partial recompense for not finding any relics of IB's Hasik.

'We used to eat it when I was a boy,' he told me. 'You could buy a sackful for next to nothing. Then they started exporting it. Do you know how much it fetches? Dried, 270 riyals a kilo.' About £200 a pound. A snip when you think of the cost of tiger penises. 'Even the women collect abalone nowadays. At first they'd just wade in and feel around for it in the crevices in the rocks. These days they go diving, like the men. Fully clothed, of course.' I had a thrilling vision of the lady abalone divers, formerly mere ticklers, of Hasik, dripping like Ophelia and clattering with aphrodisiac univalves.

Instead of eating abalone we feasted on rock oysters and chitons. The latter look like something from the earlier stages of creation – flattened armoured slugs that move very slowly across the rocks. You pick them off, snap them and gouge out with your thumb a pink, tongue-like *médaillon* of crunchy flesh. Al-Habshi said that oysters and chitons, *zikt* and *shanah* as he called them in the Mahri tongue, were an old staple of the coast and islands. I grazed off the rocks until I could eat no more; I was making up for missing out on those other old favourites, cormorants and boobies.

Al-Habshi then remembered that there was yet another old site, further west and over a headland. We crossed the rocks and came to a small bay, dead still, dead quiet. Above the beach there were several boat-shaped graves, one with an outer enclosing wall like that of Sayyid Ali Hajj on Hallaniyah. There were also a number of ruins which looked like the remains of dwellings. I hunted in vain for celadon; then, scrabbling among the stones, I found IB's fish bones: plaster-white, pitted and brittle, piles and piles of broad flat fragments half covered by blown sand.

Time which antiquates Antiquities, and hath an art to make dust of all things, hath yet spared these minor *Monuments.* They were less than minor: they were minimal. But, for a moment, I felt I had unearthed a colossus.

★

Back in Salalah, Qahtan, his *shaykh*, a goat and I went for a picnic on a mountainside from which only three of us returned. (I shall put it in writing: contrary to Sir Wilfred Thesiger's statement in *Arabian Sands*, the Khawar are a noble clan and generous to strangers.) My mention of the leopard spoor in Wadi Hadbaram elicited a long story from Qahtan about a three-hour wrestling match between a leopard and a Mahri. It ended with the Mahri sticking his hand down the leopard's throat and ripping out its gorge, which he carried in triumph to hospital. The man, however, soon tired of newfangled treatments and discharged himself. He stewed his victim and plastered his wounds with leopard lard.

I was reluctant to leave, reluctant to wear trousers again (for most of the past month I had lived in waistcloths), reluctant to say farewell to friends. But I was in danger of becoming a stationary thing, of little worth. As we parted, Habibah told me I'd be missed; not only by her, Muhammad and Nadia, but also by several Dhofari ladies of her acquaintance who had been discussing, she said, the exceeding whiteness of my legs.

On second thoughts, perhaps it was time to get back into trousers.

After performing the Mecca pilgrimage once more IB left Jeddah by sea, bound for India; 'but', he wrote, 'that was not decreed for me'. He ended up instead at Aydhab, from where he retraced his earlier route, via Cairo, to Syria. From the Syrian port of al-Ladhiqiyyah he sailed to Alanya, and began a tour of the Turkoman sultanates of Anatolia.

Anatolia

Hajji Baba, the Skystone and Other Mysteries

'When he attended the *sema*, the dome of the mosque would
rise into the air and he would see the revolutions of the angels.'

al-Nabhani (d. 1931), *Jami karamat al-awliya*, on the dervish
Sumbul al-Rumi

A T THREE O'CLOCK in the morning my neighbour the travesty
artiste made an intimate suggestion on the balcony of the Yayla
Hotel ('Cheap and Comfort'). Half Turk, half Greek, male during
the day and female when he performed, as he did nightly, at the
Banana Club, he was way beyond the brief of inverse archaeology.
I politely declined the suggestion.

Sleep was not among the few amenities on offer at the Yayla. Since
midnight the hotel had shaken to an incessant, seismic beat – *boom-
shagga-boom-shagga-boom* – from Pub 13 across the road. 'What are
they doing?' I asked the travesty artiste, as a stream of young men
went in.

He sighed. 'Dancing, and looking for girlfriends.'

We sat and drank *rakı* and talked about cleavage simulation. At four
o'clock I went to my room and lay down. The bedsprings rattled to
the disco beat, like drumsnares. Finally, at five, Pub 13 fell silent. In
the stillness, rock gave way to Prufrock, and I asked myself what I was
here for. It was not my first existential crisis; but nowhere had it been
as profound as here in Alanya.

Mediterranean Turkey was doubly foreign. Like IB, I had left the
Arabophone world; unlike him, I also seemed to have entered one

where they spoke an entirely different cultural language – a sort of Euro-Teutonic. Most of the tourists in Alanya were *ur* Germans but even some of the Turkish visitors affected rimless spectacles and *gemütlich* lapdogs. Sauerkraut was served with everything; every other building seemed to be a disco. One nightclub, the Whiskey Go Go, offered 'Sex on the Beach'. To be fair, it was not an activity but a pop group; but it seemed to sum up the ineffable crassitude of the place. Where was the Alanya of IB?

Gone.

So it appeared, anyway, as dawn broke. But later that morning, swimmy with lack of sleep, I climbed the road to the headland and came to another Alanya. It began with a gateway, the entrance to IB's 'magnificent and formidable citadel, built by the exalted Sultan Ala 'l-Din'. As I wrote down the inscription above the gate I wondered if IB had also stood here with pen and notebook.

Ala 'l-Din, the Seljuk Sultan of Rum, was keen to leave his mark. He gave the ancient Coracesium not only a new citadel but also a new name – al-ʿAlāʾiyyah, after himself. (An inexplicable Turkish aversion to voiced pharyngeals, glottal stops and geminate semi-vowels soon deformed this into 'Alaya'; the intrusive *n* is probably part of a process by which the place will eventually become 'Almanya', or Germany.) At the same time, according to a helpful information board at a café beside the gate, Ala 'l-Din was busy with the traditional Turkish sport of Armenian-bashing: 'He purifies the coastal regions from Armenians,' it said, in a frisky historic present surrounded by winking fairy lights.

IB arrived in Alanya a century later, in 1331. The glorious line of the Seljuks of Rum had ended twenty years earlier when the last sultan, pressed by creditors and by the Tatar Ilkhan of the Two Iraqs, took poison. That other great Turkish dynasty, that of the Ottomans, was still in its infancy. The Ottoman baby was rapidly turning into a hyperactive toddler; but for the moment it shared Anatolia with nine other statelets, founded by rival Turkoman chieftains among the ruins of the Seljuk sultanate. Western European travellers thought the Turkomans uncouth and bestial; Ludolph von Suchem went as far as to call them 'in all respects mean, and with the same customs as *Frisians*'. IB, however, was among co-religionists; moreover, he now had a taste for princes, however petty or newly Islamized. In Turkey he was in for a multiplicity of sultans. I had little idea of what remained from their short-lived princedoms. I knew there were plenty of Seljuk and Ottoman remains; but what had the Karamanoğulları, the Aydınoğulları, the Candaroğulları (or İsfendi-yaroğulları) and their fellow Turkoman dynasties left behind, other than their very long names? In the annals of Anatolia they were little more than a parenthesis.

Alanya, away from the sauerkraut and Sex on the Beach, was magnificently Seljuk. I explored the citadel, contouring with its walls around the headland and losing myself in lanes loud with the racket of crickets. Down at sea-level a fat Seljuk tower loomed over the harbour like a giant biscuit barrel. Nearby was a vaulted dockyard. It squatted in the water, solid as a Victorian viaduct, each arch big enough to admit a Seljuk warship; the inside eddied with light and shadow, part grotto, part undercroft and slippery with seaweed.

IB arrived here from al-Ladhiqiyyah on a Genoese merchantman. 'We travelled with a favouring wind,' he remembered, 'and the Christians treated us honourably and took no passage-money from us.' Earlier writers had also praised the Genoese mariners, who enjoyed a virtual monopoly on Mediterranean shipping. 'They are a dark-eyed people with the same colouring and finely shaped noses as the Arabs,' wrote the twelfth-century geographer al-Zuhri. 'Indeed, they are the Quraysh of the Christians,' he went on, paying them the highest possible compliment – Quraysh are the tribe of the Prophet. For their part the Genoese occasionally gave their sons orientalizing names like 'Turco' and 'Soldan', so the admiration must have been mutual.

Now, though, a different sort of Frank dominated the Mediterranean. I sat in the dockyard and watched them jet-skiing, parascending, and bungee-jumping off a crane across the bay. In a way I envied them – not their frantic forms of relaxation, but their conviviality. I faced a prospect of one-night cheap hotels, empty *rakı* bottles and no company save the shade of IB and my diary, mute tyrant of my evenings. IB himself had come to Turkey with a *rafiq*, a travelling companion, a Tunisian called Abdullah al-Tuzari. (He was to remain with him until his death in Goa a dozen years later, a dim figure of whom, beyond the slender facts of his name and the time of his demise, we learn next to nothing.) I could have done with my own flesh-and-blood *rafiq*, someone with whom I could speak the same language.

*

Antalya, along the coast, was less furiously touristic. Ottoman houses, and streams – 'springs of excellent water,' IB wrote, 'sweet and very cold in summer' – tumbled down the hill to a perfect harbour. Looking on to the town from above, I could make out bits of the walls which according to IB had divided the various communities of the port – Franks, Byzantines, Jews and Muslims. Now, fragmented, they made a dot-to-dot puzzle within the scattered jigsaw of gardens and pantiled roofs. Above all this rose Sultan Ala 'l-Din's Yivli Minare, the Fluted Minaret, like a chunky propelling pencil.

As usual, IB was more interested in people than in buildings, and he remembered a meeting on the second day of his stay in Antalya. A young cobbler came up to him, 'wearing shabby clothes and a felt bonnet', and invited him to dinner. Despite his appearance, the man was leader of the Akhis, a sort of cross between a guild, a dining society and an Islamic YMCA. IB was duly treated to 'a great banquet, with fruits and sweetmeats, after which the Akhis began singing and dancing'. The welcome was to extend across Anatolia. IB praised the Akhis not only for their hospitality, but also for their ardour 'to restrain the hands of the tyrannous and to kill the agents of the police'. Strange as this may sound, in fourteenth-century Islamic cities the constabulary were a byword for corruption, and no figure was more hated than the copper's nark.

The Akhi network disbanded not many decades after IB's Anatolian visit, but I was pleased to discover near the harbour a small mosque built by a certain Akhi Yusuf. The imam showed me the founder's tomb. I wondered if I had discovered IB's shabby and generous cobbler, but found out via the imam's Qur'anic Arabic that Akhi Yusuf had lived a good eighty years too early. It was a curious conversation, full of long pauses and verilies – the Islamic equivalent of talking Latin with a pre-Vatican II priest.

Still in search of Akhi memorabilia, I tried a different tack. IB described the furnishings of the Akhis' hospice with unusual precision. Among them were 'five candelabra of the kind called *baysus*, each in the form of a brass column with three feet, which supports a brass lamp with a tube for the wick'. A visit to Antalya Museum, however, while it turned up candlesticks Roman and Ottoman (and exotica such as mystical flagellation aids and Santa Claus's jawbone) produced no *baysus*. It also reminded me how much had happened in Asia Minor: a lot, and much of it far longer ago than the fourteenth century. The quantity of classical statuary alone was astonishing: beneath a portico stood a long line of emperors and demigods, all facing the doorway to the restoration workshop. It was the first time I had seen a museum where the exhibits, and not the visitors, queued. That parenthesis in history in which IB had visited Anatolia was, I now realized, a mere interjection.

That evening, I was sitting in the hotel restaurant feeling lost – linguistically, culturally, temporally – when a strange encounter took place. Not knowing how to summon the waiter in Turkish, I called him in the Arabic of San'a ('*Ya Izzay!*' carries better than 'Er, excuse me ...'). At this, two men on the next table suddenly turned and stared at me as if I had been the risen Lazarus.

After the initial shocks – theirs of discovering an Englishman who spoke Yemeni Arabic, mine, more unnerving, of finding out that they were Israelis – we exchanged histories. The Israelis had been born in Tel Aviv to Yemeni parents: Yirham's came from a town towards Aden, Reuben's from a village near San'a. We spoke in Arabic. Now and again, Reuben would hold up his hand and ask me to repeat something; then he would say the phrase to himself, shaking his head gently. 'You see,' he explained, 'when I hear you ... I remember my father and mother. Your speech was their speech', his voice cracked, 'exactly.'

I had released a warm flood of nostalgia. 'When my great-grandmother died,' said Yirham, 'she was a hundred and five. And her last words were, "I want to go back to Yemen."'

'We're always saying that,' Reuben added. 'Life isn't easy. We orientals don't get on with the Shiknaz, the Ashkenazis. And Tel Aviv is all rush. A hundred times worse than London. Yemen ... Yemen we remember as somewhere unhurried. All that sitting around, telling stories, chewing *qat*.'

'You make it sound like the Promised Land,' I said.

They nodded.

Reuben excused himself. He returned with a damp towel. 'Israeli *qat*,' he announced.

I sat there until late at night, on the terrace of the Sun Rise Hotel, with the Zionist Enemy, exchanging jokes, proverbs, lines of songs, all of us missing Yemen, I a Yemen from which I had been absent too long, they a Yemen they had never seen, taking what Turkish law – if it had heard of it – would have regarded as a highly illegal drug. It was probably the worse *qat* I have ever chewed; but we were talking the same language.

★

The following morning Reuben and Yirham headed back to the land which, for them, had failed to live up to its promise. I left the coast for Konya, drawn like IB by a remarkable man: Jalal al-Din al-Rumi, known to the Turks as Mevlana, 'Our Master'. Born in 1207 in the northern foothills of the Hindu Kush, the future Mevlana and his family moved to Anatolia to escape the advance of the Tatars. He was brought up in the scholarly, Persianized surroundings of Seljuk Konya and became a legist and professor. And then something very strange happened. In IB's version of the story, a seller of sweetmeats came into the room where Mevlana was lecturing and offered him a cake. Mevlana abandoned his lecture and disappeared with the sweet-seller. 'After many years he returned; but he had become demented, and would speak only in Persian rhymed couplets which no one could understand. His disciples used to follow him and write down that poetry as it issued from him, and they collected it into the book called the *Mathnawi*.'

'Speaking crazily, weeping crazily, laughing crazily,' said Mevlana, in the *Mathnawi*, of another returned wanderer, 'men and women, small and great, were struck with bewilderment.' He could have been describing his own reappearance in Konya, spouting rhyming stories that inhabit the borderlands between comedy, philosophy and madness. The *Mathnawi* is the masterpiece of a holy fool. Gradually, the reader slips into a magical-real world in which a dialogue between a king and a slave on accident and substance, or a housewife having a metaphysical chat with a chickpea, seem utterly normal. There are violent swings of scale: 'Once upon a time there was a huge, enormous city, only its size was no more than the size of a saucer. Very huge it was, very wide and very long, really tremendous, tremendous as an onion.' As IB suggests, it is nonsense − but the nonsense of the 'pole', or spiritual axis of his age, the nonsense of Carroll and Blake that talks of many things, of an immense world of delight closed by your senses five.

Mevlana would often utter his couplets while dancing, or as he revolved around a pillar in his college. After his death the order he had founded − the Mevlevis, the so-called Whirling Dervishes −

continued the dance and made it the central feature of a balletic, hieratic and mystical ritual known as *sema*. For six centuries, Konya was the pivot of the dervish world. Then came Atatürk, who in 1925 banned the Mevlevis, Stalinistically, for 'reactionary conspiracy'. They were permitted to whirl again in 1953, but only once a year on the anniversary of their master's death. The Mevlevis, one of the most important of all the mystical brotherhoods to spring out of medieval Islam, were now seen by the authorities as potentially subversive Morris dancers. Business, however, saw them as a money-spinner: along the Konya road, the pirouetting dervish had become a favourite logo on eateries and service stations. I was going to miss the annual Mevlana Festival, and it didn't bother me one bit.

It was good to be away from the coast, from the fruity smells of sweat and sun-oil, ripening at the end of a long summer. Perhaps the traveller al-Maqdisi overstated things when he wrote that all cities on the sea are hotbeds of fornication and sodomy, but I knew what he was getting at. Inland Konya, in contrast, was a picture of continence, a city of beards and of foreheads lumpy from praying. It was also continental: heat radiated from the ground, but there was a hint of a chill in the air, of steppe winds from the east. The year was on the turn; I was back in Asia, and back in the Islamic world.

Mevlana's mausoleum-complex was closed, but I walked around it in the fading light, my eyes fixed on the conical turquoise dome that floats above that spiritual omphalos, that adytum of dervishes, the tomb of the saint. A dumpy woman stood at the door, stooping to read the opening times. I went to do the same and realized that she was murmuring, clutching the door handles in supplication, not reading but praying.

*

Come, come again, and again . . .
Come, be you unbeliever, idolator or fire-worshipper . . .
Our hearth is not the threshold of despair;
Even if you have broken your vow of repentance a hundred times,
Come again.

The quotation hung above the entrance to Mevlana's tomb-chamber. We took him at his word, Turks, trippers and travel writers, and piled into the mausoleum, this spiritual Alice's Restaurant, carrying our shoes in white plastic bags. The whiff of rancid trainers mingled with the odour of sanctity; devotees raised their hands in supplication before the tombs of Mevlana, his family and followers – a fleet of them, sailing for salvation, each with a turban at the masthead – while tourists raised their cameras to get a better shot. In the adjoining hall where the Mevlevis had once whirled in their *sema* ceremony, broody peasant women clucked at the preserved underpants of defunct dervish-masters. In the mosque, a tourist ran his video camera along cases of open manuscripts as if scanning barcodes at a supermarket checkout.

IB described Mevlana as 'a saint of high rank'. This is an understatement. His mana was so concentrated that even a sip of spring rainwater in which a corner of his turban had been dipped was held to transmit high-calorie blessings. The distribution of this water became an annual event, held in April; a year or two after IB's visit to Konya, Abu Sa'id, Tatar Ilkhan of the Two Iraqs, presented the Mevlevis with a vessel worthy of the ceremony. I found the April Cup in a corner of the tomb-chamber. 'Cup' was also an understatement. It stood waist-high, and was of dark bronze and hard to see in the gloom. Then I stooped down to inspect it more closely, and saw that the entire surface was inlaid with silver and gold. One cartouche stood out from the rest, polished by passing fingers: it showed a slender enthroned ruler between two Mongol pages. The ruler's features were almost worn away; but I wondered if this might be a portrait of the donor – the boy-king over whom Sultan al-Nasir sighed, 'the most beautiful of God's creatures', as IB remembered him from their meeting in Baghdad – Abu Sa'id, calligrapher, lutenist and descendant of Genghis Khan. Portrait or not, with its barbaric, almost Texan proportions married to such exquisite decoration, the April Cup overflowed with the spirit of the late Mongol age.

IB mentioned the Mevlevis' 'vast hospice in which food is served to all wayfarers'. In my imagination I had seen myself here, discussing mysteries over tripe soup. The hospice was much enlarged in Ottoman times, and Mevlevis still stirred the cauldrons in the kitchen; but the cooks were waxworks, the cooking fires lit only by red light bulbs. The mysteries had evaporated.

I gave up on dervishes and decided to look for other survivals from IB's time. The traveller admired the carpets of the region, 'which have no equal in any country, and are exported to Syria, Egypt, Iraq, India, China and the lands of the Turks'. Almost incredibly, carpets woven for the Great Mosque in Konya – probably when Sultan Ala 'l-Din built the main prayer-hall a century before IB's visit – were still in use there until the 1900s. I had read that some of them were pre-served in the Mevlana complex. A thorough search had, however, drawn a blank. I tried the mosque: perhaps I would find a carpet, even a tiny fragment, in its original setting. As Battutian relics went, a carpet on which the traveller might have prayed would be the equiv-alent of the True Cross.

In the mosque I found a superb minbar in a forest of columns – bunches of asparagus tied with ribbons, all of stone – but not a stitch of a Seljuk carpet. Next door stood two polygonal mausolea with pointed roofs, stark as spacecraft in the hard sunlight. The authorities had recently restored one of them, and commemorated the work above the original Arabic foundation text – IN ROMAN CHAR-ACTERS. 'Vandals!' I hissed. 'Is nothing sacred?'

I wandered crossly around Konya, haunted by the omnipresent face of Atatürk, axer of Arabic, dissolver of dervishes, iconoclast. As night fell my annoyance increased. Some national celebration was taking place and the streets of Konya were hung with illuminations: roses, tulips and – tip-toeing through them in dolly-mixture neon – dervishes. I returned, nauseated, to the hotel, hardly suspecting that I was about to enter a Konya, a universe, which IB knew.

My entrée came via the combination, unlikely anywhere but in Turkey, of a wrestler and a carpet merchant. The wrestler was performing physical jerks in the hotel foyer; when he had finished, we fell into conversation about Seljuk Konya. He had heard about the Great Mosque carpets but didn't know what had become of them. 'Let's ask my friend Kamil,' he suggested. 'He runs a carpet shop and knows everything about Konya.' And, I thought, remembering the patter of these salesmen in Alanya and Antalya, there'll be apple tea in six languages and no obligation to buy.

We met Kamil on the street. The wrestler passed me on to him, and the two of us walked together towards his shop. 'Where are you from, my friend?' he asked. I could predict the coming half-hour with accuracy.

'Britain. But I live in Yemen.'

All of a sudden, there on the pavement, Kamil took my arm and turned me to face him. His eyes filled with tears, the cords of his neck tightened, and he began to sing – a slow, sobbing dirge. Several passers-by stopped and listened. I recognized the words 'Yemen' and 'flower'. When he had finished, he wiped his eyes and we walked on as if nothing had happened.

'I'm sorry,' I said, wondering if I had found another exile from Yemen, 'you'll have to explain.'

'It is difficult,' Kamil said. 'But it means roughly: "This is Yemen. Its flower is . . . *çemen*." I don't know what it is in English, but it is not sweet. Bitter. "They go there and do not return. I wonder why." It is about our Osmanlı soldiers who went to your Yemen and didn't come back.' I lived, of course, in the graveyard of the Ottomans: Yemen, where, a hundred years ago, Anatolian conscripts had died by the thousand; Yemen, whose flower, as I found out later from the dictionary, is bitter cumin; a place whose name is, a century on, as sadly, musically evocative for the Turks as Picardy is for us.

In the shop Kamil gave me the foreseen apple tea and a display of his stock (there was no obligation to buy), following my reactions with the searching eye of all carpet sellers and other psychoanalysts. The phrase 'You like this one', which began as a question, gradually became a conjecture, then a gentle imperative. Uncannily, he knew exactly what I liked. I steered the discussion, however, on to IB and the Seljuk carpets of Ala 'l-Din's mosque. Kamil thought they might have been taken to Istanbul. He then asked me what else my Arab traveller had to say about Konya.

I gave him a summary of IB's account of Mevlana and his dervishes. 'And now,' I concluded, 'they are gone. Or at least they're no more than a tourist attraction . . . '

'No! You are wrong,' Kamil interrupted. 'God protects those who love him. And tonight,' he smiled arcanely, 'God willing, you will meet them.'

God willed it. At ten o'clock Kamil and I walked along a shadowed side-street near Mevlana's mausoleum. 'You are not the first unbeliever I have brought here,' Kamil confided. 'And you should know that the others have left as converts.'

I swallowed. 'I thought you said there was no obligation to buy.'

We entered a gate, crossed a courtyard and came to a door with many pairs of shoes at the threshold. We added ours and went in. Inside was a small lobby which three men – one middle-aged and clean-shaven, one in his twenties, tall and bearded, and a youth – were using as a changing-room. I had a glimpse of tight white trousers, soft boots, high fawn caps; the tall man was adjusting the folds of a long white skirt. It was a uniform I had already seen – on the waxwork dervishes in Mevlana's museum-mausoleum. The men were utterly absorbed in their robing and seemed not to notice us. We passed from here into a large room lined with more men and boys, all in mufti, sitting cross-legged on low mattresses around the walls. There had been a low hum of voices; as we entered, the room fell silent. After a lot of wriggling, a couple of boys ended up on the floor and Kamil and I were squeezed into the line on either side of an old man with a shaven head. I had hoped to be an unobtrusive observer; instead, I was sitting almost in the lap of Shaykh Nuri Kılcı, usually known as Hajji Baba, master of the Mevlevi-Kaderi dervishes.

For a moment Hajji Baba appraised me, bright-eyed and bushy-bearded, both gnome-like and gnomic. We exchanged a few Arabic pleasantries, then he switched into Turkish with Kamil interpreting. The whole room was looking and listening.

'What is your name? *Tim?* What is a "Tim" doing here, among us?' Kamil interjected some words of explanation, and Hajji Baba's eyes narrowed. 'You have lived in Yemen for fifteen years and you are not a Muslim? Who are these Yemenis that they have not directed you in the true path? You need stronger, younger men who will beat you!' He slapped me on the back of my neck, gently, then grinned. Suddenly his expression changed to one of the utmost gravity. 'Look at yourself,' he said softly. 'Your hair is going grey. You might die tonight. And then you will go to the Eternal Fire. You do not know yourself. First know yourself, then you will know God and take Him into your heart. Your heart is a palace for Him. You are beautiful: make yourself more beautiful still!' He took my shoulders, pulled me downwards and tenderly kissed the top of my head.

Throughout this monologue the audience hung on Hajji Baba's utterances. The only movement was of a boy who brought us tea, approaching on his knees. I, however, had only one concern: not to belch. On account both of our close proximity and the very large raw onion I had eaten with my supper, it would not have been a pleasant experience for the *shaykh* of the Mevlevi-Kaderis.

I soon forgot the turmoil in my gut, for the *sema* had begun. A man on our right chanted a litany in Turkish interspersed with Arabic. While this was happening, I was at last able to study the *sema*-goers. There were perhaps seventy of them, mostly in early middle age but with a sprinkling of older and younger men, and a few boys. What was remarkable about them was, like IB's cobbler host in Antalya, their ordinariness. I tried to imagine how they had spent the day: driving taxis, selling carpets, keeping accounts, extracting teeth. They looked as unlikely a set of mystics as you might meet anywhere.

The litany ended, and a flute began to play. It was a simple melody but mesmeric, like a Satie *Gymnopédie*. 'Listen to this reed, how it makes complaint, telling a tale of separation ... The cry of the reed is fire, it is not wind ... It is the fire of love that has set the reed aflame; it is the surge of love that bubbles in the wine!' Divine love, separation of soul from Creator, ecstatic champagne: with this allegory Mevlana returned from his travels. No one, said IB, could understand him; now, as we listened, it began to make sense.

The *sema*-goers intoned the Islamic creed, then other phrases which ended on a long *glissando* syllable, *huuuu*; as it died away they prostrated themselves. Some sobbed. I noticed Hajji Baba give a sign, and two drums began to beat, insistently. The whole room chanted *la ilaha illa 'llah*, There is no god but God. Faster and faster it went; then another almost imperceptible sign from Hajji Baba and the rhythm changed, and the chant, to a simple *Allah ... Allah ...* The men rocked back and forth. At first I remembered the swaying dancers at al-Husayn's *mawlid* in Cairo; but the dervishes of Konya soon left them standing – the rocking became more vigorous, even violent. A youth opposite snatched breaths between *Allahs* with loud sobs and gulps, and sweat flew from him: he seemed on the verge of hyperventilation, of collapse, and I now thought of IB's Shrieker, a dervish of Bursa who died of ecstasy. And still the intensity increased.

Just this side of frenzy the two elder dancers appeared. They crossed the room on their knees and kissed Hajji Baba's hand. He stroked their faces, then they rose and began to turn, pirouetting on the left foot and propelled by the right, which rose and fell in time with the drums. As their speed increased their skirts billowed out and became perfect cones of white. Their arms were outstretched, right palm upwards, left downwards. I knew from my reading on the der- vishes that their hands were meant to transmit *barakah* from heaven to earth – rather like spiritual lightning-conductors. Books, however, had not prepared me for what now took place – a gradual emptying of the mind of everything but these two revolving figures, cycle and epicycle, and that deafening throb: *Allah ... Allah ...* , the great iamb, the music of the spheres.

Eventually the dancers retired, kissing once more the hand of their gnostic conductor, and others came on – those prosaic mystics in trousers and sweat-stained shirts. The last to dance was the youth I had seen robing earlier. In seconds he was a conic blur, weightless, on the point of levitation. Thus he remained, time in suspense, until at last Hajji Baba nodded to the drummers and the rhythm slowed, the corolla of skirts folded, the heartbeat became still. In the silence and acrid-sweet stink of sweat, someone began to recite from the Qur'an. I looked from face to face around the room and remembered that IB had described the scene, and such voices, 'that work upon men's souls and at which hearts are humbled, skins creep, and eyes fill with tears'. The recitation began: '*Ha-Mim Ayn-Sin-Qaf*. Thus Allah, the

Mighty One, the Wise One, inspires you as He inspired others before you.' Again, the mystic letters.

When the reading finished, Hajji Baba turned to me and asked how I felt. After the catharsis of the *sema*, I could only honestly say that I felt empty.

'Then,' he said very quietly, 'with what will you fill this emptiness?'

We looked at each other, the crowd suddenly absent – like potential lovers. Shocked, I looked away. The room flooded back.

I heard Hajji Baba speaking, then Kamil translating. 'He says your *nafs* is too strong, that it is making you fight against Islam. You know the meaning of *nafs*?'

I nodded. 'For a moment I entertained the idea of spending the rest of my life in the service of this *shaykh*,' wrote IB of the island-hermit of Abbadan; 'but I was dissuaded from it by my importunate *nafs*.' By his worldly, appetitive spirit.

Hajji Baba spoke again. 'And', said Kamil, 'he says that your head is too full of books.'

Mats were spread and laid with peaches, melons, grapes and cucumbers. Hajji Baba picked the ripest and sweetest fruit and passed it to me on a plate – the *simat* of the dervishes, the food served to all wayfarers, unbelievers and idolators included. After we had all eaten, he recited Mevlana's grace and we dispersed into the midnight streets, shivering after the bath-heat of the room, shirts stiffening with sweat-frost. As Kamil and I were leaving, Hajji Baba patted my shoulder and said, 'I think you will not sleep tonight.'

He was right. A pair of tomcats growled and scrapped under the bedroom window. My stomach growled and scrapped. And my mind span and pulsed, noisy with the strangeness of it all: of looking for a carpet and finding the *sema*; of glimpsing a world IB had known, officially dead but living on in the back streets of Konya; and of hearing the language of the coast – a language of love, dance, wine, ecstasy – spoken in the dialect of angels.

Some time after three the microcosmic belch broke out, tremendous as an onion. Then someone chucked a bucket of water over the cats. The spinning ceased, the pulse slowed; sleep came.

★

'The Sultan of Akridur makes a practice of attending afternoon prayers in the congregational mosque every day.' I entered the mosque, the *Travels* open in my hand. 'He sits with his back to the wall of the *qiblah*.' I sat, sultanically, against the wall facing Mecca. 'The Qur'an readers take their seats in front of him on a high wooden platform.' I looked up: there it was, a double-decker dais. It was an extremely unusual piece of furniture, but I had missed it when I came in – my nose was stuck in the text. Perhaps Hajji Baba was right, and my head was overstuffed with books.

So far, IB would have had no trouble recognizing Akridur, the Turkish Eğridir, west of Konya, set on a lake surrounded by apple orchards and the peachy mountains of Pisidia. 'We lodged there in a college opposite the mosque.' I crossed from the mosque to the college, exactly opposite, entered through its superbly carved portal and found myself in . . . *a tourist bazaar*. As I walked around the courtyard, peering into the little rooms that opened off it, I wondered where IB had stayed. In jeans, or sunglasses? In leather jackets, or tie-dyed T-shirts? Only the eagles knew – stone ones, perched above the courtyard on reused Byzantine capitals, looking down with ancient, pterodactylic *Weltschmerz*.

Eğridir was an *urbs in rure* with a good sprinkling of chic women in jeans. But as I travelled south-west towards IB's next destination, Gölhisar, 'Lakecastle', the demography became increasingly bucolic. Jeans gave way to elasticated floral print trousers; the women inside them grew in volume. In Burdur market the sellers of peppers were, to a woman, deeply upholstered and covered in chintz. At the same time, the buses that I rode diminished in size and shared the roads with carts and tripping horses. The wider world impinged little, although I noticed that the usual amulets dangling from one rear-view mirror – 'Muhammad' in Arabic script, and an anti-Evil Eye eye of blue glass – had been joined by an Internet Explorer 4 CD: a mixture of faith, superstition and technology.

I tried to pronounce, *sotto voce*, the names of villages we passed. At Höyügü, I realized I would need a lot of practice to develop the necessary embouchure. At least my ignorance of Turkish was shared with IB. He claims to have picked it up later but Gibb, in an uncharacteristically wry footnote, dismisses the claim as 'fanfaronade'.

We passed from a land of bright lakes and orchards to one of muted colours – swatches of yellow stubble, brown earth, black burnt stubble, grey road and two-tone trees in silver and dark green – then entered a luminous upland plain fringed with cream hills. Mindful of

Hajji Baba's comment about books, I had suppressed the tic that made me turn to the *Travels* every few minutes. But as the bus neared Gölhisar, I reread IB's description of it: 'a small town surrounded on every side by water in which there is a thick growth of rushes. There is no way to approach it except by a path like a bridge constructed between the rushes and the water, and broad enough only for one horseman. The city is on a hill in the midst of the waters and is formidably protected and impregnable.' As in Eğridir, I was impressed by IB's ability to recall a scene over twenty years later, with neither notebooks nor, for this Anatolian back-of-beyond, independent sources to jog his memory.

The only problem was that Gölhisar bore no resemblance whatsoever to IB's description. True, there was a hill with some ruins on it; but the hill stood on sloping ground, so any lake would have had to defy gravity. The Arthurian vision of castle and rushy mere evaporated.

In my Turkish equivalent of Indo-Arabic, I asked at the bus station whether I was in the real Gölhisar. The ticket man looked momentarily surprised (I suppose it is rather ill-mannered to turn up in a place and immediately accuse it of being an impostor); then he laughed, and explained that we were, without doubt, in the unique and genuine Lakecastle. I was also able to elicit the following information: there was a castle but no lake at Lakecastle; a lake, Gölhisar Gölü, existed, but it was five miles from the town; at Lakecastle Lake, however, there was no castle – let alone a castle on an island, for there was no island.

I began to wonder if IB had got it wrong. Certainly, there are problems with his Anatolian itinerary. At one point, for example, he strikes off east and travels as far as Erzerum. 'We stayed there for three nights,' he says, 'then left for the city of Birgi, where we arrived in the late afternoon.' Even allowing for IB's tendency to elasticate time, as an account of an eight-hundred mile journey it is undeniably terse. But, while this blip could be the result of enthusiastic editing, it was far harder to reconcile IB's Gölhisar with the place I was in. Even so, there was something – a verisimilitude – about his description of Gölhisar. I caught a bus to the turn-off for the lake, and set out to look for the invisible island.

The lane was paved with cowpats and perfumed with aniseed. A mile or so off the main road I came to Yamadı, a village of tottering balconies decked with pepper ropes and chilli necklaces. The village ended with a cuboid tomb-chamber, ogivally roofed, and an old lady. I asked her who was buried in the tomb, hoping for a Battutian lead; she answered at length, patting the building now and then while I grinned and nodded encouragingly. Having understood nothing, I said in Turkish 'I don't speak Turkish,' uttered a sonorous Arabic prayer, and passed on.

After another mile or two, I saw a corner of lake and made for a hill that overlooked it. It would be the perfect vantage point for spotting vanished islands. Near the hill I had another one-sided conversation, with a man working in a sugar-beet field. As he spoke, I noticed a large dyke running through the field. Cattle grazed in water meadows beneath the hill, which was fringed with rushes. Drained land . . . I had solved the problem of the missing island: it was the hill. 'Is there a road?' I asked, pointing towards it. In reply, the farmer led me to a raised track – IB's 'path like a bridge'.

As I crossed the causeway – it had been enlarged, clearly at a recent date, to tractor width – I congratulated IB on his powers of recollection, and reproved myself for doubting them. The only thing missing now was his town and its fortifications. I quartered the hill and found plenty of potsherds of a burnished red ware that looked far older than the fourteenth century and, alarmingly, dozens of recently sloughed snakeskins; but not a trace of a medieval building. A defensive tower on the summit, looking out over the undrained part of Lakecastle Lake, turned out to be a square rock outcrop.

There was only one area left to explore, a wide terrace at the base of the hill, north of the causeway. And here, at last, in a field of tomatoes, I spotted something that could only have been Islamic and medieval – a bit of blue-glazed faience tile. It was a minor yet pleasing monument. But if it came from IB's Gölhisar, what had happened to the rest of the town?

I found a clue at the head of the causeway. Here stood a big new barn, as yet unroofed, built partly of large and finely worked blocks of ashlar. Like the burnished sherds they had a pre-medieval look to them; other bits of masonry that lay about nearby – fluted column drums, part of an acanthus frieze – were unquestionably classical. The enlarged causeway also incorporated some dismembered ancient buildings. Probably, I surmised, IB's Gölhisar had been no more than a classical or Byzantine site recycled and given Islamic touches; now it had itself been recycled, and possibly not for the first time. I thought back to the *madrasah* at Eğridir where IB had stayed, constructed from bits of Byzantine buildings and a Seljuk caravanserai, and now turned into a mini-complex of boutiques. It was all part of the same process, cycle and recycle. Nothing was ever sacred.

*

My discoveries were hardly earth-shattering. But at night over my diary and *rakı*, that melancholy spirit, I thought again that it would have been good to share them with a *rafiq*, a travelling companion. Instead, I shared them with ghosts – with IB, and with less substantial future ghosts: you.

At the same time I didn't envy IB, who seems never to have had a minute to himself. His arrival in Denizli even sparked off a fight between rival Akhi groups, each desperate to earn honour by looking after the stranger. 'The altercation', he says, 'grew so hot that some of them drew knives.' (I too was the object of a minor altercation in Denizli – between the touts of rival *pensions*.)

As well as enjoying the energetic welcome of the Akhis, IB schmoozed with sultans. He gives us an insight into his technique: questioned by a prince about other rulers he had met, IB realized that 'his idea was that I would praise those of them who had been generous and find fault with the miserly. I did nothing of the kind; on the contrary, I praised them all.' These courtierly skills usually earned IB a meal, a robe and some cash. On one occasion, however, they provoked an overdose of hospitality. During his fortnight in the generous thrall of Sultan Muhammad ibn Aydın of Birgi, IB admitted, 'I began to weary and wished to take my leave.' By the time he did, he had collected some of his most vivid Anatolian memories – of a stone that fell from the sky, a mountain camp under the walnut trees, and endless presents of butter in sheep's stomachs.

IB's Birgi was the capital of a principality that included Ephesus and Smyrna; today it has shrunk to a dot on the map, on a hill above the Little Meander. A footnote in Gibb refers the reader to *Murray's Guide* of 1895 and to the learned Phippson's slightly later five-volume *Reise und Forschungen in westlichen Kleinasien*. Cavalierly, I had failed to consult either work. Birgi was thus a surprise, a cascade of pantiles down a hillside in which, out of an island of firs, rose an immense, metropolitan mosque. It was built of large ashlar blocks the colour of shortbread; the minaret was a tall cylinder of ginger brick diapered with voided blue lozenges. I looked for an inscription and found one over the main door: 'Built by the Amir ... the Holy Warrior, the Fighter at the Frontiers, Sultan Muhammad ibn Aydın, in the year 712' – IB's hospitable captor himself, 'one of the best, most generous, and worthiest of sultans'.

'You can read Arabic?' said a voice by my side. I turned and nodded to the speaker. 'I am studying Arabic at high school,' he continued. 'Islamic high school. But it is not one of my best subjects. However, I am always first in English, and nearly first in history. I think you are interested in the history of Birgi?'

It all came out in a flood – IB, his travels, mine – which only ran out at Birgi, the Sultan, the stone that fell from the sky, the camp under the walnut trees, the stomachs of butter. The boy looked at me solemnly. I wondered what he saw: bore, or maniac?

'We shall look for these things together,' he said.

Yalçın took me into a mausoleum by the mosque. Several tombs lay under a dome, again of ginger and blue brick. 'Here is Sultan Muhammad. It is written that he died in 1334, in an accident while hunting,' he said, translating from a typed card by the tomb. 'And look, here are his sons – Isa, Ibrahim and Ghazi Umar Bey. It says that Ghazi Umar fought on the island of Chios, and that he was a friend of ... "Cantacuzene".'

This last, surprising piece of information about Ghazi Umar, whom IB met here in Birgi and then in Smyrna, I confirmed later from Gibbon's *Decline and Fall*. The Turkoman prince's friendship with the Byzantine Emperor John V Cantacuzene was compared, the historian wrote, 'in the vain rhetoric of the times, to the perfect union of Orestes and Pylades'; the Emperor, for his part, looked on Ghazi Umar with 'sentimental passion'. On one occasion, Gibbon went on, the prince rescued the Empress Irene from the Bulgarians. She invited him to visit her but, 'by a peculiar strain of delicacy, the gentle barbarian refused'. (A fictionalized version of Umar also appears in the *Decameron*, in which, less delicately, he rapes the Sultan of Babylon's daughter.) As yet unaware of these ramifications, I simply enjoyed meeting the mortal remains of characters from the *Travels*, and doing so in live and enthusiastic company.

The prayer-hall of the mosque was a perfect arrangement of dark and light, an airy cuboid beneath a walnut ceiling. Beside a *mihrab* of turquoise and black tiles stood a pulpit, also of walnut, richly carved and patinated dark chocolate. As we admired it, we were joined by the imam. 'I preach from this every Friday,' he said, with understandable pride. He pointed out three gilded bosses on the side of the pulpit. 'The earth, in the middle,' he explained, 'and beside it the sun and the moon. These', he said, indicating a ring of smaller gilded polygons around the bosses, 'are the planets.'

'I think Sultan Muhammad was interested in astronomy,' Yalçın said.

I went to my bag and pulled out Gibb's translation of the *Travels*. ' "Have you ever seen a stone that fell from the sky?" ' the Sultan asked IB. ' "I have never seen one, nor ever heard tell of one," ' the traveller replied. 'Then they brought in a great black stone, very hard and with a glitter in it. I reckoned it a hundredweight. The Sultan ordered the stonebreakers to be summoned, and at his command four of them beat on it as one man, four times, with iron hammers, but made no impression on it. I was astonished at this phenomenon, and he ordered it to be taken back to its place.'

As I read, Yalçın translated for the imam. Then I asked if the meteorite was still in existence; it was, after all, not the sort of thing that would get thrown away. But they had never seen the *göktaşı*, the skystone, nor heard tell of it.

The double doors of the pulpit bore a fine Arabic inscription. It was a *hadith*, a saying of the Prophet: 'O God, I seek refuge with You from work that does not profit, from hearts that are not humble, from prayers that are not answered, from appetites that are not sated.' This time it was the imam who translated for Yalçın. And, as he did so, another scene from the *Travels* played itself out: 'The Sultan asked me to write down for him a number of *hadiths* of the Prophet. Then he commanded the professor to write an exposition of them for him in the Turkish language.'

I looked around the prayer-hall. Sultan Muhammad had clearly been an avid *hadith*-collector: each window was furnished with walnut shutters, each shutter carved like the pulpit with a saying of the Prophet. It was a most legible building and, for one put up by a minor Turkoman warlord in a parenthesis in history, thoroughly civilized.

While the mosque was gloriously intact, the secular monuments of Sultan Muhammad seemed to have disappeared completely. IB described an audience-hall 'with an ornamental pool in the centre and a bronze lion at each of its corners, spouting water from its mouth'. Here, long-haired Byzantine pages served their delicate barbarian masters with sherbert and biscuits in gold bowls. Yalçın and I made do with *ayran*, diluted yoghurt, in a tea-garden north-west of the mosque. It overlooked a dry watercourse that flowed in the spring when the snow melted up on the slopes of Bozdağ.

'If I could be Sultan of Birgi,' Yalçın day-dreamed, 'do you know where I would build my palace? Right here, in this tea-garden.' He was probably right. We had combed Birgi and found no better site. He had also asked everyone we met whether they knew about the *göktaşı*, the skystone. Although we had drawn a blank, I could not have wanted a more dogged research assistant. 'Is it very important for you to find it?' he asked.

It was the sort of question, like those concerning the song the sirens sang or the Sphinx's inscrutable smile, that one ought to ask but didn't. 'Well . . . I suppose it's important to look.'

'Then I shall dig for it!' he said, with a sudden heroic gesture that took in Birgi, Bozdağ and half the Little Meander valley. 'But first,' he continued, back to his serious self, 'we must look for the campsite.'

★

When IB arrived in Birgi, 'the Sultan was passing the summer on a mountain thereabouts on account of the great heat. We climbed up to the mountain by a road that had been hewn in its side, and reached his camp just before noon. There we alighted, by a stream of water shaded by walnut trees.'

'There is IB's road,' Yalçın said, pointing to a track terraced into the flank of the mountain. It was the following morning, and we were looking up at the massif of Bozdağ squatting over the town on its great sunburnt hunkers.

IB was not a happy camper; he soon grew restless in Sultan Muhammad's summer retreat. Still, he carefully described his accommodation, 'a tent which is called by them a *kharqah*, made of wooden laths put together in the form of a cupola and covered with pieces of felt; the upper part can be opened to admit light and air'. The design is old enough to have appeared in Aeschylus, whose Scythians 'dwell in latticed huts high-poised on easy wheels' – a reference to the mobile version of the yurt that IB saw later in the land of the Golden

Horde. Formerly this mini geodesic dome was found from Anatolia to Manchuria. Now, although the Turks themselves have abandoned these round tents, they still survive elsewhere in Asia (and have even recently crossed the Bering Strait to Oregon where, as New Age housing, the tepee is *passé*).

We set off up the track. Below us an early sun raked across the roofs, minarets and gardens of Birgi; further below, a haze hung over the Little Meander. We climbed quickly into the cooling air, browsing on wild figs and green walnuts. Eventually the old road merged with a new asphalted one. Yalçın flagged down a tractor and we bounced the rest of the way up, sitting in a scoop at the back. 'It's not cheating,' he pointed out. 'IB was riding a horse.'

I was surprised to find Bozdağ a substantial settlement of concrete houses and tea-gardens. 'The rich people in Birgi and Ödemiş come here for the summer,' Yalçın explained, 'just like the Sultan. Only they have villas now, not tents.' IB, the unhappy camper, would have approved.

After lunch we set out along a stream, looking for a campsite shaded by walnut trees. Yalçın led the way, slashing through the undergrowth with his stick. Often we were forced to walk in the stream itself. 'This is Vietnam!' he said. 'Like the American films. Write in your notebook, "And Yalçın led me into water many metres deep, and we swam it bravely!"' I did, although the stream was no more than a trickle. Several hours later, stung by nettles and covered with old man's beard, we gave up. We hadn't found the place; or perhaps we had found it many times, for the entire valley was over-hung with walnuts, old ones, perhaps even Battutian ones.

We sat under one of them and went through the text again; but there were no more clues. 'We have looked,' said Yalçın, 'and maybe we have found. We shall never know. But I think that if everything was written in the book, there would be no reason to come and look.'

I caught the last bus out of Birgi, the only passenger. The driver asked me if I had found my *göktaşı*, my skystone. I shook my head, and looked back at Birgi: the last of the light was catching Sultan Muhammad's minaret; Bozdağ was growing indistinct, a little furry, like moleskin. What I had found, and left behind, was my *rafiq*.

★

I have said that there are no ghosts in Islam; perhaps it would be more correct to say that there are no Muslim ghosts. 'The story goes', wrote the traveller Abu Hamid of Granada,

> that in the time of the Prophet, Abdullah ibn Umar went on a journey. He set out alone on his she-camel. As he was passing the battle-site of Badr where the pagans of Mecca were killed, the ground suddenly split open. 'There rose up', he said, 'a human being, blackened and smouldering from head to toe. He had a chain about his neck that dragged behind him, and he cried out to me, "Abdullah! Give me water! *Give me water!*" My camel shied at the apparition. Then there rose up another man. He pulled the first one back towards him with the chain, saying, "Do not give him water, for this is Abu Jahl, the enemy of God!" Then he drove Abu Jahl back into his grave with a whip, and the ground closed over him.' Abdullah ibn Umar was ter-rified, and abandoned his journey. When he told the Prophet of what he had witnessed, the Prophet made it a rule that there-after no one should ever travel alone. He said, God's blessings and peace on him, 'One's company for the devil, two for a pair of devils; three's company for travelling.'

IB took the decree to heart. As well as al-Tuzari, his Tunisian *rafiq*, he had gathered along the way a group of even shadowier, nameless 'companions'. In Ephesus he bought 'a Greek slave-girl, a virgin, for forty gold dinars'; in Smyrna Ghazi Umar, son of the Sultan of Birgi, gave him a slave named Nicholas, 'five spans tall'; shortly after this in Balikesir he bought another slave, Margarita. All these were in addition to the slave Michael, part of a going-away present from Sultan Muhammad that also included a hundred gold dinars, a thousand silver dirhams, a complete wardrobe and a horse. The companions had to make do with a robe each and some dirhams.

IB was no longer the callow spiritual backpacker who had left Tangier six years earlier. He was turning into a swell, and getting – at least in retrospect in the *Travels* – increasingly blasé about Turkoman princes: that of Gerede was 'one of the middling class of sultans ... of fine character, but not liberal' (he gave IB a horse and a robe), his counterpart of Balikesir (gift rating: a silk robe) 'a worthless person' who ruled over 'a rabble of good-for-nothings for, as they say, "Like king like people" '.

Although most of the names in IB's good sultans guide have slipped out of the historical conscious, there are exceptions. Sarukhan of Manisa (no gift rating, as he was busy paying his respects to the air-dried corpse of a recently deceased son) has a hotel named after him, and a park. He even has a statue, thickly moustached, turbaned and wearing a sort of trench-coat. Apart from the turban, the statue bears a striking resemblance to Earl Haig. And then there was Orkhan ('he sent me a large sum of money'), son of Othman the eponymous Ottoman.

In Orkhan, IB sensed the enormous energy that galvanized an empire and a six-hundred-year dynasty: 'It is said that he has never stayed for a whole month in any one town. He fights with the infidels continually and keeps them under siege.' Faced with such boundless machismo there was little the infidels, the Byzantines, could do. They had entered the long, couch-potato period of their decline, and left the business of war to Catalan mercenaries who were less interested in fighting the Turk than in plundering the cities they were paid to defend. Orkhan had taken the city of Bursa in northwest Anatolia only five years before IB's visit; by the time of his death twenty-eight years later, his armies were thumping on the gates of the Balkans.

I once met a descendant of Orkhan's who lived in Henley-on-Thames and worked as a chartered accountant. Now, I had higher hopes of Battutian resonances from his illustrious ancestors, still in their old capital of Bursa. I was disappointed. Both Orkhan's and Othman's mausolea had been rebuilt after an earthquake in 1855 in Great Exhibition-orientalist taste, all mother-of-pearl, pastel shades and chandeliers. Orkhan's funerary turban was wrapped in cellophane, like an outsized toffee-apple.

There was something trumpery, almost flippant about these tombs. The rest of Bursa, however, seemed weighed down by its own *gravitas*, and was predominantly brown. The Great Mosque, a fine fourteenth-century building, had been painted with *trompe-l'oeil* drapes in several shades of brown; a nearby civic building was encased in dark brown wood, like a Bavarian *Rathaus*. The leaves were turning brown, and the city smelt of autumn, rich pastries and dead empires. My mind kept returning to that airy shortbread mosque in Birgi, built by a man who preferred camping on Bozdağ to campaigning against Byzantium. I left Bursa to its brown study and headed for the Black Sea.

By now, IB too had stopped divagating, and was set on the port of Sinop and a passage to the Crimea. Sultans were thinner on the ground in northern Anatolia, and here the *Travels* has more to say on the sort of people who, without mausolea, would otherwise have sunk into the anonymous mulch of dead humanity. There is the doctor of Islamic law, famed locally for his knowledge of Arabic, who turned out not to know a word of the language: 'These travellers', he squirmed, in Persian, 'speak the ancient Arabic speech and I know only the new Arabic.' There is IB's Christian landlady in Göynük, who tried to sell him a job-lot of saffron; and the servant sent to the market for Arabic *samn*, clarified butter, who came back with Turkish *semen*, animal fodder. And there is that timeless character of travelogues, the rip-off merchant: 'He used to steal some of the money for our expenses,' IB remembered of his Arabic-speaking guide on the road to Kastamonu. 'We had to put up with him because of our problem of not knowing Turkish, and it got to the stage where we would openly accuse him and say to him at the end of each day, "Well, Hajji, how much have you stolen from the kitty today?" He would tell us, and we would laugh at him and make the best of it.'

I made my way to Kastamonu in the company of peasants, on buses scented with garlic, damp wool and woodsmoke. Over the past months I had met enough dead medieval notables to last several life-times; but in Kastamonu I was keen to find another one, the aged and pious *shaykh* Dada Amir Ali. 'I found him lying on his back,' wrote IB. 'One of his servants helped him to sit up, and another raised the eyelids from his eyes. On seeing me the *shaykh* addressed me in pure Arabic, saying, "You are heartily welcome!" I asked him his age and he said, "I was an associate of Caliph al-Mustansir, and at his death I was thirty years old. My age now is one hundred and sixty-three years." I asked him to invoke a blessing on me; he did so, and I with-drew.' (Gibb points out that the *shaykh's* arithmetic was shaky: he could have been no more than 123 lunar years old – a mere 119 solar years.)

Since Kastamonu billed itself as 'an interest point of religious tourism', and Dada Amir Ali sounded a likely candidate for saint-hood, I spent a day religiously rambling around the town in search of his tomb. The expedition turned up several other Dadas, or 'Grandads', including one under an apple tree in an old lady's back garden. I didn't find my Dada; but I came across another curiosity called Aşıklı Sultan, a Seljuk killed in an attack on Byzantine Kastamonu in 1116. One end of this holy warrior's grave was pro-vided with a small window: poking out beneath the glass was a pair of small, mummy-like feet. I was immediately reminded of the similar, and roughly contemporary, 'crusader' in the vault of St Michan's church in Dublin. Having – as one does – once shaken the crusader's hand, I was now tempted to tickle Aşıklı Sultan's toes. There was something irresistible about them: they looked like strips of biltong. The glass panel was, however, firmly fixed.

★

'You know Diogen?' asked the manageress of the Villa Rose. 'He lived here, in Sinop. This Diogen, one day one big colonel came to him. And Diogen says, "Hey, you get away. I want the shine!" '

The story of the meeting between the colonel – in fact Alexander the Great – and Diogenes, the Cynic of Sinop, was followed by others, less well known. I learned that the city's original inhabitants were Amazons and that Bilal, a local saint whose tomb IB visited, used to walk about with his head under his arm. The Villa Rose suited such rococo history: it was an ordinary seaside bungalow that had mutated, sprouting Corinthian columns, Louis Farouk *fauteuils* and aspidistras. A clock made from a gilded lobster hung on the dining-room wall, and next to my table stood a statue of a nude girl frotting her backside against a herm.

Diogenes was, of course, a celebrated al fresco masturbator, and something of this tendency to public relaxation survived in Sinop until IB's time. 'I passed one day by the gate of the congregational mosque,' he recalled, 'outside which are stone benches where the inhabitants sit. I saw here several high-ranking officers, with an orderly in front of them holding a bag filled with a substance resembling henna. As I watched, one of the officers took a spoonful of it and ate it. I had no idea what it was, but the person with me told me it was hashish.' Hash-fiends apart, IB thought well of Sinop, 'a superb city which combines fortification with beautification'. I had arrived after sunset so could not yet assess its beauty; but even in the dark I could see the silhouettes of battlements. To the east, the towers of Trebizond have gone; the towers of Sinop survive, looming even over its bus station.

In the morning I drew the curtains for my first sight of the sea: it was invisible beneath a mist. During breakfast, the mist lifted to reveal grey fishing boats on grey water beneath grey air – the Black Sea, grey on grey like a Monet Thames. As IB observed, Sinop stands at the landward end of a peninsula, 'a mountain projecting into the sea'. I walked to the isthmus and explored the defences, walls and towers of rusticated masonry where lizards darted across the stones. Although a road had been punched through the wall that cut off the narrowest part of the isthmus, the vaulted gate where IB awaited permission to enter the city was still intact. Inside, however, it had become a café, with pink velvet tablecloths scarred with a pox of fag-burns. Down by the harbour the Sea-gate, still a gate, echoed to an Iron Maiden track played at full volume from an adjoining tower; the site of IB's lodgings, a hospice of the Akhis outside the gate, had become a 'Family Tea-Garden'.

Beside the door of the Great Mosque I was pleased to find the stone benches where IB had watched his Sinopean dope-heads, now much worn down by centuries of bottoms. Inside, though, the building had altered. According to the *Travels* Sulayman Pervane, the old ruler of Sinop, had always said his prayers on top of a marble cupola over the ablution fountain; this, however, had been replaced with a workaday wooden canopy. Neither had the prayer-hall been improved by a cladding of blue clapboard. I muttered, on IB's behalf, about change and decay.

Not far from the mosque, I spotted a portal surmounted by a sort of cinquelobate doily, all done in marble. An inscription identified the building as a college founded by IB's Pervane. Expecting to find it recycled as another boutique mini-complex, I tried the door. It was locked. Clearly very exclusive ... perhaps a *salon de couture*, or a recording studio? I rapped loudly. The door was opened by a boy with a grave expression; beyond him I saw a spacious colonnaded quadrangle with a marble fountain in the centre. The boy, I noticed, was holding an Arabic copybook. '*Al-salam alaykum,*' I said.

'*Wa alaykum al-salam wa rahmat Allah wa barakatuh,*' he replied.

How much he understood of my introduction to IB I don't know; but I passed the entrance exam. Inside, seven other boys emerged from rooms around the court. We began a solemn progress through what I soon realized to be that great rarity – a functioning medieval *madrasah*. Eight bunk beds occupied one room, eight bars of soap were positioned at regular intervals around the fountain. Here, protected from Iron Maiden and other excesses, the boys had their characters formed by cold water and Qur'an lessons. IB would have been delighted.

The tour ended beyond a door in the corner of the court, in a space roofed with corrugated iron. In contrast to the rigorous tidiness of the rest of the *madrasah*, it was littered with junk. Several lambs' feet and a desiccated oesophagus had been chucked on a finely inscribed tomb. Wondering whom this might contain, I began to read the inscription: 'This is the tomb of Ghazi ... ibn Mas'ud Çelebi ... '

It was an unexpected discovery. Ghazi Çelebi, son of Mas'ud II, the last Seljuk Sultan of Rum, is probably the fourteenth century's only documented frogman. 'He was brave and audacious,' IB reported, 'and endowed by God with a special gift of endurance under water.' The Ghazi used this gift to deadly effect, diving beneath Byzantine vessels and holing them with a drill. Neither my Turkish nor the boys' Arabic was up to testing IB's information, so I drew a sketch of the scene. They were totally mystified. The other part of the account, I decided, would be even further beyond my powers as an illustrator. According to IB, Ghazi Çelebi, in true Sinopean style, died stoned. Having one day eaten more hashish than was good for him, 'he went out hunting and pursued a gazelle. But he spurred his horse on too hard and was intercepted by a tree, which struck and crushed his head. So he died.' I recited a prayer for the soul of this remarkable man, and bade farewell to my puzzled hosts.

The memory of my failed attempt at long-distance sea travel in Oman was still fresh, and I put off the business of looking for a boat to the Crimea with one last bit of inverse archaeology. 'On top of the peninsula', said IB, 'is a hermitage dedicated to al-Khadir and Ilyas. Beside it is a spring of water, and a prayer made there is answered.' (Strictly, al-Khadir and Ilyas – Elijah – are not a double act but two faces given to the same indistinct character; if this were not enough, Arab Christians also identify al-Khadir-Elijah with St George.) Al-Khadir has a way of popping up at geographical extremes – deserts, high peaks, IB's own Tangier at the end of Africa – and Sinop, at the most northerly point of Asia Minor, is no exception. For years the Americans snooped across the Black Sea from a radar base out on the headland, and by chance a Turkish ex-employee came to tea at the Villa Rose. I asked him if he knew of the hermitage.

He shook his head and laughed. 'To hell with old ruins! You go to the beach. Have a swim. Enjoy yourself!'

I said I could think of few more enjoyable activities than looking for ruined hermitages. My hostess, however, looked concerned. 'It is so, so far!'

'It's only about six kilometres.'

'Six kilometres by car, maybe. By walking, *much* further.'

Undeterred, I set off the following day along the promontory. Despite a rising tideline of apartment blocks, much of the landward end was covered, as IB noticed, with figs and vines. A road wound upwards but ended at a gate and a large sign that said MILITARY ZONE – ENTRY PROHIBITED. I about-turned, then struck out across country that clattered with dry thistles. Wind sang in power-lines overhead. Towards the end of the peninsula there was another military installation, set on the last high peak and containing several golf-ball radar domes. And there, tantalizingly far inside the perimeter fence, I spotted the ruins of an old building. For a moment I considered marching up to the gate, flourishing the *Travels* and trying to gain entry. Instinct told me this was the hermitage; prudence, however, and cowardice, prevented me from trying to find out. Instead, I climbed down to the end of Turkey, a sheer drop overhung with lichen-covered rocks, and ate chocolate biscuits.

Once more the horizon had been air-brushed out by mist. For centuries, Arab geographers had had only the haziest notions of what lay beyond it. There were reports of an outlet at the north to the Circumambient Ocean, and of sea-monsters four days' journey in length. In IB's time, knowledge of the dim transpontine regions had improved. There was a steady traffic from them into the central Islamic lands, most importantly in slaves. The Mamluk aristocrats of Cairo – Sultan al-Nasir's father Qalawun, Qawsun, Bashtak and most of their fellows – were shipped from the northern Black Sea ports. But the interior was little known.

I wondered why IB had crossed to the steppe empire of the Golden Horde. He offered no clues. Fate had set his journey in motion, a growing love of travel had kept it moving; but what about the itinerary? From the *Travels,* one would imagine he existed in a purely accidental world: he was in Turkey, then he went to the Crimea. Reading between the lines, however, I suspect that two pieces of information were on his mind: that Özbeg, Khan of the Golden Horde, was a recent and keen convert to Islam; and that, his territories being vaster by far than those of all the princelings of Anatolia combined, he was rich.

I walked back to Sinop along the lower slopes of the promontory. Cows munched at the scrub between unfinished shells of buildings. As I was passing an inhabited villa, a man watering the garden invited me for coffee. Vural spoke only Turkish and German but his daughter, Hale, was a fluent English-speaker. They had never heard of the hermitage, but knew much about the other monuments of Sinop. 'The one that's impressed me most', I said, 'is Pervane's *madrasah*. Not just the building, but the fact that it's still in use.'

Vural caught the gist of this, and was wrinkling his nose even before Hale translated. When she did, he smiled darkly and muttered something about '*arabische Mikroben*'. To illustrate the point, he darted into the garage, came out with a can of flyspray and directed imaginary blasts towards the town. '*Paff! . . . Paff!*'

It hardly needed an explanation; but Hale said, 'What he means is that these places are dangerous. The boys will grow up and try to spread *shari'ah*, Islamic law.' We talked on, I the infidel defending Islamic tradition and continuity, Vural the Muslim vehemently attacking these subversive institutions, until a sudden blast of wind off the sea set the power-lines shrieking. It was cold, a first breath of winter, 'when the Land of al-Rum is like glittering glass, its air like stinging hornets'. Our looking-glass debate came to an end.

I walked on briskly and stopped for an early supper at the Pasha Battery, a Crimean War fort that advertised itself as a restaurant and casino. In the empty dining-room, the waiter pressed champagne and whisky on me. I said I'd just have a beer. 'And have one yourself,' I offered, thinking that the place needed cheering up a bit.

He smiled. 'I don't drink. You see, I'm at the İmam Hatip Lisesi. I'm going to be a mosque preacher, *in sha Allah*.'

I told him that a casino seemed a strange choice of workplace for a future *khatib*. I certainly couldn't imagine the Arabian microbes at the Pervane *madrasah* or my *rafiq* Yalçın, also at Islamic high school, plying people with hard liquor. The waiter merely shrugged. Perhaps there was no choice.

At the far end of the restaurant there was a small stage with a two-manual electronic organ. Later, inspired by the beer, and since there was still no one else about, I asked the waiter if he would switch it on. 'You play?' he asked. I said I did.

He also turned on some coloured lights and a revolving disco globe. And there I sat, in a vaulted Ottoman arsenal, playing Bach's D minor Toccata to a pre-recorded *boom-shagga-boom* with the volume just this side of feedback. I was getting my own back on Pub 13.

★

'Our stay in Sinop lasted about forty days', IB remembered, 'while we were awaiting an occasion to travel by sea to the Crimea. We then hired a vessel belonging to the Greeks but remained eleven days more, waiting for a favourable wind.' IB's seven-week wait didn't bode well. Down in the harbour there were a few smallish fishing vessels, but little activity except on the mole, where boys dangled lines into water thick with jellyfish.

I asked around for boats to Kırım, the Crimea. The only response was the tongue-click and the languid raising of eyebrows which in Turkey denotes not surprise, but negation. At length I found a small elderly man, the owner of a fishing boat, who had a little English and a lot of wombat-coloured hair poking out between his shirt buttons. 'Russian boats go Yalta,' he told me. 'Cucumbers, melons, fruits. But not now. Customs problems. Pay too much Kırım. Also economy problems.' As he spoke, the hair wriggled fascinatingly. 'Now Sinop local fishing only. Often no fish. No money no honey. Try Trabzon. Try Istanbul better.'

I thanked the hirsute talking telegram, and decided to try Istanbul.

★

I began on the quay at Karaköy, in the marble halls of Turkish Maritime Lines. They ran an occasional service to Samsun, just east of Sinop, and a summer cruise to Smyrna, Alexandria, Messina and various other Mediterranean fleshpots, and looked alarmed at the mention of the Crimea.

The streets behind the quay looked more promising. All the signs were in Cyrillic characters; import–export men wearing shades and mobile phones stood in the doorways of shops that sold chandeliers and surveillance devices. A black and chrome Chevrolet Impala cruised past, aglitter with fins.

Between the quayside buildings I spotted a ship, the *Doktor Ivan Popov*, and wondered if this might be part of the ex-Soviet research fleet which, I had heard, now kept the Ukraine and points north supplied with fridge-freezers. But how to find out?

I tried an agency which offered 'БИЛЕТЫ something something СТАМБУЛ–ОДЕССА'. Inside, Mr Öner could offer me tickets not only to Odessa, but also to Novorossiysk. 'And the Crimea?' I asked, hopefully.

'It is not now a regular destination,' he said. 'Try the Chamber of Shipping.'

In which my inquiry was answered with a decisive *yok*.

I was sitting there, wondering what to do next, when an English-speaking seaman came over and struck up a conversation. I told him all about IB; he gave me a look of profound sympathy. 'Perhaps you go to the dock and sit,' he suggested. 'Wait for a ship from Kırım.' I asked how long I might have to wait. 'Maybe one week, maybe more ...'

I pictured myself camping out on the quayside among the fridge-freezers, growing seedier by the day and clutching a bit of card: YALTA (SEVASTOPOL WILL DO).

'Your man Ibn was here very long ago,' said the sailor. 'Now you go to Atatürk International Airport and you fly.'

This time I had absolutely no doubt about what IB would have done.

IB sailed from Sinop across the Black Sea to the Crimea, part of the vast territories of the Tatar Golden Horde. After a visit to the ruler Özbeg Khan, whose tented capital was at the time in the northern foothills of the Caucasus, he set out for Constantinople. IB spent a month in the Byzantine capital then, probably in October 1332, turned east and headed once more for that elusive goal – India.

The Crimea

Fourteenth-century Features

'I was come into a new world.'

Friar William of Rubruck (13th century), on entering the land
of the Golden Horde

IT WASN'T THE age of the Crimean Air plane that was alarming, but the colour scheme. The walls and curtains, in two shades of blue – pleasing enough, rather Oxbridge – were teamed with a fudge-coloured carpet and blood-clot seats. Several of these collapsed under my fellow passengers. They were all Turks, all male and all very excitable, and the cabin was filled with whoops and cheers.

Crimean Air, according to the boarding pass, was my reliable partner for journeys to Tashkent, Krasnodar, Minsk, Murmansk, Chelyabinsk – what a poetical boarding pass! – Novosibirsk, Windhoek ... *Windhoek?* As my mind boggled at the idea of Crimeans in the Kalahari, an air hostess appeared through the cockpit door. She was wearing a retina-jangling red trouser-suit, and looked very strict. Chatter ceased, and she began reciting the safety procedure.

As she spoke my eye fell on a large heap of ropes, nets and floats beside her at the front of the cabin. There seemed to be no explanation for their presence, unless they were some sort of primitive life-saving device in case of a forced landing in the Black Sea. I shuddered, remembering a description by a contemporary of IB of the Sea of Nitush (early on in the history of Arab geography, a copyist had got the dots wrong on بنطس, Pontus, the classical name for the Black Sea – he wrote نيطش; at that moment the wind must have changed, for Nitush it remained): 'it is a dark and frightful sea, stormy and great of wave, seething furiously, a swift wrecker of ships, and frequented by waterspouts.' Even if we escaped drowning, bobbing in our net like the Jumblies in their sieve, there was another horror, perhaps worse: the notorious Pontine sea-fart, an enormous submarine stink-bomb said periodically to explode in the Black Sea's lower depths, bubbling up and gassing anyone unfortunate enough to be in the vicinity.

IB himself had a bad experience on the Black Sea. 'A storm blew up against us. We were in sore straits, with destruction staring us in the face. I was in the cabin, along with a man from the Maghrib named Abu Bakr, and I bade him go up on deck to observe the state of the sea. He did so and returned, saying, "I commend you to God".' It didn't exactly inspire confidence.

The air hostess finished speaking and, with perfect timing, a voice from the back of the plane exclaimed the Turkish equivalent of 'I commend you to God'. There was a ripple of laughter, followed by a nervous silence as the plane taxied. Within a few minutes, however, we were climbing over the northern mouth of the Bosphorus, out over an innocent, blue Black Sea.

My neighbour opened his briefcase, took out a publication called *Mega-Pasha*, and was soon engrossed in an illustrated feature showing odalisques in bridal veils and knickers. I opened the *Travels*.

IB survived the storm and landed at the eastern end of the Crimea. 'This wilderness', he wrote, describing the steppe, 'is green and grassy, with neither tree nor hill, high or low, nor narrow pass nor firewood. What they use for burning is animal dung, and you can see even their men of rank gathering it up and putting it in the skirts of their robes.' Mandeville also mentioned the Tatars' manure-mania: 'They eat Cattes, and all maner of wyld bestes, rattes & myce, and they have but lyttle wodde, and therefore they dyght theyr meate with horse dounge & other bestes dounge . . . and they be ryght foule folke, and of evyll lyking.'

IB's opinion of the Tatars was higher. Although their customs were scarcely less strange to a Tangerine than to an inhabitant of Hertfordshire, they were at least ruled over by an enthusiastic convert to Islam – Özbeg, Khan of the Golden Horde and in-law to both the Mamluk Sultan and the Byzantine Emperor. The traveller was to meet him later, in the foothills of the Caucasus; for the moment his goal was Tuluktumur, Özbeg's governor of the Crimea, who held court in its cognate capital of al-Qiram. My intention was to look for traces of IB's Tatars, but I was also keen to meet their modern-day descendants: expelled from the Crimea by Stalin in 1944 for 'collaboration' with the Germans, 250,000 Crimean Tatars had returned home after the break-up of the Soviet Union – albeit to a frosty reception from the Russian and Ukrainian majority.

Among my other Battutian destinations was Kaffa, 'one of the world's celebrated ports', renamed Feodosia when Catherine the Great took the Crimea from its last ruling khan. When IB was there, Kaffa was a trading enclave under a Genoese governor and populated by Genoese, Venetians, Florentines, Turks, Russians, Egyptians, Greeks, Circassians, Armenians, Alans and Provençals. It was his first experience of a mainly Christian town, and it was a shock. One aspect of Feodosia particularly fascinated me: it was supposedly the place from which the Black Death spread to Europe, the Levant and North Africa. Most important of all, I wanted to investigate one of IB's strangest overnights – in a church in eastern Crimea, where he and a monk talked icons.

As I walked out of the arrivals hall at the airport of Simferopol, the present Crimean capital, all these plans began to crumble. I was ridiculously ill-prepared. All I had to guide me was a slim Russian phrase-book, the *Travels*, various jottings from Arab geographers – none later than the fourteenth century – and the name of a hotel eighty miles away in Feodosia. I asked the Turks if they knew how to get there. They were surprised. 'Feodosia? *Keffe?* It's not good. Come with us to Simferopol.' They described some of the capital's temptations, mercantile and fleshly. I was not tempted. The Turks boarded a bus and I was left alone, delighted by their use of the pre-Catherinian name but wondering if I would ever make it to Feodosia – let alone Kaffa.

A large and grizzled taxi driver sauntered up to me and spoke in Russian. 'Feodosia . . . ?' I inquired, tremulously. He smiled, and beckoned. A replay of scenes during my last days in Turkey flashed through my mind: faces aghast at the mention of the Crimea, fingers drawn across throats, a warning heard in Kastamonu – 'Never, never go out at night in Kırım. They eat people.' The afternoon was waning. I followed the taxi driver, wondering whether I would end up dyghted with dung somewhere out in the huge silence of the steppe.

Vitaly was, of course, charming. We were soon discussing – God knows how – the merits of various bars in Aden, which he had visited as a sailor in 1972. The Crescent, I agreed, was decidedly *horrorshow* – my Burgessian approximation to the Russian for 'good'. We recalled too the Rock, and the Sailor's Club; but conversation – like the bars of old Aden – soon ran dry. Vitaly put on a cassette of bitter-sweet Slavic disco music.

The road was fast but potholed. We headed east through colourless steppe under a vast sky, smooth and grey as a flat-iron. At first it looked as if it would never quite meet the earth; but soon a horizon appeared to the south – a line of mountains behind which, Vitaly said, lay the sea. The Crimea took on shape: that of a prodigious pasty, rolled flat in the middle, crimped at the edge.

There were occasional villages of small cement-block houses, and people with vegetables in buckets by the side of the road. Some sold honey, one of the Crimea's medieval exports. Amid the strangeness of arrival, it was something to latch on to. Then, abruptly, we entered a region of deciduous forest. In Turkey, autumn had been at its melancholy outset; here it was crimson and yellow, fierce and fiery. I had crossed from the land of a mousy Pan to the realm of red-headed and more primitive gods. As we drove past Stary Krim, IB's city of al-Qiram, I noticed a brand-new mosque near the road. Further into the town rose another minaret. Its profile took me back across the sea, across Anatolia, and I realized that it must belong to the mosque built by Özbeg in 1314 – within a year or two of the one put up by Sultan Muhammad ibn Aydın of Birgi. Something else to latch on to. '*Allah! Allah!*' Vitaly wailed. '*Krimsky Tatar . . . mullah!*'

It was still not dark when we reached Feodosia. I had forgotten how far north we were – as far north as Bordeaux. I shivered; but boys and girls wandered about in the endless twilight in shorts, displaying endless, non-Tatar legs. For the next half-hour we cruised the town, asking in vain for my hotel. This was not a simple matter. When I had booked the room (a requirement for getting a visa) through an agent in Manchester, it had been called the Torgtehbiznes; I had recently telephoned the agent from Turkey to change my dates, and learned that it was now called the Fiord. When, finally, we found it, there was no indication on the blank frontage that it was a hotel at all, and certainly no name. Even the staff didn't seem to know what it was called. Incredibly, though, they were expecting me.

I behaved like a newly arrived Martian. They had to show me how to use the room-key, double-headed like Zeus's axe, and how to switch on the light. I then locked myself in the loo and had to be

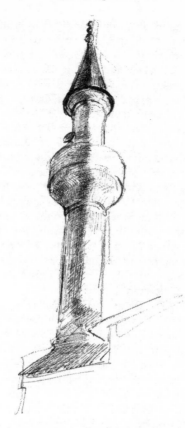

rescued. As I was searching for an appropriate form of thanks in the phrasebook, one of the other guests gently closed it, said, 'No! *This* . . . ' and flourished a bottle of vodka.

He was right. Vodka – and Crimean *champanskaya*, and *konyak*, and scotch from me – were great facilitators of communication. An impromptu party began. We ate curds with sour cream and sugar, and the little dumplings called *pelmeni*, and oily *shprotti* – which my new vodka-based fluency told me were Slavonic 'sprats'. Despite these stomach-lining snacks, the drink took me by stealth. Sprats, shprats, shprotts: it seemed eminently reasonable.

And then it happened, quite unexpectedly: I was dancing. My

partner was a plump platinum blonde, comfortably into her fifties, less so into a lamé sheath dress. As we swayed in a tight clinch – an unusual tactile experience, both metallic and pneumatic – she ruffled my hair, pointed to herself and cooed, *'Babushka!'* Then, pointing to me she added, throatily, 'I *loahv* you!'

Some time later I prised myself free, but she carried on dancing with increased vigour. I had several stiff shots of vodka to recover. The room began performing elaborate double *entrechats*. I excused myself for the night. But she was still up there strutting her stuff, pogoing alone to the bitter-sweet Slavic disco beat. Some *babushka*.

I awoke early to the sound of leaves being swept on the street. My head, too, was littered with dead matter. I went for a walk to clear it. In the middle of town I found a market, already busy with head-scarved women selling fruit and vegetables, almonds and walnuts, berries and dried camomile. Seeing this, I could understand the appeal of the Crimea for the Tatars. It had everything – bountiful forests and mountains and, inland, broad flat grazing for the herds. For a nomad people who were getting a taste for the fruits of settled life, it was perfection in miniature.

The market was a thoroughly peasant place, but nearby was a different Feodosia, of low stuccoed villas with classical pediments, peeling madder washes and cats in windows. I stopped and listened: someone was playing the 'Minute Waltz' on a slightly out-of-tune piano, beautifully, *rubato*. It ended with a whirl of *accelerando*, then a silence broken only by the spin of falling leaves.

I wandered down to the docks, IB's 'wonderful harbour where some two hundred ships lay, both ships of war and merchantmen' – now silent too, home to a bare half-dozen small vessels. It was going to be hard to find out where hushed, provincial Feodosia and noisy, cosmopolitan Kaffa intersected, if indeed they still did.

Back in the hotel a woman was waiting for me. She was in chic early middle age and wore a frock with red polka dots. She extended her hand. 'My name is Nina Suvorova. The proprietress of this hotel summoned me.' Her English was carefully poised. 'She thought that you were perhaps a little . . . lost, and that you might welcome some guidance.' She looked at me quizzically and pursed her lips, which matched the polka dots.

'Well, I must say I'm a bit perplexed on the language front,' I admitted. 'By the way, your English is excellent.'

'That is because I am a teacher of the English language,' she explained.

I told her that I too had been one, years ago. 'Ah, then perhaps you know Bonk? But no, of course not. His grammar is for the Russian-speaking learner. It is indispensable. I always say to my students, "Let us begin with Bonk!"' She smiled so radiantly that I could imagine no more delightful guide.

We set out immediately. Nina hadn't heard of IB; but I soon realized that, as far as more recent history went, I had no need of a guidebook. 'This', she said, pointing to a seafront façade covered with gambolling cherubs, 'is the Astoria Hotel. It was constructed in 1914. You may wish to note that seven years later it was the scene of the conference that ended the Civil War. The last of the White Russians departed from here, from Feodosia.' A statue of Pushkin, freshly decorated with flowers, inspired her to recite a verse; Lenin we passed by without comment. We strolled along the harbour, further than I had been on my earlier sortie, until we came to a tapering tower. 'And this is the Tower of St Constantine. The noted nineteenth-century marine painter Aivazovsky, who was a great benefactor to Feodosia, recalled very scenically the arrival of Catherine the Great at this tower, after the capture of the Crimea by Potemkin from the hand of the last Tatar khan. The date of the khan's surrender, if you would like to note it, was 8 April 1783. It was Catherine who restored to our city its original Greek name of Feodosia ... '

I was staring up at the building, following its cornicing of brick merlons, only half listening. Nina paused. 'And the date of the tower?'

'It was constructed by the Genoese in the fourteenth century ... ' I felt a tingle of excitement '... The tower – I think one says more precisely "bastion" – was part of the city wall. Here the wall turned inland from the sea, protecting the Genoese from attackers from the steppe to the east.' So this was the intersection, where Feodosia met Kaffa.

We sat on a bench in a park behind the bastion. Nina was back to Aivazovsky; but my mind was elsewhere, trying to reconstruct the dreadful event which had taken place – right here – a decade and a half after IB's visit.

The year was 1346. Özbeg Khan had been dead five years; the new ruler of the Golden Horde was his son Janibeg, whom IB had met on his trip to the Caucasus foothills. The uneasy co-existence of Tatars and European traders had broken down. Janibeg's forces first attacked the Genoese colony of Azov, on the mainland 250 miles to the north-east; now they were besieging Kaffa, and making little impression on it. Then disaster struck: the attackers were themselves attacked – by the Black Death. The siege collapsed, the European colony was safe. As a parting shot, Janibeg ordered his catapulteers to lob the bodies of the plague victims over the walls.

Walls which had withstood live Tatars were no defence against dead ones. A city under siege, enclosed, tightly packed, is the human equivalent of a Petri dish: even before the Tatars had left, the plague was galloping through Kaffa. Fearing another siege, many of the surviving Italian merchants sailed for home. With them went *Pasteurella pestis*, released from the thinly populated steppe into the crowded Mediterranean basin, to gorge itself on Europe, North Africa and the Levant.

Some commentators have branded the account, written by a contemporary Italian chronicler, a legend; others have pointed out that the epidemic would have spread in any case. The pest investigators Dols and Ziegler, however, do not doubt that the siege of Kaffa was a factor in the westward journey of the Black Death. And if the account is true in detail, then Janibeg was by no means the first commander to use biological weapons. In medieval Europe, besieged towns were regularly bombarded with dead cows, the victims of rinderpest. The idea is much older: according to Arab geographers the notorious scorpions of Nusaybin, now on the Turkish-Syrian border, are said to be descended from ancestors which the Sassanian army shot over the battlements in earthen pots in AD 363.

As Nina dilated on painters and poets, my thoughts flicked between the procession to the Mosque of the Footprints in Damascus, plague pits in Bristol, and the sickening *whump* of corpses landing here, where we sat on a bench in a tree-lined avenue.

' . . . And now we shall visit the burial place of Aivazovsky. I hope you are not tiring.'

'No, no. I was just thinking of IB.'

'Ah, Battutah. I believe you are thinking often about your Battutah.' She made him sound like a rival for her affection.

Unexpectedly, the burial place of Aivazovsky also rang Battutian bells – loud ones, and not only metaphorical. It was in a fourteenth-century Armenian church, approached through an arched structure like a *porte-cochère*. Nina explained that this was a bell-chamber. I immediately pulled out the *Travels* and read: 'When we alighted at the mosque of Kaffa we heard the sounds of bells on every side. Never having heard them before, I was alarmed and bade my companions ascend the minaret and chant the Qur'an, litanies, and the call to prayer.' The judge of the Muslims appeared, equally alarmed. ' "I heard the chanting and the call to prayer, and feared for your safety," he said. Then he went away, but no evil befell us.'

'Your Battutah was correct when he said that the bells were all around him,' Nina said, impressed. 'There were approximately forty churches in medieval Kaffa.'

As we wandered around the old part of the town we found more of them. One had a small tree growing out of its roof. Another lay in waste ground littered with human turds. Now they were silent; but it needed little imagination to picture the arrival of IB and his friends in what, to them, was a hell of bells. The sound is anathema to pious Muslims for, as the *hadith* says, 'The angels will not enter any house in which bells are rung.' In towns with mixed Muslim and Christian populations there could be long-running rivalries, Minarets v. Steeples. The eleventh-century poet al-Ma'arri described one such local derby:

> In Ladhiqiyyah it's all go
> For Jesus and the Prophet:
> Priest's bell clangs out *fortissimo*,
> *Shaykh* shrieks and strains to top it.

There was one mosque in Feodosia, and it turned out to be no distance from the first church. As we entered the gate – Nina, I noticed, hesitantly – I wondered if this could have been the very place where IB staged his minaret protest, and where he and his companions stayed during their visit. The building, however, was hard to date, for it was a confused jumble of ragged masonry and brickwork, much patched and altered. The confusion was increasing as we watched: a man was mixing cement for a half-built arcade along the front of the prayer-hall. Hearing our footsteps, he turned around.

For a moment, I stared. He had an almost circular face, rather flat, framed by a bobble hat and a wispy beard. His eyes were slightly feline, and set wide apart and high up in the skull. It was a strange face; and yet I had seen it many times before – in manuscripts, in silver and gold on bronze, in lustre on ceramics. It was the face of the steppe peoples, of Mamluks, Khans and Ilkhans – a young face, in its mid-twenties, but also a fourteenth-century face. '*Al-salam alaykum*,' I said.

'*Wa alaykum*', he replied, equally surprised, but in good Arabic – I could tell from that much, '*al-salam*.'

'Where did you learn Arabic?' we asked each other, simultaneously, and then both laughed. I told him, and explained what had brought me to the Crimea. The imam of the Mufti Mosque had learned his Arabic, he said, in Tataristan. Nina watched us silently. She was in Feodosia, the imam and I in Kaffa.

Inside the prayer-hall, he sketched in the mosque's history. It was founded in 1623; a century and a half later, Potemkin gave it to the Catholics among his forces who had settled here, to use as a church. Only with the return of the Tatars in the 1990s had it become a mosque once more. 'And now we are expanding,' he said, indicating a growing island of carpet on the bare floor. Suddenly he glanced at his watch. 'You must excuse me. I have to call the *adhan*. You see, we have no muezzin.' I wanted to ask him more, but God came first. After all, He had been kept waiting long enough: there were two centuries of devotions to be made up for. 'You will join us for the prayer?' he asked me, expectantly.

'I'm a Masihi,' I replied.

His face fell very slightly, like a soufflé taken from the oven, then reinflated. 'It . . . it is good to speak Arabic. I hope you will return.'

Outside, I paused at the street gate and looked back towards the bitty stonework of the prayer-hall. If this was three hundred years too late, what had happened to IB's mosque? Then, something caught my eye, in the arch above the doorway: the stones were joggled – jointed together with a slight jigsaw kink. For a building of 1623, it was a very fourteenth-century feature . . . Perhaps I was becoming obsessive, seeing fourteenth-century profiles everywhere. The call to prayer sounded out, amplified, astonishingly loud in the bell-less hush of Feodosia.

After our visit to the mosque Nina was, for once, subdued. She was back on form though when I went that evening to supper in her flat, in a block in the suburbs of Feodosia. At the door I was greeted by the earthy smell of *bortsch* and by Marco Polo – Nina's terrier. He sniffed at my trousers; I sniffed at his name.

Nina was giving a private class to a student (I noticed the indispensable Bonk between them on the table). While she took him, macaronically in English and Russian, through a reading comprehension on the manufacture of macaroni, I dipped into an English-language guidebook to the Crimea. The peninsula, I learned, is ten times the size of Luxembourg; Yalta boasts an obelisk commemorating Lenin's decree, 'On Utilizing the Crimea for the Treatment of Working People'; Planerskoye is home to a Museum of Gliding and Parachutism. There were statistics on the production of *champanskaya* and hosiery. All esoteric stuff; but, I reflected, my own interest in the Crimea – in the visit of a Moroccan who had been here for a few days in 1332 – was no less so.

Later, over supper, I realized that my close focus could also be seen as tunnel vision. I was complaining about the price of cigarettes, which had risen by a fifth in a single day. I asked Nina if she thought I'd been cheated.

She laughed. 'Have you not heard? The rouble fell, more than one month ago – down, down! Now it is affecting our economy here. We Russians, the Ukrainians, your Tatars . . . no one is safe.'

I admitted I hadn't heard. Nina shook her head slowly, as if at a hopeless student. 'Before 1991 we knew our future. Now it is shock after shock. We continue as we can; but this shock has been the hardest. Viktor Chernomyrdin – in case you do not know,' she said pointedly, 'he was the Prime Minister of Russia – compared it to the Tatar armies riding through the land, destroying. And you are not aware of it because you are busy with Battutah!'

Later, back in the hotel, I remembered Chernomyrdin's comment. So far I had met only one Tatar, but the Russian national conscious, it seemed, contained hordes of them. It was understandable, as the Tatars were the only force ever to have conquered its national home. In IB's time, the princes of Muscovy were little more than tax collectors for Özbeg; their bid for independence fifty years later was answered by the sacking of Moscow by his grandson. Chaucer heard about it – 'in the Londe of Tartarie/There dwelt a King that werried Russie'. Seven hundred years on, the Tatars were still apparently werrying the Russians. Perhaps that fourteenth-century face which for me suggested delicate ceramics and opulent metalwork had, for Nina, conjured up more threatening images.

★

I hadn't realized the savagery of economics on the rampage. The following morning, the hotel cook joined me for coffee. I pieced her story together from her few fragments of English. She had been a naval architect. Now there was no money and no more navy to design. The kitchen of the Hotel Anonymous, as I thought of it, was the only place she could find work. The brief personal history was by any standards a tragedy. And yet, like Nina, she was stoical and stylishly clothed, and she shrugged magnificently when I asked her about the future. I left her frying breakfast eggs, dressed for a tea dance, and all for eight pounds sterling a month.

I went to look for the imam but the mosque was locked. Instead, at the southern end of the town, I came across his mirror image. The setting was familiar: towers staring at the sea and wind keening through the power-lines – like Sinop, but several degrees colder, many shades greyer, and gnawed by decay. Bastions rose like shattered tombstones out of a graveyard of burnt grass and broken glass. A stream turned out to be a sewer; a children's playground was smashed and abandoned, the swings rusted into rigor mortis. Several medieval churches and chapels stood among the desolation. I entered one of them and saw the faint remnants of a fresco, a line of apostles turning their faces towards a seated Christ – faces without features, lepers' faces. There had been other figures but only the lines of their drapery survived, turning saints into shrouded spectres. There was no romance in these ruins. They looked like the aftermath not of time or economics, but of a plague.

Only one building showed any sign of being looked after, a church with a high drum-shaped lantern topped by a new and tinny metal dome. Outside it three men were mixing cement and laying paving stones. One of them had the long beard of a priest. Like the imam, he was trying to provide something to latch on to in a disintegrating world.

★

I thought I was the only foreigner in Feodosia, until Nina invited me to supper again, to meet another protégé of hers. He was an Austrian haematologist called Gerhard, and he had brought his internet girl-friend Nadia – like Nina, a Feodosia Russian. Also present was Nina's daughter Natasha, visiting from distant Nizhny Novgorod.

'I am helping Nadia', Nina explained, 'to express herself to Gerhard.' Nadia grinned and recrossed her legs. She was a strapping girl, built like a nutcracker, and looked quite capable of expressing herself without any assistance. She reminded me of the traveller Ibn Fadlan's comment on the Volga Rus: 'Never have I seen a people more perfectly formed. They are flaxen-haired, fair-skinned and tall as palm trees.' As we ate, I quoted the description; then, tactlessly, followed it with IB's own picture of the Russians: 'They have red hair, blue eyes and ugly faces, and they are a treacherous folk.'

'That is not true!' Nina retorted. Her opinion of my Battutah, never high, sank lower.

It was late when we left, and Nina warned Gerhard and me not to speak English. It seemed a strange piece of advice, but she explained that there were many bad men about at night. I remembered the worried looks in Turkey when I had mentioned my trip to Kırım. We flagged down a taxi, the only vehicle about. Nadia sat in the front and engaged the driver in conversation, Gerhard and I in the back. It was almost impossible not to speak; throughout the journey we quivered silently with *champanskaya*-fuelled giggles, while the driver threw us dark looks in the mirror.

*

The following day, as I was finishing lunch in a restaurant, I spotted the imam walking past outside. I quickly paid my bill and trotted off in pursuit, but he had disappeared. I was keen to find out more from him about the history of the mosque. Whenever I went there it was shut, and this brief sighting was my only other glimpse of him.

I was to find another clue in Stary Krim. IB had hired a wagon for the twenty-five-mile journey; I hired Viktor, a chunkily built taxi driver who, Nina intimated, might come in useful for other reasons. 'Beware!' she warned. 'Stary Krim is *not* a good place.'

My expectations of prowling post-Soviet mafiosi were unfulfilled. IB's 'large and fine' city of al-Qiram felt more like an overblown village, with small neat houses set in orchards heavy with russet fruit. We made for the minaret of Özbeg's mosque, which I had spotted on my journey to Feodosia. Again, building work was in progress – the stonework had been repointed and a fine wall was growing around the compound. The doorway of the mosque was framed by looping arabesques and bore an inscription, in which I made out 'the exalted Sultan Muhammad Özbeg Khan' and the date AH 713 – AD 1314. Below this was something instantly familiar: in the arch above the door itself, the stones interlocked with the same jigsaw joints that I had seen in Feodosia. The similarity in profile seemed too close for coincidence. I couldn't prove it, but I felt certain that the Feodosia mosque of 1623 incorporated a much earlier structure – the very one in which IB had stayed and made war on the churchbells.

An elderly Tatar approached as we were inspecting the doorway. At first he eyed us warily; but when I greeted him in Arabic, he smiled. He could do no more than return the greeting, so I switched to my meagre Turkish. Thanks to the Turkification of the Golden Horde under Özbeg I was able, seven centuries on, to hold a makeshift conversation with Kamal. The mosque, I learned, had an imam-preacher and a muezzin; the community was pouring money into the building, to restore and beautify it. The building, though, was heavily padlocked, and the key 'unavailable'. I never saw inside the Tatar holy of holies.

Wondering what had happened to the notables IB met – the governor Tuluktumur, his sons Qutludumur and Sarubak, the *shaykh* Zadah al-Khurasani, and others in a list of similarly magniloquent names – I asked Kamal if he knew of any tombs. He smiled grimly, glanced sidelong at Nina and Viktor, and said something about Russians. When I told him I didn't understand he began a vigorous mime of digging. Nina spoke to him in Russian, then said, 'He was telling you about the archaeologists.' I looked at Kamal, who was still grim-faced, and thought: one man's archaeologist is another man's bodysnatcher.

We found what was left of the graves at a house on Lenin Street. Viktoria and Aleksandr, the resident Russian scholars, were personally innocent of grave-robbery – the despoliations had taken place years before. They took me around the 'lapidarium'. Several of the gravestones were dated, tantalizingly, to the 1330s – the decade of IB's visit; I looked in vain for names on his list. Saddest of all, the Tatar nobles and their cosmopolitan camp-followers had ended up as jumbles of bones wrapped in newspaper. In life, they had been sticklers for protocol: IB remembered the governor's major-domo announcing arrivals in the audience chamber, ' "*Bismillah*, our lord and master, the *qadi* of *qadis* and of magistrates, the elucidator of cases and of rules of law, *bismillah* . . . *Bismillah*, our lord So-and-So al-Din, *bismillah* . . ." ' Now they mingled, promiscuous, anonymous, unceremonious as cod lots, in sheets of old *Pravdas*. This charnel-house, this graveyard of a graveyard, was a sundering of people, of history, from place. Perhaps it was no less calculated than Stalin's expulsion of live Tatars.

My spirits rose as we drove down a track in the woods to investigate another Battutian lead. 'Outside this city', the traveller heard, 'was a Christian monk living in a monastery, who devoted himself to ascetic exercises. He was able to fast for forty days at a stretch, after which he would break his fast with a single bean. He also had the faculty of revealing secret things.' IB's host, Shaykh Zadah, pressed him to visit this prodigy, 'but I refused. Afterwards, however, I found out the truth of what was said about this monk, and regretted not visiting him.'

'I know where this place is,' said Nina, when I had read the passage out in the archaeologists' house. 'It is the Armenian monastery of Surb-Khatch, Holy Cross.' The archaeologists had disagreed, pointing out that Surb-Khatch was built in 1338 – six years too late for IB. I was sceptical about dates. The mosque in Feodosia, after all, had every appearance of being a refoundation of an earlier building.

We arrived at Surb-Khatch, its drum dome rising out of a clearing in the forest. My suspicions about dates were confirmed by a scholarly looking young man who was working on its restoration, and who told us that it had been enlarged from an earlier monastery. Nina translated IB's account of the ascetic; the man smiled and spoke. 'He says that Battutah was right,' she explained. 'It was the custom of Armenian monks to break their fasts on beans.'

None of this, of course, was proof that we had found IB's monastery. But, as we crossed a small walled courtyard and entered the church, the question slipped from my mind.

I had never seen anything like it. The west door was surmounted, like the mosques of Stary Krim and Feodosia, by a joggled arch: pure Mamluk. A blind arch higher up was carved with thick, interlacing strapwork; above this were two pierced, tea-strainer bosses: pure Seljuk. Inside, the column capitals and recesses either side of the altar were decorated with *muqarnas*, the tiers of shell-like indentations with stalactite projections that are as Islamic as the call to prayer.

There was even a *mihrab*, an Islamic prayer-niche, again rich with *muqarnas*; above it, in a tondo, was a nosediving dove. I blinked, and realized it was a font, let into the wall. I recalled the orientalizing entrance to my old parish church, built a decade or so before Surb-Khatch; but this was an entire building in which the architectural language had been written in the wrong script. It was utterly unexpected, totally successful, and made stranger still by its setting in the forest. Surb-Khatch was an architectural Briar Rose, of mixed parentage and extraordinary beauty.

Outside the church, the young man led us to a spring of water issuing from a wall fountain. 'This', Nina translated, 'is called "the Practical Spring".'

I asked her why. There was another short exchange. 'Because', she said, 'its water makes you practical.'

I drank deeply.

★

Sounds of the steppe: a steady *birr . . . birr . . . birr . . .* of crickets overlaid with the off-beat rapping of other insects, and with the calls of unseen birds – *chuckety-chuckety-chuck, fweet . . . fweet.* They all came together, a laid-back, melodious jam session. And in the interstices, when for fractions of seconds the voices seemed to catch breath, you could hear the hiss of silence.

We had gone east out of the Crimea proper into its appendix, the antepeninsula of Kerch, following a straight wide road empty of traffic. At first we could see both seas, the Black, to the south, and the Sea of Azov to the north. They were the colour of slates in rain, the land ahead a watery blue. The air was warm. Now as we stood by the side of the road I deconstructed, then reconstructed the landscape. Mentally, I removed asphalt, power-lines, the few trees; then placed on the virgin grass herds of horses, a line of wagons moving slowly, lone figures stooping to collect dung in the skirts of their robes.

We resumed our journey and passed the Tatar settlement, or re-settlement, of Arma-Elli, a sudden place in the void, neat with palings; crossed the Cimmerian Dyke, dug in the Bronze Age as a last-ditch defence against the advancing Scythians, redug in the 1940s against the Germans, now filled with brambles; drove through Gornastayevka, once Marienthal, a colony of Swiss legionaries set up by Catherine the Great. For such an empty place it was busy with history.

Seventy miles from Feodosia we reached the outskirts of Kerch. They began with a post-industrial scene of grassy slag-heaps – except that the mounds were Scythian barrows where dead noblemen were buried with their households, strangled for the occasion. Then the road descended into a wasteland planted with clumps of apartment blocks. Finally we turned on to a grand seaside boulevard, hushed – like Feodosia – but for the sound of bells: not a peal or a carillon, but a chorus of muffled anvils. I remembered, for the first time in months, that it was Sunday.

'We made for a harbour called Karsh,' wrote IB, recalling his arrival in the Crimea, in Europe, 'intending to put in there. But some persons who were on the mountain made signs to us not to enter. Fearing that we might run into danger, we turned back along the coast. As we approached the land I said to the master of the ship, "I wish to descend here," so he put me ashore. I saw a church so we made towards it.'

The church was the scene of one of the most mystifying exchanges in the *Travels*, and I was keen to visit it and pick up clues to solve the mystery. The only possible candidate for it, according to the archaeologists of Stary Krim, was the eleventh-century St John the Baptist; there were, and had been, no other churches further along the coast. We reached it just as the sound of its bells began to die away, *calando* . . . *perdendosi*. *Tacet*. I could imagine no greater contrast to the Armeno-Mamluk church in the woods. St John's, its vanilla stone banded with brick the colour of ripe pink peaches, was the product of an architectural *gelateria*.

A service had just begun, so Nina suggested a visit to the nearby museum. The museum director agreed that St John the Baptist was the only possible contender for IB's church. She then took us on a tour of the collection. It was rich in red-figure ware and sculpture from the time of the Bosporan Kingdom, the small but energetic empire run here by Greeks and locals which spanned the Kerch Strait – the Cimmerian Bosphorus, hence the kingdom's name. The director's running Russian commentary on the exhibits was inlaid with Greek – *rhyta* and *kylices* and *oenochoes*. At one point she grasped a statuette of Aphrodite, turned it around, patted the goddess's rump and pronounced her – with a twinkle in her eye – *kalipygaya*. I was mildly shocked.

Later, we returned to the church. The service was over, and we

entered the west door via a small phalanx of antique almsmen who crossed themselves creakily as we passed by. 'In the church,' IB remembered, 'I found a monk, and on one of the walls I saw the figure of an Arab man wearing a turban, girt with a sword, and carrying a spear in his hand. In front of him was a lamp, which was alight. I said to the monk, "What is this figure?" and he replied, "This is the figure of the Prophet Ali." I was filled with astonishment.'

As well he might have been. A Christian icon – and surely it must be, with the lamp burning before it – showing not only an Arab, but the Prophet Muhammad's cousin and son-in-law, promoted by a monk to prophethood? It was an enigma which I had spent some time turning over, viewing it laterally, vertically, diagonally. The turban might have been a halo seen in the flickering half-light of the church; the spear and sword were attributes of warrior saints and archangels. But why Ali? Obviously, IB had misheard. 'This looks like a natural confusion with Elias [Elijah],' said Gibb in a footnote, 'the Greek genitive of which is Elía.'

The problem was that the iconography simply didn't fit. In the restored church in Feodosia, a helpful icon painter had produced his catalogue of patriarchs and saints by numbers. We turned to an image of Elijah. The prophet was shown with a narrow face and long pointed beard; he had no sword or spear. In Stary Krim the archaeologists had agreed that the identification with Elijah seemed impossible. They had then shown me a drawing taken from a medieval fresco of St Theodore Stratilates, the archetypal warrior-martyr, which fitted well with IB's description. The major difficulty here was the name, which by no stretch of the phonetic imagination could be garbled into *al-nabi Ali*.

During my earlier research, the same difficulty had applied to St George, my own original candidate for the subject of IB's icon. I had then moved on to archangels and turned up a fourteenth-century icon of Gabriel with turban-like halo and spear. His wings could, in poor lighting, have become an Arab-style cloak. Archangel Gabriel ... *al-nabi Ali* ... -eli-Gabrieli. To be honest, I was flailing around in the dark just as much as IB.

The church had been restored recently. Elderly ladies were polishing and sweeping and fussing about the bookstall. One of them told me via Nina that St John the Baptist was the oldest church in the world; then she added, with a sly smile, 'It's older than the Vatican, you know.'

An irredeemable schismatic, I went off to examine the iconostasis. I had hardly dared to hope that IB's Prophet Ali might have survived; as it was, all the icons were brand-new. At least, I thought, iconography was a fairly conservative art and there might be some clues. There was St George, with sword and spear, but for his name the perfect Prophet Ali; there were the archangels Gabriel and Michael. And there was another category, which I hadn't considered: bishops. Their bulbous Orthodox mitres could easily be mistaken for turbans, their long slender croziers for spears. But what about the sword? As I was pondering the question, the iconostasis door opened.

Father Boris, with his straggly grey beard, parchment-coloured hands, cassock and black velvet cap, looked like an alchemist. I explained why I had come to Kerch and tried out my thoughts on the possible identities of IB's icon. While Nina translated, the priest cocked his head to one side and gave out little donnish sniffs of consideration. He thought for a while, then spoke. 'To me it seems most likely that your traveller was looking at a bishop. The mitre and crozier, as you say, could have changed in his imagination into a turban and spear. As for the sword, there is one possibility that comes to mind: St Nicholas, whose remains are at Bari.' And whose jawbone, I remembered, I had seen in Antalya. 'He is a patron and defender of the oppressed, and as such he is sometimes shown with a sword.'

Nikolai ... *al-nabi Ali* ... Nikolai. Father Boris watched me as I mouthed the words.

'Have I answered your question?' he asked.

'Perhaps,' I said, unconvinced.

Father Boris took my hand. 'What was the name of your traveller? Battutah ... Then, you are welcome as a second Battutah!'

I thanked him, then read the final part of IB's passage: 'We spent the night in that church, and cooked some fowls, but we could not eat them because they were among the provisions we had taken with us on the ship, and everything that had been on board was impregnated with the smell of the sea.' As Nina translated, Father Boris's eyebrows rose. I quickly explained that I didn't intend to emulate IB to the letter. We parted at the door, Father Boris chuckling with relief.

The enigma of the icon remained unsolved. But I left the church with a strange feeling: that, in a sense, I had continued IB's conversation where he had left off, two-thirds of a millennium ago.

'I think you will find nothing more of your Battutah,' Nina said, intent on dragging me away from the fourteenth century. 'Let us climb the Acropolis of Kerch and visit the palace of Mithridates Eupator, ruler of the Bosporan Kingdom. There is also an interesting memorial to the brave partisans who fought the Germans.'

As we climbed, I realized that this must have been IB's mountain – 'Some persons who were on the mountain made signs to us not to

enter [the harbour] ... We turned back along the coast.' On the
summit, Nina pointed out the columns of King Mithridates and
the partisans' obelisk. But I was contemplating a more chimerical
history – the arrival of IB's ship in the sweep of bay beneath us,
heading for the harbour to the north-east; frantic waving from this
hilltop; a change of course – under oar? there would have been no
room to tack; the ship's boat taking the traveller and his party ashore,
dropping them just down there, where St John's overlooks the sea,
facing east towards Asia.

It was a superb vantage-point, this hill at the end of a continent
above the shimmering Cimmerian Bosphorus: just the place for a
shrine to al-Khadir. I thought of the peninsula at Sinop 'on top of
which', wrote IB, 'is a hermitage called after al-Khadir and Elijah'.
Or rather, al-Khadir also known as Elijah. Also known, to the
Christians, as St George.

And there – like the key you hunt for through your pockets, only
to find you have left it in the lock – was the answer: Elijah/Elias alias
Ali *was* George.

It was such an obvious solution that I dismissed it from my mind
instantly. And yet, as we sat on the hilltop in the autumn sunshine, it
reinsinuated itself. The Crimea in IB's time was a place where
doctors of Islamic law studied the fasting habits of Christian ascetics;
where, in an Armenian monastery church, a font could pass muster as
an Islamic prayer-niche; where, Nina had told me, the Genoese mint
in Feodosia struck bilingual coins – heads Latin, tails Arabic. In so
culturally bilingual a setting, what could have been more natural than
for IB's monk to translate St George into one of the other persons in
that trinity of identification, Elijah? Or for that matter into Ali
himself – who, like George, was the consummate holy warrior and
gentleman? Three centuries on, talking religion with the traveller
Pietro della Valle, Shah Abbas of Persia argued forcefully that Ali and
St George (and, for good measure, St James the Greater) were one
and the same. Perhaps IB hadn't misheard.

★

On my last night in Feodosia, Nina held a farewell dinner party.
Gerhard the haematologist was there, and strapping Nadia, tall as a
palm tree. Natasha, Nina's daughter, invited me to visit her: 'Come,
Timochka, to Nizhny Novgorod, and bring Battutah with you.' Put

like that it was hard to refuse; but Nizhny Novgorod was all but in what IB called the Land of Darkness, and I was not to be persuaded. Neither was Nina, when I suggested she rename Marco Polo, her terrier, 'Battutah'.

Next morning I awoke once more to the sound of the sweeping of leaves. I bade farewell to the Hotel Anonymous and set out for the airport with Nina in Viktor's taxi. We left several hours earlier than necessary, as Nina wanted to show me Bakhchiserai, successor to Stary Krim as capital of the Crimea. By the time it was founded the Golden Horde had fragmented into separate khanates, and it was here that the rulers of the Crimean fragment ran slowly to seed in their *bahçe-saray*, their pleasure-garden palace.

After lunch in the outskirts of Simferopol, I was obliged to ask Viktor to stop at the nearest public lavatory. Shortly after, he pulled off the road, pointed to a cement-block building and spoke to me with a grisly smile. 'Viktor fears that you will not find it pleasant,' Nina explained.

Viktor was right. Inside was a stink uncircumscribable by adjectives and a man straining, trousers down, over one of three adjacent holes. 'Oh sorry,' I mumbled, blushing. I turned on my heel and fled.

When I had recovered from the shock, a snatch of modified Irving Berlin came to mind:

> And I just can't find the bowel-relief I seek,
> If we're there together, squatting cheek-to-cheek.

(As it happens, public defecation has a long and distinguished history in these parts. The traveller Ibn Fadlan described the King of the Volga Rus as 'sitting on an enormous throne encrusted with gems, from which he never descends. With him are forty slave-girls of the royal bed, with whom he copulates in full view of his courtiers. And if he wishes to answer a call of nature, his chamberpot is also near to hand.')

We passed through Alma Vale – eponym, via the Crimean War, of dozens of roads in Victorian suburbia. Bakhchiserai also lay in a valley. The palace was really a series of kiosks – perhaps a throw-back to the Tatars' tented origins – together with a mosque and a small cemetery, all dispersed among gardens and courtyards. Broad eaves shaded walls painted with curlicues and other Ottoman-style decorative etceteras. Nina stood beside an elaborate wall-fountain and recited a verse by Pushkin, in which he admired its 'poetical tears'. It was all rather whimsical and – considering the masters of Bakhchiserai sprang from the loins of Genghis Khan – decadent.

I only realized just how early the decay had set in when we approached the khan's audience hall. The entrance was framed by a stucco doorcase. Flat pilasters topped by fiddly acanthus supported an inscribed lintel and a heavy classical cornice with a line of egg-and-tongue mouldings. The whole thing ended in a bloated tympanum that sprouted frothy little panaches. It was coloured in preposterous, prawn-cocktail pink. The inscriptions were in Arabic script; the design was undiluted Renaissance camp.

Then again, 'decay' might be the wrong word. Perhaps it was more a case of symbiosis. Once more, I remembered the orientalizing porch of my parish church in Bristol, that strange Indo-Perso-Saraceno-Gothic growth. This was merely its converse – executed,

according to a plaque beside the door, by a visiting Italian craftsman in 1503.

That date, however, was ominous. Vasco da Gama was founding the first European colony in the Indian Ocean, Amerigo Vespucci discovering that those transatlantic islands were no Indies, but a new world. There would be no more symbiosis. The old world IB had known was about to be slowly, mercilessly throttled.

Constantinople

Talking about Jerusalem

'O mankind! We created you from male and female, and made
you into nations and tribes, that you may know one another.'

Qur'an, chapter 49, verse 13

'OUR ENTRY INTO Constantinople the Great was made about
noon or a little later, and they beat their church-gongs until the
very skies shook with the mingling of their sounds. When we
reached the first of the gates of the king's palace we found it guarded
by about a hundred men. I heard them saying, "*Sarakinu! Sarakinu!*" '

Sarakenoi. Saracens. Muslims. IB had entered the city that for over
six centuries had been the most elusive goal of Islamic conquest.
During his Anatolian trip he had been within eighty miles of it.
When eventually he got there, it was three thousand miles later and
in the grandest style possible.

From the Crimea IB had travelled to the mobile metropolis of
Özbeg Khan. He found it in transit near the spa of Beş Dağ, Five
Hills; now, translated literally as Pyatigorsk, it is the Baden–Baden of
southern Russia. 'We saw a vast city on the move, complete with
mosques and bazaars, the smoke of the kitchens rising into the air,
and horse-drawn wagons transporting the people. On reaching the
camping place they took down the tents from the wagons and set
them on the ground, for they are light to carry, and so likewise they
did with the mosques and shops.' At the heart of the camp stood
Özbeg's Golden Pavilion, 'covered with plaques of gold, in the centre
of which is a couch covered with silver gilt and encrusted with
precious stones'. This was nomadism *de luxe*.

Özbeg's *ordu*, or camp (origin of both 'horde' and Urdu, the camp language of Hindustan) inspired a long excursus on the manners and customs of the Tatars. IB was unimpressed by their cuisine, mainly millet porridge, horsemeat and macaroni pudding. *Qumizz*, koumiss, the fermented mares' milk of the Tatars, he found disgusting. One aspect of Tatar life, however, fascinated him. 'In this country I witnessed a remarkable thing, namely the respect in which women are held by them; indeed, they are higher in dignity than men.' Unveiled, they were magnificent in bejewelled conical headdresses that nodded with peacock feathers – 'anyone seeing their husbands would take them for their servants'. Doyenne of these ladies was Taytughli, Özbeg's number one sultana. 'He spends most of his nights with her,' the traveller confided, 'and I was told for a fact by a trustworthy individual, a person well acquainted with matters relating to this queen, that the Sultan is enamoured of her because of a peculiar property in her, namely that he finds her every night just like a virgin.' (This earns a double exclamation mark in Dr Abdelhadi's edition of the *Travels*.) Apparently, this gynaecological quirk ran in Taytughli's family, said to be descended from a woman who tempted Solomon and was banished to the steppe. IB was clearly itching to get down to some fieldwork; but, he says wistfully, 'nothing like that ever came into my hands'.

Taytughli was also tight of fist, 'the stingiest of the sultanas'. Of the other three, the most generous was Bayalun. She showered IB with presents – money, horses and, a great rarity in Tatar lands, bread. She also showered him with tears: 'She asked about us and our journey hither and the distance of our native lands, and she wept in pity and compassion and wiped her face with a handkerchief that lay before her.' One can understand her sympathy, as she herself was far from home. Bayalun, part of that extraordinary fourteenth-century network of nuptial alliances, was the daughter of the Byzantine Emperor.

On her marriage to Özbeg, Bayalun seems to have been given the dubious honour of being renamed after her mother-in-law. Her baptismal name is a mystery; since the Emperor's other daughters can be accounted for, she was probably illegitimate. In the Byzantine documents, only a single chance survival mentions the marriage. It is a letter dated 1341 from a monk in Constantinople to a brother monk in Thrace, warning him that the Scythians are about to invade ('Scythians' is a glorious anachronism for 'Tatars'). The source of this intelligence was highly placed, the writer says – no less than the wife of the Scythian king, the daughter of the Emperor Andronicus III. A brief Arabic reference by IB's contemporary al-Umari also confirms the marriage. Özbeg, he says, took tribute from the Byzantines 'until the time he allied himself to them in marriage, whereupon he removed the burden of that tax'.

IB had found in Bayalun the most unexpected soul-mate, a fellow stranger in the alien world of the Tatars. He had also found his passport to Constantinople. Bayalun was pregnant, and when Özbeg gave her permission to give birth at home, IB 'begged of him to allow me to go in her company to see Constantinople the Great for myself. He forbade me, out of fear for my safety; but I solicited him tactfully and said to him, "It is under your protection and patronage that I shall visit it, so I shall have nothing to fear from anyone." He then gave me permission.'

Özbeg lived up to his expected gift-rating. IB's going-away present included 1,500 gold dinars, ingots of silver and 'a large collection of horses, robes and furs'. Jingling with cash, cushioned by miniver and sable, he set out from the Golden Horde to the Golden Horn, across the steppe with Bayalun and her retinue of six thousand.

★

Following my own Anatolian trip I had crossed the Sea of Marmara to Constantinople the Great in the company of a large Bulgarian Turkish woman, a practitioner of *t'ai chi* with a not unpleasing moustache. *Eheu fugaces!* We travelled by hydrofoil, and the journey was over before I could discover more.

Is there an arrival more intoxicating? Domes bursting out of a backlit skyline; pavements tacky with mussel liquor, air with sardine fumes and diesel, light with vapour; a city resonant with the honk of *vapurs* as they dash over the water tacking Europe to Asia – the sound too of another city of arrivals and departures, on the brink of another continent: Tangier, where the journey had begun.

IB's first sight of Constantinople was of its Land Wall, a four-mile line of bastions gazing out to Thrace. He had crossed southern Russia, the Ukraine, Moldavia, Romania and Bulgaria in the uneventful comfort of the royal wagon train. At the Byzantine border the princess parked her mobile mosque and celebrated her homecoming, like any Western expat returning from Islamic lands, with bacon. She may have put aside her Islamic mores, but she did not forget her Muslim guest: at her instigation, a servant was beaten for giggling at IB and his companions as they prayed. Bayalun knew what it was like to be a stranger.

Behind the walls, Constantinople was in a state of terminal louche-ness. It had never really recovered from the events of 1204 when Enrico Dandolo, that unsavoury nonagenarian Doge, had redirected the Fourth Crusade to pillage the imperial city. More recently, a sense-less squabble had weakened it further. In 1320 the future emperor, IB's Andronicus III Palaeologue, killed his brother in a spat over a woman. Their father died a week later, apparently of a broken heart; their grandfather, Andronicus II, excluded the young prince from the suc-cession. The prince made war on him, and five years later was recog-nized as co-Emperor. In 1328, the younger Andronicus deposed the elder and put him in a monastery, ending a reign described by Gibbon as 'prolix and inglorious'. Indeed, the Palaeologue dynasty as whole, wrote the historian, was 'prolix and languid'.

Writing at the time of IB's visit, al-Umari comes across as a sort of Arabic Gibbon:

They may be great in number, but their most powerful ammu-nition is wine and soft bread, their most reliable *matériel* brocade and silk. The only blows struck are on cymbal and lute, the only thrusts are in the direction of swelling breasts and pliant under-bellies. Blood they spill, but from the wound of the wine-jar's mouth; their glorious dead are but dead drunk, fallen in battle with the bottle. Their most valiant assaults are on the dinner table; their only active service takes place between mattress and bedsheet.

IB was blithely unaware of the supposed moral decline. What caught his eye was something quite different: 'Most of the inhabitants of this city are monks, devotees and priests, and its churches are numerous beyond computation. They display great magnificence in building them, constructing them of marble and mosaic work.' The Palaeologues, their empire withering about them, with their comic-opera politics and ragtime army, presided over one of the greatest periods of Byzantine art. Now back in Istanbul, I visited the monastic church of Christ of the Chora, not far from the Adrianople Gate where IB entered the city. It is hard to identify exactly the churches he saw but I felt sure that this one, rebuilt a decade before his arrival and one of the masterpieces of the age, would have been on his tour. From the outside, like the pop-up book *madrasah* I had seen in Morocco, it gave nothing away.

Inside, I found I had walked into a glittering cosmic cocktail party. Prophets and angels, saints and sinners jostled in mosaic and fresco on walls and vaults above a dado of rare marbles, a divine levee in levitation. There was the host of the party – Theodore Metochites the Logothete, rebuilder of the church, dwarfed by a gigantic striped turban. I was the only visitor, and in the silence the images were almost audible: the rustle of shrouds as Christ dragged the dead from their tombs, the polyphonic moan from Hell – a fiery red smear filled with indistinct, twisting bodies. IB heard other sounds. 'A boy', he wrote, perhaps of this very place, 'was sitting on a pulpit reading the gospel in the most beautiful voice I have ever heard.'

Also as in the Moroccan *madrasah*, the silence was soon shattered. This time they were French. I went to find the Palace of Blachernae.

On his arrival, IB was taken to meet the Emperor. He was led by the sleeves through mosaic-covered halls, past ranks of silent courtiers, into the imperial presence. Andronicus III questioned him, via a Syrian Jew, on his travels. 'He was pleased with my replies and said to his sons, "Honour this man and ensure his safety." ' First, though, IB had a request – for a guide-interpreter, 'that I might see the city's wonders and curious sights and tell of them in my own country'. As always, the charm worked. IB left the palace on a richly caparisoned horse, accompanied by fanfares and by an imperial dragoman and parasol.

As medieval Islamic tourism went, a city break in Christian Constantinople was something of a rarity. But IB was by no means the only Muslim in the capital. 'Muslims in Constantinople', wrote al-Umari, 'are shown respect and hospitality. Indeed, some are resident in the city. Praise God, they suffer no contempt or scorn, but are allowed to have their mosques and imams.' He added, perhaps wishfully, that any emperor who mistreated the Muslim community risked being deposed by the Patriarch. The tradition of respect was a long one. Ibn Rustah, writing in about 900, says that the Emperor would invite all the Muslim prisoners-of-war to Christmas dinner. 'Huge amounts of food were served, both hot and cold. As it was brought in the Master of Ceremonies called out, "By the life of the Emperor's head, I declare this banquet entirely free of pork products!"' On leaving, the prisoners were each given two gold dinars and three silver dirhams.

I found the Palace of Blachernae next door to a football pitch and a piece of waste ground dotted with goats. There were no fanfares; only a man trying out his novelty car horn at the gate. Neither were there whispering guards or silent courtiers, mummified in cloth of gold and etiquette. And there were no tourists. The place looked totally unvisited; but a bulky woman bumbled out of her cement bungalow, plonked impertinently in the palace courtyard, and took 300,000 lira off me. (Inflation is nothing new: IB noticed that the Byzantine gold hyperperon, debased under Andronicus, 'is not good coin'.) Only one bit of the palace remained, a three-storey arcaded façade of grey stone chequered in rusty brick. Behind it, the floors had gone and the walls were cobwebbed and fire-blackened. IB remembered seeing 'mosaics of creatures both animate and inanimate'; I scanned the ground, looking for tesserae among the rubbish, until I saw a glint of gold. I stooped down ... A curtain twitched in the bungalow: the Mistress of Blachernae was watching. The gold tessera was a discarded sweet-wrapper.

*

Of all the churches IB visited, only one is immediately identifiable. 'It is called in their language *Aya Sufiya*. I can only describe its exterior. As for its interior I did not see it.' But what an exterior! – a scrummage of vaults, semidomes and buttresses, a rippling architectonic musculature hefting up the huge central cupola like the world on Atlas's shoulders.

Not that IB noticed. Or rather, what remained in his memory was two-dimensional: marble paving and *pietra dura* in the temenos of the church, gold and silver plaques on its doors. Also he recalled people – judges, pen-pushers from the Patriarchate, churchwardens, sweepers and lamplighters. IB's is not a photographic memory, but that of a miniaturist in which figures are set against richly decorated planes. Two figures are central, one of them IB himself. I stood before the west front of Hagia Sophia, among the chattering coach parties and fallen conkers, and tried to picture their meeting. It is one of the most extraordinary in the whole literature of travel.

Account of the King Jirjis, who became a Monk. This king invested his son with the kingdom, consecrated himself to the service of God, and built a monastery outside this city, on the bank of its river. I was out one day with the Greek appointed to ride with me when we chanced to meet this king, walking on foot, wearing hair-cloth garments, and with a felt bonnet on his head. He had a long white beard and a fine face, which bore traces of his austerities; before and behind him was a body of monks, and he had a pastoral staff in his hand and a rosary around his neck. When the Greek saw him he dismounted and said to me, 'Dismount, for this is the king's father.' When the Greek saluted him the king asked about me, then stopped and said to the Greek (who knew the Arabic tongue), 'Say to this Saracen, "I clasp the hand that has entered Jerusalem and the foot that has walked within the Dome of the Rock and the Church of the Resurrection, and Bethlehem",' and so saying he put his hand upon my feet and passed it over his face. I was amazed at their belief in one who, though not of their religion, has entered these places. He then took me by the hand and as I walked with him asked me about Jerusalem and the Christians living there, and questioned me at length. I entered with him into the enclosure of the Great Church. When he approached the main door, there came out a number of priests and monks to salute him, for he is one of their great men in the monastic life, and when he saw them he let go my hand. I said to him, 'I should like to go into the church with you,' but he said to the interpreter, 'Tell him that every one who enters it must needs prostrate himself before the great cross, for this is a rule laid down by the ancients and it cannot be contravened.' So I left him and he entered alone and I did not see him again.

The monk was of course not the Emperor's father but his grandfather, Andronicus II. Deposed in 1328, he had remained for a time, Lear-like, losing his sight, in the echoing emptiness of Blachernae, until forced to take on the monk's habit. Gibb and others have pointed out two further problems in IB's account. The first is that the elder Andronicus's monastic name was not Jirjis, George, but Antony; the second that, however we stretch the elastic chronology of the *Travels*, by the time IB arrived in Constantinople the ex-Emperor was dead.

The name is not so worrying. After all IB dictated the *Travels* more than twenty years on, without notes, and to have remembered any Greek names at all would have been a remarkable feat. Some of his stabs are far from the mark. For example, the Golden Horn appears as 'Absumi' – probably a garbled version of *potamos*, river. 'Andronicus', with its unArabic consonant cluster -*ndr*-, could conceivably be lopped and deformed by an Arab and by the passage of time into 'Jirjis'. (I am grasping at a phonemic straw; but then, several people in Yemen are convinced that my name is Ahmad Kandash. Work that one out.)

Timing, however, is a greater problem. Andronicus-Antony died in February 1332; IB, according to Gibb, could not have arrived in Constantinople before September. Perhaps then IB misunderstood the monk's identity, or was misled; perhaps the monk was another member of the imperial family; or perhaps, *pace* Gibb, the conundrum of IB's chronology *could* be twisted into a solution, like a four-dimensional Rubik's Cube.

Does any of this matter? Whoever Jirjis was, the meeting – a meeting – did take place. The details are convincing – the pastoral staff, the rosary, the coarse garments, the hand held then released. Gibb himself, a canny and not unsceptical scholar, admits the passage bears the 'unmistakable stamp of truth'. And it is a meeting that takes place still: with Umm Baha in the Egyptian desert, the old stationer of Aleppo, Hajji Baba of Konya, the Imam of Feodosia; and with Hasan in San'a, with whom I often saunter around predestination and free will, Aquinas and Mu'tazilism, keeping in step until we come to the inevitable Qur'anic threshold – 'Whoever adopts a *din* other than Islam, it will not be accepted of him.' *Din* is religion; *din* is also custom, the rules of the ancients. Meetings, and partings.

In the course of a year of travelling I had been inside mosques from Tangier to the Crimea. In the seventeen I have lived in San'a, a place where the rules of the ancients still apply, I have never entered a single one. I think I knew how IB felt, standing at the door of Hagia Sophia, peering into the great murmuring vault.

Inside, it was chilly. The paving and panelling, all of marble, exuded a thin film of sweat. The floor, white, worn and polished by feet, seemed to flow like molten wax. The walls were of many colours and patterns – thrushes' eggs, liver sausage, trout-skin, blood slides. Paul the Silentiary enumerated the sources of the marble: Carystus, Phrygia, Sparta, the Iassian hills, Lydia, Lybia, the lands of the Moors and the Celts and of Atrax. I looked ahead and up, into the vast emptiness. It is a space that could swallow Nôtre-Dame, that ingests even tour groups, breaking their voices down into a low ambient hum.

It wasn't always so empty. 'Immense was the supply of heads and bones, crosses and images, that were scattered by this revolution over the churches of Europe,' said Gibbon of the pillage of Constantinople and Hagia Sophia by Dandolo's 'crusaders'. But Byzantium, if Ludolph von Suchem is to be believed, had limitless stocks: when the Emperor's Catalan mercenaries asked for a bonus payment in the form of holy relics over a century after the Venetian sack, 'he granted their prayers, set up as many bodies of saints as the Catalans numbered heads, and the gentlemen stood afar off and chose each a body in turn, according to their rank'.

With the Ottoman conquest of 1453 and the conversion of Hagia Sophia to a mosque, the new Islamic broom swept the relics and images away. The mosaics were whitewashed over. Now, though, the whitewash is being removed. My eye was drawn to the focal point of the apse, to a patch of cobalt and gold. As I strained to make it out, someone switched on a spotlight and the image sprang out of the gloom: the Virgin and Child. The Child was turning in His mother's lap, raising His fingers – to catch her hand, or to bless? I climbed to the gallery for a better look.

From close to, Christ seemed a miniature boy rather than an infant – too old for laps. He looked slightly upwards, almost smiling. Mary gazed off to the right, the north, as if at some distant event, detached, resigned. I think her hand was feeling for His, to cling on; but it was hard to say – the movement was arrested, a single frame caught between motion and stillness, divinity and humanity.

It was a strange image, full of emotion but devoid of sentiment, beautiful and disturbing at once. Stranger still was that it was flanked by a pair of hanging roundels bearing the Arabic words 'Allah' and 'Muhammad', sombre as funerary hatchments. The meeting was surprising, but utterly logical: mystic letters, God and His prophet in Arabic script, floating next to the Logos in human form. If al-Khadir, Elijah and St George could get together, then why not God in His abstract and fleshly forms?

More surprising, on reflection, was that it had taken secularism to reveal this happy double theophany – the militant secularism of Atatürk that had turned the church-mosque into a museum and stripped away both the rules of the ancients and their whitewash. There was, I remembered, an Islamic precedent. The Ka'bah at Mecca, wrote al-Harawi in his pilgrim guide, 'had originally contained images of the angels and the prophets, of the Tree of Paradise, of Abraham, and of Jesus the son of Mary and his mother. In the year in which he occupied Mecca, the Prophet gave orders that these images should be obliterated, with the exception of that of the Messiah and his mother.' Not long after the Prophet's death, the Ka'bah was burned. Among the victims of the fire was the Madonna of Mecca, Our Lady of the Ka'bah.

Here the juxtaposition survived, more eloquent than a septuagint of sermons. And could there have been a setting more appropriate than the junction of Europe and Asia, and a building dedicated to Hagia Sophia, Divine Sagacity? It was strange to think that out there, right now, people were at each other's throats, doctrinally, physically, hounding each other with dogmas, and had been for the last fourteen centuries. Strange, and blackly funny. Someone deserves an alpha for wit, an omega for taste. The Devil, presumably.

★

After a month in Constantinople IB said farewell to his princess, turned east once more and set off to milk the teats of Time. It was time also for me to part from him, at least for the moment. My note-books were bursting – 856 pages of A5, closely written – and I hadn't even reached the end of the first *sifr*, or volume, of his *safar*, his journey. (*Sifr* is originally a scroll, something you unroll as you read it; *safar* is the unscrolling of the earth beneath you as you travel. *Sifr* and *safar*, reading and rolling, riding and writing: that process as circular as the round world and as old as Gilgamesh.) God willing, IB and I would meet up again somewhere between here and China. We had come a long way since our first meeting in the Greater Yemen Bookshop, but there was much further still to go, and more wonders to look for. Many more: 'For God', said old Captain Buzurg of Ramhurmuz, 'created his wonders in ten parts; and nine of these ten are in the East.'

I went to a travel agent's to confirm my ticket. As I was waiting, someone came in and asked in French about a flight to Belgrade. I turned and saw a man in his early twenties, small and wiry, beady and feral as a ferret. He wore hip black jeans, a small black backpack and a black triceps-revealing T-shirt. Judging by his accent and colouring, he had to be a Maghribi. He was clean shaven but his armpits, I noticed, were unIslamically hairy. There was something puckishly attractive about him.

He wasn't getting very far, so I translated from the travel agent's English into Arabic. Jamal replied in Arabic heavily sauced with French. 'Tell him', the agent said, 'that he can't get a single. He must buy a return.'

'Why?'

'This is the rule. He has an Algerian passport.'

I translated. Jamal decided to give up.

We left together and strolled through the Byzantine Hippodrome. Jamal talked of his passion for kung fu, I of mine for IB.

'It's a good thing you didn't try to follow IB through Algeria,' he said.

'You mean the problems?'

He nodded. 'I've got problems there myself,' he confided. 'I can't go back. You see, I got into trouble with the police.' He pointed to his crotch.

My mind somersaulted through the possibilities.

'I was in prison. They burned my prick with cigarettes.'

In answer to my wordless question, he pulled a wallet from his pocket and extracted a grubby passport-sized photograph. It showed a young man with a bushy, Islamic-puritan beard. The face looked familiar. 'Who is it?'

Jamal laughed. 'It's me! They locked me up and tortured me, all because I was a Muslim with a beard.'

I stared at him, astonished. The transformation was almost unbelievable; but the faces were indeed the same. 'And now?'

'I'm a Muslim without a beard.'

We walked on. 'If I can get to Belgrade, I'll cross from there to Italy, and from Italy to France, *in sha Allah*. I've got a diploma in animal health, and I want to carry on studying, get a degree.'

Over tea in a café, Jamal talked more about his future. I wasn't taking it in – I was still dizzy from the revelation of his past. I just watched and listened to this prodigy, this kung fu fundamentalist. He had successfully repackaged himself. That, I supposed, was what it was all about: packaging. You have a beard, you get tortured; you have an Algerian passport, you can only get a return. Rules of the ancients.

Suddenly he looked at his watch. 'I'd better get going. You know what the Prophet said, God bless and protect him? "Seek knowledge, even if you have to go to China." '

'Or France,' I said.

We entrusted each other to the safekeeping of God.

I watched him walking away, rucksack bobbing, until he was swallowed up by the pavement crowds. I would never raise IB's ghost; but there went his spirit, restless as ever.

Bibliographical Note

There are some thirty known manuscripts of the *Travels*. The earliest may be in the hand of IB's editor and amanuensis, Ibn Juzayy. From the provenance of the manuscripts, it seems that the work circulated mainly in North Africa. Abridgements were however known in the Levant and one of these, written in Aleppo in the seventeenth century, appeared in an English version in 1829. (The translator, the Reverend Samuel Lee, began his career as a carpenter's apprentice in Shropshire, picked up eighteen languages in his spare time, became Chaplain to Cambridge Gaol and ended up in the professorial chairs of both Arabic and Hebrew.)

Defrémery and Sanguinetti's edition of the complete Arabic text appeared in Paris between 1853 and 1858 (a reprint was published in the same city in 1979). It has been translated into many languages, including Swedish, Armenian and Chinese, and even retranslated, for unfathomable reasons, from Spanish to Arabic. The Hakluyt Society accepted H.A.R. Gibb's proposal for a five-volume English version as long ago as 1922. Gibb died in 1971, shortly before the publication of Volume III. Professor Beckingham had by this time taken over the project; the fourth and final volume of text appeared in 1994. Beckingham himself died in 1998; Volume V, consisting of indexes, was published in 2000 under the supervision of Professor A.D.H. Bivar. All five volumes are available via the Hakluyt Society, c/o The British Library, London. (Gibb also produced a single-volume abridgement in 1929, reprinted in London in 1983.)

Dr Abdelhadi Tazi, in his Arabic edition (Rabat, 1997), has synthesized much of the Western scholarship on IB and made it available to the Arab reader, adding many valuable insights of his own. His Introduction is long and fascinating, his indexes extremely useful.

For a full bibliography of works on and pertinent to the *Travels*, the reader of English can do no better than to consult Ross E. Dunn's excellent *The Adventures of Ibn Battuta*, a historian's view of the work 'within the rich, transhemispheric cultural setting of medieval Islam' (Berkeley and Los Angeles, London and Sydney, 1986). The IB bibliography is still growing, and in surprising directions: a collection of papers published by the Ecole Supérieure Roi Fahd de Traduction and entitled *Ibn Battuta* (Tangier, 1996), includes feminist, Jungian, post-imperial/-colonial and ethno-semiotic analyses of the text. If he knows about it, the old Tangerine must be perplexed, but not a little pleased.

Acknowledgements

Many people helped me during my travels. They include, in Morocco, Muhammad Dahduh of the Abdullah Gannun al-Hasani Library, Abdelmajid Domnati, William and Arlene Fullerton, Hasan Ridwan and, especially, IB's effervescent editor, Dr Abdelhadi Tazi of Rabat; in Egypt, Rachel Davey, Toby Macklin, Muhammad Nur and Lionel Thompson; in Syria, Hikmat Hilal and Abdullah al-Jumahi; in Oman, Claudia Cooper, Steve Dover, Abdullah al-Fadli, Michael Gallagher, Thumna al-Gandel, Shahina Ghazanfar, Colin Hepburn, Qahtan Khawar, HE Malallah al-Liwati, Dr Isam al-Rawas, Awfit al-Shahri, Ali al-Shikayli and, above all, my old friends Muhammad Ali Williams Nur and his wife Habibah; in Turkey, Yalçın Karaca and Hugh Pope; and, in the Crimea, Viktoria Arkhiptseva, Aleksandr Gavrilov and, in particular, Nina Suvorova, without whom I would have been utterly lost.

Various forms of assistance were also given by Tim Callan, the Reverend Dr Mark Chapman and Linda Collins, Stephen Day, the Reverend Canon Paul Iles, Brendan MacSharry, and Tim Morris and Ianthe Maclagan. Jay Butler, Michael Maclagan, Christopher Tanfield and Bruce Wannell helped with aspects of the text. My agent, Carolyn Whitaker, and my editor, Gail Pirkis, were assiduous in their long-distance communications and indulgent of my whims. Martin Yeoman drew the decorations from an eclectic range of sources. The Authors' Foundation and the Society of Authors provided a generous grant. The Hakluyt Society kindly gave permission for me to quote from their English version of IB's *Travels*, translated by the late Professors Sir Hamilton Gibb and Charles Beckingham. (All who study IB are indebted to Gibb and Beckingham, and to the nineteenth-century editors of the *Travels*, Defrémery and Sanguinetti. If there is a special corner of heaven for Arabists, they are there, and probably still poring over the text.) Perhaps most important of all, Hasan al-Mujahid al-Shamahi of San'a was a first, unlooked-for link with the world of IB.

To all of the above I extend my grateful thanks.

Bayt Qadi, San'a
August 2000

Index

Note: page numbers in *italics* refer to illustrations. Arabic *ibn/bin*, 'son of . . .', is abbreviated to b.

Index